Trial of Frederick Bywaters and Edith Thompson

Filson Young

Trial of Frederick Bywaters and Edith Thompson
Trial of Bywaters and Thompson
Filson Young
HAR01530
Monograph
Harvard Law School Library
Edinburgh and London: William Hodge & Company, Limited, 1923

The Making of Modern Law collection of legal archives constitutes a genuine revolution in historical legal research because it opens up a wealth of rare and previously inaccessible sources in legal, constitutional, administrative, political, cultural, intellectual, and social history. This unique collection consists of three extensive archives that provide insight into more than 300 years of American and British history. These collections include:

Legal Treatises, 1800-1926: over 20,000 legal treatises provide a comprehensive collection in legal history, business and economics, politics and government.

Trials, 1600-1926: nearly 10,000 titles reveal the drama of famous, infamous, and obscure courtroom cases in America and the British Empire across three centuries.

Primary Sources, 1620-1926: includes reports, statutes and regulations in American history, including early state codes, municipal ordinances, constitutional conventions and compilations, and law dictionaries.

These archives provide a unique research tool for tracking the development of our modern legal system and how it has affected our culture, government, business – nearly every aspect of our everyday life. For the first time, these high-quality digital scans of original works are available via print-on-demand, making them readily accessible to libraries, students, independent scholars, and readers of all ages.

The BiblioLife Network

This project was made possible in part by the BiblioLife Network (BLN), a project aimed at addressing some of the huge challenges facing book preservationists around the world. The BLN includes libraries, library networks, archives, subject matter experts, online communities and library service providers. We believe every book ever published should be available as a high-quality print reproduction; printed on-demand anywhere in the world. This insures the ongoing accessibility of the content and helps generate sustainable revenue for the libraries and organizations that work to preserve these important materials.

The following book is in the "public domain" and represents an authentic reproduction of the text as printed by the original publisher. While we have attempted to accurately maintain the integrity of the original work, there are sometimes problems with the original work or the micro-film from which the books were digitized. This can result in minor errors in reproduction. Possible imperfections include missing and blurred pages, poor pictures, markings and other reproduction issues beyond our control. Because this work is culturally important, we have made it available as part of our commitment to protecting, preserving, and promoting the world's literature.

GUIDE TO FOLD-OUTS MAPS and OVERSIZED IMAGES

The book you are reading was digitized from microfilm captured over the past thirty to forty years. Years after the creation of the original microfilm, the book was converted to digital files and made available in an online database.

In an online database, page images do not need to conform to the size restrictions found in a printed book. When converting these images back into a printed bound book, the page sizes are standardized in ways that maintain the detail of the original. For large images, such as fold-out maps, the original page image is split into two or more pages

Guidelines used to determine how to split the page image follows:

- Some images are split vertically; large images require vertical and horizontal splits.
- For horizontal splits, the content is split left to right.
- For vertical splits, the content is split from top to bottom.
- For both vertical and horizontal splits, the image is processed from top left to bottom right.

Notable British Trials

Frederick Bywaters

and

Edith Thompson

NOTABLE BRITISH TRIALS SERIES

Madeleine Smith. Edited by A Duncan Smith
Dr. Pritchard. Edited by William Roughead
The Stauntons. Edited by J B Atlay
Franz Muller. Edited by H B Irving
The Annesley Case. Edited by Andrew Lang
Lord Lovat. Edited by David N Mackay
Captain Porteous   Edited by William Roughead
William Palmer. Edited by Geo H Knott
Mrs. Maybrick. Edited by H B Irving.
Dr. Lamson. Edited by H L Adam
Mary Blandy. Edited by William Roughead
Glasgow Bank Directors   Edited by W Wallace
Deacon Brodie. Edited by William Roughead
James Stewart. Edited by David N Mackay
A. J. Monson. Edited by J W More
Oscar Slater. Edited by William Roughead
E. M. Chantrelle. Edited by A Duncan Smith
The Douglas Cause. Edited by A F Steuart
Mrs. M'Lachlan   Edited by William Roughead
Eugene Aram. Edited by Eric R Watson
J. A. Dickman. Ed by S O Rowan-Hamilton
The Seddons. Edited by Filson Young
Sir Roger Casement. Edited by Geo H Knott
H. H. Crippen. Edited by Filson Young
The Wainwrights   Edited by H B Irving
Thurtell and Hunt. Edited by Eric R Watson
Burke and Hare. Edited by William Roughead
Steinie Morrison. Ed by H Fletcher Moulton
George Joseph Smith. Edited by Eric R Watson
Mary Queen of Scots. Edited by A F Steuart
Neill Cream   Edited by W Teignmouth Shore
Bywaters and Thompson   Edited by Filson Young

IN PREPARATION

Henry Fauntleroy   Edited by Horace Bleackley
H. R. Armstrong   Edited by Filson Young
S. H. Dougal. Edited by Gilbert Hair
Catherine Webster   Edited by Elliot O Donnell
Adolf Beck. Edited by Eric R Watson
Ronald True   Edited by Donald Carswell
Dr. Philip Cross. Edited by P J O Hara

Particulars may be had from the Publishers

Wm Hodge & Co., Ltd   Edinburgh and London

Edith Thompson

TRIAL OF
FREDERICK BYWATERS
AND
EDITH THOMPSON

EDITED BY

FILSON YOUNG

EDINBURGH AND LONDON
WILLIAM HODGE & COMPANY, LIMITED

MADE AND PRINTED IN GREAT BRITAIN
BY
WILLIAM HODGE AND COMPANY, LTD.
GLASGOW AND EDINBURGH
1923

TO

HERBERT AUSTIN

CLERK OF THE CENTRAL CRIMINAL COURT

A TRIBUTE OF

FRIENDSHIP AND REGARD

FROM

THE EDITOR

PREFACE

THE extraordinary interest which the public took in the trial of Frederick Bywaters and Edith Thompson was the subject of much adverse comment at the time. It may be that the present-day fashion of sensation-mongering in trials and dishing up crime for the delectation of the Sunday morning lie-a-bed is to be reckoned among the less worthy of the uses to which the craft of writing can be put. Yet it is the public interest in justice which alone keeps it reasonably pure, and although we cannot all attend Courts of law, we are all concerned in what is transacted there. Unfortunately the public ear is only open when a crime or trial is coloured by what are called ' sensational ' circumstances. But there are many circumstances other than those described by that disagreeable word that repay the closest attention, and should be pondered over by serious people, and for that reason this case has been considered worthy to be included in the Notable Trials Series. In order that the reader should have material upon which to judge the main issue in the case, I have thought it desirable to publish in full not only that portion of the letters on which the case was founded, but also the other and equally illuminating portion of which nothing was heard in Court. The material upon which my appreciation of this case rests consists of official and unofficial documents, observation and impressions of the persons concerned in it, studies of the locality, and conversations with relatives and friends of the two defendants. I am obliged to the Director of Public Prosecutions, Sir Archibald Bodkin, for his kindness in giving me access to the transcripts of the shorthand notes prepared for the Court of Criminal Appeal, and to Mr. Justice Shearman for revising the proofs of the edition of his charge to the jury which appears in these pages.

F. Y.

LONDON, *November*, 1923.

CONTENTS

	PAGE
Introduction,	xiii
Table of Dates,	xxxii

The Trial—

FIRST DAY—WEDNESDAY, 6TH DECEMBER, 1922

Indictments,	2
Discussion on the Letters,	3
The Solicitor-General's Opening Speech for the Crown,	8

Evidence for the Prosecution

John Ambrose Henry Laxton	17	Dr. Percy James Drought,	22
Robert Taylor,	18	Mrs. Lilian Bywaters,	23, 33
Dora Finch Pittard,	18	William Eustace Graydon,	25
Percy Edward Clevely,	18	Ernest Foster,	27
John Webber,	19	Mrs. Fanny Maria Lester,	27, 29
Dr. Noel Maudsley	20	Frank Edward Mynill,	29
Walter Grimes,	20	Arthur Newbury,	30
Walter Mew,	21	Herbert Carlton	30
Richard Halliday Thompson	21	Mrs. Lilian Vallender,	31
Cyril Geal,	22		

SECOND DAY—THURSDAY, 7TH DECEMBER, 1922

Evidence for the Prosecution (continued)

Edith Anne Brown,	32	Alfred Scholes,	33
Amelia Augusta Lee,	32	Percy James,	33
Rose Jacobs,	32	John Hancock,	34
Charles Higgins,	33	Richard Sellars,	35
Frank Page,	33		

Statements by the Prisoner, Edith Jessie Thompson,	35
Statements by the Prisoner, Frederick Bywaters,	37

THIRD DAY—FRIDAY, 8TH DECEMBER, 1922

Evidence for the Prosecution (continued)

Leonard Williams,	41	John Webster,	42
Henry William Forster,	42	Dr. Bernard Henry Spilsbury,	42
Charles Caldwell Taylor,	42		

Evidence for the Prisoner Bywaters

Frederick Edward Francis Bywaters,	45

CONTENTS

Evidence for the Prisoner Thompson

	PAGE
Mrs. Edith Jessie Thompson,	73

Fourth Day—Saturday, 9th December, 1922

Evidence for the Prisoner Thompson (continued)

Mrs. Edith Jessie Thompson,	97
Avis Ethel Graydon,	104
Mrs. Ethel Jessie Graydon,	105

Closing Speech for the Prisoner Bywaters

Mr. Cecil Whiteley	105

Closing Speech for the Prisoner Thompson

Sir Henry Curtis Bennett,	112

Fifth Day—Monday, 11th December, 1922

Closing Speech for the Prisoner Thompson (continued)

Sir Henry Curtis Bennett,	112

Closing Speech for the Prosecution

The Solicitor General	126

Charge to the Jury

Mr. Justice Shearman	133

The Verdict	156
The Sentence,	156

APPENDICES

I. Letters from Edith Thompson and Frederick Bywaters put in Evidence at the Trial,	161
II. Letters from Edith Thompson not put in Evidence at the Trial,	219
III. Court of Criminal Appeal—Rex v. Bywaters,	251
Court of Criminal Appeal—Rex v. Thompson,	255

LIST OF ILLUSTRATIONS

Edith Thompson (from a sketch by Julius M Price),	*Frontispiece*	
Sir Thomas Inskip, K C ,	*facing page*	8
Frederick Bywaters,	,,	45
Edith Thompson,	,	73
Mr Cecil Whiteley,	,,	105
Sir Henry Curtis Bennett, K C ,	,,	112
The Hon Justice Shearman,	,	133
Edith Thompson,		161
Frederick Bywaters,		192

INTRODUCTION

I

On the midnight of October 3-4, 1922, Mr Percy Thompson, a London shipping clerk, and his wife Edith were walking from Ilford Station along the Belgrave Road towards the street called Kensington Gardens, where they lived. The road along which they were walking was straight and monotonous, and at that hour of the night almost deserted. The people who had come out by the same train had dispersed in different directions, and soon this couple, tired enough, as we may suppose, after a long day's work and an evening at the theatre, found themselves almost alone. Their relations were not cordial, although they lived outwardly on quite good terms. It is probable, therefore, that they walked for the most part in silence, each occupied with private thoughts, and that the silence of the night was unbroken but for the sound of their footsteps along the paved road divided only by the patches of light that waxed and waned as they passed the successive lamp-posts. But they were not alone. Other footsteps were hurrying after theirs, footsteps of fate indeed, whose overtaking meant the death of the three persons who encountered in that place. The hurrying footsteps were those of Frederick Bywaters, a youth of twenty, home on leave from his work as a ship's writer on board the s s " Morea " After a few words of altercation he drew a knife and stabbed Percy Thompson to death—or rather, left him in a dying condition sunk against the wall at the side of the road. He then ran away. Edith Thompson, after an attempt to minister to her husband, ran to find help, and met other people returning home late also, who had been walking some distance behind along the same road. On their return with a doctor they found that Thompson was dead.

This is the simplest possible statement of the crime which was the subject of the inquiry set forth in the following pages. I do not propose here to recapitulate in narrative form a story which is fully unfolded in the trial itself. I propose only to discuss some aspects of it which were not, and could not be, the subject of inquiry in a Court of law, but which have some bearing on any dispassionate examination of the case in its relation to general human justice as distinct from technical justice.

Bywaters and Thompson.

II

This is a story of passion, and, strange to say, is for that very reason regarded as disreputable in itself by many people. It is, on the contrary, the passion in it which alone invests what would otherwise be a story of sordid crime with any dignity or psychological interest. The crime was essentially sordid and commonplace—the husband stabbed to death by his rival in his wife's affections in the presence of and (so the prosecution alleged) with the approval of that wife. It would be difficult to imagine any circumstances which would afford a shade of justification or excuse for this extremely primitive proceeding. But the case as a whole was not sordid, because the murder formed such a small part of it, and the emotional antecedents of the act itself, illuminated by a series of the most remarkable letters that have been made public in modern times, lift the whole story out of the commonplace. Nothing is commonplace if we know enough about it. It is commonplace for a jealous man to kill his rival, but it is not commonplace to be able to trace back his emotional history and be aware of the emotional force that ultimately swept him away on its tide.

Criminal lawyers have an incorrigible instinct for melodrama, and they are apt to see, or rather to present every one in the light of martyr, hero, or villain. Some of them seem to have a quaint theory that human nature is divided into two kinds of people: on the one hand, plain, decent people, the stuff of which judges and juries are made, who are shocked and horrified at any transgression of the moral law, and can hardly believe that persons should be found wicked enough to transgress it; on the other hand, blackguards and devils degraded by such things as passion, guilty, outside the licensed degrees, of a thing called love, and generally and deservedly in trouble of some kind until they are swept within the meshes of the law. The Ilford case was no exception to this rule. The three persons concerned were duly presented in the melodramatic way. The good, patient and unoffending husband, the manly young fellow corrupted and debauched by the experienced woman of the world, and the black-hearted sorceress, weaving her spells, casting her nets, and bringing ruin on every one connected with her.

Now we cannot pretend to know the inner hearts and lives of these three people, but we can get a little nearer the truth than that. The unhappy victim of this savage assassination seems to

Introduction.

have been a fairly inoffensive person, and the worst I have heard of him from those who knew him is that he was stupid and vain. But there is ample evidence that in his married life—which was a very unhappy one for him as well as for his wife—he had cultivated the art of being disagreeable with considerable success. The circumstances of the marriage were in themselves not conducive to happiness. Husband and wife earned their living separately. They left the house at a quarter past eight in the morning and did not return until seven in the evening. There were no children, and they had thus practically nothing in common except the dormitory side of existence, which seems to have resolved itself into a chapter of bitter squabblings, and the deeper trouble that underlies the persistent attempts of a husband to take as a right something that should only be given. It is not to be wondered at that a weak character such as Thompson's expressed itself in this dilemma with acrimony, with meanness, and sometimes with violence. He was the one with the real grievance, and he seems to have made the most of it.

It is when we come to the characters of Bywaters and Mrs. Thompson that we are at once confronted with an element of the unusual. Neither of these persons was at all like what the general public thinks. Bywaters was not the innocent young lad that his defenders presented to the jury; Edith Thompson was not the corrupt, malignant sorceress portrayed by the prosecution. A great deal of play was made about their respective ages, and it was suggested that she was an experienced woman corrupting a young lad. That is not the way I see it. Bywaters was twenty and she was twenty-eight, but in some ways he was the elder of the two, as he was certainly the more masterful. He was an almost excessively virile, animal type. He had knocked about the world, he had knowledge of life, and an exceptionally strong will. You will read in the course of the trial a great deal about the woman's influence on him; but I am convinced that his influence upon her was at least as great as hers upon him, and probably greater, and they came upon their undoing because of a certain exaggerated difference between them. Bywaters, as I read his character, was totally devoid of imagination; actions were his only realities. Edith Thompson had an excess of imagination. To her actions were unimportant. Her chief consciousness was hardly ever in what she was doing at the time, but inhabited a world of dreams and make-believe. If this aspect of the characters of the two people concerned be kept in mind, I think it will make many things clear which must otherwise remain obscure.

III

But it is not enough to say that Edith Thompson had too much imagination. We must look more closely at her than that, for she is the sole key to this mystery, and without understanding of her the whole story cannot be justly read. There are people to whom everything is common, and to a great part of the public Mrs. Thompson was a common and commonplace woman. But there were people present at the trial who are connoisseurs in women and scholars of their character, and who are able to recognise, behind the most sordid disguises, the presence of that something which lifts a woman out of whatever class she may naturally belong to and sets her in a class apart—the class of influencing, compelling, driving, beckoning women, who have power over men, and, through them, over the world. To such students it was clear that Edith Thompson belonged to that company, and no one who read, for example, Mr. James Douglas's marvellously sensitive, acute, and discerning analyses, written during the course of the trial, can have any doubt as to the power of a personality which, from the dismal *decor* of the dock, could so act on an intelligence that no experience can de-humanise. She was compact of contrasts and contradictions. She was called a hysterical woman by many people engaged in the case, but through five days of acute trial I saw no sign of hysteria in her. She was remarkable in this way, that quite above her station in life, quite beyond the opportunities of her narrow existence, she had power of a kind that is only exercised by women possessed of a high imaginative talent; she had that peculiar quality of attraction which over-rides beauty and prettiness. She was not what is called a beautiful woman, nor always even pretty, but she had a certain character, certain movements of infinite grace, a head finely poised on a beautiful neck, and the secret of looking like a hundred different women according to the nature of her environment. There is one simple test by which you may judge the kind of woman that Edith Thompson was. No two photographs of her looked like photographs of the same

Introduction.

woman, from different angles of view, in different clothes she appeared like different people. Put her in a housemaid's dress and she would look like a housemaid, place her in tragic circumstances and she became a tragic actress. She was, to that extent, Everywoman, and she had the secret of the universal woman. The three portraits of her in this book are like portraits of three different people; if you asked me which she was like, I would say she was like none of them, and like them all, but the one which best represents her character is the pencil drawing made of her by a distinguished artist as she sat in the witness-box, and that is not the portrait of a common or commonplace woman. If she had been a Frenchwoman she would have been long ago taken out of her humble working life and been at once the slave and the ruler of some connoisseur in extravagant caprice. Stage, costumes, jewels, and victims would have been provided for her. As it was, a bookkeeper in a milliner's shop, she had to find her own stage, her own empire, her own drama. She had to find her own victims, and in the end she herself was the chief victim of her own tragic personality.

IV

Bywaters was a clean-cut, self-possessed, attractive-looking youth of twenty, with a good character and record. At the opening of this drama which developed into a *crime passionel* he was a ship's writer or clerk who had become the friend and intimate of Mr and Mrs Thompson. He was nineteen years of age, eight years younger than she. She and her husband did not agree. They were physically incompatible, and saw very little of each other—as little as she could help. The husband had employment in a shipping office, and she was book-keeper in a milliner's shop in Aldersgate Street. She had no particular home life or duties, and such as she had she sought to avoid as much as possible. Her acquaintance with young Bywaters ripened rapidly into friendship and then love. He was often away at sea for long periods, and during these periods she used to write to him letters of a kind characterised by Mr Justice Shearman as "gush," which lovers and friends at a distance love to receive, letters telling him her thoughts as they rose in her head, what she was doing, what she was reading, what she was thinking, and breathing throughout a curious passion, half of the mother, half of the slave-mistress, that gives its supreme interest and power to this correspondence. They also contained a great deal of reference to attempts at the administration of poison to her husband, which belong to the criminal part of the case and which for the moment I will leave aside. But as to the general contents of these letters I would say, paying all respect to the comments of a learned, humane, and impartial judge that they are true love letters, and that the emotion in them is both deep and true. They contain passages of actual beauty, to find the match for which you would have to look in the love letters of people far above her in poetic and literary attainments. The love they breathed being illegal, was as a matter of course the subject of unsympathetic reference in a Court of law. "Insensate, silly affection," the judge called it. Love may be unwise, but it can never be silly, and how something that is founded on passion and emotion can be insensate I will leave the legal mind to decide. Lest I be accused of speaking disrespectfully or unreasonably of an eminent and admirable judge, I will quote one passage which seems to me fairly typical of the judicial treatment of emotional matters. "You have been repeatedly told," he said, "that this was a case of great love, and we have had for days both speeches and questions with reference to this love. Just at the end of the letters comes this passage 'He has the right by law to all that you have the right to by nature and love.' *If that nonsense means anything, it means that the love of a husband by his wife means nothing because marriage is acknowledged by law.*" Just read again the simple sentence from Mrs Thompson's letter. Surely it is a brief and exact statement of the position as it existed between these three, and is, therefore, not nonsense. "I have no doubt," added his lordship, "that the jury and every proper-minded person is filled with disgust by such expressions." Disgust at what? At the statement itself, or at the suggestion that there can be any right but that of law? It seems to me that love and nature are both things that have very definite rights of their own, although it is the business of the law to restrain them if it can. In any case, the number of judges who can with advantage intercalate their judicial utterances with these little homilies on life and conduct is so inconsiderable as to make the practice, upon the whole, undesirable.

Introduction.

V

It is these letters, however, that focus our interest in the sequence of events that led to the death of Thompson. With regard to the incriminating passages in them, in which the strangest descriptions are given of alleged attempts at poisoning the husband, I think the explanation is quite simple. Mrs Thompson's dramatic sense, aided by her imagination, and quite remarkable fluency in writing, led her, in order to keep her image commandingly before the absent lover, to represent herself as engaged, for his sake, in the dreadful task of poisoning her husband. She wished him to believe that there was nothing she would stop at, though, in fact, she had no intention whatever of running the risks that such attempts would have involved. It is certainly inconsistent with her character, as I conceive it, that if she had really intended to poison her husband she would have philandered with the idea on paper, and written reams of incriminating matter. She would have done it and said (or written) nothing about it. A Borgia does not write, she acts. With Edith Thompson words took the place of actions. In her words she was speculative, adventurous, indirect, in her actions she was logical, direct, and—even in her transgressions—conventional. She was a woman who could play with ideas to any extent, while her actions remained quite limited and almost normal. She lived two lives, one, this dream life, the life of the heroine of the letters, the other a commonplace routine life of some one who passed daily as in a trance from Ilford to Aldersgate Street, and back from Aldersgate Street to Ilford, and who, sitting at her desk apparently keeping accounts, was really engaged in weaving an imaginative web that should stretch across half the seas of the world, and bind her lover with its gossamer threads.

By keeping these letters Bywaters brought ruin to the writer. She kept none of his, she was too loyal for that. It is extremely probable that he entered into this grim and shocking game of correspondence about poisoning meaning it as little as she did, and it is probable that they both found an erotic stimulus in giving full play on paper to their jealousy. And when the letters ceased, and they met again they had worked themselves up too far, what had been grim play had to become grim earnest, and to avoid anti-climax this jealous lad was forced to the climax of the knife.

As the trial proceeded, and all this obvious pretence was exposed and stripped, whatever attraction it may have had for them faded away. As the words, pleading and passionate, were read and re-read until every one in Court was familiar with them, one could see the miserable consciousness growing in both of the accused persons that what she at anyrate had meant to be lovely and happy, all they had dreamed of hoped for and fought for, had come to terrible nemesis and confusion. Such humiliation, quite apart from any suggestion of guilt, is the inevitable result of dragging emotion into a Court of law. It has no place there, it cuts a pitiful figure there, and that which may have been true and beautiful in its living environment becomes false, horrible, and deadly there.

VI

Let us now consider the way in which the legal problem posed before the Criminal Court was dealt with. The trial can hardly be regarded as a classic from a legal point of view. A fastidious jurist might even describe it as slovenly, in that the scheme of the prosecution seemed never to have been either clearly conceived or clearly presented to the jury, while those conducting the defence found themselves in such a dilemma, as a consequence of the strategy adopted, as to leave little opportunity for anything beyond ingenious quibbling on Mr Cecil Whiteley's part and emotional eloquence on the part of Sir Henry Curtis Bennett. The Treasury counsel engaged in the prosecution were Mr Travers Humphreys and Mr Roland Oliver, but owing to the nature of the case and the fact that both prisoners were to be tried together, it was decided to send down the new Solicitor-General, Mr (now Sir) Thomas Inskip, K.C. This officer's practice had largely lain apart from the criminal law, and he was not much at home in the handling of a case like this. It is possible, moreover, that he had very little time in which to study his brief, but whatever may have been the cause, his handling of the case was loose and uncertain. There was a certain irony in the fact that sitting beside him as his junior, and almost idle throughout the case, was Mr Travers Humphreys—a man whose mind seems to me the hardest, brightest and most exact of those engaged in criminal work for the Treasury. Mr Humphreys had practically nothing to do except occasionally to read the long extracts from the letters which took so many hours. It was a curious occupation for him, thus to be reading aloud these passionate utter-

Introduction.

ances in the presence of the woman who wrote them, and it is to his credit that, much as he disliked the task, his reading of those letters was by no means unsympathetic and some of their haunting phrases that were repeated so often in Court will remain associated in my memory with the tones of Mr Travers Humphreys

The legal interest in the case centres round the matter of the letters, and the way in which they were to be used The question as to the trying of two prisoners together for the commission of one crime which was made a point of appeal by the defendants, and which took an acute form in the case of the trial of the Seddons,[1] is one on which the existing law is clear, though not satisfactory The woman was charged with murder, her alleged part in it being that of a principal in the second degree If a jury were satisfied that she was present and supported, instigated, assisted or commanded the accomplice by whose actual hand the deed was done, they could find her guilty of murder equally with her accomplice Whether, in such a case the two are tried separately or together is a matter entirely in the discretion of the Court before which they are brought and if any hardship or injustice ensues to one or other of the accused persons through the weight of evidence offered against both pressing unduly against either the only remedy lies in the Court of Appeal

In this case there could be no doubt whatever as to who actually committed the murder The case against Bywaters was as clear as any case of murder could be, and there was practically nothing to be pretended in his defence except that he was the instrument and agent animated by a powerful and compelling influence And for his counsel to press that defence would have been inevitably to fortify the attack on the woman and embarrass her defence—which he was expressly instructed not to do What the prosecution desired was to bring the crime home not only to Bywaters but to Mrs Thompson, and the only way in which they could do this was to bring in the letters written by her to Bywaters, and so strangely preserved by him They were necessary as evidence (a) that she desired Thompson's death (b) that she was for a period of consecutive months engaged in endeavouring to compass that death, (c) that she was in conspiracy with Bywaters right up to the day of the murder to bring that death about, and (d) that she was

---

[1] See "Trial of the Seddons" in the Notable Trials Series —Ed

present when the crime was committed, and knew beforehand that it was to be committed. It was chiefly the way in which the letters were presented that lays the prosecution open to criticism. The letters do not seem to have been carefully enough analysed and the bearings of the really essential passages marshalled into any sort of sequence. The mass of the correspondence was, so to speak, thrown before the Court, and prosecuting counsel browsed through it, taking advantage of anything which seemed likely at the moment to assist the particular aspect of the case which he was presenting. The result was a great deal of confusion, a great waste of time, undue emphasis on certain passages of the letters which would not bear the weight of the construction sought to be placed on them, and the neglect of other passages which, while they would have served the purpose of the prosecution equally well, would have been more helpful and illuminating in discovering the truth. A defect in form of this kind, inherent in the design of the case for the prosecution, affects the form of the proceedings throughout. It confuses the defence, which has to follow the track of the prosecution, and it makes it very difficult for the judge to deliver a clear charge to the jury, since he also has to follow the original wandering course, retrace his steps, and traverse over and over again the same ground as it is approached from different angles and for different purposes. All these defects will be apparent to a student of the trial as it appears set forth in the following pages.

VII

But if the defects of the prosecution were serious, the defects of the defence were fatal. As I have already indicated, there was really no case for the defence of Bywaters, and Mr Cecil Whiteley's final speech is interesting chiefly for its ingenuity, and might serve as a model of what can be done and said in the defence of a murderer who is practically found standing over his victim with the weapon in his hand. But the case of Mrs Thompson was very different. No one suggested that she had committed the murder, and the only evidence that she had ever intended any murder was furnished by herself in a series of letters so fantastic that it should not have been impossible to find an explanation of them that might satisfy a jury. It seems to me that Sir Henry Curtis Bennett lost one of the opportunities of his lifetime when, after the confused and

Introduction.

uncertain opening of the Solicitor-General, he did not for once do what counsel are so often telling juries they are doing, but, in fact, so seldom do—leave the prosecution to prove its case and attempt no positive defence. Let me say at the earliest possible moment that there is no suggestion that Sir Henry was personally responsible for the line of defence or for the consequences. Mrs. Thompson insisted upon going into the witness-box and giving evidence. For counsel to give actual advice on such a subject in a matter of life and death is to take a greater responsibility than is, perhaps, right, but I think if I had been in Sir Henry's place and found that my client was determined to go into the witness-box, I should have asked her to brief another counsel. No one can ever foretell the effect which the evidence of a defendant in a murder charge will have on the case, but an experienced lawyer could have foretold, and must have known, the very great difficulty that the prosecution would have in getting a conviction against Mrs. Thompson if she did not herself give evidence, and contented herself by merely denying, through her counsel, that she had anything whatever to do with the killing of Percy Thompson, and throwing upon the prosecution the onus of proof that she had.

The dilemma is an acute one. On the one hand there is the adverse comment which the judge in his summing up is entitled to make on the silence of the accused person: the jury are asked to draw the inference that if there was any true story to tell, the accused would be the first to wish to tell it. There is the advantage, in the case of an attractive woman, of the effect of her personality and the appeal to humanity through the pathos of her position, although, in my own opinion of modern juries, the value of that effect should not be put too high. On the other hand, there is the terrible danger of the cross-examination to which the accused giving evidence is subjected: the risk of the one word too much, or the failure of mental endurance at a critical moment, that may turn the scale of opinion against the accused. And, of course, there is always the possibility, if a person who has not given evidence is convicted, of the awful misgiving that if he or she had gone into the witness-box the jury might have found a different verdict. The reasons against Mrs. Thompson going into the witness-box were, however, so strong that when she insisted on doing so she threw away her case. There is nothing about which our law is so scrupulous as in seeing that the facts of a case against which no

Bywaters and Thompson.

defence is made except that of denial are proved against the prisoner beyond all shadow of doubt. The case for the prosecution on the indictment was that Bywaters and Mrs. Thompson, "on the fourth day of October 1922 in the county of Essex, and within the jurisdiction of the Central Criminal Court, murdered Percy Thompson." That is what the jury were asked to find. If the defence had said, on behalf of Mrs. Thompson, "I did not murder Percy Thompson, I had nothing to do with it, I had no knowledge of it, and I was stunned and horrified when it took place, and I defy the prosecution to introduce any evidence with which that denial is not absolutely compatible," and had rested on that, I do not think you would have found a British jury to convict her. For all the evidence (apart from the letters, with which I shall deal later) supports the theory that Mrs. Thompson did not plan or prepare this murder in any way, that she did not suggest it to Bywaters, and that when it took place it caused her surprise, horror, and dismay. There is the evidence that she had planned the next day to go with her husband to Paddington Station to meet a servant from Cornwall whom they had engaged—the servant who did, in fact, arrive on the afternoon of the very day on which Thompson was killed. There is the evidence of John Webber, of which I think nearly enough was not made in the trial. He lived at 59 De Vere Gardens, Ilford, and at what must have been the moment of the murder, and 30 or 40 yards away from the spot where it was committed he heard a voice raised in the silence of the night—a woman's voice, crying, "Oh don't, oh don't!" in the most piteous manner. He was retiring to bed, but so impressed was he by this cry that he put on his clothes and went out into the street, where he met the little crowd of three hurrying to the spot where Mrs. Thompson was holding up her husband. That is evidence, surely, not that Mrs. Thompson assisted and approved of the crime, but that she tried to prevent it; yet I think the only bearing of this evidence alluded to by the judge was that it went to prove that Mrs. Thompson was present and a witness of the murder. It does not seem to me that that is the true value of this piece of evidence, or that nearly enough weight was given to it as bearing out what I believe to have been the fact, that Mrs. Thompson, however much she might have desired that a kind Providence would remove her husband from her path, was just as horrified as any one else when she saw that the furious assault of Bywaters upon him was, in fact, a murderous assault.

Introduction.

VIII

But Mrs Thompson did go into the witness-box and tell her story. Roughly, it was the same story as Bywaters had told, with minor discrepancies of detail which are unimportant. They had both naturally, not knowing how far the police were in possession of the facts, and being desirous not to incriminate one another, made false or incomplete statements on arrest. But when they came before a jury they attempted no denial of the main facts, they attempted to explain them. But remember that they were both trying to explain something which, in the light of an ordinary Court of law, was inexplicable—namely, the meaning of the fantastic passages in their correspondence. With regard to that correspondence, I think the defence made another mistake in not having the whole of the letters put in as evidence instead of that portion of them selected by the prosecution. The effect of this would have been twofold. The proportion of the "poison and glass" passages to the whole correspondence would have been seen to be very small, whereas the jury had the impression that the greater part of Mrs Thompson's correspondence consisted of discussions as to the best and most convenient method of murdering a husband. In the second place, other matter would have appeared which would inevitably have suggested a very different explanation of many of the passages relating to drugs and poisons. Is it not clear, on a careful study of these letters, that this unhappy woman was on more than one occasion, sometimes with the advice and assistance of Bywaters and sometimes without it, engaged in taking measures to counteract the results of intercourse, either with her husband or with Bywaters? Turn to the passage on page 204, and again to passages in the letters which will be found on pages 220, 221, 222, 224, and 226. There is no doubt in my mind as to the nature of the actions to which these letters refer, and the words "daring" and "risking," of which so much play was made by prosecuting counsel when they occurred in that final letter—" I am still willing to dare all and risk all if you are "—occur here in quite obvious connection with the other matter. Of course, Sir Henry Curtis Bennett was aware of all these passages and of the value they might have. But there he was in another dilemma, for if he were to introduce them and put the construction indicated by them on many other passages adduced as evidence of murderous intention, he would have had to present his client to the jury, not only as an adulteress, but as an abortionist, and he no doubt thought that the prejudice created in their minds by that admission would outweigh any advantage to be gained by such explanation of the poison passages as it might afford. There again one may be glad that one had not to make that decision, but the meaning of these passages cannot be ignored by any student of the case, and they throw a very considerable light on other passages which, without that light, are obscure or inexplicable.

IX

The explanation given by the two accused persons of the incriminating passages in the letters was either that they referred to a suicide compact between them, or to the intention to take what was to Mrs Thompson the extreme step of leaving her husband and going away with Bywaters, or to the various attempts that they undoubtedly made to get Thompson to divorce her. Thin as these explanations sometimes appeared in Court, they are far thinner when read in print. There are, no doubt, passages which are quite truly explained by one or other of these answers, but there are other passages that quite obviously have nothing to do either with suicide or elopement. In my opinion, the real explanation of the passages relating to definite attempts on the husband's life by means of poison, glass, &c, is that these two people were playing in their letters a very dangerous kind of game, in which Mrs Thompson's too fertile imagination cast her for the rôle of that tragic heroine with whose existence in fiction she was very familiar. The most genuine kind of lying in the world is purely fantastic lying, which arises from a desire to escape from the uninteresting actualities of life. In this way children lie, telling you of some marvellous thing which they have seen or done. The fact is merely that the world as they found it at the moment was not sufficiently interesting to satisfy their imaginations, and so they invented a world that was. So with this woman. Her life during the long absences of Bywaters on his voyages was dull compared with the life that she imagined for herself. For remember this about her, she was a woman with a single idea and ambition: the ambition of a happy and open union with the man she loved. If there is one thing that runs like a continuous thread throughout this corre-

Introduction.

spondence, it is that ambition. It was a passion with her, it was the real inspiration of her life at this time. The question naturally occurs to any sane person why did she not leave Thompson and go and live with Bywaters? The sane person ignores Respectability, which was her god, and Romance, which was her goddess. To indulge the goddess would have been to offend the more powerful god, and there are questions of finance entangled with Respectability which powerfully abet that deity. Yet the woman to whom open disrepute is a deterrent from her dearest wishes would surely be unlikely to substitute murder for it! We are here in the very toils of sentimentality. The lesson seems to be that a woman who takes Respectability for her god and Romance for her goddess, and enlists a practical young man in their service, may possibly find herself in a morass from which the only extricating agent is a rope.

But her passion for a prosperous and respectable union was so great that what she did apart from it, the way in which she spent her days, the way in which she amused herself was of very little importance to her. She was capable of being a lively and amusing companion, and there are many humorous passages in these letters that suggests her intolerance of dulness, and the rather mischievous pleasure she took in shocking people. There are passages on pages 234 and 238 that are particularly illuminative of this quality. She was a very attractive woman, and in her business life she was extremely capable, and came constantly into contact with a large circle of acquaintances, among them the buyers in large establishments (for she was a very successful saleswoman), and in the course of this independent existence she had many opportunities of amusement of which it is clear that she availed herself. It was a method of passing the time and speeding the hours of what was to her the unreal part of her life, as apart from the real dream-world that she entered when she began to write to her lover. The profound sense of the triviality and unimportance of everything she did apart from him breathes through her accounts of dances, dinners, expeditions.[1] It is this sense of proportion so lacking in other ways, which gives the light touch to her little thumbnail sketches, full of wit and characterisation, of people that she met

---

[1] At one of these, at Henley, she describes herself as being "the guest of an M P, Mr Stanley Baldwin."— Ed

Bywaters and Thompson.

X

There was, of course, every reason for putting Bywaters in the witness-box. He had a story to tell and he was the only person who could tell it. To tell it in his own words was his only possible chance. But putting Mrs Thompson in the witness-box was quite another thing. Her real case was a mere denial. Instead of that, the defence were forced to make an attempt to disprove the case for the prosecution, instead of leaving them to prove it, and were also forced to try and prove Mrs Thompson's explanations from the witness-box when they should have been content with resting on denial. You cannot prove a negative. To attempt to do so on oath is to lay yourself open to a damaging cross-examination.

Only a study of the letters will reveal the truth about the relationship between these two people. In the matter of influence, I think that in absence hers was the stronger, but when they were together his was obviously the dominating will. "Why will you never do anything that I ask, darling? You still have your own way always." It is obvious that during his last absence he was becoming less enthusiastic, and attempting to turn the relationship into a platonic one. I believe him to have been a virile degenerate, quite capable of blackmail, and that one reason why he so carefully kept all these letters, while she destroyed his, was that if and when he wanted to get rid of her he would have something to hold over her in the way of threat. At anyrate, she was obviously terrified at the thought of losing him, and her last letters revealed this anxiety. But when he returned and they came together the passion flamed out again, and all question of turning it into a platonic friendship vanished in the excitement of their re-union. In the heat of that excitement the mind of Bywaters forged the intention to put an end somehow or other to the existing situation. I believe his account of what happened to be substantially correct, and that it was in a kind of agony of jealousy and despair that he sought Thompson on that night, with the idea of forcing him to come to some arrangement, and that some taunting word fanned his jealous hatred into fury, and that having once struck he struck again, with the will and intention to murder.

Introduction.

Having regard to the way in which the case was conducted and to the very definite trend of the judge's summing up, it became increasingly likely that the jury would find both the prisoners guilty of murder. Nevertheless, the verdict with regard to Mrs Thompson came as a shock to most people who heard it. Even then, after sentence had been passed, few people thought that it would actually be carried out. But things loosely or wrongly done in the beginning have a way of continuing on their course, so that it is very difficult to give them another direction; and although an extensively signed petition was presented to the Home Secretary on behalf of Mrs Thompson, he found himself in the dilemma which was the inevitable sequel to the method of the prosecution and the defence. So much prejudice had been created, the jury had so evidently been allowed to take for granted that Mrs Thompson was the real inspirer and originator of this crime, that to let her escape the consequences while visiting them upon Bywaters, seemed, in the forced and sentimental atmosphere concerning influence that had been raised, a matter of gross injustice. The recent record of the Home Office with regard to reprieves had not been a fortunate one, and this particular incident happened at a moment when, in order to justify past weaknesses, a little show of "firmness and determination" was indicated. Decent opinion was genuinely shocked and horrified at the thought of Mrs Thompson's execution, but indecent opinion, which sometimes in matters like this seems to have more voice and more influence, was all for the sensation afforded by the execution of a young and attractive woman whose hands at anyrate, were innocent of blood.

The demeanour of the two tragic protagonists in the terrible interval between the rejection of their appeals to the Court of Criminal Appeal and the day of their death was characteristic of both. Bywaters was dauntless, self-satisfied, matter-of-fact, and, apparently, unmoved and unaffected by any imaginative sense of what was in store for him. A letter written to his mother a few hours before his execution was as firm, precise, and neat in calligraphy, and as conventional and unemotional in content, as that of a banker acknowledging a deposit. As far as I know, he neither desired nor attempted to write to Mrs Thompson, nor she to write to him; at anyrate the prison regulations permitted no communica

Bywaters and Thompson.

tion between them. They parted in the dock. They who had shared so much, shared the last awful moments of their ordeal, and thereafter never shared anything more, unless they can be said to have shared the tremendous and simultaneous extinction that awaited them—him at Pentonville, and her half a mile away at Holloway—on the morning of 9th January.

Mrs. Thompson hardly ever spoke of him, or of anything personal. She lived in prison in the same kind of agonised trance as had enwrapped her through the trial. When her relations visited her she tried to talk of commonplace and impersonal things as they all did, with the result that there must have been a good deal of unreality and play-acting about these artificially cheerful interviews. Only once, when her mother spoke to her about the letters and said, "How could you write such letters?" did she say something of deep significance in this case—"*No one knows what kind of letters he was writing to me.*"

He went to his death with firmness and assurance; she was taken to hers in a state of collapse, and, I hope, of merciful oblivion. For on the most sober consideration of the case, her execution seems to have been without other than merely legal justification, and to have been the result of a kind of frozen moral inertia which seized those whose business and responsibility it should have been to avoid an act that although technically justifiable on legal grounds, was, in the considered judgment of sober public opinion, as essentially unjust as it was inexpedient.

XII

There was so much false diagnosis about this case that I should like to make one assertion in the name of things as they are, instead of as they might be wished, or ought, to be. This crime was a consequence of frustrated passion. "Guilty passion" the judge and counsel called it. Well, these two people never felt particularly guilty but they did feel hampered. Life on £4 or £6 a week may afford opportunity for the birth and development of illegal passion; it did not in this case afford much opportunity for the indulgence or satisfaction of it, in more than snatched meetings at a tea shop, walks in municipal parks, and in that romantic intercourse which consists in outpourings of the heart on paper. If they had belonged to another class, where people have leisure and freedom, we should

Introduction.

never have heard of them except, perhaps, in the Divorce Court. The sordidness of their case was the killing, not the loving. That part of the story was real, and the long letters from "Peidi," telling of her thoughts, her hopes, her trials, the books she was reading, all those trivial jottings that are the soul of true and frank correspondence (and it is only a very small part of the letters that contained the criminal matter), were the expression of a true emotion, incomprehensible, perhaps, to people who have forgotten (and how soon we forget!) the power of youthful passion, but really very simple, and possibly pardonable to people who have not forgotten.

Age is eternally jealous of youth, impotence is jealous of passion, law is jealous of liberty, those who have found happiness within the pale are apt to look with suspicion and misgiving on those who dare to seek and find happiness without the pale. Intellect affects to despise emotion, yet a real and deep emotion, however wayward, is a more vital thing than are the sterile and negative barriers within which, necessarily, but in vain, the social state tries to confine it. That is why we have Courts of law, for a world ruled only by emotion would be a dreadful place. The lesson of it all surely is never to let emotion escape from its own sphere, to wander into the dreadful wilderness that ends in the Court and the prison house. Mr. Justice Shearman frequently referred to Bywaters as "the adulterer," apparently quite unconscious of the fact that to people of Bywaters's generation, educated in the ethics of dear labour and cheap pleasure, of commercial sport and the dancing hall, adultery is merely a quaint ecclesiastical term for what seems to them the great romantic adventure of their lives. Adultery to such people may or may not be "sporting," but its wrongness is not a matter that would trouble them for a moment. Sinai, for them, is wrapped in impenetrable cloud. And if we are not prepared to adapt the laws of Sinai to the principles of the night club and the *thé dansant*, I see no other alternative but to educate again our young in the eternal verities on which the law is based.

Leading Dates in the Bywaters and Thompson Case.

1914		—Edith Graydon employed at Carlton & White's, London
1915	January 15	—Percy Thompson married to Edith Graydon
1918	February	—Frederick Bywaters joins Merchant Service
1920	July	—The Thompsons move to 41 Kensington Gardens, Ilford
1921	June	—Bywaters goes with them to Shanklin, I.W.
,,	,, 18	—He returns to live with them as a lodger
,,	August 5	—He quarrels with Thompson and leaves
,,	September 9	—He leaves in s.s. *Morea* for the East (Correspondence between Bywaters and Mrs. Thompson)
,,	October 29	—Bywaters returns to England
,,	November 3	—He visits the Thompsons
,,	December 11	—He sails again in the *Morea* (Correspondence continued)
1922	January 6	—He returns home
,,	,, 20	—He sails again
,,	February	} Correspondence continued
,,	March	
,,	,, 16	—Bywaters returns home
,,	,, 31	—Bywaters sails again in the *Morea*
,,	April	} Correspondence continued
,,	March	
,,	May 25	—Bywaters returns in the *Morea*
,,	June 9	—Bywaters sails again for the East
,,	July	} Correspondence continued
,,	August	
,,	September 23	—Bywaters arrives at Tilbury, works on ship, and sleeps at home
,,	,, 25	—He meets Mrs. Thompson
,,	,, 29	—He leaves ship and goes to his mother's home
,,	October 2	—He meets Mrs. Thompson by appointment
,,	,, 3	—They have tea at Fuller's, and leave together at 5.15 The Thompsons go to the theatre Bywaters spends the evening at the Graydons, and leaves about 11 p.m. Percy Thompson murdered at Ilford about midnight
,,	,, 4	—Mrs. Thompson visited by police 3 a.m. Bywaters arrives at his mother's house early a.m. He goes to town He spends the evening at the Graydons, where he is arrested. Statement to police Mrs. Thompson arrested
,,	,, 5	—She makes a statement Post mortem on the body of Thompson Bywaters is charged, and makes a second statement
,,	,, 9	—Knife found in Seymour Gardens
,,	,, 12	—Letters found in Bywaters's chest on board s.s. *Morea*
,,	November 3	—Thompson's body exhumed. Post mortem
,,	,,	—Bywaters and Mrs. Thompson before Magistrate. Committed for trial
,,	December 6-11	—Trial at the Old Bailey
,,	,, 21	—Appeals of Bywaters and Mrs. Thompson heard and dismissed
1923	January 9	—Frederick Bywaters hanged at Pentonville and Edith Thompson at Holloway

THE TRIAL

WITHIN THE

CENTRAL CRIMINAL COURT,

OLD BAILEY, LONDON,

WEDNESDAY, 6TH DECEMBER, 1922

Judge—

MR JUSTICE SHEARMAN

Counsel for the Crown—

THE SOLICITOR-GENERAL
MR TRAVERS HUMPHREYS
MR ROLAND OLIVER

(Instructed by the Director of Public Prosecutions)

Counsel for the Prisoner Frederick Bywaters—

MR CECIL WHITELEY, K.C.
MR HUNTLY JENKINS
MR MYLES ELLIOTT

(Instructed by Mr Barrington Matthews)

Counsel for the Prisoner Edith Thompson—

SIR HENRY CURTIS BENNETT, K.C.
MR WALTER FRAMPTON
MR IVOR SNELL

(Instructed by Mr F. A. S. Stern)

[*Copy Indictment No 1**

The King

AGAINST

FREDERICK EDW^D FRANCIS BYWATERS

AND

EDITH JESSIE THOMPSON

CENTRAL CRIMINAL COURT

Presentment of the Grand Jury

F E F BYWATERS and E J THOMPSON are charged with the following offence —

STATEMENT OF OFFENCE

MURDER

Particulars of Offence

F E F BYWATERS and E J THOMPSON on the 4th day of October, 1922, in the County of Essex, and within the jurisdiction of the Central Criminal Court murdered Percy Thompson

---

[*Copy Indictment No 2*†

The King

AGAINST

FREDERICK EDW^D FRANCIS BYWATERS

AND

EDITH JESSIE THOMPSON

CENTRAL CRIMINAL COURT

Presentment of the Grand Jury

F E F BYWATERS and E J THOMPSON are charged with the following offences —

FIRST COUNT

STATEMENT OF OFFENCE

Conspiracy to Murder contrary to sec. 4 of the Offences against the Person Act, 1861

Particulars of Offence

F E F BYWATERS and E J THOMPSON on the 20th day of August, 1921, and on divers days between that date and the 2nd day of October, 1922, in the County of Essex, and within the jurisdiction of the Central Criminal Court, conspired together to murder Percy Thompson

---

* This is the Indictment upon which there was Conviction

† The accused were not tried on this

SECOND COUNT

STATEMENT OF OFFENCE

Soliciting to Murder contrary to sec 4 of the Offences against the Person Act, 1861

Particulars of Offence

E J THOMPSON on the 10th day of February, 1922, and on divers days between that day and the 1st day of October, 1922, in the County of Essex, and within the jurisdiction of the Central Criminal Court, did solicit and endeavour to persuade and did propose to F E F Bywaters to murder Percy Thompson

THIRD COUNT

STATEMENT OF OFFENCE

Inciting to commit a misdemeanour

Particulars of Offence

E J THOMPSON on the 10th day of February, 1922, and on divers days between that day and the 1st day of October, 1922, in the County of Essex, and within the jurisdiction of the Central Criminal Court, did unlawfully solicit and incite F E F Bywaters unlawfully to conspire with her, the said E J Thompson, to murder Percy Thompson

FOURTH COUNT

STATEMENT OF OFFENCE

Administering poison with intent to murder contrary to sec 11 of the Offences against the Person Act, 1861

Particulars of Offence

E J THOMPSON on the 26th day of March, 1922, in the County of Essex, and within the jurisdiction of the Central Criminal Court, did administer to and cause to be taken by Percy Thompson certain poison or other destructive thing unknown with intent to murder the said Percy Thompson

FIFTH COUNT

STATEMENT OF OFFENCE

Administering a destructive thing with intent to murder contrary to sec 11 of the Offences against the Person Act, 1861

Particulars of Offence

E J THOMPSON on the 24th day of April, 1922, in the County of Essex, and within the jurisdiction of the Central Criminal Court, did administer to and cause to be taken by Percy Thompson a certain destructive thing, namely, broken glass, with intent to murder the said Percy Thompson

First Day—Wednesday, 6th December, 1922

Mr WHITELEY—My lord, before the prisoners plead to this indictment I have a submission and an application to make, and that is that in the interest of each of these prisoners there should be two separate trials. The first indictment charges them both as principals with the murder of Percy Thompson. I have had an opportunity of reading the depositions and the exhibits. In my submission it is clear that there must be a question of the admissibility of evidence which may be evidence against one prisoner and may not be evidence against the other, and that the introduction of such evidence must of necessity prejudice the case of the other prisoner.

Sir H. CURTIS BENNETT—I desire to associate myself with the application of my learned friend.

The SOLICITOR-GENERAL—I hope that your lordship will refuse the application.

Mr JUSTICE SHEARMAN—I can see no ground for granting the application.

The CLERK OF THE COURT—Frederick Edward Francis Bywaters and Edith Jessie Thompson, you are charged together on indictment with the offence of murder, the particulars being that on the 4th October in this year you murdered Percy Thompson. Frederick Edward Francis Bywaters, are you guilty or not guilty?

The PRISONER BYWATERS—Not guilty.

The CLERK OF THE COURT—Edith Jessie Thompson, are you guilty or not guilty?

The PRISONER THOMPSON—Not guilty.

(The jury were duly sworn.)

Sir H. CURTIS BENNETT—My lord, before the Solicitor-General starts to open the case to the jury I have an objection to make to certain evidence that I understand the Solicitor-General desires to mention to the jury in his opening.

Mr JUSTICE SHEARMAN—The jury will retire and you can make your objection.

(The jury retired.)

Sir H. CURTIS BENNETT—There are two indictments, as your lordship knows, one indictment charges both the defendants with the crime of wilful murder, and then there is the second indictment with a number of counts charging conspiracy to incite murder and other charges. I understand that the indictment which is to be proceeded with is the first indictment. On that indictment I understand the prosecution desire to open to the jury certain letters which were found in the possession of the defendant Bywaters written

Bywaters and Thompson.

by the defendant Thompson. I appear for Mrs. Thompson and, on behalf of Mrs. Thompson, I object to the opening of those letters to the jury or, in fact, to the admissibility of those letters at any time in evidence as against Mrs. Thompson upon the first indictment.

The charge in this indictment is a charge of murder, and, no doubt, the Solicitor-General is going to suggest to the jury that the actual blow which was struck was struck by Bywaters. I do not think that he is going to suggest that any blow was struck at all by Mrs. Thompson.

Mr. Justice Shearman—Struck, as I understand by the evidence, in the presence of Mrs. Thompson.

Sir H. Curtis Bennett—In the presence of Mrs. Thompson. Now, the letters that I am taking objection to contain certain passages which make it appear that Mrs. Thompson was writing to Bywaters suggesting to him that he should send her certain material for the purpose of giving it to her husband to cause his death, and also suggestions that she was herself administering certain things to her husband. I submit that the admissibility of letters such as those cannot be acceded to until the prosecution have, first of all, showed that Mrs. Thompson took some active part in the murder, if it was murder, of her husband.

Mr. Justice Shearman—That is for the jury to decide, the matter of conspiracy.

Sir H. Curtis Bennett—Yes, my lord. If there were some act committed by Mrs. Thompson, the prosecution might then argue to your lordship that they were entitled to put these letters in evidence, either to show intent to rebut the defence of accident, or to show a system; but, until some act, some definite act, is proved by the prosecution as against Mrs. Thompson, then I submit that all these letters go to show is that if the letters really mean what they are said to mean, Mrs. Thompson is a person who would not be likely to commit the offence which is charged against her.

Mr. Justice Shearman—I wish you would give me a sample, because a great many of the letters contain quite different matters, I mean matters of affection showing the relations between the parties. Do you object to these too?

Sir H. Curtis Bennett—In some letters, where there is matter which I object to, there is also a great deal of matter which I should really welcome; but I cannot, of course, say that part of a letter is evidence and part is not.

Mr. Justice Shearman—You are at present arguing on letters which are suggesting a desire to kill this man or give assistance in killing him. Give me an example.

Sir H. Curtis Bennett—Exhibit 18 is one. "I took possession of it, and when he missed it and asked me for it I refused to give it him," &c. (reads). That is a sample. I was submitting that evidence of that sort is only admissible against Mrs. Thompson for the purpose

Discussion on the Letters.

of showing either that some act of hers was done with intent, or that that act was part of a system, or to rebut the defence that it was an accidental act on her part. Your lordship will remember, as having been one of the Court that this matter was fully discussed in the case of *The King v Armstrong* which was heard in the Court of Criminal Appeal. The decision was that Armstrong having been in possession of arsenic at a time when his wife, in fact, died, the prosecution were entitled to say, ' You were not in innocent possession, as you say you were, of that arsenic, and we can show that you were not in innocent possession of it because, in the month of October, your wife having died in February, you were using it again for the purpose of trying to kill some one." That was the decision in that case, but there, of course, there was the evidence that Armstrong was in possession of poison, and it was the defence of Armstrong that he was in innocent possession of such poison and, therefore, it was necessary to show from the point of view of the prosecution that that defence which Armstrong was putting forward was a defence which was not a true defence upon the evidence which they had available to put before the jury, and so the Court of Criminal Appeal held. Now, in my submission, this is a very different case. I am in this difficulty, I do not know how the Solicitor-General is going to open this case to the jury

Mr JUSTICE SHEARMAN—Only in one indictment. It is a very difficult question when evidence becomes admissible in rebuttal of defence. Putting that aside altogether, is not this particular matter evidence of felonious intent? I am putting aside the question which you and I will both take care of, evidence against one prisoner is not evidence against another that I think, the jury will fully understand before the case is over. But is not this evidence of a felonious intention of this lady who it is alleged, was present at the murder?

Sir H CURTIS BENNETT—Not upon this indictment. It would be evidence, I agree, and I should not be able to object to these letters upon the second indictment. Supposing these letters really mean what upon the face of them they look to mean. This letter that I am referring you to (exhibit 18) was in fact written on 24th April of this year. Now, the death of Mr Thompson took place in the early morning of 4th October of this year. Can it be possibly said that a letter written, even if it does mean what it looks to mean on the face of it, upon 24th April of this year can be evidence that upon 4th October Mrs Thompson, who certainly struck no blow, was a party to the killing of her husband six months after? There is surely a *locus pœnitentiæ* for every one and if a letter is written and is even meant to convey that Mrs Thompson was anxious in April that her husband should die, can it possibly be said to be evidence that she, although present and not striking any blow upon 4th October, was in fact a party, a principal, to the killing of her husband? I submit not

Bywaters and Thompson.

Mr Justice Shearman—It is conceivable, is it not, that she was not a principal in the first degree, but in the second degree? It makes no difference

Sir H Curtis Bennett—No, my lord It is conceivable, of course, that the case for the prosecution may be presented either that she was a principal in the second degree, or an accessory before the fact, and I want to deal with it upon that basis, because I assume that that is the way it may be put

Mr Justice Shearman—An accessory before the fact—you will correct me if I am wrong—in fact becomes a principal in the second degree

Sir H Curtis Bennett—If present she would become a principal in the second degree, if not present and had taken some previous part in the matter, then she would be an accessory before the fact It is really an academic question, the position of Mrs Thompson But the fact remains that the prosecution desire to put this letter and other letters of a similar sort, over dates which vary from November, 1921, until August, 1922 before the jury for the purpose, not of showing that something which Mrs Thompson did constituted murder, but of proving as they suggest, that she was guilty of murder These letters, in my submission, are the only evidence of murder (if they were evidence) as against Mrs Thompson at all The whole of the rest of the evidence relating to that night of 3rd October and the early morning of 4th October is absolutely consistent with Mrs Thompson having been taken by surprise in the attack which was made upon her husband, and knowing nothing whatever about it at all If the prosecution can show some act by Mrs Thompson which has to have light thrown upon it to show whether or not it is an innocent act or a guilty act, then those letters might be admissible but before they become admissible they have got to show some such intent, and in my submission the writing of those letters months before October is too distant from the date of the alleged crime and cannot be said to be evidence as to what Mrs Thompson was doing upon 3rd October

Mr Cecil Whiteley—On behalf of Bywaters I also wish to object

Mr Justice Shearman—There are some letters written by him

Mr Cecil Whiteley—There are only three letters written by Bywaters, and I have no objections to their admissibility On the subject that the letters written by Mrs Thompson which were found in the possession of Bywaters ought not to be admitted in evidence in this case, my grounds for making the submission are quite shortly these—The fact that they were in his possession is, of course, no answer by the prosecution until the prosecution can show that the contents of those letters really are relevant to the issue which is before the jury Now, I do not suppose it is going to be suggested that they are being put in on the question of identity Your lordship

Discussion on the Letters.

will remember the decision in *Thompson* in the House of Lords. I do not suggest that is the ground on which it is suggested, because there is no question of identity, therefore the only possible ground on which they can be admitted is on the ground of felonious intent.

Mr. JUSTICE SHEARMAN—Is your contention at present that they are not evidence against your client, or not evidence at all?

Mr. CECIL WHITELEY—They are not evidence against my client or at all, because the effect of those letters by Mrs. Thompson in January to May of this year is too remote for there to be any connection between what is said in those letters and the assault on the deceased man in the early morning of 4th October.

The SOLICITOR-GENERAL—My learned friend Sir H. Curtis Bennett has taken two objections, as I understand it. One of them is that the letters are not admissible because they are not evidence against his client, and the second objection is one which I should have thought was more for the jury than your lordship—as to their weight.

Mr. JUSTICE SHEARMAN—That is for the jury.

The SOLICITOR-GENERAL—The question is, are they admissible?

Mr. JUSTICE SHEARMAN—First of all, are they admissible against the lady?

The SOLICITOR-GENERAL—As regards Mrs. Thompson, I submit they are admissible because she is being charged as a principal in the second degree, and they are admissible to show that she gave the incitement without which we say the murder would not have been committed, and that is the way in which she is brought into the case. She is indicted, as the law permits, as a principal in the murder, although she did not strike the blow. The crime is one where one hand struck the blow, and we want to show by these letters that her mind conceived it and incited it, the evidence of that is the letters that Mrs. Thompson wrote to the man who struck the blow. The case of *The King v. Armstrong* is, as your lordship said, a very different case indeed. There it was a question as to whether letters or evidence which showed a crime against B had been contemplated was in any way evidence against A, and it was said that a certain foundation ought to be laid before you could bring evidence of the other matters. That is not the case here. Those letters are evidence of the particular crime which is charged, namely, that she prompted the crime and incited the crime, and she is therefore a principal in the second degree. As against Bywaters, the letters are found in his possession; they are evidence of motive.

Mr. JUSTICE SHEARMAN—You will of course prove that he received them. You say they are evidence against her on what ground?

The SOLICITOR-GENERAL—I say they are evidence against her because he received them; it is then a question as to whether we ought to attach any weight to them, but it is certain he received them and that he kept them, it is evidence of motive and intention, and the letters may be necessary, and, indeed in this case are necessary

Mr JUSTICE SHEARMAN—I think they are evidence of intention and motive It is a very difficult question

Sir H CURTIS BENNETT—As I understand, the reason given for the admissibility of this evidence is that these letters show a direct incitement to this crime Now, the letters may upon the face of them show incitement to the crime of either poisoning or destroying Mr Thompson by means of giving him glass In my submission, there must be some nexus between those letters and what they contain and the killing as it took place The killing which is alleged to have been murder took place by a stab, as is alleged, by Bywaters on Mr Thompson Now, where is the connection between that act of murder and these letters which are written months beforehand? In my submission, there is no nexus between them at all, and the proper way to deal with these letters is to deal with them under an indictment which actually charges a direct incitement, to use my friend's words, to murder Upon that indictment, clearly admissible, upon this indictment, in my submission, not

Mr JUSTICE SHEARMAN—I think these letters, letters such as the ones to which Sir Henry Curtis Bennett referred, are admissible as evidence of intention and evidence of motive, and I shall admit them Objection can be taken in the proper way when they come up Only one other matter I do not think you can contest the letters showing the affectionate relations between the parties are not evidence of motive in so far as they show affection

Sir H CURTIS BENNETT—The letters, as I have pointed out, contain both

Mr JUSTICE SHEARMAN—You cannot object to them in that way?

Sir H CURTIS BENNETT—I am objecting to them on that ground

(The jury returned into Court)

Opening Statement for the Crown.

The SOLICITOR-GENERAL—May it please your lordship, members of the jury—on 4th October, a little after midnight, Percy Thompson was stabbed to death on his way home from Ilford station, near which he lived He was in a dark part of a road, not over-well lit at the best of times, when he was struck, first of all, apparently, from behind, and then in front, by some assailant The only person present was his wife, Mrs Thompson, who is now in the dock She is charged with Bywaters, who is said by the prosecution to have been the assailant, with the murder of Percy

Sir Thomas Inskip, K C
Solicitor General

Opening Statement for the Crown.

The Solicitor-General

Thompson. You will be able to distinguish as to the relevancy of the evidence as between Bywaters and Mrs. Thompson. I give you that warning before I come to the facts in order that you may the more closely, if possible, follow the evidence which I shall open, and which shall be given. I ask you to dismiss from your minds any suggestions that you may have heard about the case in other places.

The deceased man, Percy Thompson, aged thirty-two, was a shipping clerk, and had been engaged with the same firm for twelve or thirteen years. He married in January, 1915, Miss Graydon, whose parents were living at Manor Park. There are no children of the marriage. Mr. and Mrs. Thompson lived at two or three different places after their marriage and at the time of the incident that I am going to refer to they were residing at 41 Kensington Gardens, Ilford, which they had bought in July, 1920. Mrs. Lester, who had occupied the house previously, continued to live there as a lodger. Mrs. Thompson was a little younger than her husband—she is twenty-eight years old now—and, perhaps because there were no children or for other reasons, she was carrying on her employment with a firm of wholesale milliners in Aldersgate Street, being book-keeper and manageress for the firm, and a capable and industrious servant.

The prisoner Bywaters is only twenty years of age. He was engaged for some time in the service of the P. & O. Company on the "Morea" as a laundry steward, and his employment necessitated his absence from England for considerable periods. When in this country he lived with his mother, Mrs. Bywaters, who at one time resided in Manor Park. At the time of the incident with which we are concerned his mother had removed to Upper Norwood. Bywaters, whose ship came to Tilbury Dock, found it more convenient to live with the Graydons at Manor Park, and in that way, no doubt, he became acquainted with Mrs. Thompson. He had also been at school with the Graydons. The acquaintance of Bywaters with the Thompsons became more intimate after a certain date in 1921. In June of that year he accompanied them on a holiday to Shanklin, in the Isle of Wight. He returned with them to their house at Ilford, and continued to stay with them until some date in August, when an incident happened which made him desire to leave, and Mr. Thompson to direct that he should leave, the house. It appeared that the relations between Mr. and Mrs. Thompson, formerly happy, had become less happy, and there was a quarrel between them which resulted in Bywaters leaving their house. On 21st September Bywaters left in his ship, returning in the autumn and departing again in November. About this time there were a number of letters written by Mrs. Thompson to Bywaters, the origin of which may have been the holiday in 1921. I say that because throughout these letters there

Bywaters and Thompson.

The Solicitor General

is a constant return to a certain date—27th June 1921—mentioned by Mrs Thompson as a date which marked a crisis or change in the relations between her and Bywaters. Whether that was the origin of what happened afterwards or not is not necessary for you to decide. The fact of importance for the moment is that during his absence there was a passionate and ardent correspondence between these two persons which showed that they were engaged, or intended to engage, in an intrigue. Of course, Mrs Thompson still lived with her husband, but the letters as I have said were of a passionate nature. All these letters were found in the possession of Bywaters by the police, and taken from his pocket or from his room where he lived with his mother on the day or day after the murder, or found in a "ditty box" on the ship. There is one letter which I wish to read. It bears no date, and it refers to one incident in connection with racing which enables the prosecution to fix an approximate date. It appears to have been written to Bywaters when he was some distance from the United Kingdom. It was written, as the prosecution know from the racing incident referred to, after the running of the November Handicap, which was on 26th November, 1921, and the internal evidence in the letter shows that it was written before Christmas. In that letter (exhibit 27) there appears the following:—

'It is the man who has no right who generally comforts the woman who has wrongs.' This is also right darlint isn't it? as things are, but darlint, it's not always going to be is it? You will have the right soon won't you? Say yes.

There is a more significant passage in the letter, the first of many such, indicative of the intention or desire on the part of the writer to take active measures. It is for you, members of the jury, to say what this passage means:—

The time goes slowly enough in all conscience—I don't seem to care who spends the money, as long as it helps me to dance through the hours. I had the wrong Porridge to day, but I dont suppose it will matter, I dont seem to care much either way. You'll probably say I'm careless and I admit I am, but I dont care—do you?

The unexpectedness of the passage, the inappropriateness of that passage as it stands, is startling. It will be for you to say whether the line of thought that was in Mrs Thompson's mind was that the existence of her husband was a bar to the happiness she thought she could attain.

I turn now to a letter of 3rd January (exhibit 13), in which Mrs Thompson says:—

Immediately I have received a second letter, I have destroyed the first and when I got the third I destroyed the second and so on, now the only one I have is the 'Dear Edie' one written to 41

Opening Statement for the Crown.

The Solicitor-General

Let me here explain that 41 is the number of the house in Kensington Gardens, Ilford, where Mrs Thompson lived. I should add that she sometimes received letters at Aldersgate Street.

> The only one I have is the 'Dear Edie' one written to 41, which I am going to keep. It may be useful, who knows? I've surrendered to him unconditionally now—do you understand me? I think it the best way to disarm any suspicion, in fact he has several times asked me if I am happy now, and I've said 'Yes quite' but you know that's not the truth, dont you.

When she says "surrendered to him" she is undoubtedly referring to her husband. In another part of the letter she says, "You won't always be 'the man with no right,' will you—tell me you won't." Some of the passages are indicative of nothing more than guilty passion between the parties, but the letters are important when you come to decide the question as to whether Mrs Thompson had any reason to get rid of her husband.

Bywaters was at home on 7th January, and left again on the 20th. While he was at home no letters so far as is known, passed between the parties. Soon after he left the letters began again. I read now from the letter of 10th February (exhibit 15)—

> Darlint—You must do something this time—I'm not really impatient—but opportunities come and go by—they have to—because I'm helpless and I think and think and think—perhaps—it will never come again.
> On Wednesday we had words—in bed—Oh you know darlint—over that same old subject and he said—it was all through you I'd altered. About 2 a.m. he woke me up and asked for water as he felt ill. I got it for him and asked him what the matter was and this is what he told me—whether its the truth I dont know or whether he did it to frighten me, anyway it didn't. He said—someone he knows in town (not the man I previously told you about) had given him a prescription for a draught for insomnia and he'd had it made up and taken it and it made him ill. He certainly looked ill and his eyes were glassy. I've hunted for the said prescription everywhere and cant find it and asked him what he had done with it and he said the chemist kept it. I told Avis about the incident only I told her as if it frightened and worried me as I thought perhaps it might be useful at some future time that I had told somebody. What do you think, darlint.

The passage is perhaps dark, but light is thrown on it by a later paragraph, which reads—

> It would be so easy darlint—if I had things—I do hope I shall.

One of the features of the case is the number and character of the newspaper cuttings that have been found. They are cuttings of a very great variety.

Mr JUSTICE SHEARMAN—Sent to Bywaters?

The SOLICITOR-GENERAL—Yes. Along with the letter dated 10th February there was a newspaper cutting referring to the poisoning

Bywaters and Thompson.

The Solicitor General

of a curate and his household by hyoscine. In the same letter there was another newspaper cutting headed "Poisoned chocolates for University Chief. Deadly powder posted to Oxford Chancellor. Ground glass in box." I ask you to notice the latter phrase. Another letter contained a cutting, "Beautiful Dancer Drugged. Visit to Chinese Restaurant," giving an account of the poisoning of a woman by cocaine who was suspected of having had cyanide of potassium administered to her. I ask you carefully to note that in her letter of 22nd February (exhibit 16) she writes—

> I suppose it isnt possible for you to send it to me—not at all possible, I do so chafe at wasting time darlint.

What "it" refers to is entirely for you, and whether it has any significance I leave to your determination. You will distinguish between expressions of devotion and those which appear to indicate an intention to get rid of the husband. That is the letter containing the cutting about the death of a "Beautiful Dancer."

On 14th March she writes again, exhibit 20—

> I ask you again to think out all the plans and methods for me. I wait and wait so anxiously now—for the time when we'll be with each other even though it is only once—for 'one little hour.'

With this letter there was enclosed a newspaper cutting which had reference to another poisoning case. It will be for you to say what she indicated. In March Bywaters returned to this country and sailed again at the end of the month. The letters then indicated the strength of the desire and a greater determination on the part of Mrs Thompson to take action against her husband. On 31st March, the day Bywaters sailed, when you might expect passion to be at its height, she wrote (exhibit 50)—

> After tonight I am going to die   not really   but put on the mask again darlint until the 26th May—doesn't it seem years and years away? It does to me and I'll hope and hope all the time that I'll never have to wear the mask any more after this time. This time really will be the last you will go away—like things are, won't it? We said it before darlint I know and we failed   but there will be no failure this next time darlint, there mustn't be—I'm telling you—if things are the same again then I am going with you—wherever it is—if its to sea—I am coming too and if it is to nowhere—I'm also coming darlint. You'll never leave me behind again, never, unless things are different.

In that letter two possibilities are presented. I suggest that the phrase "if things are the same again" means 'if my husband is still alive, and I cannot be with you except by leaving him, I will go with you.' In the other case how were things to be different except by the destruction of her husband's life?

The next letter is a long and ardent one, and it contains pas-

Opening Statement for the Crown.

The Solicitor-General

sages of great importance. I refer to the letter of 1st April, exhibit 17, where the following appears:—

> Don't keep this piece. About the Marconigram—do you mean one saying Yes or No, because I shant send it darlint. I'm not going to try any more until you come back. I made up my mind about this last Thursday. He was telling his mother etc. the circumstances of my 'Sunday morning escapade' and he puts great stress on the fact of the tea tasting bitter 'as if something had been put in it' he says. Now I think whatever else I try it in again will still taste bitter—he will recognise it and be more suspicious still and if the quantity is still not successful it will injure any chance I may have of trying when you come home. Do you understand? I thought a lot about what you said of Dan. Darlint, don't trust him—I don't mean don't tell him anything because I know you never would—What I mean is don't let him be suspicious of you regarding that—because if we were successful in the action—darlint circumstances may afterwards make us want many friends—or helpers and we must have no enemies—or even people that know a little too much. Remember the saying 'A little knowledge is a dangerous thing.' Darlint we'll have no one to help us in the world now and we mustn't make enemies unnecessarily. He says—to his people—he fought and fought with himself to keep conscious—'I'll never die, except naturally—I'm like a cat with nine lives' he said and detailed to them an occasion when he was young and nearly suffocated by gas fumes. I wish we had not got electric light—it would be easy. I'm going to try the glass again occasionally—when it is safe. I've got an electric light globe this time.

In the letter of 24th April, exhibit 18, Mrs. Thompson writes—

> I used the "light bulb" three times, but the third time—he found a piece—so I have given it up—until you come home.

That is the suggestion carried into effect. You are not being asked to say whether she attempted to poison her husband; all you are asked to consider is whether Mrs. Thompson incited Bywaters to kill her husband, and the letters are important from that point of view. They are important to show that she so worked and preyed on the mind of this young man by her suggestions that, although it was his hand that struck the blow, it was her mind that conceived the crime.

On 1st May she wrote to Bywaters at Port Said, exhibit 19—

> I don't think we're failures in other things and we musn't be in this. We musn't give up as we said. No, we shall have to wait if we fail again. Darlint, Fate can't always turn against us and if it is we must fight it — You and I are strong now. We must be stronger. We must learn to be patient. You said it was enough for an elephant. Perhaps it was. But you don't allow for the taste making only a small quantity to be taken. It sounded like a reproach was it meant to be? Darlint I tried hard—you won't know how hard—because you weren't there to see and I can't tell you all—but I did—I do want you to believe I did for both of us. I was buoyed up with the hope of

Bywaters and Thompson.

The Solicitor General

the "light bulb" and I used a lot—big pieces too—not powdered—and it has no effect—I quite expected to be able to send that cable—but no—nothing has happened from it and now your letter tells me about the bitter taste again Oh darlint, I do feel so down and unhappy Wouldn't the stuff make small pills coated together with soap and dipped in liquorice powder—like Beechams—try while you're away Our Boy had to have his thumb operated on because he had a piece of glass in it that's what made me try that method again—but I suppose as you say he is not normal I know I feel I shall never get him to take a sufficient quantity of anything bitter No I haven't forgotten the key I told you before

If ever we are lucky enough to be happy darling I'll love you such a lot I always show you how much I love you for all you do for me

All that lying and scheming and subterfuge to obtain one little hour in each day—when by right of nature and our love we should be together for all the twenty-four in every day

What effect would letters of this sort have on a young man whose affections she was engaging? On 18th May (exhibit 22) she makes yet another of the almost innumerable suggestions to encompass her husband's death This time the suggestion comes from a book that members of the jury may possibly have read, written by Robert Hichens, " Bella Donna " She quotes the following from it —

It must be remembered that digitalin is a cumulative poison and that the same dose harmless if taken once, yet frequently repeated, becomes deadly

The letter goes on—" Is it any use?" She refers constantly to this book and the lesson it is to teach to them as a possible method of taking her husband's life On 23rd May (exhibit 23) she says—

I'd like you to read 'Bella Donna' first you may learn something from it to help us then you can read "The Fruitful Vine"

On 9th June Bywaters went away and did not return until the following September On 13th June she writes (exhibit 24) about an apparent illness of her husband—

Darlingest Boy—I'm trying very hard—very very hard to B B * I know my pal wants me to On Thursday—he was on the ottoman at the foot of the bed and said he was dying and wanted to—he had another heart attack—thro me Darlnt I had to laugh at this because I knew it couldn't be a heart attack When he saw this had no effect on me—he got up and stormed—I said exactly what you told me to and he replied that he knew that s what I wanted and he wasnt going to give it to me—it would make things far too easy for both of you (meaning you and me)

It may be suggested that there is nothing to show any want of

---

* B B apparently means " be brave "—Ed

Opening Statement for the Crown.

The Solicitor-General

harmony between Mr and Mrs Thompson except natural quarrels. After reading that passage it does appear that there was a bitter antagonism. There is a postscript to Mrs Thompson's letter of 4th July (exhibit 26)—' Have you studied bichloride of mercury," which I am told is a deadly poison. There is another letter in which there is reference to a passage in " Romance " where she says—

> Then we were pals—this year we seem no further advanced. Why should you not send me something? You still have your own way always. If I do not mind the risk why should you.

There is in that connection a more significant passage in which it appears that she was the dominating influence in the crime. She was 28, and the man was only 20. The letter in question contains the following :—

> From then onwards everything has gone well with our lives. Darlint I should not mind if I could feel some day I could make up to you for some of the unhappiness I have cost you—I feel it shall come right but there is no conviction in it, why cannot we see into the future.

I suggest that through the correspondence it becomes clear that it was Mrs Thompson who was urging Bywaters on to commit the crime in some way or other in order to secure the happiness upon which her passion was set. He may have been reluctant or not, but can you, members of the jury, have any doubt after hearing these letters that she was not reluctant? The time comes when apparently she is determined that there shall be a culmination of the whole idea. It appeared that the man was cooling in his affection, or passion or his readiness to commit the crime. He was approaching this country and in a letter (exhibit 28) she says, " I think I am fearfully disappointed about you not getting in on Friday." She also refers to it being 109 days since she has seen him. Further on in that letter she says—

> Darlingest boy,—I don't quite understand you about " Pals." You say " Can we be Pals only, Peidi, it will make it easier." Do you mean for always? because if you do, No, No, a thousand times. We can't be " pals " only for always darlint its impossible physically and mentally. It must be still " the hope of all " or ' the finish of all." If you still only mean for a certain time and you think it best, darlint it shall be so—I don't see how it will be easier myself.
> You sound very despondent when you say about " Time passes and with it some of the pain—Fate ordained our lot to be hard." Does some of the pain you feel pass with time? Perhaps it does—things seem so much easier to forget with a man—his environment is always different—but with a woman it's always the same. Darlint my pain gets less and less bearable—it hurts more and more every day, every hour really. No, I don't think the man who mistook me for " Romance " was decent darlint, but I do think he was quite genuine in mistaking me, I don't think it

Bywaters and Thompson.

The Solicitor General
was a ruse on his part Yes, darlint you are jealous of him—but I want you to be—he has the right by law to all that you have the right to by nature and love—yes darlint be jealous, so much that you will do something desperate

Bywaters' ship arrives at Tilbury on 23rd September, and she sends him a telegram, "Can you meet Peidi Broadway 4 p m" That she was not content even then to leave the man alone appears from another newspaper extract dated 20th September, headed " Chicken Broth death Rat poison consumed by fowl kills woman " This was a reference to the death of a woman who was said to have taken poison in chicken broth There is no doubt that Mrs Thompson and Bywaters did meet on 25th September and the death of Percy Thompson took place on 4th October They met outside the premises where Mrs Thompson was employed Bywaters was seen by a Mrs Vallender outside the premises and they were seen afterwards in Fuller's shop It seems that on the Sunday or Monday before the crime Mrs Thompson wrote to Bywaters The letter (exhibit 60) is undated, and it commences—

Darlingest lover of mine, thank you thank you, oh thank you a thousand times for Friday—it was lovely—its always lovely to go out with you And then Saturday—yes I did feel happy All Saturday evening I was thinking about you I tried so hard to find a way out of to-night darlingest but he was suspicious and still is—I suppose we must make a study of this deceit for some time longer I hate it Don't forget what we talked in the Tea Room, I'll still risk and try if you will—we only have $3\frac{3}{4}$ years left darlingest

That is a rather cryptic reference to a period that Mrs Thompson mentions more than once She speaks sometimes of four years, then fifteen months have passed, and now she says there are three and three-quarter years I ask—what did they talk about in the tearoom? I put it that there was a long course of suggestion resulting in a desire to escape from the position, and a fresh suggestion was made in the tearoom On 2nd October, in the morning, Bywaters was rung up by a woman Mrs Bywaters answered the telephone and Bywaters was summoned to it He left the house that morning, and was seen with Mrs Thompson in the afternoon On 3rd October Bywaters was again rung up on the telephone He left the house, wearing a grey overcoat, and was seen with Mrs Thompson at Fuller's between four o'clock and 5 15, at which hour they left the shop together He spent the evening at the Graydons' house while Mr and Mrs Thompson went to a theatre with a Mr and Mrs Laxton, Mr Laxton being an uncle of Mrs Thompson Mr and Mrs Thompson went back to Ilford after the performance (The Solicitor-General described the circumstances of the attack on Mr Thompson and pointed out that there were no signs of a struggle) Other theatre-goers were attracted to the spot and heard Mrs Thompson exclaim, " Oh, my God, will you help me? My husband is dying "

Opening Statement for the Crown.

The Solicitor-General

Referring to the occasion when at Ilford police station Mrs. Thompson saw Bywaters, the Solicitor-General said—She was much agitated and exclaimed "My God, what can I do? Why did he do it? I did not want him to do it. I must tell the truth. I saw my husband struggling with Freddy Bywaters." Bywaters at first declared that he knew nothing about the matter, but when told that Mrs. Thompson was being charged with him he said 'Why Mrs. Thompson? She was not aware of my movements. I met Mr. and Mrs. Thompson in the road. I said to him, You have got to separate from your wife.' He said, 'No.' I said, 'Yes.' We struggled, and I took my knife from my pocket. We fought and he got the worst of it. She must have been spellbound as I never saw her move. The reason I fought Thompson is because he never acted like a man to his wife. I could not go on seeing her live like she did. I did not intend to kill but only to injure him.'

A post-mortem examination showed that there were practically no traces of any poison. There was a trace of morphine, but the presence of that might be due to other reasons, and it has no significance in the case. Nor was there any trace of glass in the body.

(The Solicitor-General read the statements by the accused.) I suggest to you, members of the jury, that you will have to consider whether the hand that struck the blow was moved, was incited, to the crime by Mrs. Thompson. It is no answer that the whole of the incitement should come from Mrs. Thompson. It may be that the passion of the young man may have led him in that direction. There is the undoubted evidence in the letters upon which you can find that there was a preconcerted meeting between Mrs. Thompson and Bywaters at the place, but supposing you were not wholly satisfied that there was a conspiracy made to effect the murder at this place and time, if you are satisfied that Mrs. Thompson incited the murder and that, incited and directed by her controlling hand, Bywaters committed the murder, then it will be my duty to ask you, after hearing the evidence, to find her who incited and proposed the murder as guilty as Bywaters who committed it.

Evidence for the Prosecution.

JOHN AMBROSE HENRY LAXTON, examined by Mr. TRAVERS HUMPHREYS—I live at South Tottenham. The deceased Percy Thompson was my nephew by marriage. From time to time I met him and his wife, the prisoner Thompson. On Tuesday 3rd October, I met them both by arrangement at the Criterion Theatre, I think the arrangement was made by my wife about a week or a fortnight beforehand. After the performance was over we left Mr. and Mrs. Thompson at the Piccadilly Tube station, about quarter to eleven or eleven o'clock. They were going to Liverpool Street, and went down a different lift from what we did.

Bywaters and Thompson.

John A H Laxton

Cross-examined by Sir H Curtis Bennett—I had gone on several occasions before to the theatre with Mr and Mrs Thompson So far as I could see they appeared to be on good terms The party upon the particular evening to which I have spoken was an ordinary happy theatre party, and when Mr and Mrs Thompson left us at the tube station they appeared to be upon their usual terms

Robert Taylor, examined by Mr Roland Oliver—I am a police constable of the K Division and am accustomed to making plans I have prepared a plan of the neighbourhood of Belgrave Road and Kensington Gardens Ilford, which is now produced I have shown by dots the actual scene of the crime, nearly half-way between Endsleigh Gardens and Kensington Gardens I also show the street lamps in the neighbourhood The place where the actual killing was done is a dark part of the road at night The spot I have marked on the plan as the scene of killing is only 54 yards from Thompson's house, 41 Kensington Gardens At this point the pavement is 7 feet wide, and the roadway is 26 feet wide

Dora Finch Pittard, examined by Mr Travers Humphreys— I live at 59 Endsleigh Gardens, Ilford A few minutes before midnight on 3rd October I arrived with some friends of mine at Ilford station and I proceeded to walk home by Belgrave Road When I was between De Vere Gardens and Endsleigh Gardens I saw a woman running towards me—the prisoner, Mrs Thompson She cried out, " Oh, my God! Will you help me, my husband is ill, he is bleeding " I asked her where he was, and she said he was on the pavement I took Mrs Thompson to the house of Dr Maudsley, at the corner of Courtland Avenue, and then I went back to Kensington Gardens, Mrs Thompson being just in front of me Finding a man lying on the pavement, I asked Mrs Thompson what had happened to her husband, and she said " Oh, don't ask me, I don't know Somebody flew past, and when I turned to speak to him blood was pouring out of his mouth " Mrs Thompson was very agitated and incoherent

Cross-examined by Sir H Curtis Bennett—When I first saw Mrs Thompson she was running hard in my direction

It was quite clear to you that at that time she was in a hysterical condition?—Yes, she was very agitated

It was quite obvious to you that what she wanted was to get help for her husband?—Yes, I suppose so

Percy Edward Clevely, examined by Mr Travers Humphreys —I live at 62 Mayfair Avenue, Ilford I was one of the party which included the last witness, Miss Pittard While walking

Evidence for Prosecution.

Percy Edward Clevely

through Belgrave Road we met the prisoner, Mrs Thompson, who seemed to come out of the darkness, as it were. She spoke about her husband having fallen down, that he was ill, and she wanted help, and she asked where we could find a doctor. We went to Dr Maudsley's house, and, on returning, we found the deceased lying on the pavement with his back propped up against the wall. I asked Mrs Thompson how it had happened, and she said she could not say—"Something brushed past," or "flew past," or words to that effect, "and he fell down."

Cross-examined by Sir H Curtis Bennett—When Mrs Thompson first came up, was not the first thing she said, "Do you know a doctor, do you know a doctor?"—No, I think the first thing was that she asked for help. She asked for a doctor, and said that her husband had fallen down. On the way back from Dr Maudsley's Mrs Thompson ran on in front of us to get back to her husband. When we got there we found her kneeling down with him.

When you asked her what had happened, was she in a very agitated condition?—Yes, she was certainly very excited and agitated.

And hysterical and incoherent in her statements?—Yes.

John Webber, examined by Mr Roland Oliver—I am a sales manager and live at 59 De Vere Gardens Ilford. About 12 30 in the morning of 4th October, just as I was about to retire to bed I heard a woman's voice saying, "Oh, don't, oh, don't," in a most piteous manner. On hearing that I went out into the street, and I saw two ladies and a gentleman coming towards me in the direction of Dr Maudsley's house. One of the ladies was running in front of the other two. After they had passed me I saw a match being struck, and I went up to the place and found a man sitting against the wall. Mrs Thompson was there alone with him, and I asked her if the man had had a fall, but she said she did not know. I asked her if I could be of any assistance to him, and she said, "Don't touch him, don't touch him, a lady and a gentleman have gone off for a doctor." After that Dr Maudsley came with Miss Pittard and Mr Clevely. I helped the doctor to undress the man. I heard the doctor ask Mrs Thompson if he had been ill, and where they had come from. She told him that he had not been ill, and that they had come from the Criterion Theatre.

Cross-examined by Sir H Curtis Bennett—I have no doubt whatever that the voice I heard, "Oh, don't oh, don't," was the voice of Mrs Thompson. It was about three or five minutes afterwards that I saw the three persons coming towards me. Mrs Thompson, who was in front, was sobbing and running hard. When I went across to where Mr Thompson was sitting on the pavement I found Mrs Thompson there, evidently waiting for

Bywaters and Thompson.

assistance. I asked her if he had had a fall, and she said "Yes—no—I don't know."

It was quite evident, was it not, that she was in a very agitated state at that time?—I should say she was almost hysterical.

Dr. NOEL MAUDSLEY, examined by Mr. TRAVERS HUMPHREYS—I live at 62 Courtland Avenue, Ilford, which is at the corner of Belgrave Road. I was called up by Miss Pittard in the early morning of 4th October, and I went to a spot about half-way between Kensington Gardens and Endsleigh Gardens. I there saw a man lying on the pavement, with Mrs. Thompson standing by his side. I struck a match and made an examination of the man. I first examined his pulse, and found that he was dead. I should think about five or eight minutes would elapse from the time I was first called to the time I actually got to the body. When I examined the man I should say he had been dead somewhere about ten minutes. Mrs. Thompson was in a confused condition, hysterical and agitated. I asked her if her husband had been taken ill coming home in the train or coming along the road, and she said no. When I told her that her husband was dead she said, "Why did you not come sooner and save him?" I saw no wounds; there were no bleeding points to observe, but the blood was welling out of his mouth. I did not see any indications of a struggle having taken place.

Cross-examined by Mr. CECIL WHITELEY—I never directed my attention at all to the wounds from which this man was suffering; I made no examination.

WALTER GRIMES, examined by Mr. TRAVERS HUMPHREYS—I am a sergeant of the K Division of the Metropolitan Police. About 3 a.m. on 4th October I went to Mrs. Thompson's house and asked her if she could explain to me what had happened on the road home from the station. She said, "I don't know, I can't say; I only know that my husband suddenly dropped down and screamed out, 'Oh!' I then rushed across the road and saw a lady and gentleman, and asked them if they would help me, and they went with me to the doctor." Later on in the morning I asked her if she was carrying a knife in her handbag at the time, and she replied, "No." I then asked her if she or her husband saw or spoke to any person when they were coming through Belgrave Road, and she replied, "No, I did not notice any one."

Cross-examined by Sir H. CURTIS BENNETT—I was along with Sergeant Mew when this conversation took place with Mrs. Thompson at three o'clock in the morning. At that time she appeared to be very distressed and inclined to be hysterical. Sergeant Mew asked her, "Can you account for the cuts on your husband's neck?" Mrs. Thompson said, "No. We were walking along, my husband

Evidence for Prosecution.

Walter Grimes

said, 'Oh' I said, 'Bear up' thinking he had one of his attacks. He then fell on me and walked a little further, he then fell up against the wall, and then on to the ground." Sergeant Mew then asked her if her husband carried a knife.

WALTER MEW, examined by Mr TRAVERS HUMPHREYS—I am a police sergeant. I went to Belgrave Road shortly after 1 a m on 4th October. Mrs Thompson was there beside the body of her husband. After the body was removed by some other officers I went with her to her home, 41 Kensington Gardens, which was quite close by. On the way there she said "Will he come back?" and I replied, "Yes." She then said, "They will blame me for this." At three o'clock on that same morning I returned to 41 Kensington Gardens and saw Mrs Thompson again. I asked her, "Can you account for the cuts on your husband's neck?" She replied, "No. We were walking along and my husband said 'Oh' I said, 'Bear up,' thinking he had one of his attacks. He then fell on me and walked a little further. He then fell up against the wall, and then on to the ground." I asked her, 'Did he have a knife?" And she replied "No I did not see a knife or anything." I noticed that her coat and her clothes and face had signs of blood on them, which would be natural if she had been holding up her husband or anybody else who was bleeding.

Cross-examined by Mr CECIL WHITELEY—I went to the mortuary to which the body was taken, and I saw the clothes taken off the deceased man's body. He was wearing a blue suit. There was a hip pocket on the right-hand side of the trousers.

Cross-examined by Sir H CURTIS BENNETT—The upper part of Mr Thompson's clothing was saturated with blood. The blood which I saw on the clothes of Mrs Thompson was quite consistent with her having assisted her husband and having propped him up against the wall in the position in which he was found.

By Mr JUSTICE SHEARMAN—When she said, "Will he come back," I thought she meant would they bring her husband's body back.

Cross-examination continued—I do not think she realised at the time that her husband was dead.

RICHARD HALLIDAY THOMPSON, examined by Mr TRAVERS HUMPHREYS—I live at 49 Seymour Gardens, Ilford. The deceased, Percy Thompson, was my brother. He was thirty-two years of age at the time of his death. I last saw him alive on the night of 2nd October. At that time he appeared to be in good health. His wife and he had been living at 41 Kensington Gardens, Ilford, for something over two years. I was called in the early morning of 4th October to go to 41 Kensington Gardens, and I got there between quarter to two and two o'clock. I had been told that my brother

Bywaters and Thompson.

Richard Halliday Thompson

had had a seizure and was dead. When I got to the house I found my sister-in-law there; she was in a very agitated condition. I asked her if she could give me a rough idea of what had happened and how my brother had met with his death. She stated that he was walking along and suddenly came over queer, fell against the wall, and slid down saying "Oh." She told me that her husband had been complaining of pains in his leg on the way from the station. She went to get the nearest doctor, and on her way she met a lady and gentleman, and asked them to obtain assistance for her. I understood then that they went with her to the doctor's, and he was rather a long time coming, and she complained about it. When the doctor arrived her husband was dead. I understood her to say that the doctor said he had died from hæmorrhage. I do not think I asked her any other questions.

Cross-examined by Mr CECIL WHITELEY—My sister-in-law was a Miss Graydon. I have known her for many years. My brother and his wife frequently visited the Graydons at 231 Shakespeare Crescent. I think they usually went there on a Friday. I have never met the prisoner Bywaters at the Graydons' house.

Cross-examined by Sir H. CURTIS BENNETT—My brother joined the London Scottish in 1916, and was discharged because he was suffering from heart trouble and was totally unfit for service.

CYRIL GEAL, examined by Mr TRAVERS HUMPHREYS—I am a police constable. At 12.30 a.m. on 4th October I, with the assistance of another constable, took the body of the deceased man Thompson to the Ilford mortuary and assisted to undress the body. I did not find a knife or any other weapon in the possession of the deceased man. Except for the cuts in the clothing caused by a knife, I did not find that the clothing had been torn at all.

Dr PERCY JAMES DROUGHT, examined by the SOLICITOR-GENERAL.—I am divisional surgeon to the Ilford Police Division. On 5th October I made, by direction of the Coroner, a post-mortem examination of the body of Percy Thompson. I found on the body on the left side below the ribs, four slight cuts on the skin. I also found on the front of the chin two slight cuts parallel to one another, two slight cuts on the right side of the lower jaw, and on the inner side of the right arm, at the elbow, there was a cut $3\frac{1}{4}$ inches long. I then found a stab in the back of the neck 2 inches deep and $1\frac{1}{4}$ inches wide, that was above the clothing. Then there was a stab at the back of the neck slightly to the right $2\frac{1}{2}$ inches deep and $1\frac{1}{4}$ inches wide, passing upwards towards the right ear.

By Mr JUSTICE SHEARMAN—These were two separate stabs.

Examination continued—The result of the second stab was that there was about half a pint of blood in the stomach which had come from the artery in the neck, the carotid artery, which had

Evidence for Prosecution.

Dr Percy James Drought

been severed. I should say that the wounds at the back and round the neck required a considerable force. Those at the front were superficial, and did not require so much force. I came to the conclusion from the bloodstains that the assailant was on the footpath when the blows were struck. With regard to the slight wound at the front, the assailant must have been in front and then got round to the back with the deeper ones. The stab that cut his carotid artery is more likely to have been struck from the back than from the front. It would have been possible for the man to walk after the blow that severed the artery was struck, but not for very long. I do not think he would be able to speak very much. I should think that the man would die in about a couple of minutes after the severe stab was delivered. The wounds which I saw could have been inflicted by the knife which is now produced.

Cross-examined by Mr CECIL WHITELEY—In my opinion, the wound on the neck, the fatal wound, was received from behind.

But it is doubtful?—It is doubtful. I am quite clear that the fatal wound was the last blow that was inflicted.

Mrs LILIAN BYWATERS, examined by Mr ROLAND OLIVER—I am a widow, and reside at 11 Weston Street, Upper Norwood. The prisoner Bywaters is my son. He was twenty on 27th June of this year. For some years past he has been employed as a ship's writer by the P. & O. Company. When the ship was in port and his duties did not necessitate his staying with the ship he used to live with me. Once in the summer of last year he stayed away for about a fortnight. He told me that he had been staying with Mr and Mrs Thompson at Ilford, and that he had gone with them to the Isle of Wight for a holiday. I believe this was in July of last year, but I could not say for certain. For the last year or more he has been on the P. & O. ship "Morea." When she was in port she was generally at Tilbury, and my son always stayed with me except on the one occasion I have spoken to. I believe he sometimes slept on board. I know the Graydon boys through their going to school with my son. I believe that he once stayed for a short time with the Graydons at Manor Park, but I could not say for certain. I know Mrs Graydon slightly, and have been in her company once or twice at the outside. The last time I saw her before this affair was early this year, but I did not speak to her then.

Coming to the last time that my son came home from sea, the "Morea" got in on 23rd September, and my son remained with the ship, working there for some days, but sleeping at home. I think he stopped working on the ship on Friday, 29th September. That day he just went up to town, as far as I know, and came back home to sleep some time after nine o'clock in the evening. On the Saturday morning he went up to town and came back to tea. On Sunday 1st October, he stayed at home all day. On the Monday

Bywaters and Thompson.

Mrs Lilian Bywaters

morning he went up to town. Before he went out there was a telephone message. I answered the telephone and spoke to a woman. I do not know whose voice it was. As the result of speaking to that woman my son came downstairs from his bedroom and spoke through the telephone. He went up to town just after eleven o'clock, I think, and he came back at night with the 11 5 train from Victoria. I had been in town myself that day, and I came back in the same train. Our station is Gipsy Hill. On the Tuesday the telephone rang just before nine o'clock, and my son answered it. I do not know whether it was a man or a woman who rang up. My son left the house a little before twelve. I went to bed about half-past ten that evening; my son had not returned then. Later on the front-door bell rang. I could not say what time it was; I think I was sleeping when the bell rang. I called out, "Is that you, Mick?" and he answered, "Yes, Mum." Next morning I said to him, "You were late last night, were you not?" and he said, "Yes." I asked him "Did you go to sleep in the train?" and he said "Yes, and went on to Norwood Junction," two or three stations further down the line. He did not say how he had got back from there. On the next day, Wednesday the 4th, I went up to London with my son and left him at the corner of Cheapside, just past Nicholson's, between half-past two and three o'clock in the afternoon. That was the last time I saw him before he was in custody. About eleven o'clock that evening I saw Inspector Page when I got home, and I took him to my son's bedroom. I saw him take some letters out of a suitcase, and also two pieces of paper out of my son's coat.

By Mr JUSTICE SHEARMAN—I believe the last train to our station leaves Victoria at ten minutes past twelve, but I could not say for certain.

Cross-examined by Mr CECIL WHITELEY—My husband was a ship's clerk also. He joined the Army in December, 1914, and was killed in the war. After my husband was killed I started a milliner's business in Upper Norwood. My boy has been with me always except at the time he has been at sea and the time he was staying with the Thompsons. When he was at school he got a splendid character, every report was marked "Excellent." After leaving school he went to some shipping agents in Leadenhall Street, and remained with them for about nine months. He left there with an excellent character, and went to another firm of shipping agents, with whom he remained until February, 1918, when he joined the merchant service as a writer. Since then he has been at sea most of the time, with intervals of about a fortnight, and his certificate of discharge at the end of each voyage shows that his character for ability was very good and for general conduct also very good. He has been practically all over the world. I have two daughters as well as my son. When he came back the last time his ship arrived on 23rd September, and he came straight back that day to my house at Westow Hill

Evidence for Prosecution.

Mrs Lilian Bywaters

Although he was working on the ship until 29th September, he always slept at home. On Saturday, 30th, he came home to tea about four o'clock, and he did not go out again until about eleven o'clock on the Monday morning. I was not aware until I heard recently that he visited the Graydons' house on the evening of 2nd October, nor was I aware that he visited the Graydons again on the Tuesday evening. On the following day, 4th October, he was with me in London until after two o'clock, when he left me at St. Paul's Churchyard.

Has he always been an excellent son?—One of the best that a mother could have.

WILLIAM EUSTACE GRAYDON, examined by Mr TRAVERS HUMPHREYS—I reside at 231 Shakespeare Crescent, Manor Park. The female prisoner is my daughter. She was married to Mr Thompson on 15th January, 1915, and she will be twenty-nine years of age on Christmas Day. There are no children of the marriage. She has been living for the last two years at 41 Kensington Gardens, Ilford, and I saw both her and her husband there from time to time. I have known the prisoner Bywaters for two and a half or three years to the best of my recollection. When he was at home between his voyages he used to come to our house from time to time, and he stayed for a period with us while he was waiting for a ship. I think that would be in the summer of 1921. When he returned from his voyage on 23rd September of this year he visited us on several occasions. He was at our house on Monday, 2nd October, about 6.15 or seven o'clock in the evening, and left about ten, or possibly a little later. He came about the same time on Tuesday, 3rd, and left about the same time. I remember my unmarried daughter, Avis, saying in the course of that evening and in the presence of Bywaters that the Thompsons had gone to a theatre, but he made no comment. I saw Bywaters again at our house next evening, the 4th, about seven o'clock. He had a copy of the *Evening News*, and he asked me if I had seen the paper. I said "No." Then he said, "This is a terrible thing if it is true." I surmised what he was referring to and said "I am afraid it is only too true."

Did you know at that time that Mr Thompson had been killed by somebody?—I knew Mr Thompson was dead. While Bywaters was at my house that evening some police officers came and took him away.

Cross-examined by Mr CECIL WHITELEY—My daughter and her husband were weekly visitors at our house; they practically always came on a Friday. Bywaters was known to me and my family for some considerable time, and he was a frequent visitor at our house. He came back from his last voyage on 23rd September, but he did not come to see us until Monday, 2nd October, when he came round

Bywaters and Thompson.

William Eustace Graydon

about 7.30 in the evening. It is quite probable that he would stay talking to me and my family until about 10 or 10.30—perhaps not quite so late. My son Newenham was there, but he may have gone out during the evening. Bywaters spoke to me that evening about some tobacco that I had agreed to get for him. He came again about seven o'clock in the evening of Tuesday, 3rd October, and he remained until ten or thereabouts. During the whole time he was talking to me and to my wife and my daughter Avis. I cannot recollect Mrs Thompson's name coming up during that conversation. I have no recollection of any comment being made upon the tobacco pouch that he had. I was not present in the room during the whole time that he was there, and it is possible that something may have been said about the tobacco pouch when I was not in the room.

Was he exactly the same on that evening as he had always been on previous evenings?—Quite.

Nothing unusual about him?—Nothing whatever.

Cross-examined by SIR H. CURTIS BENNETT—I knew my son-in-law for about seven years before his marriage.

During the whole of the time you knew him had he complained of heart attacks?—He had complained of various attacks, generally his heart. I have never seen him myself in a heart attack.

I show you an enclosure (exhibit 15a), which was in a letter written by your daughter to Bywaters. It is a cutting from the *Daily Sketch* of 9th February 1922, and it is headed "Curate's household of three. Mystery of his death still unsolved. Wife and doctor. Woman asked to leave the Court during man's evidence." Have you got that?—Yes, I see that that report refers to a Dr Preston Wallis, who was my doctor since about 1900.

From 1900 until 1915, when your daughter got married, Dr Preston Wallis would have been her doctor?—He would. Exhibit 15b is apparently a continuation of the same report—"Poisoned curate. Resumed inquest to-day following analyst's investigation." Bywaters lived for some time at Manor Park, up to 1916 or thereabouts. I could not say whether Dr Preston Wallis was also the Bywaters' doctor. Exhibit No 24, which is now shown me, is in my daughter's handwriting, and is dated 13th June, 1922—

I rang Avis yesterday and she said he came down there in a rage and told Dad everything—about all the rows we have had over you—but she did not mention he said anything about the first real one on August 1st—so I suppose he kept that back to suit his own ends. Dad said it was a disgraceful thing that you should come between husband and wife and I ought to be ashamed. Darlint I told you this is how they would look at it—they dont understand and they never will any of them.

Thompson never came to me and made any complaint as to the conduct of Bywaters with my daughter, that is the purest imagination—

Evidence for Prosecution.

William Eustace Graydon

Dad was going to talk to me Avis said—but I went down and nothing whatever was said by any of them I told Avis I shd tell them off if they said anything to me I didn't go whining to my people when he did things I didn't approve of and I didn't expect him to—but however nothing was said at all Dad said to them " What a scandal if it should get in the papers " so evidently he suggested drastic measures to them

There is no truth whatever in those two paragraphs As a matter of fact, I had no idea that my daughter and her husband were not on good terms Whenever I saw them together they always appeared to be quite happy and fond of each other

Re-examined by the SOLICITOR-GENERAL—I cannot remember any particular theatre being mentioned when my daughter mentioned the fact that the Thompsons had gone to the theatre or were going to the theatre on the night of 3rd October It would not be necessary or convenient for Bywaters to go through Ilford in order to get from my house in Manor Park to Upper Norwood

By Mr JUSTICE SHEARMAN—The ordinary way would be by the District Railway from East Ham to Victoria

Re-examination continued—There is no route that I know of that would take him through or near Belgrave Road in order to get to Upper Norwood I had no knowledge of Dr Farnell, the Vice Chancellor of Oxford University He is quite a stranger to me

By Mr JUSTICE SHEARMAN—I had never heard of any trouble about Bywaters coming between Thompson and my daughter

ERNEST FOSTER, examined by Mr TRAVERS HUMPHREYS—I am a detective constable In the evening of 4th October I went to Mr Graydon's house in Manor Park, and I there saw the prisoner Bywaters I said to him " We are police officers Is your name Frederick Bywaters? " and he said, Yes I said " I wish you to accompany us to Ilford police station for the purpose of being interviewed in connection with the Ilford murder ' He made no reply, and I conveyed him to Ilford police station, where he was detained

Cross-examined by Mr CECIL WHITELEY—Sergeant Williams, Mr Graydon and I think, Mr Newenham Graydon were present in the room when I said I wanted Bywaters to go to the Ilford police station It is possible that Bywaters may have said, " Certainly," but I did not hear him I did not hear him say " Certainly, I will do anything I can to help you "

By Mr JUSTICE SHEARMAN—At any rate he went quietly?—Yes

Mrs FANNY MARIA LESTER, examined by Mr TRAVERS HUMPHREYS —I live at 41 Kensington Gardens, Ilford I lived at that house before Mr and Mrs Thompson came about two years ago Mr Thompson bought the house, and I became their tenant of part of the house, Mr and Mrs Thompson occupying the two rooms upstairs and some rooms downstairs Both Mr and Mrs Thompson used to

Bywaters and Thompson.

Mrs Fanny Maria Lester

go to their business in London, leaving about quarter-past eight in the morning. Generally Mrs Thompson came back to the house first, about quarter to seven, or perhaps before that. Sometimes Mr Thompson was very late in getting home, about ten or eleven. I remember them going for a holiday to the Isle of Wight in June of last year. When they came back from their holiday they brought the prisoner Bywaters with them, and he remained for some time, but I could not say whether it was as a paying guest. He left on the Tuesday after the August Bank Holiday. Mr Thompson had his breakfast in bed that morning and Bywaters and Mrs Thompson had their breakfast downstairs. Bywaters went away for good after Mr and Mrs Thompson had gone out. Mrs Thompson showed me her arm, it was black from the shoulder to the elbow. When she showed me her arm I asked her what was wrong, and she said, "Mr Thompson and Mr Bywaters were having a few words and I interfered, and he pushed me on one side—shoved me up against the table." I think Bywaters left the house within a day or so after that, and he did not come back again.

By Mr JUSTICE SHEARMAN—He came back to the house once again on a Saturday afternoon but I could not say when, and he saw both Mr and Mrs Thompson.

Examination continued—I would not say that Mr and Mrs Thompson were on very good terms at any time. I used to hear them having very high words at times. I remember Saturday, 30th September. Mr and Mrs Thompson went away together in the morning and Mrs Thompson returned about half-past ten. She stayed in for a time and then went out again. She came back in the middle of the day and cooked Mr Thompson's dinner. He came home to dinner. On Sunday, 1st October, Mrs Thompson was in during the day and cooked their dinner. They went out together with some friends, I think, in the afternoon. On Monday morning, 2nd, they both went away the same as usual and they came back about seven o'clock. On Tuesday they both went away as usual and the next time I saw Mrs Thompson was when she was brought back after midnight. When she was brought back she only said that they would not let her go with him, or they would not let her bring him home—they had taken him away from her and if they would let her go to him she would make him better. The Thompsons' rooms are lighted by electric light. They did not keep a servant, Mrs Thompson cooked the food. A servant came on this day, 4th October, for the first time.

Cross-examined by Mr CECIL WHITELEY—I am quite clear that Mrs Thompson came back about twenty minutes past ten on the Saturday forenoon after having gone out with her husband. She remained in the house for about twenty minutes and she was back again at one o'clock. From that time to the Monday morning she and her husband were together as far as I know.

Evidence for Prosecution.

Mrs Fanny Maria Lester

Cross-examined by Sir H Curtis Bennett—Mrs Thompson complained to me that the housework was too much for her, and she told me that she was going to get a servant. The servant actually arrived to take up her situation on the evening after the death of Mr Thompson. When Mrs Thompson was brought back to the house in the early morning of 4th October she was in a very prostrate condition.

As far as you could form an opinion did you come to the conclusion that she did not realise that her husband was dead?—Yes, she said so.

You did come to the conclusion that she did not realise that her husband was dead?—Yes. The words she used were "They have taken him away from me, if they would let me go to him I could make him better."

It looked clearly as if she thought he was still alive?—Yes. I never prepared any of the food for Mr and Mrs Thompson. Mrs Thompson prepared all the meals that they had at home.

Frank Edward Myhill, examined by Mr Travers Humphreys—I am employed as a clerk under the Board of Trade in the General Register of Shipping and Seamen, Towerhill. I produce exhibit 32, a certificate relating to the British ship "Orvieto," and exhibit 33, a similar certificate relating to the British ship "Morea." Exhibit 34 is a log of the "Orvieto" and exhibit 35 is a certified extract showing the ports of call on the voyage. Exhibit 36 is a special log of the "Morea" on a journey between 9th September 1921, and 29th October, 1921, and exhibit 37 is an extract showing the ports of call. Exhibits 38 and 39 are the log and extract showing the ports of call on the voyage which started on 11th November, 1921, and finished on 6th January, 1922. Exhibits 40 and 41 are the log of the "Morea" and a certified extract showing the ports of call on the voyage which started on 20th January, 1922, and ended on 16th March. exhibits 42 and 43 relate to a voyage of the "Morea" beginning on 31st March and ending on 25th May 1922, exhibits 44 and 45 relate to a voyage of the same ship beginning on 9th June, 1922, and ending on 23rd September. Exhibit 46 shows the beginning and end of these various voyages and also the rating of the prisoner Bywaters. On the first voyage he was rated as mess room steward, on the next a writer, the next a writer, and the last a laundry steward.

Cross-examined by Mr Cecil Whiteley—Bywaters was for three fortnights in London this year. The records show on each voyage his ability and conduct as very good.

Mrs Maria Fanny Lester, recalled, further cross-examined by Sir H Curtis Bennett—My husband died in the beginning of May of this year. Up to that time I prepared porridge for my husband's

Bywaters and Thompson.

Mrs Fanny Maria Lester

breakfast, and Mr Thompson used to take a plate of porridge out of it as I made enough for two. Mr Thompson had a gas fire put in the drawing room.

Re-examined by Mr CECIL WHITELEY—Sometimes Mrs Thompson would have the porridge as well as her husband.

ARTHUR NEWBURY, examined by Mr TRAVERS HUMPHREYS—I am chief clerk in the pursers' department of the P. & O. Steamship Company. I have seen the prisoner Bywaters. After the arrival of the steamship "Morea" at Tilbury on 23rd February of this year, he, as ship's writer, had to be in attendance during the day, but he would not sleep on board while the ship was in dock. He left the ship on 28th September and his leave started from the morning of the 29th. He was due on board on 5th October, but he would not be supposed to sleep on board until the night before the ship left dock. She left on 13th October.

HERBERT CARLTON, examined by Mr ROLAND OLIVER—I carry on business under the name of Carlton & Prior as a wholesale milliner at 168 Aldersgate Street. The prisoner Mrs Thompson was in the employment of my firm. I should think she has been with me for about eight or ten years. She acted as book-keeper and manageress, and she was a very capable woman. During the time she was with me she was earning £6 a week, and then I gave her a bonus at holiday and Christmas times. Her hours were from 9 to 5, and on Saturdays from 9 to 12.15. I have seen the prisoner Bywaters on two occasions, the first time being when he was with Mrs Thompson in our showroom about eighteen months ago. The next time I saw him was on the Friday before the death of Mr Thompson. I saw him in the porchway of our house about half-past four or quarter to five. I was downstairs in the basement; Mrs Thompson called down about ten minutes to five that she was leaving, and I allowed her to go. I was aware that she was married and that her name was Mrs Thompson, but in business she used her maiden name, Miss Graydon. In fact she was in our employ before she was married. She did not come to work on Saturday, 30th September, as she had asked for the day off and I gave it to her. She came on Monday, 2nd October, and Tuesday, 3rd October, and left at the ordinary time. I did not see her again until after she was in custody. I have seen one or two registered letters for Mrs Thompson addressed to my firm. I could not say whether they came from abroad. I handed them to her. I am quite familiar with Mrs Thompson's handwriting and I have had an opportunity of examining the original exhibits in this case. Exhibit 65 is a list of the documents which are in her handwriting.

Cross-examined by Sir H. CURTIS BENNETT—There was no question at all of Mrs Thompson leaving my employment. She was

Evidence for Prosecution.

the sort of lady who with her business capacity would probably be able to get employment anywhere quite easily

Mrs LILIAN VALLENDER, examined by Mr ROLAND OLIVER—I work at Carlton & Prior's and I know the prisoner, Mrs Thompson I also know the prisoner Bywaters The first time I met him was at Shanklin in the Isle of Wight in June, 1921 He was staying there with Mr and Mrs Thompson and Mrs Thompson's sister The next time I saw him was last summer near our premises in Aldersgate Street, about five o'clock in the evening I saw him again that week in Aldersgate Street I did not see him after that until Monday, 25th September Mrs Thompson told me that he was outside, and I went across the road to Fullers' shop and had coffee with him This would be about five o'clock Mrs Thompson came over afterwards and I left the two of them in Fullers I saw him again on 29th September in Fullers but Mrs Thompson was not with him When I came back to the office she was dressed ready to leave

Second Day— Thursday, 7th December, 1922

EDITH ANNIE BROWN, examined by Mr ROLAND OLIVER—I am employed at Fullers, Limited, confectioners, 42 Aldersgate Street, which is just about opposite Carlton & Prior's. I know both the prisoners by sight, and I have seen them together in our teashop. On 29th September Bywaters came to our shop alone, and was joined by the witness Miss Vallender, and later by Mrs Thompson. I next saw Bywaters at our shop on Monday, 2nd October, Mrs Thompson was not there on that day. On Tuesday 3rd, I saw them both together in our shop. They left together about quarter-past five. One day a woman brought Bywaters a note. I think it was on the Friday, but I cannot be certain.

Cross-examined by Mr CECIL WHITELEY—There used to be two employees at Fullers' shop, now there are three. The busiest time is between twelve and two. We do not have very many customers in at tea-time.

AMELIA AUGUSTA LEE, examined by Mr ROLAND OLIVER—I am a waitress at Fullers, in Aldersgate Street. I remember the prisoner Bywaters, but not the female prisoner. I remember seeing the male prisoner in the tearoom during a week in the early part of the year. I also saw him in the tearoom on the Friday previous to the Ilford murder. He came into the shop alone, and then later on he was joined by Miss Vallender. I saw him again on the following Monday along with a lady. I also saw him on the Tuesday. After he had been in for about an hour a lady came and joined him—not the same lady who had coffee with him on the Monday. I should think that this would be between four and five o'clock. They went out together.

ROSE JACOBS, examined by Mr ROLAND OLIVER—I am employed at Carlton & Prior's, in Aldersgate Street, and I know the prisoner Mrs Thompson. I also know the prisoner Bywaters. I have seen him twice in our place at Aldersgate Street. (Being referred to exhibit No 9)—That is a note written in my presence by Mrs Thompson on the firm's paper, "Come in for me in half an hour.—Peidi." Mrs Thompson asked me to take that note over to Bywaters, who was sitting in Fullers' tearoom, and I did so. As far as I can remember, this was between four and half-past four o'clock, and it was on Friday, 29th September, although the note is dated 30th September. After Mrs Thompson was arrested I found exhibit No 11, a box, on her desk. It was locked when I found it. It was opened by Inspector Hall in my presence, and it contained some letters and cards which he took possession of.

Evidence for Prosecution.

Charles Higgins

CHARLES HIGGINS, examined by Mr. ROLAND OLIVER—I am a porter employed by Carlton & Prior. (Shown exhibit No. 10—"Wait till one, he's come, Peidi.")—I remember Mrs. Thompson, on Monday, the day before the crime, asking me to take that note to a man in a blue overcoat who would be outside Aldersgate Street station. There was another note about quarter of an hour afterwards.

Mrs. LILIAN BYWATERS, recalled, further cross-examined by Mr. CECIL WHITELEY—I remember in August, 1921, my son coming home and having a conversation with me about Mrs. Thompson. He told me that Mrs. Thompson led a very unhappy life with her husband, and he asked me if I could tell him how she could get a separation from her husband. I said I could not tell him how to get a separation, but that there was no law to compel her to live with a man if she was unhappy with him.

By the SOLICITOR-GENERAL—I believe that was after my son had been living with Mr. and Mrs. Thompson.

FRANK PAGE, examined by Mr. TRAVERS HUMPHREYS—I am a detective inspector at New Scotland Yard. On 4th October I went to 11 Westow Street, Norwood, the house of Mrs. Bywaters, the mother of the prisoner Bywaters. I saw her in the evening, and in her presence I searched the bedroom occupied by the prisoner Bywaters. In a case in the bedroom I found the two notes (exhibits 9 and 10). In a suitcase in the bedroom I found some letters from Mrs. Thompson (exhibits 28, 47, 54, 58 and 60). I also found the telegram (exhibit 58). Exhibit 59 appears to be the original telegram of which 58 is a delivered copy.

Cross-examined by Mr. CECIL WHITELEY—I do not know how many of Mrs. Thompson's letters were found in the possession of Bywaters.

ALFRED SCHOLES, examined by Mr. TRAVERS HUMPHREYS—I am a detective inspector of police employed by the Port of London Authority. On 12th October I went to the s.s. "Morea," which was then lying at Tilbury Docks. I went into a cabin and took a locked box (exhibit No. 8), which I eventually handed over to Sergeant James. That box was opened in my presence. It contained a number of letters which were taken away by Sergeant James. It also contained a photograph of Mrs. Thompson.

PERCY JAMES, examined by Mr. TRAVERS HUMPHREYS—On 12th October I received some keys from Inspector Hall. With one of those keys I opened the box which is exhibit 8, locked it again, took it away, and handed it to Inspector Hall.

Bywaters and Thompson.

John Hancock

JOHN HANCOCK, examined by Mr. TRAVERS HUMPHREYS.—I am a detective constable. I received a number of letters from Inspector Hall, which I examined and had copied. There were also a number of newspaper cuttings in some of the letters. On 9th October I found a knife (exhibit No 1) in a drain on the north side of Seymour Gardens, Ilford, about 250 yards from Kensington Gardens, Ilford. I handed it to Inspector Hall. I did not find any sheath. It is an English knife. I received three letters from the witness Miss Jacobs (exhibits 14, 30 and 51). These letters are signed by Bywaters. I searched the house at 41 Kensington Gardens, and I found a bottle (exhibit 61) in a small drawer in Mr. and Mrs. Thompson's bedroom. It has a label, "Aromatic tincture of opium." I handed the bottle to Mr. Webster, the analyst.

Cross-examined by SIR H. CURTIS BENNETT—Altogether I found 62 letters, including telegrams, and of these 32 have been put in as exhibits in this case. In the different letters there were some 50 enclosures, cuttings from newspapers, referring to a variety of subjects. Of those cuttings about ten referred to cases which were more or less in the public eye at the time. I have with me a list of the names of the cuttings. It includes the following:—

The Poisoned Curate	Do Women Dislike the Truth?
Curate's Household of Three	Does Courtship Cost too Much?
Helping the Doctor	Do Women Fail as Friends?
The Poisoned Curate	Advent of Loveless Women
Women who Hate all Men	University Mystery
Do Men like Red Haired Women?	False Friendship
Drugs for Brother in Hospital	An Ideal Love Letter
Event of the Season	Women on the Rack
Two Women	Women who Always Act
Battle of Calves and Ankles	Girl's Death Riddle
Patient killed by Over dose	Men and Marriage
Girl's Drug Injection	Masterful men
Fuel Control and Love-making	Winning Her, Winning Him
Holiday Death Pact	Asking her twice
My Sweet Offer	July Marriages
Flat Mystery	The Wedding Season
Their Married Life	Keeping Her
Rather the Devil for a Father	What does She Do with Him?
Defence in Disputed Baby Case	Do not Marry a Genius
Crimes against Love	Dangerous Women
Chicken Broth Death	Woman the Consoler
Poisoned Chocolates	The Ideal Dance Partner

The Best Wines that I have drunk

The little bottle which has been produced, containing aromatic tincture of opium, was found by me in the small drawer in the chest of drawers in the bedroom which was occupied by both Mr.

Evidence for Prosecution.

John Hancock

and Mrs. Thompson. I did not see any of Mr. Thompson's collars and ties in that drawer. It contained envelopes, notepaper, photographs, and gloves. I could not say whether it was his drawer or her drawer.

RICHARD SELLARS examined by Mr. TRAVERS HUMPHREYS—I am a divisional detective inspector of police, K Division. At 11 a.m. on 4th October I saw Mrs. Thompson at her house, 41 Kensington Gardens, Ilford. I said to her, "I am an inspector of police. I understand you were with your husband early this morning in Belgrave Road. I am satisfied he was assaulted and stabbed several times." She said, "We were coming along Belgrave Road, and just past the corner of Endsleigh Gardens, when I heard him call out 'Oh-er!' and he fell up against me. I put out my arms to save him and found blood, which I thought was coming from his mouth. I tried to help him up. He staggered for several yards towards Kensington Gardens and then fell against the wall and slid down; he did not speak to me. I cannot say if I spoke to him. I felt him, and found his clothing wet with blood. He never moved after he fell. We had no quarrel on the way, we were quite happy together. Immediately I saw blood I ran across the road to a doctor's. I appealed to a lady and gentleman who were passing, and the gentleman also went to the doctor's. The doctor came and told me my husband was dead. Just before he fell down I was walking on his right-hand side, on the inside of the pavement, nearest the wall. We were side by side. I did not see anybody about at the time. My husband and I were talking about going to a dance." At that time Mrs. Thompson was in an agitated condition. About 7 p.m. on the same day I saw the prisoner Bywaters at the Ilford police station and took possession of the overcoat he was wearing, which is the one now produced. I saw Mrs. Thompson again a little later in the same evening, after she had made her first statement to me, and I afterwards took her to the Ilford police station. I spoke to her again on the next day, 5th October, and asked her if she would give me any further information regarding her husband's assailant. She said, "I will tell you if I possibly can," and she made a voluntary statement which was typewritten, read, and signed (exhibit No. 3). That statement is as follows :—

EDITH JESSIE THOMPSON, 41 Kensington Gardens, Ilford, age 28, married, states—

My husband's name is Percy Thompson. He is a shipping clerk employed by Messrs. O. J. Parker & Co., Peel House, Eastcheap, E.C.

I am employed by Carlton & Prior, millinery manufacturers, 168 Aldersgate Street, E.C., as a book keeper. We have been married six years and have no family. We were married in the beginning of the year 1916. In that year my husband joined the London Scottish Regiment, he was discharged

Bywaters and Thompson.

as medically unfit a few months later and did no foreign service. I have always been on affectionate terms with my husband. I remember Tuesday, 3rd October, 1922. We both went to our respective businesses that day. I met my husband by appointment at a quarter to six, in Aldersgate Street, that day, we went to the Criterion Theatre, we there met my uncle and aunt, Mr and Mrs J Laxton, we left the Theatre about 11 p m , we all four went to the Piccadilly Circus Tube, we there separated, my husband and I went to Liverpool Street, and we caught the 11 30 train to Ilford, we arrived at Ilford about 12 o'clock, we then proceeded along York Road, Belgrave Road and when we got between De Vere and Endsleigh Gardens, (we were walking on the right hand side) my husband suddenly went into the roadway. I went after him, and he fell up against me, and called out " oo-er " He was staggering, he was bleeding and I thought that the blood was coming from his mouth. I cannot remember whether I saw anyone else there or not. I know there was none there when he staggered up against me. I got hold of my husband with both hands and assisted him to get up against the wall. He stood there for about a minute or two and then slid down on to the footway, he never spoke, I fell on the ground with him. I cannot remember if I shouted out or not. I got up off the ground and ran along to Courtland Avenue, with the intention of calling Dr Maudsley, but on the way I met a lady and a gentleman and I said to them something to this effect, " Can I get a doctor or help me, my husband is ill " The gentleman said, " I will go for the doctor ' Dr Maudsley arrived shortly after, although it seemed a long time. The doctor examined my husband and said that he was dead. An ambulance was sent for and the body was removed. I was accompanied to my home by two Police Officers.

I know Freddie Bywaters, I have known him for several years, we were at school together, at least I wasn't but my two brothers were. He is residing with his widowed mother at 11 Westow St , Norwood. He is a ship's writer and periodically goes away to sea. He has been for a very long time on visiting terms with my family. In June, 1921, Bywaters came to reside with my husband and myself at No 41 Kensington Gardens. He came as a paying guest. I think he paid 25s or 27s 6d per week. He was with us up to the beginning of August, 1921. I remember August Bank Holiday 1921. My husband and I quarrelled about something, he struck me. I knocked a chair over. Freddie came in and interfered on my behalf. I left the room and I do not know what transpired between them. As far as my recollection goes, Freddie left on the following Friday, but before he left my husband and he were friends again. We have been in the habit of corresponding with one another. His letters to me and mine to him were couched in affectionate terms. I am not in possession of any letters he writes to me. I have destroyed all as is customary with me with all my correspondence. The letters shown to me by Inspector Hall and addressed to Mr F Bywaters are some of the letters that I wrote to Freddie, and were written to him without my husband's consent. When he was at home in England, we were in the habit of going out occasionally together without my husband's knowledge.

This statement has been read over to me. It is voluntary and it is true.   (Sgd)   EDITH THOMPSON.

After making that statement, Mrs Thompson and I left the

Evidence for Prosecution.

Richard Sellars

room, I took her to the matron's room. In doing so we passed the library, where Bywaters was detained. She saw him as she passed, and she said, "Oh, God, oh, God, what can I do? Why did he do it? I did not want him to do it." She further said almost immediately after, "I must tell the truth." She was a little hysterical, and I said "You realise what you are saying, what you might say may be used in evidence." She then proceeded to make a statement, which again was written down and signed (exhibit No. 4). It is as follows:—

> When we got near Endsleigh Gardens a man rushed out from the Gardens and knocked me away and pushed me away from my husband. I was dazed for a moment. When I recovered I saw my husband scuffling with a man. The man whom I know is Freddie Bywaters was running away. He was wearing a blue overcoat and a grey hat. I knew it was him although I did not see his face.

After taking Bywaters' coat from him it was examined by Dr. Drought, and after he had examined it I said to Bywaters 'We shall detain you and retain possession of your overcoat.' He said "Why I know nothing about it." He commenced to speak further, and I said, 'If you wish to make a statement it will be better to put it in writing.' I cautioned him and he made a statement which he signed in my presence (exhibit No. 5).

4th October, 1922

FREDERICK EDWARD FRANCIS BYWATERS, 11 Weston Street, Upper Norwood, aged 20, Laundry Steward, states—

I have known Mr Percy Thompson for about four years and his wife Edith, for about 7 years. Mr Thompson is a shipping clerk, his wife is in a millinery business, and they reside at 41 Kensington Gardens Ilford. I stayed with them from June 18th 1921 to the 1st August, 1921. The first week that I was there, I was there as their guest and the remaining weeks I paid 25s. per week. The cause of my leaving was that Mr Thompson quarrelled with Mrs Thompson and threw her across the room. I thought it was a very unmanly thing to do and I interfered. We had a quarrel and he asked me to leave, and I left. I had always been exceedingly good friends with Mrs Thompson. I was also on visiting terms with the mother of Mrs Thompson, a Mrs Graydon, who resides with her husband and family at 231 Shakespeare Crescent Manor Park. After I left Mrs Thompson I went back to reside with my mother at my present address. On the 7th September 1921, I got a position as writer on board the s.s. 'Morea.' I sailed on the 9th September and returned to England the end of the following month. Shortly after I came back from the voyage I called on Mr and Mrs Thompson at their address. Mrs Thompson received me quite friendly, Mr Thompson a little coldly, but we parted as friends. The same evening I called on Mrs Graydon and I there again saw Mr and Mrs Thompson, who were visiting her. I have never called upon Mr and Mrs Thompson since that time. I have met them once or twice at Mrs Graydon's since, the last time being in June last. Since

Bywaters and Thompson.

that date I have never seen Mr Thompson I have met Mrs Thompson on several occasions since and always by appointment They were verbal appointments On Monday last I met her by appointment at 12 30 at Aldersgate Street We went to lunch at the Queen Anne's Restaurant, Cheapside After lunch she returned to business and I have not seen her since Mr Thompson was not aware of all our meetings, but some of them he was I have known for a very long time past that she had led a very unhappy life with him This is also known to members of Mrs Thompson's family I have written to her on two occasions I signed the letters Freddie and I addressed her as "Dear Edie" On the evening of Monday 2nd October I called on Mrs Graydon and stayed there till about 10 o'clock I never mentioned the fact that I had lunched with Mrs Thompson that day, and as far as I know Mr Thompson was not aware of it I left my home yesterday morning about a quarter to twelve I was dressed in the same clothes that I am now wearing I went up West and remained there until the evening I was alone and never met anyone that I knew I then went to Mrs Graydon's, arriving there about 7 I left about 11 o'clock my impression is that it had gone 11 Before leaving I remember Mrs Graydon's daughter Avis saying that Percy (Mr Thompson) had 'phoned her up, and I gathered from the observations she made that he was taking his wife to a theatre that night and that there was other members of the family going When I left the house I went through Browning Road, into Sibley Grove, to East Ham Railway Station I booked to Victoria which is my usual custom I caught a train at 11 30 p m and I arrived at Victoria about 12 30 a m I then discovered that the last train to Gypsy Hill had gone, it leaves at 12 10 a m I had a few pounds in money with me but I decided to walk I went by way of Vauxhall Road, and Vauxhall Bridge Kennington, Brixton, turning to the left into Dulwich, and then on to the Crystal Palace and from there to my address at Upper Norwood, arriving there about 3 a m I never noticed either 'bus or tram going in my direction On arriving home I let myself in with a latchkey and went straight to my bedroom My mother called out to me She said, "Is that you, Mick?" I replied, "Yes," and then went to bed I got up about 9 a m and about 12 I left home with my mother I left my mother in Paternoster Row about half past two I stayed in the City till about 5 I then went by train from Mark Lane to East Ham and from there went on to Mrs Graydon's arriving there about six The first time that I learned that Mr Thompson had been killed was when I bought a newspaper in Mark Lane before I got into the train to go to East Ham I am never in the habit of carrying a knife In fact I have never had one I never met a single person that I knew from the time that I left Mrs Graydon's house until I arrived home Mrs Thompson has written to me two or three times I might have received one letter from her at home The others I have received on board ship I have destroyed these letters She used to address me as "Dear Freddie," and signed herself "Peidi" I occupy the back bedroom on the top floor at my address, and that is where I keep all my clothing When I said that I was dressed in precisely the same clothing yesterday as I am to-day, I meant it to include my undergarments, with the exception of my collar and handkerchief, which are at home

This statement has been read over to me, is voluntary and is true

(Sgd) FREDERICK E F BYWATERS

Evidence for Prosecution.

Richard Sellars

Having made some further inquiries I again saw Bywaters on the evening of 5th October and said to him, "I am going to charge you and Mrs Thompson with the wilful murder of Percy Thompson." He said, "Why her? Mrs Thompson was not aware of my movements." I said, "If you wish to say anything I will take it down in writing." I again cautioned him. He made a statement which I read to him and which he signed. It is exhibit No 6, and it is dated 5th October—

FREDERICK BYWATERS states—

I wish to make a voluntary statement. Mrs Edith Thompson was not aware of my movements on Tuesday night 3rd October. I left Manor Park at 11 p m and proceeded to Ilford. I waited for Mrs Thompson and her husband. When near Endsleigh Gardens I pushed her to one side, also pushing him further up the street. I said to him "You have got to separate from your wife." He said "No." I said "You will have to." We struggled. I took my knife from my pocket and we fought and he got the worst of it. Mrs Thompson must have been spellbound for I saw nothing of her during the fight. I ran away through Endsleigh Gardens, through Wanstead, Leytonstone, Stratford, got a taxi at Stratford to Aldgate, walked from there to Fenchurch Street, got another taxi to Thornton Heath. Then walked to Upper Norwood, arriving home about 3 a m. The reason I fought with Thompson was because he never acted like a man to his wife. He always seemed several degrees lower than a snake. I loved her and I could not go on seeing her leading that life. I did not intend to kill him. I only meant to injure him. I gave him an opportunity of standing up to me as a man but he wouldn't. I have had the knife some time, it was a sheath knife. I threw it down a drain when I was running through Endsleigh Gardens.

Later the two prisoners were charged with the murder of Percy Thompson. When the charge was made Thompson made no reply while Bywaters said "It is wrong, it is wrong." On 12th October I received a ditty box (exhibit No 8) from Sergeant James. The prisoner Bywaters gave me the key which opened the box. I received from Inspector Page of New Scotland Yard and also from Sergeant Hancock a number of letters. Inspector Hall also handed to me three letters written by Bywaters. I have seen Bywaters write, and to the best of my belief exhibits Nos 14, 30 and 51 are in his handwriting.

Cross-examined by Mr CECIL WHITELEY—Bywaters was taken to the Ilford police station on the evening of 4th October.

Were you in sole charge of this case or was there any other officer concerned?—Superintendent Wensley came down but I was practically in sole charge of it. He was not present with me at every interview I had with Bywaters. He was present with me when Bywaters gave the long statement (exhibit No 5). He was not present when I took the statement No 6. When Bywaters was

Bywaters and Thompson.

brought to the station in the evening of the 4th Superintendent Wensley and I were there, and we both saw him. We were in the company of Bywaters that evening for about an hour and a half. Practically the whole of that period was occupied by the taking of the statement. There was a typist present in the room.

You do not suggest that this was a statement dictated by Bywaters?—Practically. He wished to make a statement, and I said we would take it down in writing.

No questions asked?—Yes.

Is it not clear from the statement itself that questions were put to him and his answers are incorporated in that statement?—Not wholly, practically. Both Superintendent Wensley and I asked the questions. We left Bywaters about nine o'clock. I do not think either of us saw him again that evening. I do not remember seeing him. I believe he slept in the library that evening. On the next day, 5th October, about 3 p.m., I took a statement from Mrs Thompson (exhibit No 3). The second statement of Mrs Thompson (exhibit No 4) was taken about half-past four or quarter to five.

Was it before those two statements that Mrs Thompson saw Bywaters and said "Why did he do it I did not want him to do it"?—Yes, after she was returning from the room where she was taken. Superintendent Wensley was not present when she said that. No steps were taken by the police to prevent Mrs Thompson and Bywaters seeing each other.

It was after Mrs Thompson had seen Bywaters and after she had made the statement (exhibit No 4) that you went back into Bywaters' room and the statement (exhibit No 6) was taken?—Yes. I wrote it down myself. Before that statement was taken I told him that I was going to charge him and Mrs Thompson with this crime.

By Mr JUSTICE SHEARMAN—Did you know by that time that he had seen that she was there too?—Yes.

You told us that she caught sight of him, but nobody has told us that he caught sight of her. Do you know if he did?—I could not say, because my attention was centred on her.

Cross-examination continued—I certainly think that Bywaters did see Mrs Thompson, but I cannot say positively.

No doubt they had seen one another, and the very first thing he said directly you said that both of them were going to be charged was, "Why her? Mrs Thompson was not aware of my movements"?—Yes.

And when you charged them both together that evening Bywaters said "It is wrong, it is wrong"?—Yes.

Cross-examined by Sir H CURTIS BENNETT—I first of all saw Mrs Thompson at 11 a.m. on 4th October, the morning that Mr Thompson died, and at that time she made a statement which I noted in my notebook. At that time she had no knowledge, as far as I know, that any inquiries were being made as regards Bywaters

Evidence for Prosecution.

She did not say anything about anybody having knocked her or pushed her aside. After making that statement I asked her to come to the police office, and she was kept there from twelve o'clock on the 4th until the afternoon of the 5th, when I took from her the long statement (exhibit No. 3).

At that time, as far as you know, she had no knowledge that Bywaters was at the station?—I could not say, but I should not think so.

Nobody had told her as far as you know?—No, but I gleaned that she did on account of the letters.

What?—I gleaned that she did on account of the letters. The letters were on the table where we took the statement, and she must have known on account of Bywaters' letters.

By Mr. JUSTICE SHEARMAN—She identified her own letters to Bywaters.

Cross-examination continued—She identified them in the statement (exhibit No. 3). That statement took about an hour and a half. After the statement was taken she had to pass the room where Bywaters was being detained in order to get to the matron's room.

Directly she saw Bywaters there she said this, "Oh, God, oh God, what can I do? Why did he do it? I did not want him to do it", and then almost immediately afterwards, "I must tell the truth"?—Yes.

And then it was that, having said "I must tell the truth," you cautioned her, and then she said "When we got near Endsleigh Gardens a man rushed out from the gardens and knocked me away, pushed me away, from my husband. When I recovered I saw my husband scuffling with a man. The man who I knew as Freddie Bywaters, was running away. He was wearing a blue overcoat and a grey hat. I knew it was him, although I did not see his face." That is right?—Correct.

So that directly she had in fact seen Bywaters was at the station she made this second statement?—Yes.

LEONARD WILLIAMS, examined by Mr. ROLAND OLIVER—I am a detective of K Division. On 6th October I took the prisoner Bywaters and certain property from Ilford to Stratford Police Court. When at the Court he said, pointing to the property, "Have you a knife there?" I said "No." He said, "Have they found it?" I said "I do not think so." He said, "I told them I ran up Endsleigh Gardens, but coming to think of it after I did it I ran forward along Belgrave Road towards Wanstead Park, turning up a road to the right. I am not sure whether it was Kensington Gardens where they lived or the next road. I then crossed over to the left side of the road, and just before I got to the top of Cranbrook Road end I put the knife down a drain, it should be easily found."

Bywaters and Thompson.

Henry William Forster

HENRY WILLIAM FORSTER examined by Mr ROLAND OLIVER—I am a director of Osborne & Co., tool merchants, 165-166 Aldersgate Street. (Shown knife, exhibit No. 1) We sell at our shop knives identical with that, the price being 6s. We call them hunting knives, and they are sold in leather sheaths.

Cross-examined by Mr CECIL WHITELEY—We have carried on business in Aldersgate Street for about seventeen years, and during all that time we have been selling knives similar to that.

CHARLES CALDWELL TAYLOR, examined by Mr ROLAND OLIVER— I am a detective sergeant of the Salford Police. I attended the Manchester November Handicap on 26th November, 1921. A horse called "Welsh Woman" was running on that date.

JOHN WEBSTER examined by Mr TRAVERS HUMPHREYS—I am senior official analyst to the Home Office. On 11th October I received Bywaters' overcoat (exhibit No. 29) and examined it for the presence of blood. I found a large number of stains of human blood on the right and left sleeves of the coat. I also examined the knife (exhibit No. 1) and found that there were several areas which gave reactions for blood both on the handle and on the blade. The traces were not sufficient for me to say whether it was human blood or not. On 4th November I received from Dr Spilsbury some bottles and jars containing some of the organs of the deceased Mr Thompson. In the liver and kidneys I found a small trace of an alkaloid giving a reaction for morphine. The bottle labelled "aromatic tincture of opium" (exhibit No. 61) contains morphine. It would be used as a sedative for killing pain, and it is a thing that anybody might properly have in use. Assuming that the deceased used it a day or two before his death, it is possible that a minute trace would be found.

I want to ask you with regard to some matters which are mentioned in the letters. Is hyoscine a poison?—Yes.

Cocaine, potassium cyanide, sodium antimonyl tartarate, bichloride of mercury, and digitalin—are these all poisons?—Yes.

Cross-examined by Sir H. CURTIS BENNETT—Aromatic tincture of opium is quite an ordinary thing. Up till twelve months ago it could be purchased at any chemist's, but now it is necessary to have a medical prescription. It is something akin to chlorodyne. If a person suffered with the heart, chlorodyne or tincture of opium would produce relief. Chlorodyne contains traces of morphine.

Dr BERNARD HENRY SPILSBURY examined by the SOLICITOR-GENERAL—I am senior pathologist to the Home Office. I made a post-mortem examination of the exhumed body of Percy Thompson on 3rd November. Dr Drought, a divisional police surgeon, was present. The body was that of a well-nourished man. I found cuts

Evidence for Prosecution.

Dr Bernard Henry Spilsbury

in the neck and in the throat. The skull and the coverings of the blood vessels were normal, but the heart was slightly enlarged. So far as I could tell at the time, the other organs of the body were healthy.

By Mr JUSTICE SHEARMAN—The cuts which I found were stabs, with the exception of one on the right arm, which was a cut.

Examination continued—I did not find any signs of poisoning, nor did I find any scars in the intestines. I am aware that glass has been mentioned in this case and in the letters as possibly being administered to Percy Thompson. If glass had been administered I would not necessarily expect to find indications in the organs. The administration of glass, broken or ground, would produce different results. Large fragments of glass if given might produce injury by cutting the wall of the gullet, or the stomach, or the intestines, and if those injuries did not prove fatal a scar or scars might be found on the walls afterwards. If given in a powdered form the immediate effect of the powder would be to produce innumerable minute injuries to the delicate membranes lining the stomach and intestines in all probability setting up an acute illness, but if that did not occur, or if recovery followed, the glass would disappear entirely from the system, with the possible exception of that small portion known as the appendix in which it might lodge and remain for a long time.

In this case did you find any indications of powdered glass in the abdomen?—No there were none. I found no indication of the presence of glass either in large pieces or in powdered particles.

Is the negative result of your examination consistent with glass having been administered?—Some time previously yes. It is possible that glass in large pieces could have passed through the system without such injury as to leave any signs behind. It would pass away in the food and in the excrement. What I found as the negative result of my examination is consistent also with particles of glass having been passed through the system. As to other poisons I would not expect necessarily to find indications of poisons if they had been administered some considerable time before. Some poisons would leave no traces at any time even if death occurred shortly after administration. Others would produce effects which would last for a few days, and in the case of a few poisons a few weeks, but after the end of that time there are very few poisons which would leave any indications except poisons which were corrosive or which were markedly irritant poisons. Neither hyoscine or cocaine is markedly irritant. Cyanide of potassium is an irritant, it would either kill quickly or recovery would occur within a short time. Sodium antimonyl tartarate is an irritant poison and I think it probably would be difficult to detect any traces after ten days or a fortnight. Bichloride of mercury is an intense irritant poison and it might show traces for a very long time. In

Bywaters and Thompson.

Dr Bernard Henry Spilsbury

the kidneys and bowel there might be evidence of it after certainly some weeks and possibly some months after its administration. Digitalin has no irritant effect.

By Mr JUSTICE SHEARMAN—Used in small quantities it is a stimulant.

Examination continued—Morphine would not leave any traces.

Cross-examined by Sir H CURTIS BENNETT—Does it all come to this that there has been no trace whatever in the post-mortem of any glass having been administered, either in large pieces or powdered?—That is so.

And as far as poisons are concerned, there is no trace whatever of any poison ever having been administered, except of morphine, which I have dealt with?—That is so.

No trace of any poison being present and no changes suggestive of previous attempts to poison?—Quite. Glass if taken would pass through the gullet into the stomach, and then through the duodenum, and so on through the intestines to the cæcum. Off the cæcum is the appendix.

On its journey through those parts of the body would not a large piece of glass tend to cut or make a scar?—It would tend to cut or to pierce the wall. The scar would come afterwards.

You would find a scar remaining afterwards, would you not?—You might do so. I made a very careful examination to see if there was any scar anywhere, and I could not find any. There is no outlet from the appendix except the one opening into the bowel. I made a careful examination of the appendix and found no trace at all of glass of any sort, powdered or otherwise. If any of the poisons mentioned in my examination had been given in appreciable doses, illness would have resulted, the degree of illness depending upon the amount. There are not many of the poisons which have been put to me to-day which would leave any permanent effect at all. Some of course, would leave a trace for a time.

At any rate there was no trace, either post-mortem or by analysis, of any poison ever having been given?—No.

Mr TRAVERS HUMPHREYS—I have been consulting my learned friends in order to see if they desire us to call the remainder of the witnesses, Edgar Edwards, Robert Gilham, William Mould, Henry Palmer and Detective-Inspector Rixon.

The SOLICITOR GENERAL—That will be the case for the Crown.

[The letters exhibits Nos 49, 12, 62, 27, 13, 15, 16, 20, 50, 17, 18, 19, 21, 22, 51, 23, 66, 67, 68, 24, 53, 25, 69, 26, 52, 63, 54, 28, 55, 47, 48, 58, 59, 9, 60, 10, 64, 14, 30, 31 were read]*

Sir H CURTIS BENNETT—The jury, of course, will understand that in addition to those letters there are 33 other ones on which the prosecution do not rely and which are not put in.

---

* See Appendix

Frederick Bywaters

Evidence for Prisoner Bywaters.

Evidence for the Prisoner Bywaters.

FREDERICK EDWARD FRANCIS BYWATERS (prisoner on oath), examined by Mr CECIL WHITELEY—When I arrived from my last voyage I went to stay with my mother at Weston Street, Norwood. My mother had been living there about two and a half years, and previous to that she was living in Manor Park. The Graydons were also living in Manor Park. I met the Graydon boys at school and got to know the family in that way. I have been on good terms ever since with the Graydon family. Between 26th February and 4th June last year I was away on a voyage to Australia. I arrived at Tilbury on 4th June, and I went for a holiday to the Isle of Wight. Mr and Mrs Thompson and Avis Graydon were also taking a holiday there, and we met friends, Mr and Mrs Vallender, who has been a witness in this case. I was in the Isle of Wight for one week. On 18th June I went to stay with the Thompsons at 41 Kensington Gardens, on Mr Thompson's invitation, and I stayed with them in their house until 5th August.

How did you come to leave?—There was a quarrel on 1st August, the Bank Holiday, between Mr Thompson and his wife over a very trivial matter; it was a pin that caused the trouble. Mr Thompson threw his wife across the morning room and on her passage across the room she overturned a chair. I was standing outside and heard the bang and ran inside.

By Mr JUSTICE SHEARMAN—Then you did not hear the quarrel. I thought you said you heard the quarrel?—The quarrel started in the garden.

Examination continued—Mrs Thompson, who was sewing, said, "I want a pin," and I said, "I will go and get you one." I went inside and got the pin, and when I came outside again into the garden they were arguing. The argument dropped for the time being and we went inside to tea. Thompson came in and created further trouble, and then there was a struggle.

Had you been taking Mrs Thompson about?—No.

You had been out with her?—With Mr Thompson. As the result of the row I left at Mr Thompson's request and my own inclination. I was in London between 5th August and 9th September.

Just tell us at once, Bywaters, were you taking Mrs Thompson out during that time?—I was meeting her occasionally.

What was the state of your feelings to her and hers to you?—We were friends. I think her husband knew that we were meeting.

Had you then fallen in love with her?—I was fond of her. I had never mentioned it to her, though.

When was it first that you were in love with one another?—Well, I suppose it was just before I went away in September. I was away from 9th September to 29th October, and during that time I got letters from Mrs Thompson and I replied to them.

Bywaters and Thompson.

Frederick E. F. Bywaters

I do not want to go into any detail, but were you writing to one another love letters?—Yes. When I came back on 29th October I remained in London for just a fortnight, until 11th November. During that time I saw Mrs. Thompson practically every day.

I ought to have asked you this before: before you left in August did you have any conversation with Mr. Thompson in the presence of Mrs. Thompson as to separation or divorce?—Yes, on this day of the trouble, 1st August, there was a conversation between the three of us about a separation. Mr. Thompson said to his wife, " We will come to an agreement and have a separation," and she said, " Yes, I should like that, but you make a statement and then whine back to me and retract that statement, you have done that before." When I came back in October Mrs. Thompson and I spoke about the desirability of her getting a separation from her husband. I said to her, " Can you not come to any amicable understanding or agreement with your husband to get a separation," and she replied, ' I keep on asking, but it seems no good at all." On that visit home in the end of October and the beginning of November I went to Kensington Gardens on a Saturday afternoon and made a request to him that he should have a separation. I had taken Mrs. Thompson out previously, apparently he had been waiting at the station for her and he had seen the two of us together. He made a statement to Mrs. Thompson, " He is not a man or else he would ask my permission to take you out," and she repeated that statement to me the following day. In consequence of that I went and saw Mr. Thompson, and as he had said that I had run away from him, I told him that I did not see him at the station. Mrs. Thompson was present part of the time.

At that time was anything discussed between you and Mr. Thompson about a separation or divorce?—Yes, that was the theme of the conversation. I said, " Why do you not come to an amicable agreement, either have a separation or you can get a divorce," and he hummed and hawed about it. He was undecided and said, " Yes—No—I don't see it concerns you." I said, ' You are making Edie's life a hell. You know she is not happy with you." He replied, ' Well, I have got her and I will keep her." Eventually I extracted a promise from him that he would not knock her about any more and that he would not beat her, but I could get no understanding with regard to a separation or divorce. I met him again on Saturday evening at the Graydons. I left with my ship on 11th November and I was away until 7th January.

Look now at the letter (exhibit 62) and at this passage—

All I could think about last night was that compact we made. Shall we have to carry it thro'? Don't let us darlint.

What was the compact?—Suicide.

Who suggested that?—Mrs. Thompson had suggested it.

Evidence for Prisoner Bywaters.

Frederick E. F. Bywaters

Did you ever make any agreement that you should commit suicide?—Well, I suggested it as a way of calming her, but I never intended to carry it out.

Then the letter goes on—

I'd like to live and be happy—not for a little while but for all the while you still love me. Death seemed horrible last night—when you think about it darlint, it does seem a horrible thing to die, when you have never been happy really happy for one little minute.

I am going to ask you at once Bywaters, at any time was there any agreement between you and Mrs Thompson to poison her husband?—Never, there was never such an agreement.

Was there any agreement that any violence should be used against her husband?—No, the greatest violence was separation.

As far as you could tell reading these letters, did you ever believe in your own mind that she herself had ever given any poison to her husband?—No, it never entered my head at all. She had been reading books.

Had you some quinine on board?—Yes, I used it myself. It was in the form of 5 grain tabloids, white.

Did you ever give any of that quinine to Mrs Thompson?—I did.

Apart from that quinine did you ever give her any other drug?—No, I did not.

Did you ever give her any poison of any sort or description?—No, nothing at all. The quinine has a most bitter taste, very unpleasant. There were other two letters which I got before I came back on 7th January, one of them being exhibit 27, with which Mrs Thompson enclosed a number of cuttings. That was a habit of hers—instead of sending a newspaper she would send cuttings that appeared to be interesting. The cuttings were with regard to cases of all sorts which I was interested in reading. I got back from my voyage on 7th January and I was on leave until the 20th. During that fortnight I saw Mrs Thompson frequently and the question of getting a separation or a divorce was discussed between us. She still complained of being ill-treated; she said, " Things are just the same, they get no better. She said that the chances of getting a separation were very small; that Thompson would never agree to it. I was away again from the 20th January to 17th March. During that time I got the letter (exhibit No 15)—

Darlint—you must do something this time—I'm not really impatient—but opportunities come and go by—they have to—because I'm helpless and I think and think and think—perhaps—it will never come again.

I hardly know what that refers to.

" You must do something." What was it she had been wanting you to do?—Take her away.

Bywaters and Thompson.

Frederick E. F. Bywaters

It is suggested by the prosecution that that means that you were going to do something in connection with her husband. Is there anything in that?—It is entirely wrong.

Did she ask you more than once to take her away?—Oh, yes.

Tell us about it. Was it a genuine demand by her or not?—Well, she appeared to want to go away, but she used to get very hysterical. She was of a highly strung nature.

By Mr Justice Shearman—Did she ask you to take her away or not?—Oh, yes.

Examination continued—When she said, "Try and help me," in what way was it she had asked you to help her?—In regard to getting a separation.

On 14th March she writes you the letter (exhibit No. 20) in which there is the following passage:—

I am not going to talk to you any more—I can't and I don't think I've shirked have I? Except darlint to ask you again to think out all the plans and methods for me and wait and wait so anxiously now—for the time when we will be with each other—even tho' it's only once

What were the "plans and methods" which she had asked you to think out?—Going away together, or the separation.

Was there any discussion as to what she was to do abroad?—She would go abroad to a millinery business. My wages were about £4 a week. I was visiting various countries and various cities, and Mrs Thompson was writing to me at these various countries and various places. I was to make inquiries as to the prospects of her obtaining situations in these places. Bombay was mentioned, also Australia, where there might be an opening for her. She also mentioned Marseilles to me. I came back on 17th March, and was at home for a fortnight. It would be at that time that I gave Mrs Thompson the quinine. I was seeing her constantly then. When I went away on 31st March she wrote me the letter (exhibit 50) in which she said—

This time really will be the last you will go away—like things are won't it? We said it before darlint I know and we failed—but there will be no failure this next time darlint there mustn't be

What "failure" had there been?—The failure to get a separation—failure to take her abroad.

"You will never leave me behind again, never unless things are different." What does that mean?—That means unless she could get a separation I would not go to sea any more alone. I would not leave her again unless I took her with me—go with me you see.

In Mrs Thompson's letter dated 1st April (exhibit 17) she talks about an electric light bulb. Did you pay any attention to that at all?—No. I think she was trying to put herself in the same place as Bella Donna in the book "Bella Donna."

Evidence for Prisoner Bywaters.

Frederick E. F. Bywaters

Did you attach any importance to it at all?—No, I thought it was mere melodrama.

Then in the letter of 24th April (exhibit 18) she says, " I used the ' light bulb ' three times " Then look at the letter of 1st May (exhibit 19), " We shall have to wait if we fail again " What does that mean?—Another attempt to get a separation.

Look at this passage—

We'll wait eh darlint, and you'll try and get some money, and then we can go away and not worry about anybody or anything You said it was enough for an elephant Perhaps it was But you don't allow for the taste making only a small quantity to be taken It sounded like a reproach was it meant to be?

Just tell what the reference to the elephant and the quinine is?—Thirty grains of quinine taken by Mrs Thompson I told her it was enough for an elephant I used to take 10 grains when I was bad with malaria

Look now at the letter of 18th May (exhibit 22), which starts with a quotation from " Bella Donna " Did you attach any importance to that?—That it came from a book, that is all, it is a quotation I arrived home on 26th May

After the date of arriving home did you pay any attention at all to what she had said in these letters to you received on that voyage between March and May?—No, nothing at all I was at home for a fortnight between 26th May and 9th June, and I was seeing Mrs Thompson constantly then We were always discussing the question of a separation or divorce I went away on 9th June, and did not come back until 23rd September During the whole of that time I was getting the various letters which have been produced

Did you correspond with her as much on this voyage as you had done previously?—No, I did not The reason was I thought that if I ceased to correspond with her her life would not be so hard The references in the various letters about my not writing to her just refer to the fact that I had not written much from various ports The letters which I did write to her were similar to the three which have been produced (exhibits 14, 30, and 31)

Did you ever write a letter suggesting violence or poison?—No, never

Look at Mrs Thompson's letter of 23rd May (exhibit 23)—

I'll try to be patient darling You talk about that cage you are in—that's how I feel—only worse if it can be so

Had you written to her telling her to be patient?—Yes, oh, yes

Look at the letter of 13th June (exhibit 24)—

Darlingest Boy, I'm trying very hard—very very hard to B B

Bywaters and Thompson.

Frederick E. F. Bywaters

Does that mean " be brave "?—That means be brave I had written her a letter and told her to be brave

Then it goes on—

When he saw this had no effect on me he got up and stormed—I said exactly what you told me to and he replied that he knew that's what I wanted and he wasn't going to give it to me—it would make things far too easy for both of you (meaning you and me) especially for you he said

What had you told her to tell him?—A separation, and if she could not get a separation suggest a divorce, and she would provide him with the evidence—she would go to that extent I told her to say that, and that is what she is referring to In the letter of 20th June (exhibit 25) she says, " I wish you had taken me with you, darlint " There was a suggestion that we should go away the following year, 1923, and I had partly made arrangements in Australia When she says, " When you are not near, darlint, I wish we had taken the easiest way," she is referring to suicide, as that was the easiest way out of it Later on in the letter she says, " What an utterly absurd thing to say to me, ' Don't be too disappointed ' " I had written to her saying that I had started to make arrangements in Australia, or that I was going to make arrangements, but she could not expect too much yet, and was not to be too much disappointed

Come now to the letter of 4th July (exhibit 26)—

In one part of it [she is referring to a letter to you] you say you are going to still write to me because it will help, in another part you say—perhaps I shan't write to you from some ports—because I want to help you

You had written to her to that effect?—Yes, that I was not going to write

Why arn't you sending me something—I wanted you to—you never do what I ask you darlint—you still have your own way always—If I don't mind the risk why should you? Whatever happens cannot be any more than this existence—looking forward to nothing and gaining only ashes and dust and bitterness

What was it she had asked you to send her?—More letters

Where did the risk come with regard to these letters?—The risk was people seeing them, she did not want any one to see them, that was all There was always the difficulty as to where these letters should be sent to

Look at letter of 14th July (exhibit 52), where she says—

You do say silly things to me—' try a little bit every day not to think about me '

Is that what you had been telling her to do?—That is what I said

Evidence for Prisoner Bywaters.

Frederick E. F. Bywaters

Sometimes I think and think until my brain goes round and round ' Shall I always be able to keep you ' Eight years is such a long time

What was she referring to there?—Her age and mine She was eight years older than me, and she felt it

Look at exhibit 63, which was written on 28th August—

Darlingest boy, to-day is the 27th and it's on a Sunday, so I am writing this in the bathroom, I always like to send you greetings on the day—not the day before or the day after

What was that the anniversary of?—The 27th June, 1921, my birthday

By Mr Justice Shearman—But this is August?—Yes, it was

Examination continued—I will read the rest of the letter—

Fourteen whole months have gone by now, darlint, it's so terribly long

Was it the day in the month that it was an anniversary of?—Yes, the 27th is the anniversary

Neither you nor I thought we should have to wait all that long time, did we? Altho' I said I would wait five years—and I will darlint—it's only three years and ten months now

What was the waiting five years?—On 27th June 1921 Mrs Thompson told me she was unhappy, and I said, " Let me be a pal to you let me help you if I can " This was after we had come back from the Isle of Wight, and while I was staying in Thompson's house Mrs Thompson and I had been having an argument, and she suddenly burst into tears, and I advised her to wait, not to give up hope, and not commit suicide

But what was to happen at the end of the five years?—Well there was hardly anything definite It was just an arrangement to put off anything—her committing suicide I extracted a promise from her to wait five years, so that she should not commit suicide

During that five years was there to be any suggestion of a separation or a divorce?—Yes, five years to try and get it

And if there was no divorce or separation in five years, what then did she suggest?—Either going away entirely, the two of us going away, or suicide

Look now at the letter of 12th September (exhibit 54) This is one of the last letters she wrote to you before you got home—

I've got nothing to talk to you about—I can't think about anything at all—I can't even look forward to seeing you I don't hear from you much You don't talk to me by letter and help me and I don't even know if I am going to see you

Will you tell us how she came to write that?—I had ceased

Bywaters and Thompson.

Frederick E. F. Bywaters

corresponding with her. I had said I would not see her when I came to England, as it would not be so hard for her to bear; her life would be easier, perhaps, if I did not see her or correspond with her. I was doing that for her sake, as I wanted to help her. In the letter (exhibit 28), she says—

> You say 'can we be pals only, Peidi, it will make it easier.'

I had suggested that to her. Further on in the same letter she says—

> Have you lost heart and given up hope? Tell me if you have darlint.

That was the result of the letter I had written. I arrived in this country on 23rd September, and Mrs. Thompson wired to me to meet her.

At that date had there been any agreement that any act of violence should be done to her husband either by her or by you?—No, nothing at all.

In these letters that have been read, was there anything which incited you to do any act of violence to Mr. Thompson?—Nothing whatever.

Had it any effect on your mind at all, so far as Mr. Thompson was concerned?—No, I never considered them much.

The Court adjourned.

Third Day—Friday, 8th December, 1922.

FREDERICK EDWARD FRANCIS BYWATERS, recalled, further examined by Mr CECIL WHITELEY—My ship arrived at Gravesend on Saturday, 23rd September and I went to my mother's that evening, and continued to reside there I first met Mrs Thompson after my return on Monday, the 25th I also met her on the next three days at quarter to six in the evening at Fenchurch Street station, and I left her at quarter to seven Those were the only times I was with her during those days On Friday 29th, I met Mrs Thompson about mid-day and took her to lunch, and then she went back to her business I went to Fullers' teashop between three and four that afternoon, and I got the letter which Miss Jacobs handed to me I was in the teashop when Mrs Vallender came in Later on Mrs Thompson came in I left her that evening in Ilford about quarter to seven, and then I went home to my mother's On the Saturday morning, about nine o'clock, I took her for a walk in Wanstead Park, and left her in the park about one o'clock I went home to my mother's about tea-time, and I stayed there for the rest of the day, and for the whole of the Sunday until the Monday On the Monday morning Mrs Thompson telephoned to me (which was quite a usual thing when I was at home), and I took her for lunch After lunch she went back to her work, and in the afternoon I went to Fullers' teashop That was the day on which Higgins gave me exhibit 10, " Wait till one, he's come —Peidi " Mrs Thompson came into the teashop, and I left her at about quarter to seven, the usual time I then went to Mr Graydon's 231 Shakespeare Crescent, Manor Park I had been there on the previous Monday with a message from Mr Graydon's son in Australia I was on very friendly terms with that family On that Monday evening I stayed with them up till about 10 30 That evening I asked Mr Graydon if he would get me some tobacco, and he said that he would

Up to that time had there been any agreement between you and Mrs Thompson with reference to her husband in any way?—Only the usual agreement of trying to get a separation or divorce

Had the position been changed in any way from what it had been on your previous leave?—No, nothing at all, if anything, we were both trying to get more resigned to it

Come now to Tuesday, 3rd October Had you a knife in your possession?—Yes, I had a knife with a leathern sheath which I bought in November, 1921, and which I took with me when I went abroad I always carried it in my overcoat pocket, and it was in my pocket on 3rd October Mrs Thompson telephoned to me as usual that morning, and I took her to lunch at the Queen Anne

Bywaters and Thompson.

Frederick E. F. Bywaters

Restaurant, Cheapside. After lunch she went back to her business, and in the afternoon I went to Fullers' teashop. Mrs Thompson joined me there at about ten minutes past five; she came to the door, and I got up and went outside with her, and left her at Aldersgate Street station about half-past five. The conversation I had with her was making arrangements for the following day. She asked me if I would be in town the following day as usual.

Was that the arrangement that was come to between you?—Yes. She said she was going to a theatre with Percy and her uncle and aunt from Stamford Hill, and Miss Avis Graydon was supposed to go too, and she added, "I wish I was going with you." After leaving her at Aldersgate Street station I went to Mr Graydon's house at Manor Park and arrived there between six and half-past six. I went there in order to get the tobacco that we had spoken about, and I remained till eleven o'clock, sitting in the same room all the time. Mr and Mrs Graydon, Newenham Graydon, and Avis were in the room with me at different times. I had a pouch with me which Mrs Thompson had given me as a present on the Monday. Both Mrs and Miss Graydon noticed it. Mrs Graydon said to me, "You have got a new pouch, Freddy. Was it a present?" and I said, "Yes." She said, "From a girl, I expect?" and I said "Yes." She said "I expect the same girl gave you that as gave you the watch?" (I had got a present of a watch from Mrs Thompson two voyages previously.) I said, "Yes the same girl gave it me," and she said, "I know who it is, but I am not going to say. Never mind, we won't argue about it. She is one of the best." I said, "There is none better."

Bywaters, I know it is difficult, but I want you to tell us in your own way what your feelings were towards Mrs Thompson?—After that conversation, which happened just before I left, I was naturally thinking of Mrs Thompson. I was thinking how unhappy she was, and I wished I could help her in some manner. That was the trend of my thoughts all the way to East Ham station. When I arrived at East Ham station I thought, "I don't want to go home, I feel too miserable. I want to see Mrs Thompson. I want to see if I can help her." I turned round from East Ham station and walked in the direction of Ilford. I knew Mr and Mrs Thompson would be together and I thought perhaps if I were to see them I might be able to make things a bit better. I had spoken to Mr Thompson about this on two previous occasions only, in August and September of the previous year.

What was your object in going to Ilford?—I went to see Thompson to come to an amicable understanding for a separation or divorce.

Until that moment, had you had any intention of going to Ilford at all that night?—Oh, no. It kind of came across me all of a sudden. I arrived at Ilford station and crossed over the

Evidence for Prisoner Bywaters.

Frederick E. F. Bywaters

railway bridge, turning down York Road into Belgrave Road. When I got into Belgrave Road I walked for some time, and some distance ahead I saw Mr. and Mrs. Thompson, their backs turned to me. They were walking along Belgrave Road towards Kensington Gardens, and Mrs. Thompson was on the inside of the pavement. I overtook them, and pushed Mrs. Thompson with my right hand like that (describing). With my left hand I held Thompson, and caught him by the back of his coat and pushed him along the street, swinging him round. After I swung him round I said to him, "Why don't you get a divorce or separation, you cad?"

Where were your hands when you said that?—By my side, I had let go of him. He said, "I know that is what you want, but I am not going to give it you, it would make it too pleasant for both of you." I said, "You take a delight in making Edie's life a hell." Then he said, "I've got her, I'll keep her, and I'll shoot you." As he said that he punched me in the chest with his left fist, and I said, "Oh, will you?" and drew a knife and put it in his arm.

Did he do anything before you took the knife out?—Yes, he punched me with his left hand and said, "I'll shoot you," going at the same time like that with his right hand (describing).

Why did you draw your knife?—Because I thought I was going to be killed. After I put my knife into his arm there was a struggle. All the time struggling, I thought he was going to kill me. I thought he was going to shoot me if he had an opportunity, and I tried to stop him.

We know of the wounds he received. Have you any recollection at all as to how the wounds at the back of the neck occurred?—I have not any exact recollection, but all I can say is I had the knife in my left hand, and they got there somehow.

During all this time after you had brushed Mrs. Thompson away did you see her again?—I did not. She might have been 10 miles away for all I saw of her. After the struggle I suppose I ran away. I don't remember it definitely, but that is what happened.

At that time did you realise that he was dead?—No, he was standing up when I left him. I then made my way home. Next day I did some shopping with my mother, and came to London with her. In the afternoon I went to the city, and afterwards I went to visit Mr. and Miss Avis Graydon at Manor Park, as there had been an arrangement made on the Tuesday that she should come out with me that night.

With Mrs. Thompson?—No, not with Mrs. Thompson. I bought a copy of the *Evening News* at Mark Lane station (the station for Manor Park), and I read there an account of what had happened.

Was that the first knowledge you had that Mr. Thompson was dead?—It was. I could hardly believe it then. I have heard the evidence that Mr. Graydon has given in this Court, it is quite true

Bywaters and Thompson.

Frederick E. F. Bywaters

The police officers came and asked me to go to Ilford police station, and I went. I saw Superintendent Wensley, Inspector Hall, and a typist in the police station that evening, and I signed my first statement (exhibit 5) in their presence.

Did you yourself dictate that statement?—No, I did not, I was asked to oblige Superintendent Wensley.

Was it done in the form of questions and answers?—Yes.

You say nothing in that statement as to the meeting with Mrs. Thompson by the wall?—No.

That is right, is it not?—That is correct. I did not know what happened really. I knew Mrs. Thompson was in custody, and I wanted to help her. I was kept at the police station all night, and the following evening I signed the statement (exhibit No. 6). Before signing that statement I had been taken to Mrs. Thompson. I was taken from the library to the C.I.D. office.

You were taken past her?—No, in her presence.*

Where was it?—In the C.I.D. office. I afterwards made the statement (exhibit No. 6).

Did you hear what Mrs. Thompson said?—No, I saw her statement.

By Mr. Justice Shearman—Do you mean her written statement (exhibit No. 4)?—Yes.

Examination continued—I have no idea what happened to the sheath of my knife. The knife was found five days afterwards.

Cross-examined by the Solicitor-General—From February, 1921, to June, 1921, I was with the "Orvieto." From June until September I was at home. When I came home in June, 1921, I was eighteen years of age.

Had your acquaintance with Mrs. Thompson before that been simply as a friend of her brother?—I was a friend of Mrs. Thompson as well.

A friend of the family without any particular affection for her?—Oh, no, that is not so. Mrs. Thompson and I were always very good friends.

Was it on the holiday which you spent with her and her husband at Shanklin when you first fell in love with her?—No.

Did she declare any particular affection for you?—She did not.

Nor you for her?—No.

Are you sure of that?—I am positive.

Did you and her husband remain perfectly good friends during that holiday?—Yes.

---

* This is an example of the confusion arising from the bad acoustics of the Central Criminal Court. The witness' meaning as to his seeing of Mrs. Thompson was never made clear to the Court.—Ed.

Evidence for Prisoner Bywaters.

Frederick E. F. Bywaters

When do you say you first felt or declared your affection for her?—I first told her just before I went away in September, 1921. That was after I had left her husband's house.

Do you suggest that that was the first time you and she had declared yourselves to each other?—Yes, as mutual affection.

As being in love with each other?—Yes.

Did it go as far as that at that time?—Yes.

Look at Mrs. Thompson's letter to you of 20th June, 1922 (exhibit No. 25), and turn to the fourth paragraph. Was 20th June, 1921, spent with the Thompsons at Shanklin?—No. We were not at Shanklin then. We were at Kensington Gardens.

Look at the fourth paragraph—

It's Friday now darlint nearly time to go, I am wondering if you remember what your answer was to me in reply to my 'What's the matter' to-night of last year. I remember quite well 'you know what's the matter, I love you' but you didn't then darlint, because you do now and it's different now, isn't it? From then onwards everything has gone wrong with our lives—I don't mean to say it was right before—at least mine wasn't right—but I was quite indifferent to it being either right or wrong and you darlint—you hadn't any of the troubles—or the worries you have now—you were quite free in mind and body.

Was that a true or an untrue statement, that a year ago, in June, 1921, you and she had declared your love for each other?—That is not right.

That is untrue?—That is untrue.

Can you suggest how this woman who was in love with you, had invented an imaginary beginning for this amazing passion?—I don't quite understand you.

By Mr. JUSTICE SHEARMAN—To come down to the simpler question—did you on that day say, "I love you"?—No.

Cross-examination continued—Look at Mrs. Thompson's letter of 11th August, 1921 (exhibit 49)—

Darlingest,—Will you please take these letters back now? I have nowhere to keep them, except a small cash box, I have just bought and I want that for my own letters only and I feel scared to death in case anybody else should read them. All the wishes I can possibly send for the very best of luck to-day, from Peidi.

That letter was in fact written a few days after you had left their house at Kensington Gardens?—That is so.

Does that satisfy you that your evidence is wrong as to the date you told her you loved her?—No.

Then on 20th August, 1921 (exhibit 12), she writes—

Come and see me Monday lunch time, please darlint. He suspects Peidi.

Bywaters and Thompson.

Frederick E. F Bywaters

Do you remember when you met her?—I suppose I went on the Monday, but I don't remember

Do you remember then as to whether you and Mrs Thompson had conversations as to suspicions of her husband about you?—He was naturally jealous of Mrs Thompson's friends

Did you and Mrs Thompson have conversations about the time, or just after, you left her husband's house as to her husband being suspicious of you?—No

Did you and Mrs Thompson at that time desire that she should be separated from her husband?—Oh, yes

Was she anxious for it?—Yes

I think in your evidence-in-chief you said that you and Mr and Mrs Thompson discussed a separation?—They discussed it, I listened

Were you involved in that conversation as the lover of Mrs Thompson?—No

I may take it you did not declare yourself at any time in the conversation?—Oh, no

Were you anxious to declare yourself, or were you anxious to prevent the husband from being suspicious?—I had not those feelings then

Then I may take it that at that time you had no intention of taking Mrs Thompson away with you, or no thought of it?—I had thought of helping Mrs Thompson, I should like to help her to be more happy

Had you any thought at that time of going away with her, taking her to live with you?—No

Had you thought of that before you departed on your voyage in September, 1921?—Yes

Had you suggested that to her?—Not exactly that. I had suggested she should get a divorce or separation, and, failing that, we should go away together That was just a few days before I left in September 1921 I saw Mr Thompson again after the interview at which he and his wife discussed separation—I saw him while I was in the house, and I saw him again when I came home in November

Up till that time in November, so far as you know, had the husband any suspicions of you?—No

Were you and he perfectly good friends?—No, I cannot say that we were good friends

Were you on friendly terms?—We were acquaintances

When you met him in November did you meet as friends and part as friends?—As acquaintances We shook hands when we went, we were not bosom chums

Did you mention the question of a separation to him again on that occasion in November?—Yes

Was he angry about it?—No, I cannot say he was

Evidence for Prisoner Bywaters.

Frederick E F Bywaters

Was he pleased about it?—Well, he was not exactly pleased

Did he turn you out of the house?—Oh, no

He discussed it in an amicable way?—Yes

Did you then tell him that you were in love with his wife?—No

Did you suggest any grounds upon which either she or he was to obtain a divorce?—No

Was divorce mentioned?—Divorce or separation was mentioned

Were you not at this time attempting to keep back from him all suspicion as to your relations with Mrs Thompson?—No, I was not attempting to keep it back

Did you ever tell him up to that time?—No

Had you and Mrs Thompson at that time spoken about suicide?—Yes

Do you remember when that proposal was abandoned?—Abandoned?

Yes Was it abandoned?—Yes, the pact of suicide was abandoned

It is referred to in exhibit No 62 the letter of 18th November, 1921—

All I could think about last night was that compact we made Shall we have to carry it thro'?

Was that pact of suicide abandoned after that letter?—I never really considered it seriously

May we take it from that time forward there was no more thought of the suicide pact?—Oh yes, there was, it was mentioned

But not really entertained by you?—No

Do you say from that time forward the only idea in your mind or hers was divorce or separation?—Or suicide on her part

But the suicide, I put to you, after that letter was not seriously entertained?—Not by me, but by her it was

Except for the suicide on her part you say that you or she only contemplated separation or divorce?—That is true or me to take her away

Was the removal of her husband ever mentioned by her to you?—No

Never?—Never

Did it ever occur to you that that was a way in which you and she might come together?—No

Did her letters suggest it to you?—No

Did you tell your learned counsel that you read her letters as melodrama?—Some

What was it you understand as melodrama?—She had a vivid way of declaring herself, she would read a book and imagine herself as the character in the book

Do you mean that you read her references to poison as melodrama?—Some as melodrama, some as general knowledge

Bywaters and Thompson.

Frederick E. F. Bywaters

General knowledge?—Yes

I don't understand that. What did you understand when she mentioned a particular poison?—To what are you referring?

Are you aware, or do you remember, that she mentioned several times a poison in her letters?—Yes

Did that suggest to you a dose of poison might kill her husband?—No

It did not occur to you?—No

Did you not read those letters as meaning that the idea was in her mind?—No

Did she ever make an actual proposal to you that you and she might go off together?—Yes

When did she first make it?—I suppose it was about the November when I came home

Did you agree to the proposal or did you reject it?—I said, "Wait and see what happens"

What were you going to wait for?—To see if she could get a separation or divorce

And how long were you going to wait?—A period of five years

Did you ever mean to do anything to make a divorce possible?—No

You had no intention of taking any action?—No

Will you turn to the letter of 1st April, exhibit No 17 "I thought a lot about what you said of Dan?"—I had told Mrs Thompson about a friend of mine named Dan

That is all you had told her?—I told her of some of his business that he had told me. I had not told him anything about myself and Mrs Thompson

Then will you follow while I read—

Darlint, don't trust him—I don't mean don't tell him anything because I know you never would—what I mean is don't let him be suspicious of you regarding that—because if we were successful in the action—darlint circumstances may afterwards make us want many friends—or helpers and we must have no enemies—or even people that know a little too much Remember the saying 'A little knowledge is a dangerous thing'

What was "the action" that she there refers to?—Suicide, as far as I remember

But, Bywaters, read it again. What does "the action" mean?—Mrs Thompson had proposed to me that she did not want to make my life as unhappy as hers. She said she would sooner kill herself

Do you really suggest that "the action" means suicide?—As far as I remember, yes, it means suicide

Are you quite clear it does not mean crime?—I am positive of that

I am coming back to that letter. Look now at exhibit No 50

Evidence for Prisoner Bywaters.

Frederick E F Bywaters

This is written before 31st March and you had been home for about a fortnight at the end of January and again for a few days at the end of March?—Yes

Read what Mrs Thompson says in that letter—

This time really will be the last time you will go away—like things are, won't it? We said it before darlint I know and we failed—but there will be no failure this next time darlint, there mustn't be

Had there been a failure?—Yes

What had you tried that had failed?—Separation or divorce

Does it occur to you what was the best way to get a divorce if that was all you wanted?—Yes, I know the best way of getting a divorce

What was the best way of getting a divorce for Mrs Thompson from her husband?—To provide Mr Thompson with the information he needed

Why did you not try?—Because he would not accept

Did you provide him with the information?—She had

Had she provided him with the information to enable him to get a divorce?—She said she would provide him with the information to get a divorce

Had she tried to give him the information to get a divorce?—She said she would do it

My question was had she tried to get a divorce from her husband?—She had suggested to him she wanted a divorce, and she would provide him with the information he required if he would come to terms

I suggest to you that "failure" there refers to the same thing as "action" in the other letter—that Mrs Thompson had tried to poison her husband and had failed?—And I say that that is not true

What you say is that it refers to information or a statement she had thought of making to her husband to make him divorce her?—Yes, or separation

Were you and she really anxious that he should know that you and Mrs Thompson were lovers?—He did know

From what time did he know?—I do not know he exactly knew we were lovers He knew we were fond of each other

Did you not do your best to keep it from him from start to finish?—Oh no

Will you turn to the letter of 3rd January, 1922, exhibit No 13—

Immediately I have received a second letter, I have destroyed the first and when I got the third I destroyed the second and so on, now the only one I have is the "Dear Edie" one written to 41, which I'm going to keep It may be useful, who knows?

Bywaters and Thompson.

Frederick E. F Bywaters

Was that the letter of 1st December, exhibit 14, beginning "Dear Edie" and signed "Yours very sincerely, Freddy"?—Yes

Was that the customary way in which you wrote to Mrs Thompson at that time?—No

Was that letter written in that form in order to disarm suspicion?—No

Did you understand from the passage I have just read from the letter of 3rd January that she was going to use that letter to disarm suspicion?—No

Did you understand what was meant when she said "It may be useful—who knows"?—I do not know

Would the letter be any use to get a divorce or separation?—I think that she is referring to the latter

I take it you would agree with me the letter would not be useful for that purpose?—I do not agree with you I never said that

You do not follow me You agree with me that that letter which says "Dear Edie," and finishes "Yours very sincerely" would be of no use to enable either her or you to get a divorce?—That letter was not meant to be a means of getting a divorce It was a letter conveying Christmas greetings

Did you understand what she meant when she said "This letter may be useful, I will keep it?"—She may have kept this to show to her sister Avis, that was one of the reasons that I wrote it

Then you did write it to blind somebody?—Oh yes

Did the subject of poisons ever occur in your conversations with her when you were at home?—Sometimes

In what connection?—General conversation knowledge

Who mentioned poisons?—If she had been reading anything and poison was mentioned, and any matter that she would not understand, she would ask me what it meant

Did you know anything about poison?—I did not know very much

Did she appear to be interested in poison?—No not particularly

Did it ever strike you it occupied a prominent place in her mind?—No more than other things

Did you take an interest in poison?—I was fond of chemistry when I was at school

But chemistry and poison are two different things?—Poisons deal with chemistry Poisons come in chemistry

Did you take any interest in poisons as poisons?—No

Did you keep up your interest which you say you had in chemistry?—No, I did not She knew of that interest, though; her brother used to join me

Do you suggest then that the mention of poison in your conversation and in your letters was due to the fact that she knew you were interested in chemistry? Is that your explanation?—No, my

Evidence for Prisoner Bywaters.

Frederick E. F. Bywaters

explanation is this if she had been reading something and it occurred to her, if I had been in her presence she would have asked me what it was If I was not there, she put it in writing

Do you remember a document which you wrote out containing the troy weights, exhibit 57? " 60 milligrams = 1 grain, 18 grains = 1 gramme, 30 grammes = 1 oz " Is that your handwriting?—Yes

When did you write it?—I could not say

Why did you keep it?—Because it is useful in general knowledge

Had that any connection with the request she made to you to experiment with pills?—Oh no

Turn back to the letter of 1st April, exhibit No. 17, and listen to this paragraph—

He was telling his Mother etc the circumstances of my 'Sunday morning escapade' and he puts great stress on the fact of the tea tasting bitter ' as if something had been put in it ' he says. Now I think whatever else I try it in again will still taste bitter—he will recognise it and be more suspicious still and if the quantity is still not successful it will injure any chance I may have of trying when you come home Do you understand?

What did you understand about that passage?—That she had taken the quinine and it tasted bitter

Look at it again—

He puts great stress on the fact of the tea tasting bitter ' as if something had been put in it ' he says

To whom did it taste bitter?—Mrs Thompson

Do you suggest that, Bywaters?—I do

Do you suggest that is how you understood the letter when you received it?—I do

Now I think whatever else I try it in again will still taste bitter—he will recognise it and be more suspicious still

Do you still adhere to what you say, that she is speaking of her taste?—Yes

What did you understand him to be suspicious of?—That she was attempting to commit suicide

Did you understand her to mean that she would tell him that her tea tasted bitter and she was about to commit suicide?—Possibly she would

Is that your understanding of that passage?—That is

Look at the letter of 1st May (exhibit 19)—

I don't think we're failures in other things and we mustn't be in this

Did you understand what that referred to?—Yes

Bywaters and Thompson.

Frederick E F Bywaters

What?—Well, if you read further, "We mustn't give up as we said"

What was that?—Give up trying for a separation or divorce

> We must learn to be patient We must have each other darlint It's meant to be I know I feel it is because I love you such a lot—such a love was not meant to be in vain It will come right I know one day, if not by our efforts some other way We'll wait eh darlint, and you'll try and get some money and then we can go away and not worry about anybody or anything You said it was enough for an elephant

Do you remember saying that?—Yes

Did you say that in writing or in speech?—In speech

Are you clear about that? Did you say it in a letter or in a conversation when you were at home?—I really do not remember whether it was in conversation or in a letter

And what was it you said was enough for an elephant?—The quinine I had given Mrs Thompson

For what had you given her quinine?—She had been wanting me to get her something with which to commit suicide, as she did not want to make my life as unhappy as hers To satisfy her craving I said I would get her something, and I gave her quinine

It is your suggestion that in May, 1922, you were lending your assistance to her desire to commit suicide?—Her suggestion

You say you gave her this quinine because she wanted something with which to commit suicide Is that right?—Yes, that is so

Did you give her quinine with that object?—I did

Were you therefore willing to help her to commit suicide?—No, I knew she could not hurt herself with quinine

You were playing with her ideas?—I was pulling her leg

> You said it was enough for an elephant Perhaps it was But you don't allow for the taste making only a small quantity to be taken It sounded like a reproach was it meant to be?

That is your explanation, that you were playing a joke upon her?—That is so

She goes on—

> Darlint I tried hard—you won't know how hard—because you weren't there to see and I can't tell you all—but I did—I do want you to believe I did for both of us I was buoyed up with the hope of the 'light bulb' and I used a lot

Did you understand that as referring to a dose she herself took of broken glass?—Possibly, yes She was trying to persuade me to give her something with which to commit suicide, and I refrained I gave her this quinine so that she would not take anything herself

Evidence for Prisoner Bywaters.

Frederick E F Bywaters

But in the next passage that I have called your attention to she refers to another specific—

I was buoyed up with the hope of the ' light bulb ' and I used a lot—big pieces too

Did you understand that to mean that she had taken glass?—I understood that to be a lie from her to me

You understood even if it was a lie, that what it was a lie about was what she had taken herself?—Oh yes

By Mr JUSTICE SHEARMAN—Look at it Was she lying about what her husband had taken or what she had taken herself?—I say she was lying about what she had taken herself

Cross-examination continued—Look at the next sentence—

I quite expected to be able to send that cable

Do you suggest that after she had taken the dose that would kill her she was expecting to send you that cable?—No, I do not suggest that

What do you suggest?—That she would have sent me a cable if she had been successful in getting a divorce or an agreement of separation

By Mr JUSTICE SHEARMAN—Had you arranged with her if anything happened she should cable you?—Yes if she was successful in getting an agreement for separation

Cross-examination continued—

I quite expected to be able to send that cable—but no—nothing has happened from it

That is the glass?—No

What was it?—The approach of Thompson to get this separation

Now your letter tells me about the bitter taste again Oh darlint, I do feel so down and unhappy Wouldn't the stuff make small pills coated together with soap and dipped in liquorice powder—like Beechams—try while you are away

Is that why you were interested in Troy weights?—No

Our Boy had to have his thumb operated on because he had a piece of glass in it that's what made me try that method again—but I suppose as you say he is not normal

Who is " he "? Read the next sentence if you are in doubt—

I know I feel I shall never get him to take a sufficient quantity of anything bitter

Bywaters and Thompson.

Frederick E. F. Bywaters

Have you any doubt that you understood that to mean the husband?—I did not understand that

To whom did you understand it referred?—Perhaps she had made a mistake in the words

And meant " me "?—Yes

" I know I feel I shall never get ' myself ' to take a sufficient quantity of anything bitter " Is that how you read it?—That is right she did not like the taste of quinine

Was there any reason why she should be concerned as to leaving traces of what she was doing? Read the next sentence—

Darlint, two heads are better than one is such a true saying You tell me not to leave finger marks on the box—do you know I did not think of the box but I did think of the glass or cup whatever was used I wish I wish oh I wish I could do something

You understood that to mean at the time I wish, I wish oh, I wish I could kill myself ' Is that it?—Yes

Turn now to the letter of 18th May 1922 (exhibit No 22), the " Bella Donna letter—

' It must be remembered that digitalin is a cumulative poison, and that the same dose harmless if taken once, yet frequently repeated becomes deadly ' Darlingest boy the above passage I've just come across in a book I am reading " Bella Donna ' by Robert Hichens Is it any use?'

Did you answer her question?—No, I did not answer it

Did you attach any importance to the question?—I thought it was another manner in which she was trying to get something with which to commit suicide

You were devotedly attached to Mrs Thompson at this time?—Yes

Did it excite no apprehension in your mind when she made these repeated proposals to you to commit suicide?—I told her if she really wanted it I would get it for her, I would get her something to commit suicide

Did you understand this was a proposal that digitalin should help her to commit suicide?—Yes, I understood her to mean that would be more pleasant than quinine or the glass

What was the object of having the cumulative poison if she was going to commit suicide?—I did not see the object of having a cumulative poison, but it was not unpleasant

Did she expect you to help her to commit suicide do you know?—I do not know that she really did expect it but she often mentioned it

In the long letter I have already referred you to (exhibit 19) she says—

Do experiment with the pills while you are away—please darlint No, we two—two halves—have not come to the end of our tether Don't let us

Do you still suggest that was suicide?—Yes

Evidence for Prisoner Bywaters.

Frederick E. F. Bywaters

Look at the letter of 4th July (exhibit No. 26), "Have you studied bichloride of mercury?" Had you studied it?—I had not.

Did you study it?—I did not.

Did the question surprise you?—No.

Did you refer to it in your correspondence?—I did not.

Did you connect it again with suicide?—No.

What did you connect it with?—A general or common or garden question.

Did you still think at that time that she was pretending or contemplating to commit suicide?—No, not apparently then.

Just follow. In May she was writing letters to you which you say you understood meant suicide?—Yes.

In July she was writing to you about poison when you were in Freemantle, in Australia?—Yes.

Did you understand her to have abandoned suicide or to be still thinking of it?—I did not understand her to mean anything except that was a question. I expect she had read that somewhere, and did not know what it was and asked me if I knew.

Did you ever rebuke her about the suicide talk?—Well, I tried to pacify her.

When you were in Australia did you tell her that you had made arrangements or had begun to make arrangements for living in Australia with her?—Yes.

That was at this time, on this trip?—Yes.

Was it the arrangement which you began to make in Australia with a view to her running away from her husband?—Yes, failing separation or divorce.

Look at the letter of 24th April (exhibit No. 18), which apparently reached you at Aden on 7th May—

I used the 'light bulb' three times but the third time—he found a piece—so I've given it up—until you come home.

What did you understand by that passage?—She had been lying to me again.

She had been what?—Lying to me, lying.

What did you understand the lie was?—It was melodrama on her part, trying to persuade me that she had taken broken glass.

"I used the 'light bulb' three times but the third time—he found a piece." You understood she meant her husband had detected her in an attempt to commit suicide?—Yes.

"So I have given it up until you come home." Do you suggest that she was going to wait for your arrival home in order that you might co-operate with her in committing suicide?—I might give her something more, some quinine.

That would be a strange idea to you Bywaters, if that is right?—Yes, I do not know her idea.

Bywaters and Thompson.

Frederick E F Bywaters

In any conversation, did you ever speak about the risks you and she were running? Did she tell you she was running a risk?—Yes

Can you tell me what risk she was running?—Whenever she mentioned to her husband separation or divorce there was always trouble

What was the risk?—Of her being unhappy, her life being made more unhappy

Did she say "I am prepared to run a risk if you are"?—If I would let her, if I was agreeable

The risk she was running?—Of being knocked about

Did she tell you in her letters that so far as she could make her husband believe it, her husband thought she was a happy woman again, or something of that sort?—No she told me in her letters that was the only way she could obtain a little peace

Now I come to September Were you anxious to break off or to alter the relations between you and Mrs Thompson?—I thought if I did not see her or did not correspond with her, her life would not seem so hard

You thought if you did not write to her it would make her life easy?—Yes

You got the letter (exhibit No 28) some time about September Look at this passage—

Darlingest Boy,—I don't quite understand you about 'Pals' You say ' Can we be Pals only, Peidi, it will make it easier '

Had you said that?—Yes

Meaning no longer lovers?—If we could stifle our feelings would it be easier for her

Do you mean for always? because if you do, No, no, a thousand times We can't be 'pals' only for always darlint—its impossible physically and mentally Last time we had a long talk—I said ' Go away this time and forget all about me, forget you ever knew me, it will be easier—and better for you ' Do you remember—and you refused, so now I'm refusing darlint—it must be still 'the hope of all' or 'the finish of all'

By Mr Justice Shearman—You understand this letter as entreating you still to be her lover?—No, it was not entreating, it was stating facts that was all

Cross-examination continued—

If you still only mean for a certain time and you think it best, darlint it shall be so—I don't see how it will be easier myself—but it shall be as you say and wish, we won't be our natural selves tho' I know—we'll be putting a kerb on ourselves the whole time—like an iron band that won't expand Please don't let what I have written deter you from any decision darlint—I don't want to do that—truly I'd like to do what you think best I don't sleep much better now—the nights seem so long—I

Evidence for Prisoner Bywaters.

Frederick E. F. Bywaters

sleep for an hour and lie awake for 2 and go to sleep again for another hour—right thro' the night. A doctor can't do me any good darlint—no good at all—even the most clever in the land—unless that doctor is you and it can't be, so I'm not going to waste any more money on them. I want you for my doctor—my pal—my lover—my everything—just all and the whole world would be changed.

Then at the end of the letter—

Yes, darlint you are jealous of *him*.

Who was "him"? Did you understand him to be the husband?—Yes. I understood the husband, but I made the statement first. Mrs Thompson related to me he had taken a lady out to tea, and I made the remark "All people's tastes are alike. Do you think by this that I am jealous of him?

Yes, darlint, you are jealous of him.?—Yes.

'But I want you to be—he has the right by law to all that you have the right to by nature and love—yes darlint be jealous, so much that you will do something desperate.'—But I was not jealous.

She was appealing to you to be jealous and do something desperate?—No. "Desperate" was to take her away—that is how I read it.

Why did you not take her away?—Financial reasons.

Had you at that time ever thought of marrying her?—No.

Had you ever asked her to go with you?—There had been suggestions.

Did you ever ask her as a man to a woman to go away with you and leave her husband?—I don't know that I had asked; it was more of a mutual kind of arrangement.

You had never made a definite kind of arrangement?—No, she would not take it; she would prefer a divorce or separation.

Exhibit No 55 is an undated letter—

Darlint Pal, please try and use—pour moi, and don't buy a pouch, je vais, pour vous—one of these days.

Was that the note which was given to you when she gave you the pouch?—No.

Was the pouch given to you on 1st October?—Yes.

What does this letter refer to?—It refers to a pipe.

Was it written after you had gone home?—I had it when I was in England, yes.

With it did the next document come, a cutting from the *Daily Sketch* of 20th September, 1922—"Chicken Broth Death. Rat poison consumed by fowl kills woman"?—Yes.

At that time you were able to read English newspapers for yourself?—No, not when this was written.

I thought you said it was given to you, or handed to you, after

Bywaters and Thompson.

Frederick E. F Bywaters

you reached England?—I said I received it when I was in England I received it in Plymouth on my homeward journey When I reached Tilbury I received the telegram of 25th September (exhibit 58), " Must catch 5 49 Fenchurch reply if can manage "

You met Mrs Thompson from time to time without her husband's knowledge?—Yes

Did you speak to her of the risk that you and she were running? —Not any risk that I was running

Look at the letter written on 1st October (exhibit No 60) at the end—

Don't forget what we talked in the Tea Room I'll still risk and try if you will—we only have 3¾ years left darlingest

What did you understand the risk was that she was prepared to run?—The risk of being knocked about when she was asking for separation or divorce

What was the risk that you were to run, " I will still risk and try if you will ?— " If you will let me "

How was she going to run the risk of being knocked about by telling her husband she was going with you?—No, by asking for a divorce or separation

Then you did in fact meet her and never went near her husband? —I kept away I did not want further trouble

You met her at Fullers in the afternoon of 3rd October?—Yes

Did you have any conversation about her husband?—No

Did you not refer to him?—Only that she was going to the theatre

She did tell you that she was going to the theatre?—Yes

And she told you which theatre?—Yes

After you left her I understand you went straight to the Graydons?—Yes

Were you carrying your knife when you went there?—I was

Did you carry that knife everywhere while in England?—Yes

Did you ever use it for anything?—Cutting string or cutting things handy

Is that the purpose for which you carried it?—I bought that— it may be handy at any time

A knife of that size and character?—Yes, handy at sea

Handy at sea, but was it handy at home?—Yes

As you told us, you knew before you went to the Graydons that they were going to the theatre?—Yes

When you made your statement of 4th October (exhibit 5) did you say this—

Before leaving, I remember Mrs Graydon's daughter Avis saying that Percy (Mr Thompson) had phoned her up, and I gathered from the observations she made that he was taking his wife to a theatre that night, and that there were other members of the family going

Evidence for Prisoner Bywaters.

Frederick E. F. Bywaters

You meant by that that you had heard for the first time that at the Graydons?—I did not say that

Did you mean that?—No, I meant what I say

Do you agree with me that the meaning of that paragraph is that you gathered it for the first time from conversation?—No

Just before that you say in your statement—

I left my home yesterday morning about quarter to twelve. I was dressed in the same clothes that I am now wearing. I went up west and remained there till the evening. I was alone and never met anyone that I knew

That was untrue?—That was untrue. I objected to a lot of Superintendent Wensley's questions—I resented his questions

You mean by "resented his questions" that you told a falsehood?—Yes, I wanted to help Mrs. Thompson

Did you tell falsehoods in order to shield yourself in that statement?—No

It was your one idea to shield Mrs. Thompson?—That is so

Why did you not stick to your first statement? Why did you alter your statement?—I was told Mrs. Thompson would be released if I made that statement

And you made the second statement?—I did

Was the second statement any more true than the first?—Yes

Did you say anything as to your meeting Mrs. Thompson in your second statement?—I don't know. What did I say?

"Mrs. Edith Thompson was not aware of my movements on Tuesday night, 3rd October." At any rate, whether you intended it or not, you did not correct your previous statement that you had not seen her on that day?—No

Why did you not put into your statement of 5th October anything about the incident of the attack which you have told us to-day? Had you forgotten that?—No. When I saw Mrs. Thompson she was so ill I thought she was going to die, and I thought the sooner that I got it down the quicker she would be released and could go home with her mother

So you omitted that part of your story which was concerned with the threat to shoot and the struggle?—I did. That was my main object, I wanted to help her

Can you suggest how it helped her, to omit that important fact?—She would have been released. I did not trouble about details or anything like that. I had questions put to me and I said "Yes, you say it"

You said "Yes" to anything suggested?—Practically anything

May I say that that statement there was no more true in substance than the other statement was, or that you did not care whether it was true?—Oh, yes, it is true, part of it I said myself

Bywaters and Thompson.

Frederick E. F. Bywaters

Was it true, as you said in your statement, that you waited for Mrs. Thompson and her husband?—No. That was untrue. I had that put to me.

What you actually did was to catch them up?—Yes, I overtook them.

Are you a right-handed or a left-handed man?—Right.

Did you strike the first blow from behind?—I struck the first blow in front, his right arm.

Did the struggle take place at one spot or was he moving forward?—I could not say whether we moved. I do not imagine we stood still.

Did you say you remembered striking one blow at his throat?—I did not say that.

Do you remember striking a blow at his throat?—I do not.

And you do not remember anything, do you say, after you pushed Mrs. Thompson away?—I remember pushing Thompson up the street, and the conversation between us, and the subsequent events.

Did you not discuss in the tearoom that afternoon the possibility of meeting them that night?—We did not stay in the tearoom. She did not come into the tearoom. I left it to join her.

Did you not discuss with her something desperate?—I did not.

Did you not refer to her husband except in connection with the theatre party?—That is the only way we referred to him.

Did she tell you she had abandoned all idea of suicide?—No.

Did she make any reference to poison, or force, or violence?—She did not.

And your story is that you went out from the Graydons never intending to use violence to Mr. Thompson?—I never intended to see them when I first went out.*

You formed the idea on your way from the station at West Ham?—East Ham.

Is this true in your second statement "I only meant to injure him"?—It is hardly true. I meant to stop him from killing me.

"I did not intend to kill him; I only meant to injure him." Was that true, that you went there to injure him?—No, it is not.

"I gave him the opportunity of standing up to me as a man, but he would not." Was that true?—When I said that I referred to a back occasion, not to this occasion.

Did you on this occasion give him an opportunity of standing up to you as a man?—No, I did not suggest any violence or fisticuffs at all.

Do you mean to suggest that he made the first assault upon you?—Yes, he did.

And that you then drew your knife?—I did.

---

* He had in fact arranged to go and get some cigarettes which Mr Graydon had promised to have ready for him on the evening of the 3rd.—Ed.

Edith Thompson

Evidence for Prisoner Bywaters.

Frederick E. F. Bywaters

Is it the fact that you never saw any revolver or any gun at that moment?—I never saw it, no.

Did you continue to stab him in the expectation of seeing one at any moment?—I did not know I was stabbing him. I tried to stop him from shooting me, that is all.

Re-examined by Mr. CECIL WHITELEY.—Although I never saw a revolver I believed that he had one, otherwise I would not have drawn my knife. I was in fear of my life.

At any time have you had any intention to murder Mr. Thompson?—I have not.

Your attention has been directed to the first statement which you made (exhibit 5). Did you ever suggest in this statement or any other that the first time you heard about the theatre was at the Graydons?—No, I did not suggest that. I did not wish Superintendent Wensley to know that Mrs. Thompson and I were meeting each other.

Were you thinking of anybody else except Mrs. Thompson when that statement (exhibit 5) was taken from you?—No.

Look at the letter of 11th August (exhibit 19). "Darlingest, will you please take these letters back now?" I want you to tell the Court what those letters were?—Those letters are now in the possession of the police. They are letters written to me by a lady in Australia which I had given to Mrs. Thompson to read.

Are the two letters written by you (exhibits 30 and 31) in similar terms to all the other letters which you wrote to Mrs. Thompson when you were abroad?—Not all the letters—some.

Love letters?—Yes.

Did you ever in any letter to Mrs. Thompson say anything with regard to giving poison to her husband or anything of that sort?—I did not.

Mr. WHITELEY—That is our case.

Evidence for the Prisoner Thompson

Mrs. EDITH JESSIE THOMPSON (prisoner on oath), examined by Mr. WALTER FRAMPTON—I was married to Percy Thompson on 15th February 1915. At the time of my marriage and for some years before I was employed by Messrs. Carlton & Prior, and I continued in that employment after my marriage.

Was your marriage a happy one?—No, not particularly so. I think I was never really happy with my husband, but for perhaps two years it was better than it had been.

After a lapse of two years were there constant differences and troubles between you?—There were. My husband and I very often

Bywaters and Thompson.

Edith Jessie Thompson discussed the question of separation, long before June of 1921. I had known the family of Bywaters for some years before 1921. I cannot say that my husband knew them well, but he knew them, he had met them often. In June, 1921, I went with my husband and some friends to the Isle of Wight for a holiday. The prisoner Bywaters accompanied us, at the invitation of my husband. We remained there a week, and then we returned to our house in Ilford, along with Bywaters, who remained there living with my husband and myself, until 5th August.

During that holiday in the Isle of Wight, and while Bywaters was at your house, had you conceived an affection for him?—No. The 1st of August of that year was a Monday. I had some trouble with my husband that day, I think it originated over a pin, but eventually it was brought to a head by my sister not appearing at tea when she said she would. I wanted to wait for her, but my husband objected and said a lot of things to me about my family that I resented. He then struck me several times, and eventually threw me across the room. Bywaters was in the garden at this time and in the course of the disturbance he came into the room and stopped my husband. Later on that day there was a discussion about a separation. I cannot remember exactly what was said, except that I wanted a separation, and Bywaters entreated my husband to separate from me, but he said what he usually said, that he would not. At first he said he would, and then I said to him, 'You always tell me that when I mention the subject, and later, when it actually comes, you refuse to grant it to me.'" I do not remember any further discussion with my husband about separation between the Monday, 1st August and the Friday, when Bywaters left. I occasionally saw Bywaters after he left the house.

Have you at any time from your marriage until the death of your husband ever done anything to injure him physically?—Never.

Have you ever been in possession of poison?—Not to my knowledge.

Have you ever administered any poison to your husband?—No.

Have you ever given him ground glass in his food or in any form?—Never.

Have you ever broken up an electric light bulb and given him that?—Never.

Come now to the letters. Look first at the letter dated 11th August 1921 (exhibit 49)—

Darlingest,—Will you please take these letters back now? I have nowhere to keep them except a small cash box, I have just bought and I want that for *my own letters only* and I feel scared to death in case anybody else should read them.

What were those letters?—They were letters written to him, I understand, by a girl in Australia.

Evidence for Prisoner Thompson.

Edith Jessie Thompson

What sort of letters were they that were written by the lady in Australia to Bywaters? Were they what would be called love letters? —You would hardly call them love letters—personal letters. They were not letters of mine. I do not think I had corresponded with Bywaters before this date, but I really cannot remember.

The next letter I want you to look at is the one dated 20th August, 1921 (exhibit 12)—

Come and see me Monday lunch time please darlint. He suspects

What did you mean by 'he suspects'?—I meant that my husband suspected I had seen Bywaters. I think it was on the Friday previous to that date. I usually saw him on Fridays, and I continued to see him until he sailed on 9th September. He came back in the end of October, and remained in this country until 11th November. After he sailed I corresponded with him, and among other letters I wrote exhibit 62, which is undated.

All I could think about last night was that compact we made. Shall we have to carry it thro'? Don't let us darlint. I'd like to live and be happy—not for a little while but for all the while you still love me. Death seemed horrible last night—when you think about it darlint, it does seem a horrible thing to die when you have never been happy really happy for one little minute.

What compact were you referring to in that letter to Bywaters?—The compact of suicide. We had discussed the question of suicide some time previous to the writing of this letter, I cannot state when.

What was said about it?—That nothing was worth living for, and that it would be far easier to be dead.

Had you discussed any particular means of committing suicide?—I believe we had.

After Bywaters had sailed on that voyage did you send him from time to time cuttings out of the papers?—I did. They were generally cuttings of sensational matters appearing at the time. Amongst the cuttings that I sent there was an account of an inquest upon a girl Freda Kempton, who had died through taking an overdose of cocaine.

In your letter of 14th March, 1922 (exhibit 20) you say—

Enclosed are some cuttings that may be interesting. I think the 'red hair' one is true in parts—you tell me which parts darlint. The Kempton cutting may be interesting if it's to be the same method.

What were you referring to there?—Our compact of suicide.

Look at the letter (exhibit 27) where you say—

I had the wrong Porridge to day, but I don't suppose it will matter. I don't seem to care much either way. You'll probably say I'm careless and I admit I am, but I don't care—do you?

What were you referring to?—I really cannot explain

Bywaters and Thompson.

Edith Jessie Thompson

The suggestion here is that you had from time to time put things into your husband's porridge, glass, for instance?—I had not done so

Can you give us any explanation of what you had in your mind when you said you had the wrong porridge?—Except we had suggested or talked about that sort of thing and I had previously said, " Oh yes I will give him something one of these days "

By Mr JUSTICE SHEARMAN—Do you mean that you had talked about poison?—I did not mean anything in particular

Examination continued—We had talked about making my husband ill

How had you come to talk about making your husband ill?—We were discussing my unhappiness

Did that include your husband's treatment of you?—Yes

Now you say you probably said that you would give him something?—I did

Did you ever give him anything?—Nothing whatever My husband took porridge in the mornings It was always prepared by Mrs Lester, and never by me

Further on in that same letter (exhibit 27), you say—

You know darlint I am beginning to think I have gone wrong in the way I manage this affair I think perhaps it would have been better had I acquiesced in everything he said and did or wanted to do At least it would have disarmed any suspicion he might have and that would have been better if we have to use drastic measures

What were you meaning by the " drastic measures " you might have to use?—Leaving England with Bywaters

Look now at the letter of 3rd January, 1922 (exhibit 13), where you say—

Immediately I have received a second letter, I have destroyed the first and when I got the third I destroyed the second and so on, now the only one I have is the " Dear Edie " one written to 41 which I am going to keep It may be useful, who knows?

Why were you keeping that letter?—I wanted to show it to my people if I were asked if I had heard from Mr Bywaters for Christmas It was a letter wishing me all good wishes for Christmas and my people were certain to ask if I had heard from him Otherwise I did not keep Bywaters' letters, it being a habit of mine to destroy letters that I had received

You go on to say—

Darlint, I've surrendered to him unconditionally now—do you understand me? I think it the best way to disarm any suspicion, in fact he has several times asked me if I am happy now and I've said " Yes quite " but you know that's not the truth, don't you

Evidence for Prisoner Thompson.

Edith Jessie Thompson

What is the meaning of that paragraph?—When I wrote that letter I was expecting Mr Bywaters home in a few days, and I knew if my husband had any suspicion he was coming home he would try to prevent me from seeing him

Further on you say—

Thanking you for those greetings darlint, but you won't always be 'the man with no right' will you?

What does that refer to?—I had hopes of obtaining a divorce from my husband and that Bywaters would marry me

Turn now to your letter of 10th February (exhibit 15)—

Darlint—You must do something this time—I'm not really impatient—but opportunities come and go by—they have to—because I'm helpless and I think and think and think—perhaps—it will never come again

What did you mean by "You must do something this time"?—I meant he must find me some sort of situation or take me away altogether without one I had discussed the question of Bywaters finding me a situation and also the place where he was to look for one for me—in Bombay, Marseilles, Australia—in fact, really anywhere where he heard of anything

I want to tell you about this On Wednesday we had words—in bed —Oh you know darlint—over that same old subject and he said—it was all through you I'd altered I told him if he ever again blamed you to me for any difference there might be in me I'd leave the house that minute and this is not an idle threat He said lots of other things and I bit my lip—so that I shouldn't answer—eventually went to sleep About 2 a m he woke me up and asked for water as he felt ill I got it for him and asked him what the matter was and this is what he told me—whether it is the truth I don't know or whether he did it to frighen me, anyway it didn't He said—some one he knows in town (not the man I previously told you about) had given him a prescription for a draught for insomnia and he'd had it made up and taken it and it made him ill He certainly looked ill and his eyes were glassy I've hunted for the said prescription everywhere and can't find it and asked him what he had done with it and he said the chemist kept it

Is that a true account of something that happened to your husband? —Absolutely true He suffered from insomnia and from his heart, and he took medicines for both

Were you in any way responsible for that condition that you describe in this letter?—None whatever

You go on—

I told Avis about the incident only I told her as if it frightened and worried me as I thought perhaps it might be useful at some future time that I had told somebody What do you think, darlint His sister Maggie came in last night and he told her, so now there are two witnesses,

Bywaters and Thompson.

Edith Jessie Thompson

altho I wish he hadn't told her—but left me to do it It would be so easy darlint—if I had things—I do hope I shall

What is the meaning of that paragraph?—I wrote that to let Bywaters think I was willing to do anything to help him to retain his affections

Look at your letter of 22nd February (exhibit 16), where you write—

I suppose it isn't possible for you to send it to me—not at all possible, I do so chafe at wasting time darlint

What were you referring to there when you wrote that?—Mr Bywaters had told me he was bringing me something and I suggested to send it to me to allow him to think I was eager for him to send me something to do what was suggested I wanted him to think I was eager to help him, to bind him closer to me to retain his affections I had no idea what "it" was

This thing that I am going to do for both of us will it ever—at all make any difference between us, darlint, do you understand what I mean Will you ever think any the less of me—not now I know darlint—but later on—perhaps some years hence—do you think you will feel any different—because of this thing that I shall do Darlint—if I thought you would I'd not do it no not even so that we could be happy for one day even one hour, I'm not hesitating darlint—through fear of any consequences of the action don't think that but I d sooner go on in the old way for years and years and years and retain your love and respect I would like you to write me darlint and talk to me about this

What was the thing that you were going to do for both you and Bywaters?—I was to go away and live with him without being married to him

Come now to exhibit 50—

This time really will be the last you will go away—like things are won't it? We said it before darlint I know and we failed—but there will be no failure this next time darlint there mustn't be—I'm telling you—if things are the same again then I am going with you—wherever it is—if it is to sea—I'm coming too and if it s to nowhere—I'm also coming darlin' You'll never leave me behind again, never, unless things are different

What is the meaning of that paragraph?—That referred to my constant requests to my husband for a divorce That is what I meant when I said we had failed before We had tried to get a divorce or get him to accede to one but I meant if I had not got his consent the next time I was going away with Mr Bywaters at whatever cost and whatever it meant

Do I understand the failure was a failure to induce your husband to divorce you?—That is so

Evidence for Prisoner Thompson.

Edith Jessie Thompson

And if you were not able to persuade him to take the steps, then you were going away, at whatever cost, with Bywaters?—That is so.

The next letter I have to trouble you with is the one dated 1st April (exhibit 17)—

He was telling his mother etc. the circumstances of my 'Sunday morning escapade' and he puts great stress on the fact of the tea tasting bitter.

Was there ever any time when your husband complained to his mother about the tea tasting bitter?—Not to my knowledge.

Was this an imaginary incident then that you were recording?—Yes. My husband's mother is still alive.

Now I think whatever else I try it in again will still taste bitter—he will recognise it and be more suspicious still and if the quantity is still not successful—it will injure any chance I may have of trying when you come home. Do you understand?

Had you at that time or any time put anything into your husband's tea?—No.

Had he ever at any time made complaint that his tea tasted bitter?—No.

I'm going to try the glass again occasionally—when it is safe—I've got an electric light globe this time.

What did you mean Bywaters to understand by that?—That I was willing to help him in whatever he wanted me to do or suggested I should do or we should do. There were electric lights in the house.

Had you got an electric light bulb for any purpose of this description?—I had not.

Did you ever intend to use one?—I did not.

Did you ever at any time use one?—Never.

Look at your letter of 7th May, exhibit No. 18—

Mother and Dad came over to me to dinner—I had plenty to do. On Monday Mr. and Mrs. Birnage came to tea and we all went to the Hippodrome in the evening. By the way—what is "Aromatic tincture of opium"—Avis drew my attention to a bottle of this sealed in the medicine chest in your room. I took possession of it and when he missed it and asked me for it—I refused to give it him—he refuses to tell me where he got it and for what reason he wants it—so I shall keep it till I hear from you.

Had your sister Avis found the bottle of aromatic tincture of opium?—Yes. I had no idea it was in the house before she found it. I did not know whether my husband was using it or not. I had no idea what it was, beyond the name, and in my letter I am asking Bywaters what it is. My husband missed it and asked me about it. I believe my sister Avis took possession of the bottle and threw the

Bywaters and Thompson.

Edith Jessie Thompson

contents down the sink and then threw the bottle away. The bottle which is now shown to me (exhibit 61) is similar, but I cannot say whether it is the same.

> I used the 'light bulb' three times but the third time—he found a piece—so I've given it up—until you come home.

Is there any truth in that statement?—None whatever.

Did you at this time or any time use the light bulb?—Never at all.

Was there ever an occasion when your husband found a piece of glass in his food or anywhere?—Never.

I see in that letter you go on to refer to, and give extracts from, books you were reading. Were you in the habit of doing that?—Yes. I described in detail the characters in novels I was reading and I asked Bywaters his opinion and views upon these various characters. Among other books I read "Maria," "The Guarded Flame," "The Common Law," "The Fruitful Vine," "The Business of Life," "Bella Donna," and "The Way of this Woman."

Look now at your letter of 1st May (exhibit 19)—

> It will come right I know one day if not by our efforts some other way. We'll wait eh darlint, and you'll try and get some money and then we can go away and not worry about anybody or anything. You said it was enough for an elephant. Perhaps it was. But you don't allow for the taste making only a small quantity to be taken. It sounded like a reproach, was it meant to be.

What was it that you were referring to there as being enough for an elephant?—Some quinine that Mr. Bywaters had given me in a small bottle before he went on his voyage.

Had you given some of it to your husband?—No.

Did you at any time give anything out of the ordinary to your husband?—No, never.

In that paragraph you refer to the fact that you will wait until he gets some money. Was the want of money a hindrance to you both going away at that time?—It was.

Further on in that letter you say—

> I was buoyed up with the hope of the 'light bulb' and I used a lot—big pieces too—not powdered—and it has no effect—I quite expected to be able to send that cable—but no—nothing has happened from it and now your letter tells me about the bitter taste again. Oh darlint, I do feel so down and unhappy.

Had you administered any glass fragments of light bulbs to your husband, either in large or small pieces?—Never at all.

Had you arranged to send a cable to Bywaters about anything?—Yes, principally about if I was successful in getting a divorce from my husband.

Evidence for Prisoner Thompson.

Edith Jessie Thompson

When you say " Your letter tells me about the bitter taste again," what had that reference to?—Something Mr Bywaters had said to me about a bitter taste, I suppose

Bitter taste of what?—Of the stuff I had in the bottle

Then you proceed—

> Wouldn't the stuff make small pills coated together with soap and dipped in liquorice powder—like Beechams—try while you are away

What did you wish Bywaters to understand by that?—I wanted him to understand that I was willing to do anything he expected me to do or asked me to do—to agree with him. I wanted him to think I would do anything for him to keep him to me

Turn now to your letter of 18th May (exhibit 22). You commence that letter with a quotation about digitalin and you say you have taken the passage from a book by Robert Hichens that you are reading. Did you know what digitalin was?—I had no idea

Why did you write and ask Bywaters " Is it any use?"?—For the same reason. I wanted him to feel that I was willing to help him, to keep him to me. I have never had digitalin in my possession to my knowledge. My first knowledge of the existence of such a thing was from reading " Bella Donna." Further on in that letter, when I say " Hurry up and take me away—to Egypt—if you like, but anywhere where it is warm." I just mean what I say—I wanted him to take me away at any cost, it would not matter what happened

Was that the thought in your mind at this time, that you should go away with him?—The uppermost. I have already explained that I had been asking Bywaters to find a situation for me abroad and in one of my letters I had said that I was going whether I had a situation or not. In my letter of 23rd May (exhibit 23) I say—

> Your news about—from Bombay—and waiting till next trip made me feel very sad and down-hearted—it will be awful waiting all that time, 3 months will it be—I can't wait—yes, I can—I will, I must—I'll make myself somehow—I'll try to be patient darlint

The news from Bombay that I was referring to there was that he had tried to find me a position to go to and had failed

In that letter you tell Bywaters that you would like him to read " Bella Donna," as he might learn something from it to help you. What were you referring to in " Bella Donna " which you wished him to read which might help you both?—The book was really about Egypt, and I thought he might learn something in it about Egypt

Mr Justice Shearman—I should like to clear this up. Is not the main point of it that the lady killed her husband with slow poisoning?

The Solicitor-General—I was going to deal with it in cross-examination

Bywaters and Thompson.

Edith Jessie Thompson

Examination continued—Do you recollect in that book any particular part or character that you wished to call Bywaters' attention to?—No, not particularly

Look at your letter of 14th July, 1922 (exhibit 52)—

> About Bella Donna—no I don't agree with you about her darlint—I hate her—hate to think of her—I don't think other people made her what she was—that sensual pleasure loving greedy Bella Donna was always there If she had originally been different—a good man like Nigel would have altered her darlint—she never knew what it was to be denied anything—she never knew 'goodness' as you and I know it—she was never interested in a good man—or any man unless he could appease her sensual nature I don't think she could have been happy with nothing—except Baroudi on a desert island she liked—no loved and lived for his money or what it could give her—the luxury of his yacht the secrecy with which she acted all bought with his money—that's what she liked Yes she was clever—I admire the cleverness—but she was cunning, there is a difference darlint, I don't admire that—I certainly don't think she would ever have killed Nigel with her hands—she would have been found out—she didn't like that did she? being found out—it was that secret cunning in Baroudi that she admired so much—the cunning that matched her own If she had loved Baroudi enough she could have gone to him—but she liked the security of being Nigel's wife—for the monetary assets it held She doesn't seem a woman to me—she seems abnormal—a monster utterly selfish and self-living Darlint this is where we differ about women

Was that your true opinion about the character in that book you were referring to?—Absolutely

Turn now to your letter of 13th June (exhibit 24) Do you remember the day of that month that Bywaters returned to sea?—I fancy it was the 9th

You are writing on the Tuesday following his departure—

> I'm trying very hard—very very hard to B B I know my pal wants me to On Thursday—he was on the ottoman at the foot of the bed and said he was dying and wanted to—he had another heart attack—thro me Darlnt I had to laugh at this because I knew it couldn't be a heart attack

On that Thursday (the day before Bywaters sailed) had there been a scene between you and your husband?—Yes, in the evening Mr Bywaters had taken me out to dinner I arrived home later than I usually do, and my husband made a scene He was on the ottoman

Did he appear to have a heart attack?—Not to me, because I knew when he had a heart attack, it was entirely different In the course of that scene he said he was dying and wanted to die That scene which took place on the night before Bywaters sailed was entirely due to the fact that I had been out that night and did not return till late

That is what you mean when you say "he had another heart attack—thro' me"?—Yes, he said it was through me

Evidence for Prisoner Thompson.

Edith Jessie Thompson

Then you go on—

When he saw this had no effect on me—he got up and stormed—I said exactly what you told me to and he replied that he knew that's what I wanted and he was not going to give it to me—it would make things far too easy for both of you (meaning you and me) especially for you he said

What had you said to him while this storm was going on?—I asked him to give me my freedom, and I even went so far as to tell him I would give him the information to get it

Look at your letter of 14th June (exhibit 53) You have told us that you were asking Bywaters in your letters what was aromatic tincture of opium and what was digitalin In this letter you ask him—

Darlint, how can you get ptomaine poisoning from a tin of salmon? One of our boys Mother has died with it after being ill only three days

Had you anything sinister in your mind?—It was partly curiosity and I was stating a fact about our boy's mother

In your letter of 20th June (exhibit 25) you say—

When you are not near darlint I wish we had taken the easiest way

What was the "easiest way" that you were referring to there?—Suicide

Look now at your letter of 4th July (exhibit 26)—

Why arnt you sending me something—I wanted you to—you never do what I ask you darlint—you still have your own way always—if I don't mind the risk why should you? Whatever happens can't be any more than this existence—looking forward to nothing and gaining only ashes and dust and bitterness

What were you wishing Bywaters to understand by that paragraph?—I was asking him to send instead of bring something as he suggested

Had you any particular thing in your mind?—Nothing at all

In the postscript to that letter you say, "Have you studied bichloride of mercury?" What had you in your mind when you wrote that?—Some days previously my husband had discussed with me a conversation that he had with his chemist friend about bichloride of mercury He told me the chemist had given it to a girl in mistake and had made her ill Until my husband had discussed this with me I had never heard of bichloride of mercury, nor did I know anything about it

Your husband having related this to you, you asked Bywaters whether he had studied it?—Out of curiosity I did I never had any bichloride of mercury in my possession to my knowledge

Bywaters and Thompson.

Edith Jessie Thompson

Turn now to your letter of 28th August (exhibit 63)—

Darlingest boy, to-day is the 27th and it's on a Sunday, so I am writing this in the bathroom, I always like to send you greetings on the day—not the day before or the day after. Fourteen whole months have gone by now, darlint, it's so terribly long. Neither you nor I thought we should have to wait all that long time did we? altho' I said I would wait 5 years— and I will darlint—it's only 3 years and ten months now.

What did you mean by that—it is only three years and ten months to what?—To wait.

For what?—To live with Mr Bywaters or go away with him, or be with him only.

Had you made arrangement with Bywaters to wait for five years?—Yes.

What was to happen at the end of five years?—If he was not in a successful position to take me away or had not in the meantime found me something to go to—well, we should part.

Mr Justice Shearman—The other witness's story was that they wanted to commit suicide and he said, 'Put it off five years,' which seems to be the one sensible thing I have heard.

(*To Witness*)—Was that discussed when you wanted to commit suicide together, that you should put it off and wait five years to see how he was getting on?—We might have discussed that, but I do not remember about it.

Examination continued—I was quite prepared to wait five years.

Will you turn to exhibit 28 where you say—

Yes darlint you are jealous of him—but I want you to be—he has the right by law to all that you have the right to by nature and love—yes darlint be jealous, so much that you will do something desperate.

What do you mean by doing something desperate?—To take me away at any cost, to do anything to get me away from England.

Look at exhibit 60. Do you remember the day on which you wrote that letter?—I think it was probably on the Monday, 2nd October. I saw Bywaters on the Monday, but I could not be certain whether it was before or after the writing of the letter. On the Saturday I had told him of my engagement to go to the theatre on the Tuesday. It is quite probable that that engagement was made a fortnight before.

In that letter you say—

Darlint—do something tomorrow night will you? something to make you forget I'll be hurt I know but I want you to hurt me—I do really—the bargain now seems so one sided—so unfair—but how can I alter it.

"To-morrow night" was the night you were going to the theatre. What had Bywaters to forget?—That I was going somewhere with my husband.

Evidence for Prisoner Thompson.

Edith Jessie Thompson

What was he to do to make him forget that?—I wanted him to take my sister Avis out

You say, "I will be hurt, I know." What did that mean?—I should have been hurt by Bywaters being with a lady other than myself

In that letter you also say—

Darlingest find me a job abroad. I'll go tomorrow and not say I was going to a soul and not have one little regret

Did that really represent your feelings at that time, that you were prepared to go abroad with him at once?—Yes. We had discussed it on the Saturday

Look at the end of that letter—

Don't forget what we talked in the Tea Room, I'll still risk and try if you will

What had you discussed in the tearoom?—My freedom

Had you at any time from the month of June, 1921, to the month of October of this year any desire for Bywaters to commit any injury on your husband?—None whatever. Bywaters returned from his last voyage on 23rd September, but I did not see him until Monday the 25th. I saw him again during that week and at nine o'clock on Saturday the 30th. I left him to do some shopping, and then I rejoined him, and was with him until mid-day. We spent the morning in Wanstead Park. I did not see him again on the Saturday or the Sunday. I saw him on Monday 2nd October, I think at 2.15 outside 168 Aldersgate Street, and we lunched together. After lunch I returned to business. I saw him again in Fullers about five o'clock that afternoon, and I believe I had a coffee with him. I stayed with him until about quarter to seven, when I returned home. I did not see him again that night.

During the time you were with Bywaters on the Saturday and the Monday, apart from discussing a separation, did you discuss your husband at all?—No, I did not

Was there any mention or any indication of a possible assault being committed on him?—None whatever. On Tuesday 3rd October, I went to business as usual and I saw Bywaters about 12.30, when we lunched together. I saw him again about quarter-past five, and was with him for about quarter of an hour. After leaving him I met my husband in Aldersgate Street, and we went straight west—about quarter to six I think it was. We had a slight meal together before going to the theatre

Did you anticipate or had you any reason to think that you would see Bywaters again that day or not?—None whatever. I had made arrangements to see him on the following day at lunch time at 168 Aldersgate Street

Bywaters and Thompson.

Edith Jessie Thompson

Did you know where he was going to spend the evening of Tuesday, the 3rd?—Yes, with my people at Shakespeare Crescent, Manor Park.

Was your husband going to do anything the next day, the 4th?—Yes, we had arranged to meet a maid who was coming up from St. Ives, at Paddington station. That was a maid who was to come to relieve me of domestic duties, because I was working all day.

Had anything been said at all at your meetings with Bywaters on the 3rd about seeing him again that night?—Nothing at all.

Had he made any reference to your husband at all?—None at all. I spent the evening at the theatre, and came away with my husband. Leaving Ilford station with the 11.30 train from Liverpool Street, we walked along Belgrave Road. My husband and I were discussing going to a dance. I was trying to persuade him to take me to a dance a fortnight hence. When we got to Endsleigh Gardens a man rushed at me and knocked me aside. I was dazed. I do not remember anything about it, only being knocked aside. When I came to my senses I looked round for my husband, and I saw him some distance down the road. He seemed to be scuffling with some one, and he fell up against me and said "Oo er."

Did you take that to be an exclamation of pain from your husband?—I did. I helped him along by the side of the wall, and I think he slid down the wall on to the pavement. I looked at him and thought he was hurt.

Did you notice any blood coming from him?—Yes, from his mouth. I went to get a doctor, and going along the road I met a lady and gentleman coming towards me. I do not remember what I said to them, but I know that we went to a doctor, and then I came back to my husband with them. The doctor was a long time in coming, an awful long time.

You mean it seemed a long time to you?—It seemed a long time to me. When the doctor came I asked him if he could get my husband home, and he said, "He is dead." I could not believe it, and I still entreated him to let me take him home. I cannot remember what else I said to him.

He did not come home that night?—No, they took him away.

We know from the evidence of Mrs. Lester that you told her if they would have let you go with him you could have helped him?—Yes.

Did you still think after you had gone home that your husband was alive?—Yes, I could not realise he was dead.

Had you any idea at that time that your husband had been stabbed?—None whatever.

And the doctor does not seem to have noticed that when he came?—He did not tell me anything except that he was dead.

Had Bywaters ever at any time said anything to even suggest that he was likely to stab your husband?—Never. I did not know

Evidence for Prisoner Thompson.

Edith Jessie Thompson

that he was possessed of a knife, I had never seen it until it was produced in these proceedings. On the morning of 4th October I was seen by Detective-Inspector Hawkins, first about eleven o'clock and then about twelve o'clock. I was asked to go to the station, and I went, and there I made a statement, which is exhibit 3, as the result of questions put to me and answers given by me.

Had you noticed the previous night the person with whom your husband was scuffling?—No, I had not.

After the scuffle did you see him running away?—I saw somebody running away, and I recognised the coat and hat.

Was that the coat and hat of the prisoner Bywaters?—Mr. Bywaters. In my first statement (exhibit 3) I made no reference to Bywaters, because I was not asked about him. I remained at Ilford police station throughout the day of the 4th and the night. My mother was with me. On Thursday, 5th, I saw the prisoner Bywaters there. He was brought into the C.I.D. room where I was.* After that I made my second statement.

Why did you tell the officer you had not seen any one about in Belgrave Road?—I was very agitated, and I did not want to say anything against Mr. Bywaters; I wanted to shield him.

Was it when you saw him at the police station that you detailed the full story?—No. I made my second statement, which is the true statement (exhibit 4) after Inspector Wensley had said to me, " It is no use your saying he did not do it; he has already told us he has." The inspector then said to me ' Go back to the C.I.D. room and think about it and I will come for you in half an hour." When at the end of that half-hour Inspector Hall came to me I made my statement (exhibit 4).

You have told us when you were walking with your husband a man rushed at you and pushed you aside. Did you fall at all?—I think I must have done so. I have a recollection of getting up when I went to my husband. I had a large bump on my head, on the right side of my ear. That bruise was seen both by my mother and the matron at the police station. My mother remained with me at the police station until nine o'clock on the Thursday evening.

Had you the remotest idea that any attack was going to be made on your husband that night?—None whatever.

Or at any time?—Never at any time.

Cross-examined by the SOLICITOR-GENERAL.—Have you any clear recollection now of what happened when your husband was killed?—Except what I have said, I was dazed.

---

* As usual, there is considerable contradiction and obscurity as to the exact methods of the police and the circumstances in which these important statements were obtained.—Ed.

Bywaters and Thompson.

Edith Jessie Thompson

Is exhibit 4, the short statement, everything you remember, and is it true?—It is true

Was the statement you made to the police, which I will read to you, your recollection at the time, or was it deliberately untrue—

> We were coming along Belgrave Road and just past the corner of Endsleigh Gardens when I heard him call out 'Oo'er' and he fell up against me I put out my arm to save him and found blood which I thought was coming from his mouth I tried to hold him up He staggered for several yards towards Kensington Gardens and then fell against the wall and slid down He did not speak to me I cannot say if I spoke to him I felt him and found his clothing wet with blood He never moved after he fell We had no quarrel on the way, we were quite happy together Immediately I saw the blood I ran across the road to a doctor's I appealed to a lady and gentleman who were passing and the gentleman also went to the doctor's The doctor came and told me my husband was dead Just before he fell down I was walking on his right hand side on the inside of the pavement nearest the wall We were side by side I did not see anybody about at the time My husband and I were talking about going to a dance

Now, did you intend to tell an untruth then about the incident?—Yes

Was that to shield Bywaters?—It was

In your statement you say—

> We were coming along Belgrave Road and just past the corner of Endsleigh Gardens when I heard him call out 'Oo'er' and he fell up against me

Does that not suggest that he was taken ill, and that nobody was present?—Yes

Did you intend, when you said that, to tell an untruth?—It was an untruth

And you intended it to be an untruth?—I did, but I do not mean it was an untruth that he said 'Oo'er' and fell up against me

It is an untruth in so far as it suggests that that was the first thing that happened?—That is so

Was that again to shield Bywaters?—It was

At the time you made this statement to the police you knew that it was Bywaters who had done it?—I did I do not know what you mean by "done it" I did not know then that anything was actually done When I say I knew it was Bywaters, I mean that I recognised his coat and his hat going away

Then you left out the truth in order to shield Bywaters?—Yes, that is so

You knew if you told the truth Bywaters would be suspected?—I did

Evidence for Prisoner Thompson.

Edith Jessie Thompson

In your statement (exhibit 4) you say—

I was dazed for a moment. When I recovered I saw my husband scuffling with a man.

Is that the truth?—It is.

Then did you watch your husband and Bywaters scuffling together?—I did not watch them, I saw them. When I say "scuffling" I mean that I saw my husband swaying, moving about.

And the man there with him?—There was somebody with him, they were some distance ahead of me.

And the two were in contest or pushing?—That is so.

Or fighting?—That is so.

Did you see them fighting?—Scuffling. That is my explanation, moving about.

By Mr Justice SHEARMAN—Did you see either of them strike a blow?—It was dark, I could not.

Cross-examination continued—Was it all over in a moment?—As far as I can recollect.

Then it would not be right to say that you watched them?—Oh, I did not. I mean that I saw the two men together, and it was over.

The next sentence in your statement (exhibit 4) is—

The man who I know as Freddy Bywaters was running away. He was wearing a blue overcoat and a grey hat. I knew it was him although I did not see his face.

Do you mean by that that you recognised this man whom you only saw at a distance in the dark in front of you—that you only recognised him by his overcoat and his hat?—I did, by his back.

Do you really suggest that?—I do.

Did you not know at the beginning as soon as something happened, that it was Bywaters?—I had no idea.

Mr Justice SHEARMAN—There is her statement to the doctor, she said somebody had flashed by.

Sir H Curtis Bennett—It was to Miss Pittard and Mr Clevely.

Mr Justice SHEARMAN—"Some one flew past and when I went to speak to my husband." "Some one flew past" was the expression, and Clevely's words were 'some one flew past and he fell down.'

Cross-examination continued—Supposing these two witnesses are correctly repeating what you said to them, is that a correct impression, that "somebody flew past"?—I have no recollection of saying that. I was in a dazed condition.

Is that a correct impression on your mind, that some one flew past?—No.

All you say is that when you recovered your senses and saw some one in front of you you knew it was Bywaters?—I did when he started to move away.

Bywaters and Thompson.

Edith Jessie Thompson

Had you any doubt when you were asked by the police about it that it was Bywaters who was there and was the man?—No, I had not

May I take it that when you made the long statement (exhibit 3) you left out Bywaters' name in order to shield him?—I did so

Did you also say this in the statement " I have always been on affectionate terms with my husband "?—I cannot say that I actually said that The statement was made as question and answer

I think it was read over to you and you signed it?—It might have been, yes

At any rate, is the statement true or untrue?—It is untrue

If you left Bywaters out of that statement in order to shield him, were you afraid that if you brought his name into it he would be suspected?—I was not afraid of anything I left it out entirely

Why? What were you afraid of if you did not know your husband had been stabbed?—I was not afraid of anything

What were you going to shield him from?—To have his name brought into it

Were you not going to shield him from a charge of having murdered your husband?—I did not know my husband was murdered

Did you not know that your husband had been assaulted and murdered?—The inspector told me, but I did not realise even at that time that he was dead

Inspector Hall had told you then that your husband was dead?—He had

When you told those untruths and left out Bywaters, were you not attempting to shield him from a charge of having murdered your husband?—I did not even know my husband had been murdered When I say that I did not know, I mean that I did not realise it

I will ask you again, what were you attempting to shield Bywaters from?—From being connected with me—his name being brought into anything

Now, Mrs Thompson, is it not the fact that you knew that Bywaters was going to do something on this evening and that these two false statements were an attempt to prevent the police getting wind of it?—That is not so

Now I will go back to the early stages of your relationship with Bywaters Do you agree with me that it was in June of 1921 that you first fell in love with Bywaters?—No, I did not

Do you put it in November?—September, I said

Look at your letter of 28th August, 1922 (exhibit 63), where you say—

Fourteen whole months have gone by now, darlint, it's so terribly long Neither you nor I thought we should have to wait all that long time

Does that not satisfy you that you and Bywaters declared love to each other in June, 1921?—Not at all

Evidence for Prisoner Thompson.

Edith Jessie Thompson

You deny that?—Yes

When did you first begin to address him as your lover?—It is just what you mean by "your lover"

The terms in which a woman does not write to any man except her husband?—I cannot remember

Did you from the first time you realised you were in love with Bywaters take an aversion to your husband?—For the first time, did you say?

Did you ever take an aversion to your husband?—I did

Can you tell me the date?—I think it was in 1918

Then both before and after you and Bywaters fell in love with each other you hated—is that too strong a word—your husband?—It is too strong

Did your aversion to him become greater when you fell in love with Bywaters?—I think not

Were you happy with him after you fell in love with Bywaters?—I never was happy with him

Did you behave to him as if you were happy?—On occasions, yes

Did your husband repeatedly ask you if you were happy?—He did

And did you tell him you were happy?—I did

Was that to deceive him?—It was to satisfy him more than to deceive him

Did you seriously at that time intend to leave your husband or to give him cause for divorce?—I did

Did you ever tell him you had given him cause for divorce?—I did

When, for the first time?—I cannot remember

Were you afraid your husband would find out anything between you and Bywaters?—What do you mean by "anything"?

Were you frightened that your husband would find out anything between you and Bywaters?—Except that we were meeting and he might come and prevent us meeting

But if you had told your husband that you had given him ground for divorce, what were you afraid of beyond that?—I was afraid of my husband coming to my place of business and making scenes as he had threatened

You had told your husband that you had been unfaithful to him, or would be unfaithful to him, and given him grounds for divorce?—I did

Had he made scenes at your business when you told him that?—No, he did not, but he had threatened to do so

What was the risk you were running, the risk you so often mentioned to Bywaters? Look at your letter of 4th July (exhibit 26)—

Why arnt you sending me something—I wanted you to—you never

Bywaters and Thompson.

Edith Jessie Thompson

do what I ask you darlint—you still have your own way always—If I don't mind the risk why should you?

What risk?—That was the risk of Mr Bywaters sending me something instead of bringing something

Why was that a risk?—Well it would be a risk for me to receive anything

Not a risk to receive a letter?—I did not say a letter

What was it?—Whatever Mr Bywaters suggested

Why should you think there was a risk in his sending you something?—I did not know that I should personally receive it

Why should there be a risk in a friend or even a lover sending you a letter or a present?—I did not say it was a letter

What was it?—Something Mr Bywaters suggested

Did he suggest it was a dangerous thing?—No

Why did you think it was a dangerous thing?—I did not think it was a dangerous thing

Why did you think there was a risk?—There was a risk to anything he sent me that did not come to my hands first

Did you think it was because somebody would think there was a *liaison* going on between you and him?—No, only you would not like anything private being opened by somebody previous to yourself

You were afraid somebody might have thought there were improper relations between you and him. Is that what you are referring to?—No

I understand you did not mind your husband knowing you and Mr Bywaters were lovers?—We wanted him to realise it.

The more it came to the knowledge of your husband the more likely you were to achieve your design of divorce or separation, is that the fact?—No, that is not so. The more it came to his knowledge the more he would refuse to give it me, he had told me that

In the passage I have read you were asking Bywaters to send something which he had said, according to you, he was going to bring?—That is so

What was it?—I have no idea

Have you no idea?—Except what he told me

What did he tell you?—He would bring me something

Did he not say what the something was?—No, he did not mention anything

What did he lead you to think it was?—That it was something for me to give my husband

With a view to poisoning your husband?—That was not the idea, that was not what I expected

Something to give your husband that would hurt him?—To make him ill

And it was a risk for your lover to send, and for you to receive, something of that sort?—It was a risk for him to send me anything he did not know came to my hands first

Evidence for Prisoner Thompson.

Edith Jessie Thompson

And a special risk to send you something to make your husband ill? You appreciate that?—Yes, I suppose it was.

You were urging Bywaters to send it instead of bringing it?—That is so.

Was that in order that it might be used more quickly?—I wrote that in order to make him think I was willing to do anything he might suggest, to enable me to retain his affections.

Mrs. Thompson, is that quite a frank explanation of this urging him to send instead of bring?—It is, absolutely. I wanted him to think I was eager to help him.

By Mr. JUSTICE SHEARMAN—Eager to do what?—Eager to help him in doing anything he suggested.

That does not answer the question, you know.

Cross-examination continued—He suggested giving your husband something to hurt him?—He had given me something.

Given you something to give your husband?—That is so.

Did the suggestion then come from Bywaters?—It did.

Did the suggestion come in a letter or in a conversation?—I cannot remember.

Did you welcome it when it came?—I read it.

What?—I read it and I studied it.

Did you welcome the suggestion that something should be given to your husband to make him ill?—I did not.

Did you object to it?—I was astonished about it.

Did you object to it?—I did, at the time.

And although you objected to it you urged Bywaters to send it more quickly than he intended?—I objected at the time. Afterwards I acquiesced.

From the time you acquiesced did you do all you could to assist Bywaters to find something which would make your husband ill?—I did not.

Did you try to prevent him from finding something to make your husband ill?—I could not prevent him; he was not in England.

Did you try?—I do not see how I could have tried.

Did you discourage him?—I did, at first.

And afterwards did you encourage him?—No.

Look at your letter of 1st April (exhibit 17). What is the meaning of the injunction in that letter, 'Don't keep this piece'?—I cannot remember now.

Shall I help you to remember if you read the next passage?—It may not have referred to that piece.

Look at the original letter. You see that that injunction is written on the top of a new page?—Yes.

Did you intend Bywaters not to keep that piece of paper?—No.

"Don't keep this piece"?—I think you will see there has been something attached to that piece of paper. There are distinctly two pin marks there.

Bywaters and Thompson.

Edith Jessie Thompson

You dispute my suggestion to you that "Don't keep this paper" refers to the piece on which the following is written?—I do.

Look at the next paragraph. It is about giving your husband something bitter. I think you told your learned counsel that was an imaginary incident?—Yes.

Do you mean that you imagined it, or that your husband did?—I imagined it.

Do you mean you invented the incident altogether for Bywaters' information?—I did.

Can you tell me what the object of that was?—Still to make him think I had done what he suggested.

By Mr Justice Shearman—Had done what? Given your husband something?—Yes.

Cross-examination continued—Was it with the same object that you wrote the paragraph lower down "Don't tell Dan." You say—

What I mean is don't let him be suspicious of you regarding that—because if we were successful in the action—

Does that refer to the proposal that Bywaters had made, that you should make your husband ill?—I think not.

What do you think it refers to?—The action of my going away to live with him unmarried.

I'm going to try the glass again occasionally—when it is safe. I've got an electric light globe this time.

When was it likely to be safe?—There was no question of it being safe, I was not going to try it.

Why did you tell Bywaters you were going to try it when it was safe?—Still to let him think I was willing to do what he wanted.

You are representing that this young man was seriously suggesting to you that you should poison and kill your husband?—I did not suggest it.

I thought that was the suggestion?—I did not suggest that.

What was your suggestion?—He said he would give him something.

By Mr Justice Shearman—Give him something in his food, you answered my question a little while ago that it was to give him something to make him ill?—That is what I surmised, that I should give him something so that when he had a heart attack he would not be able to resist it.

You are suggesting now that it was Bywaters who was suggesting that to you?—Yes.

And you did not do it?—No, never.

Cross-examination continued—Why were you urging Bywaters to do something if the suggestion really came from him? In your letter of 10th February (exhibit 15) your first sentence is, "You

Evidence for Prisoner Thompson.

Edith Jessie Thompson

must do something this time "?—I was not referring to that at all I was referring to him getting me something to do, a position of some sort abroad

Let us see what the rest of the letter was. The fourth paragraph is the one that relates to the incident of your husband waking up and asking you for water as he was feeling ill. Was that a true incident?—Absolutely true

Why did you hunt for the prescription? Was that to prevent a similar incident?—Probably. I did not think it was wise for him to do those things

Was your anxiety so that you should get hold of the prescription and avert the catastrophe of taking an overdose?—Yes

Do you mean you were really frightened about your husband's overdose?—I was

Then can you explain to me the meaning of the next sentence—

I told Avis about the incident only I told her as if it frightened and worried me as I thought perhaps it might be useful at some future time that I had told somebody

Was it true that you were frightened and worried, or was it acting?—No, that was true

You were frightened and worried?—I was

Why did you take special pains to tell Avis as if you were frightened and worried?—I was worried and frightened and told my sister

Why was it likely to be useful to pretend that you were frightened and worried?—If anything had happened to my husband it would have been much better for somebody else to know besides myself

And you thought it would have been much better for you, if you poisoned your husband, if you professed anxiety to Avis previously?—I had no intention of ever poisoning my husband

Look at the next paragraph—

What do you think, darlint. His sister Maggie came in last night and he told her [I suppose " he " is your husband] so now there are two witnesses, although I wish he hadn't told her—but left me to do it

Now, that is to say you wanted again to create the impression that you were frightened by your husband's attacks?—I did not want to create the impression. I was frightened

It would be so easy darlint—if I had things—I do hope I shall

What would be easy?—I was asking or saying it would be better if I had things as Mr Bywaters suggested I should have

What would be easy?—To administer them as he suggested

" I do hope I shall " Was that acting or was that real?—That was acting for him

Bywaters and Thompson.

Edith Jessie Thompson

You were acting to Bywaters that you wished to destroy your husband's life?—I was

By Mr Justice SHEARMAN—One moment, I do not want to be mistaken Did I take you down rightly as saying, " I wanted him to think I was willing to take my husband's life "?—I wanted him to think I was willing to do what he suggested

That is to take your husband's life?—Not necessarily

Cross-examination continued—To injure your husband at any rate?—To make him ill

What was the object of making him ill?—I had not discussed the special object

What was in your heart the object of making him ill? So that he should not recover from his heart attacks?—Yes, that was certainly the impression, yes

The Court adjourned

Fourth Day—Saturday, 9th December, 1922

Mrs EDITH JESSIE THOMPSON (prisoner on oath), recalled, *cross-examination continued*—Be good enough to turn to your letter of 14th March (exhibit 20), and look at this passage—

> The mail came in 12 noon, and I thought I would be able to talk to you after then—but I don't think I can. Will you do all the thinking and planning for me darlint—for this thing—be ready with every little detail when I see you—because you know more about this thing than I, and I am relying on you for all plans and instructions—only just the act I'm not. I'm wanting that man to lean on now darlint, and I shall lean hard—so be prepared

You told me yesterday that you were anxious to let Bywaters know that you were prepared to do anything for him?—Yes.

And that he was lying to you, or you thought he was lying to you, suggesting harming your husband?—Yes.

And you were writing back to him letting him think that you agreed with him. When you say in the letter "Will you do all the thinking and planning for me, darlint—for this thing," you meant the poisoning which Bywaters had suggested?—I did not.

What was "this thing"?—The thing I referred to was my going away with him.

Did "the act" that you refer to mean leaving your husband?—"The act" meant actually going with him. I wanted him to make the arrangements regarding the passage, and all the details that would be entailed in my leaving England.

At any rate, it does not mean suicide?—No, it does not mean that. It means what I have just told you.

Further on you say, "Why not go to 231, darlint?" That is your old home?—That is my mother's house.

> I think you ought to go as usual it would be suspicious later if you stopped away without a reason known to them and there is not a reason is there?

Why would it be suspicious if he stayed away from your mother's house?—Because he was in the habit of going there when he came home.

But if you were to leave your husband, discovery would be inevitable?—Discovery, not necessarily with him though—to leave my husband with him.

Do you mean you were going to leave your husband and try and keep from your people and everybody else that you had gone away with Bywaters?—That was my intention, that is what I thought about

H

Bywaters and Thompson.

Edith Jessie Thompson

Now, the next sentence but one—

Darlint, about making money—yes we must somehow, and what does it matter how—when we have accomplished that one thing

What was " that one thing '?—To get away from England

At any rate, whatever " that one thing ' means, it had been a subject of discussion between you and Bywaters?—Yes, my leaving England

You agree that you and he had discussed this " one thing "?—Yes

That letter was written on 14th March, and addressed to Plymouth Bywaters arrived in England on 17th March?—Yes

Do you remember whether you discussed with him when he came the same thing that that letter refers to?—Probably I did It was the subject of discussion always

When he was at home, did that incident happen which you speak of as " the Sunday morning escapade " in your letter of 1st April (exhibit 17), written to Bywaters at Bombay? He had left this country, if I may remind you, on 31st March While he was at home, between 17th and 31st March, did that incident happen when your husband spoke about tea tasting bitter?—My husband never spoke of tea tasting bitter

Do you adhere to your statement that this is an invention?—Absolutely

Do you notice that you put it in inverted commas, " Sunday morning escapade "?—Yes

Why did you put those words in inverted commas if Bywaters did not know what they meant?—Well, that is what I called it—that is why I used inverted commas

Were you not referring in that paragraph to something which you and Bywaters had discussed and which had happened while he was at home?—Nothing had happened

At the end of the paragraph you say—

Now I think whatever else I try it in again will still taste bitter—he will recognise it and be more suspicious still and if the quantity is still not successful it will injure any chance I may have of trying when you come home

Does that mean trying to poison your husband?—That is what I wanted him to infer

You were wanting him to entertain the hope that when he next came home you would try again to poison your husband?—I wanted to convey that impression to his mind by the letter, although I never intended to do such a thing

Is it the fact that, whether that incident is an actual incident or not, what you were speaking of in that paragraph as something you were going to try had been discussed between you and him when you were together?—Yes

Evidence for Prisoner Thompson.

Edith Jessie Thompson

Turn to your letter of 1st May (exhibit 19), and look at this sentence—

You said it was enough for an elephant. Perhaps it was. But you don't allow for the taste making only a small quantity to be taken. It sounded like a reproach, was it meant to be?

Had he in his letter to which that was an answer again referred to this plan of poisoning your husband?—He probably had. That was in answer to his question.

Had he also told you that you must be very careful in anything you did not to leave any traces, any finger marks, on the boxes?—Yes, he did.

Had he also written to you again about the bitter taste? In a paragraph further down you say—

Now your letter tells me about the bitter taste again.

That sentence speaks for itself. Then lower down—

Our Boy had to have his thumb operated on because he had a piece of glass in it that's what made me try that method again—but I suppose as you say he is not normal.

Was not this proposal of poisoning your husband mentioned in every letter that Bywaters wrote you?—I think not.

In many letters?—I will not say how many, I don't remember.

In some?—Probably.

Was it not also mentioned between you and him whenever he came back to England?—I cannot say that for certain, I don't remember.

Do you not ever remember that he spoke to you about it?—Perhaps on one occasion.

On several occasions?—I cannot say how many.

Was it you who first mentioned the book "Bella Donna" to Bywaters?—I had read that book, but I cannot say who mentioned it first. We had discussed books we were going to read and had read.

Is the story of "Bella Donna" about a woman who married her husband and went out to Egypt?—Yes.

When they were going out to Egypt on the ship, did they meet a man called Baroudi?—They did.

Did the woman Mrs Chepstow, in that story feel attracted by the comfort and the pleasures that Baroudi could give her?—I believe she did.

Did she arrange a plot to poison her husband by slow doses, in order that she might get away to Baroudi?—I cannot say if she arranged it. There was a plot right at the end of the book.

There is a plot which is really the plot of the story, to poison her husband, without anybody finding out what she was doing?—

Bywaters and Thompson.

Edith Jessie Thompson

It is a matter of opinion whether that is absolutely the plot, is it not?

Anyway, that is an important incident in the book?—At the end, yes

Did she almost accomplish that plot or design of poisoning her husband, until it was discovered at the end by an old friend?—I really cannot remember

At any rate, you do remember that it was an important incident in the book that Mrs Chepstow should get rid of her husband, so that she might go to another man?—I do not know if it mentions that she should get rid of him to go to another man. I do not remember that being mentioned in the book

Look at your letter of 18th May (exhibit 22), where you write this extract from " Bella Donna "—

' It must be remembered that digitalin is a cumulative poison and that the same dose harmless if taken once, yet frequently repeated, becomes deadly ' The above passage I've just come across in a book I am reading "Bella Donna" by Robert Hichens. Is it any use?

You agree with me that that was a suggestion which you thought of to make to Bywaters?—I wanted him to think by that that I was still agreeing to fall in with the plan which he suggested

Were you going to undeceive Bywaters and let him realise that you were not anxious to poison your husband?—I never was anxious to poison my husband

When were you going to undeceive Bywaters?—I never studied it—I never thought about it

Did you deceive Bywaters right up to his last visit to England?—I had never any intention whatever of poisoning my husband

I will take that from you for the moment. What I was asking you was this you told me that you deceived Bywaters because you wanted to keep his love?—That is so

You deceived him into thinking that you wanted to poison your husband?—Yes

Did you continue that deception right up to his visit to England a few days before the murder?—I had never told him

Did you continue to let him think that you were prepared to poison your husband?—I never mentioned the subject. I suppose he thought I was still wanting to do so

Turn to your letter (exhibit 60) (about 1st October), the last sentence—

Don't forget what we talked in the Tea Room, I'll still risk and try if you will

Was that in connection with the same matter, the idea of poisoning your husband?—No, that was not. What we talked of in the tearoom was getting me a post abroad

Evidence for Prisoner Thompson.

Edith Jessie Thompson

Look at the sentence immediately above that where you say "He's still well." Is "he" your husband?—No. That refers to a bronze monkey I have.

He's going to gaze all day long at you in your temporary home—after Wednesday.

Wednesday was 4th October?—Yes. The temporary home was a sketch of the ship "Morea" which I was having framed.

Thursday, 5th October, was the day when Bywaters' leave ended?—I do not know. "After Wednesday" meant when I had received the sketch of the "Morea" framed. It was to be finished on the Wednesday.

At any rate I suggest to you that your statement, "I will still risk and try if you will," referred to the same matter which you had mentioned so often in the letters, the risk of using poison or force to your husband?—I had never mentioned force to my husband.

But you had mentioned it to Bywaters?—Mentioned what?

Using force, something to hurt your husband?—I never mentioned the word "force."

Did you not mention the subject to Bywaters?—I do not understand what you mean.

Did you never mention in conversation with Bywaters at these tearoom visits, on 29th September, 2nd October, and 9th October, the proposal of hurting your husband or of poisoning him?—I had not done so.

Did Bywaters never refer to all these letters that had passed between you and him containing that proposal?—I cannot say that he did. He probably did not; we did not discuss the letters when he was at home.

The SOLICITOR-GENERAL—That is all I have to ask.

Mr JUSTICE SHEARMAN—Do you cross-examine, Mr Whiteley?

Mr CECIL WHITELEY—No, my lord, I ask no question.

Mr JUSTICE SHEARMAN—You know you have the right to cross-examine.

Mr CECIL WHITELEY—Yes, my lord.

Re-examined by Sir HENRY CURTIS BENNETT—The little bronze monkey stands on my desk and is referred to in several of my letters.

Mr JUSTICE SHEARMAN—"He's still well" means the monkey?

Sir H CURTIS BENNETT—Yes.

(*To Witness*)—"He's still well. He is going to gaze all day long at you in your temporary home"—that is the picture of the ship "Morea" which when framed was going to stand upon your desk where the monkey was?—Yes.

You have been asked some questions about Robert Hichens' "Bella Donna." Was Baroudi in that book a wealthy man or a poor man?—A very wealthy man.

Bywaters and Thompson.

Edith Jessie Thompson

Was Nigel, the husband of Bella Donna, a wealthy man or a poor man?—I believe he was a wealthy man

As far as you know had Bywaters any money outside his pay?—None at all

Did you know how much that was?—I had a rough idea—about £200 a year, I think

Was your husband a better off man than that?—Not very much better I believe he got about £6 a week

Did you support yourself?—I did, absolutely

If you had run away with Bywaters would you have been able to remain at Carlton & Priors? Or was it your intention to get employment elsewhere?—Yes I had been for many years with Carlton & Priors and my remuneration was a substantial one—£6 a week and bonuses

That being the position of you, Bywaters, and your husband, as compared with Bella Donna, Baroudi and Mrs Chepstow's husband, I again put to you your description of the woman Bella Donna in your letter of 14th July (exhibit 52)—

She doesn't seem a woman to me—she seems abnormal—a monster utterly selfish and self living

Is that your true idea of that woman?—Absolutely

So much for "Bella Donna" You have been asked some questions as to a paragraph which appears in your letter of 14th March (exhibit 20)—

Why not go to 231 darlint, I think you ought to go as usual, it would be suspicious later if you stopped away without a reason known to them and there is not a reason is there?

As far as you knew had your parents or family any suspicion that you were in love with Bywaters or he with you?—Not as far as I knew

Until you finally left with him, if you ever did run away with him, did you want your parents to know of this affection or this love between you?—I did not want them to know

So in this letter you are telling him to keep visiting 231?—That is so

You were also asked some questions about a paragraph in your letter of 10th February (exhibit 15), referring to an illness of your husband You were asked whether you were genuinely frightened and worried about your husband's illness, and you said that you were Apropos of that I want to ask you a question about the aromatic tincture of opium Who was it that found the bottle of aromatic tincture of opium?—My sister

Were you present when that was destroyed?—Yes

Mr Justice Shearman—She said yesterday that she did not know what had become of the bottle

Evidence for Prisoner Thompson.

Edith Jessie Thompson

Sir H Curtis Bennett—The contents were destroyed

(*To Witness*)—Was it with your concurrence that that was destroyed?—It was

When Bywaters was away from 9th June until 23rd September of this year were you getting as many letters from him as previously?—No

What did you think from that?—I thought he was gradually drifting away from me

Did you still love him very much?—I did

Where were the letters which you received from Bywaters addressed to?—168 Aldersgate Street, my place of business

For how long were they written there?—Right up till the beginning of the last voyage, I think

Where else were they written to?—The G P O in the name of Miss P Fisher

Why did you not want them written to your home address?—I did not want my husband to see them

Whenever Bywaters' name was mentioned, or whenever your husband found that you had been meeting Bywaters, what happened as far as he was concerned?—There was usually a scene

And to prevent the risk of such a scene the letters were sent to these other places?—That is so

Now, one or two questions about the night of 3rd October and the early morning of the 4th You told my learned friend that you were pushed aside and you think you fell down?—Yes

When you fell down did you receive any injury that you found out afterwards?—I had a large bump on the right-hand side of my head

That would be the side where the wall was, where you were walking?—Yes

Have you any idea how long you were upon the ground?—Not the faintest

Then you told my learned friend that when you looked down the street some little distance you saw your husband scuffling with some one?—That is so

When you saw him scuffling with some one at that time did you recognise who the other person was?—I did not

Did you ever on that night see the face of the person who was scuffling with your husband?—Never

When was the first time that night that you saw something about that person who had been scuffling with your husband which made you think who it was?—He was going away

After he had separated from your husband?—Yes

He was going away from your husband and away from you?—Yes It was the coat and hat that I recognised

Had you any idea that night or early morning that your husband had been stabbed?—None at all

Bywaters and Thompson.

Edith Jessie Thompson

As far as you could, from the moment you got up to your husband, did you do everything you could for him?—Everything I possibly could

AVIS ETHEL GRAYDON, examined by Sir H Curtis Bennett—I am the sister of the prisoner Mrs Thompson and I live with my parents at 231 Shakespeare Crescent, Manor Park On Easter Monday of this year we were knocking apart a grand piano case in Mr Thompson's garden Mr Thompson hit his first finger and said to me, "Will you go up to my room, to my medicine chest, and get me a bottle of New Skin" I went up, and I saw something in the medicine chest that attracted my attention—a large bottle of tincture of opium (Shown bottle, exhibit 61) It was a larger bottle than that, about half a pint I did not touch it I came down with the New Skin, and I went into the morning room and said to my sister who was sitting by the fire, "There is a bottle of opium in Percy's medicine chest Nip up and get it" I then went out and put the New Skin on my brother-in-law's finger He told me to take it back which I did, and I then found that the bottle of opium had gone I came downstairs again and asked my sister, "Have you taken that bottle of opium as I asked you?" and she said "Yes" I asked her where it was and she said, "On the side there—on the sideboard" I said, "I will do away with this so there can be no more trouble," and I took the bottle and went to the scullery and poured the contents of the bottle down the sink I then put the bottle in the fire in the morning room

I want to draw your attention to a letter which has been read—Mrs Thompson's letter of 13th June (exhibit 24)—

I rang Avis yesterday and she said he came down there in a rage and told Dad everything—about all the rows we have had over you—but she did not mention he said anything about the first real one on August 1st—so I suppose he kept that back to suit his own ends Dad said it was a disgraceful thing that you should come between husband and wife and I ought to be ashamed Darlint I told you this is how they would look at it—they don't understand and they never will any of them Dad was going to talk to me Avis said—but I went down and nothing whatever was said by any of them I told Avis I shd tell them off if they said anything to me I didn't go whining to my people when he did things I didnt approve of, and I didn't expect him to—but however nothing was said at all Dad said to them 'What a scandal if it should get in the papers' so evidently *he* suggested drastic measures to them

Is there any truth in that at all?—There is none whatever

Did you ever tell her anything like that at all?—I did not

Did it ever happen?—It did not

Mr Mr JUSTICE SHEARMAN—It follows therefore that your sister invented the whole of this?—Yes, it is pure imagination on my sister's part

Mr. Cecil Whiteley

Evidence for Prisoner Thompson.

Avis Ethel Graydon

Examination continued—I remember the evening of 3rd October, the night when Mr. Thompson died. Mr. Bywaters was at my father and mother's house that evening, and I was at home. I should think he left about ten minutes to eleven or eleven o'clock. I had known Mr. Bywaters for roughly four years. As I was letting him out of the door on that Tuesday night he said to me, " I will be down to take you to the pictures to-morrow evening." That arrangement was made by him just as I was letting him out of the door. My brother-in-law told me that he and my sister were to meet their maid from Cornwall at Paddington station at five o'clock on the Wednesday evening the next evening. The name of the maid was Ethel Vernon, and in fact she arrived the next night.

Mrs. ETHEL JESSIE GRAYDON, examined by Sir H. CURTIS BENNETT —The prisoner Mrs. Thompson is my daughter. I live at 231 Shakespeare Crescent, Manor Park. During the whole of the day of the 4th October I was with my daughter at the police station. I was also with her on 5th October until she was charged. She complained to me then, two or three times, about a bump on her head. I put my hand over the place where she told me it was, and I felt a bump there.

Sir H. CURTIS BENNETT—That is the case for Mrs. Thompson.

Closing Speech for the Prisoner Bywaters.

Mr. CECIL WHITELEY—May it please your lordship· Members of the jury, the time has now arrived for me to perform the last part of the duty that has been assigned to me in presenting to you the defence to this charge of wilful murder against Frederick Bywaters. Members of the jury, I do so with considerable and with deep-felt anxiety. That anxiety is not caused from any feeling, nor have I any doubt, that you and each one of you are determined to see that so far as he is concerned so far as the other prisoner is concerned, justice will be done. The anxiety arises rather from the unprecedented and extraordinary way in which the case has been presented by the prosecution so that you must have great difficulty, when you come to consider the whole of this case, in dealing with the evidence that the prosecution has seen fit to present to you.

There is no dispute, and ever since the evening of 5th October there has been no dispute, that Percy Thompson met his death owing to a blow inflicted on him by Frederick Bywaters. That being the case, and there having been the evidence with regard to the event on that night, it is one of those cases which, if brought under ordinary circumstances, would have been left to the hands of the junior counsel for the prosecution, my learned friend, Mr. Roland Oliver. The case is straight and simple. The facts of the death proved, the

Bywaters and Thompson.

Mr Cecil Whiteley

whole question for the jury would have been whether they were justified from those facts in finding a verdict of wilful murder, or of manslaughter, or some other verdict. But no. In this case the prosecution has seen fit to introduce so far as Bywaters is concerned, a mass of evidence which I submit is really irrelevant

Is it the case for the prosecution here to-day that Mrs Thompson administered poison to her husband? Is it the case for the prosecution that Mrs Thompson administered broken glass to her husband? Is it the case for the prosecution that Mrs Thompson had incited Frederick Bywaters to murder her husband? If so, why not try those issues? Why not bring such evidence as they have on those issues and let there be a straightforward issue between the Crown and Mrs Thompson? Perhaps you will be surprised to hear that in this Court to-day there was another indictment in which charges were made against Mrs Thompson, one of the counts including a charge of conspiring with Bywaters to murder her husband and the other charging her with the particular offence. Having regard to the evidence that you have heard and the Home Office report that must have been in the hands of the prosecution when the indictment was brought forward, one can perhaps understand why those two charges were not entered into against Mrs Thompson. I ask, why were not those counts proceeded with? The reason is that the Court of Appeal have to decide an issue of life or death, and in a case so serious as murder their attention would be drawn to the evidence. Why was it done? In order to convict Frederick Bywaters of murder the prosecution had to satisfy the jury that when that blow was struck Bywaters had an intent to kill, an intent preceding the act. This presumption is rebutted by the facts before you. In this case what the prosecution have done is this—having found their difficulty in proving those counts in the other indictment, they decided to introduce her into this indictment and charge her as a principal in the alleged murder committed by Frederick Bywaters, and in order to induce you to convict her they decided to bring the whole of that evidence, but they considered that would be useless to them until they could show she was acting in concert with Bywaters. The Court of Criminal Appeal have decided that a case of murder is so serious that the attention of the jury should be drawn to that fact, and that fact alone. What a farce! In spite of the decision of the prosecution regarding those counts the prosecution are willing to wound and yet afraid to strike. Knowing what their case was against Mrs Thompson, they put in a mass of correspondence which is entirely irrelevant to the issue, and in that way they associate Mrs Thompson with the other prisoner. They have tried, by introducing evidence relating, as I submit, to counts in the other indictment, to make her equally guilty of the death of Thompson, but they cannot do that unless they satisfy you that Bywaters was acting in concert with her. The case for the prosecution, so far as she is

Closing Speech for Bywaters.

Mr Cecil Whiteley

concerned, is that she was present when the alleged murder took place, and that she aided, abetted, and assisted Bywaters in that murder, and that she counselled, procured, and commanded him to commit it. Of course, if they succeed in satisfying you, members of the jury, on evidence that you can accept in law, then she is equally responsible for the murder.

Members of the jury, the tragedy in this case, the poignant tragedy so far as Bywaters is concerned is that there is sitting next to him in that box one who is charged jointly with him, one who is dearer to him than his own life. One would have thought that the position of an accused man on a charge of murder was quite difficult enough without it being thought necessary in the interests of public justice that at the same time of his trial the woman should have been charged with him. You may have noticed that I asked no question of Mrs Thompson, although I was entitled to do so. Why did I not? For this simple reason my instructions, and those given to my learned friend, were that neither by word nor deed, in conducting this case on behalf of this man, should a word be said by us, or any action taken by us which would in any way hamper the defence of Mrs Thompson. That was the position when Bywaters was called into the witness-box. That being the state of his mind, it was an anxiety that nothing he should say should in any way hurt Mrs Thompson. Yet he had to go through the torture of being cross-examined the whole object being, in some way or other, to get evidence to connect these two together before the fatal evening of 3rd October. Happily for Mrs Thompson, and it is a matter of satisfaction to Bywaters, she is in the able hands of my learned friend, Sir Henry Curtis Bennet. I hope that nothing I say will hamper him in the way he is putting her case before you.

In my submission to you, the first and perhaps the most important, question you have to decide is this—was there or was there not any agreement between Mrs Thompson and Frederick Bywaters to murder Percy Thompson on the evening of 3rd October? Was it a preconcerted meeting, or was it not? I shall next ask you to try to eliminate from your minds altogether the facts and the evidence as to what happened that evening. The prosecution are asking you to say that before these events there was a cruel conspiracy between these two persons for which they could have been prosecuted in this Court. What evidence is there of that agreement and conspiracy? What evidence is there that Bywaters was a party to any such agreement?

Just consider the difference between the personalities of these two people sitting in the box. On the one hand you have Mrs Thompson, a woman who at the time that she met Bywaters in the Isle of Wight last June, had been married for no less than seven years—an emotional hysterical woman, a woman with a vivid imagination and one who for some years had been living very

Bywaters and Thompson.

Mr Cecil Whiteley

unhappily with her husband. She becomes infatuated with a young man no less than eight years her junior. On the other hand you have a young man who at that time was nineteen years old, on the threshold of a life that had every prospect of being successful. These two are drawn together. This man—this boy—full of life, falls in love with the woman. My learned friend the Solicitor-General, made use of the expression that there was a guilty passion between these two persons. This is not a Court of morals, and whatever view may be taken of the relationship between them from a sexual point of view is absolutely irrelevant. These two persons fall in love and declare their love with one another. On the one hand there is a married woman, whose husband is unwilling to divorce her, and on the other hand a young man whose duty takes him to sea the greater part of the year. I do not suppose it will be suggested that when he went away on 9th September or again on 11th November, or in June, there was any conspiracy between the two. I submit that the letters between February and March do not suggest that Bywaters was lending himself to any suggestion that Mrs Thompson's husband should be injured in any way, or poisoned. Fortunately, two of Bywaters' letters have been preserved, and you will assume that these letters are typical of those he had already written to Mrs Thompson. The prosecution may argue that the destroying of the letters goes in their favour, but you should remember that the destroying of the letters was the only thing that the woman would do in the circumstances—she destroyed them because she did not want her husband to see them. I challenge the prosecution to show that in any of his letters Bywaters incited Mrs Thompson to any act against her husband.

Bywaters saw Mrs Thompson constantly when at home, and he saw Mr Thompson twice. But when he realised that it was hopeless, and that there was no chance of Mrs Thompson having a separation from her husband the prosecution cannot suggest that he ever did anything else. The prosecution are bound to prove that when this boy was receiving these letters he was making himself a party to what was contained in them. How have they attempted to do it? By putting in these hysterical, emotional letters of Mrs Thompson written under all sorts of circumstances. I ask you to distinguish in the letters fact from fiction. Mrs Thompson wanted to retain the affection of Bywaters. Her object in writing the letters was to show to Bywaters, who might be going out of her life at any moment, that her affection for him was so great, her love for him so deep, that there was nothing she would stop at in order to free herself and join him. If that be the view that you take, is it unreasonable to suppose that that was the view which Bywaters also took? I ask you to try, if you can, to take out of those letters what is fact and what is fiction, what is imaginary and what is real. The prosecution must satisfy you that

Closing Speech for Bywaters.

Mr Cecil Whiteley

Bywaters was agreeing to it all. We now know that although there have been only thirty-two letters produced, there were in fact found in the possession of Bywaters no fewer than sixty-five. As I say, the letters simply conveyed to Bywaters the impression that Mrs Thompson was extremely anxious to retain his affection. Where is the evidence that Bywaters really entered into any conspiracy? What did Bywaters do when he came home? Those letters had been written for some weeks, but when he returned he did nothing. He took Mrs Thompson out, as he had done on former occasions. He was on friendly terms with the family of Mrs Thompson. He showed no hostility or violence towards Mrs Thompson's husband. Bywaters had been away from this country after 13th June for a period of three months, and it was fully four months since he received these letters upon which the prosecution rely. Far from there being any conspiracy or intention in Bywaters' mind from 6th June onwards to injure Mrs Thompson's husband, you can see clearly from every page in those letters of hers that he was trying to break away from the entanglement, and there had not been a great deal of enjoyment in it for Bywaters except when he was at home on leave. He saw the impossibility of the situation and he was gradually trying to break away, but unfortunately for him, Mrs Thompson was determined that it should not be so, and so she wrote those letters complaining of her life, and always holding out the hope that they might be able to join each other. The letters should be read from the point of view of the recipient, and not of the writer, and in that light you must come to the conclusion that, whatever her intentions may have been, whatever, in fact, she may have been doing, Frederick Bywaters was no party to it. I go on to inquire if Bywaters became a party to any such agreement after 23rd September. I contend that the whole case for the prosecution shows that he did not.

I should refer in a word or two to the excellent record of Bywaters. We do not have in the dock here a man who has been charged over and over again with crimes of violence, or a man of evil reputation. We have a man of spotless reputation and good character, and yet it is suggested that he made himself a party to a conspiracy to murder the husband. Bywaters' case to-day is that it was not until he left the Graydon's house about eleven o'clock on 3rd October that he had any intention of seeing Mrs Thompson again that night or of interviewing her husband. If you come to the conclusion, as I submit you must, that Bywaters up to that evening had never any intention whatsoever to injure Mrs Thompson's husband, and that he, on his side, had never agreed with Mrs Thompson that any violence or anything else should be done to Thompson, then your verdict so far as Mrs Thompson is concerned, is "Not Guilty," and you will have to deal with the case as it affects Bywaters.

Bywaters and Thompson.

Mr Cecil Whiteley

I proceed now to deal with what is the real issue for you, and I shall detail the events of 3rd October. Bywaters has said that he left the house on the evening of 3rd October feeling very miserable. He was thinking of Mrs Thompson, and of the complaints made to him when he came from abroad. He says that an irresistible impulse came over him that he must see her, that he must try to help her, and the only way of helping her was to see again whether he could not come to some arrangement with regard to her. She is miserable, this cannot go on; he will see once more if he cannot do something. That impulse coming over him, he walked quietly towards Belgrave Road. As to the details of what happened, the only evidence you have is that of Bywaters himself. His lordship will direct you with regard to the law concerning the various possible verdicts.

Mr Justice Shearman—You want me to leave these questions to the jury—(1) Justifiable homicide, (2) manslaughter (3) murder?

Mr Whiteley—Yes. I read the report of Bywaters' evidence of what happened when Thompson met his death. [Reads report of evidence.] How did the knife come to be in Bywaters' possession? It has been said, and there is evidence to support it, that he bought the knife in Aldersgate Street in November of last year. It is not a strange thing that Bywaters should purchase such a knife, a seafaring man, visiting seaports in foreign countries. He has told us that he was accustomed to carry it in his greatcoat pocket. There are few sailors* who do not possess a knife. If you accept that, away goes the case for the prosecution that it was purchased for the express purpose of committing a dastardly murder. If you accept Bywaters' evidence, then you should come to the following conclusions:—

That the object Bywaters had in going to meet the Thompsons on that night was in order to make some arrangement with him, and not in order to kill him.

That when he arrived at Belgrave Road he had no intention of using the knife.

That Thompson struck him a blow on the chest and said, " I will shoot you," at the same time putting his right hand into his hip pocket. What was it that would flash through the mind of a man accustomed to visiting foreign countries when he heard the threat " I will shoot you " and saw a hand turned to the hip pocket? It does not matter, I submit, whether there was a revolver or not. The question for the jury is, " What did this man believe at that time "? If you come to the conclusion that Bywaters thought that Thompson intended to shoot him and had a revolver at the time, and that in

---

* Bywaters was not a " sailor " in the technical sense. He was a clerk on board a ship, and had more use for a fountain pen than for a knife.—Ed.

Closing Speech for Bywaters.

Mr Cecil Whiteley

self-defence he took out his knife and stabbed him, having reasonable apprehension that his life was in immediate danger, then the only verdict is one of Not Guilty, as being excusable homicide

With regard to the second verdict—if you come to the conclusion that Bywaters did not start the fight with the intention of using his knife, and that he used it in the heat of passion in consequence of an attack made on him by Thompson, you are entitled to reduce this crime from murder to manslaughter

Or, again, if you are satisfied that Thompson struck him a blow on the chest, followed by the words " I will shoot you," and by a movement of his hand to his pocket, then there would be such provocation as would enable you to reduce the crime from murder to manslaughter

In considering the statement made by Bywaters I think it is necessary for you to realise that from beginning to end in this case the one thing always in Bywaters' mind was the position of Mrs Thompson and how she was suffering When he left the scene that night he did not know that Thompson was dead He did not discover it until the next day, when he bought a newspaper The time has come when there should be some alteration in the way in which persons are dealt with at police stations I am not blaming the police Superintendent Wensley is one of the most efficient officials there have ever been at Scotland Yard, and it was his duty to ascertain who committed the crime and to make all necessary inquiries What I am complaining of is that when a statement was taken in the circumstances in which it was it should be solemnly produced in this Court as if it were a voluntary statement to be used in evidence against Bywaters The thoughts of Bywaters when he made the first voluntary statement were concerned as to what had happened to Mrs Thompson I ask you to put aside altogether the statements, having regard to the circumstances in which they were made, and deal with the evidence of Bywaters as he has given it

All the time that I have been addressing you I have been conscious of a feeling that, whatever arguments I may use, the Solicitor-General has the right to the final address It is a curious position In an ordinary case in this Court where a prisoner gives evidence and calls no other evidence as to facts, his counsel has the right of addressing the last word to the jury Owing to the fact that a law officer of the Crown has been engaged to prosecute in this case, I am deprived of that privilege Apparently the privilege was considered so important by those conducting the prosecution that the services of the Solicitor-General were engaged So long ago as thirty years, defending in a criminal case, one of the most famous advocates, still alive, commented on this curious and anomalous privilege, remarking, " I hope an Attorney General may be found some day unless the law is altered as it should be, to abandon the exercise of a right which does not appear to me to be

Bywaters and Thompson.

Mr Cecil Whiteley

defensible." Of course, I know that the Solicitor-General will endeavour to be as fair in his reply as he was in his opening of the case, but I am conscious that the interests of Bywaters may suffer from the fact that the Crown has the last word.

I again challenge the prosecution to point to one stable piece of evidence, to any evidence, on which you can rely, on which you can say that that man had agreed with Mrs Thompson to do some harm or some violence to Percy Thompson. Judge this young man as you yourselves would be judged. One life has already been sacrificed in this sordid and horrible drama. Is there to be yet another? Frederick Bywaters makes his last appeal to you through me, and he says to you, "It is true, only too true, that I have been weak, extremely weak. It is true, only too true, that I allowed myself to drift into this dishonourable entanglement and intrigue with a married woman living with her husband. It is true that I had not the moral courage to cut myself adrift from it and end it all. It is true, only too true, that she confided in me, that I was flattered that she should come to me, a young man of nineteen, and confide in me. It is true that I pitied her, and that my pity turned to love. I did not realise, I did not know, I had not enough experience in this life to know, that true love must mean self-sacrifice. All this is true," he says, "but I ask you to believe, and by your verdict to proclaim to the whole world that in all this history I am not an assassin. I am no murderer."

Closing Speech for the Prisoner Thompson

Sir HENRY CURTIS BENNETT—May it please your lordship, members of the jury—at last I have an opportunity of putting Mrs Thompson's case to you. It was only at the end of four days, and near the end of the case, that the defence had an opportunity of showing to you the other side of the picture already put before you by the prosecution. It is important that you should realise what you are trying. You are trying one of two indictments. The prosecution have chosen to proceed upon the first, which charges the prisoners with murder. There was another indictment which might be tried by you or some other jury against both the prisoners, and it is important that you should know what that second indictment was. It contained five counts. It charged them with on divers dates between 20th August, 1921, and 2nd October of this year conspiring together to murder Percy Thompson;

That between 10th February of this year and 1st October Mrs Thompson did solicit, endeavour to persuade, and propose to Bywaters to murder Thompson;

That between the same dates she did unlawfully solicit and incite Bywaters to conspire with her to murder Thompson;

Sir Henry Curtis Bennett, K C

Closing Speech for Thompson.
Sir Henry Curtis Bennett

That on 26th March (I don't know why that date was chosen) she administered and caused to be taken by Thompson certain poisons or other destructive things with intent to murder; and

That on 20th April she did administer and cause to be taken by Thompson a certain destructive thing, namely, broken glass.

It is quite clear from the sections of the Act of Parliament in question (Offences Against the Person Act) what the law is in relation to the second indictment. Any person who shall confederate or agree to murder any person whomsoever, or shall solicit, encourage, persuade or endeavour to persuade, or shall propose to any person to murder any other person—that person shall be guilty of misdemeanour, and, if convicted thereof, shall be liable to penal servitude for ten years. The first three allegations in that indictment are under that section of the Act of Parliament. It is not murder, but an offence whereby they can receive a substantial term of penal servitude. The last two charges of the indictment are framed under another section of the same Act, under which a person administering or causing to be administered to any other person, or to be taken by him, certain poisons, shall be guilty of felony, and liable to penal servitude.

For some reason—you, members of the jury, may possibly understand the reason; I don't pretend to—the prosecution here have elected to put these two people into the dock together and charge them with murder. As far as I know, there is no other case in which a jury have been empanelled to try either man or woman with murder where it could not be alleged by the prosecution that that person did any act when the murder, if it were murder, was committed.* By the prosecution it is stated that Mrs Thompson was what is known in the law as a principal in the second degree, namely, a person who " aids, abets, or assists a murderer when he is committing a murder."

Mr Justice Shearman—That is not exclusive. If two people contrive a murder they are guilty of murder, even though one was not there.

Sir H Curtis Bennett—Yes, he is an accessory.

Mr Justice Shearman—You say he is not guilty of murder if he did not actually take part in it.

Sir H Curtis Bennett—I am not going to shirk any issue. It is no good when representing somebody to try and put before the jury some story which does not meet the case at all. It cannot be alleged that anything further might be charged against her.

Mr Justice Shearman—Of course a person might be regarded as an accessory before the fact.

Sir H Curtis Bennett—If the case as suggested by the prosecution were that Mrs Thompson knew what was going to happen

---

* Cf "The Trial of the Seddons" Notable British Trials.—Ed

Bywaters and Thompson.

Sir Henry Curtis Bennett

that night, and that she took the person who was to be murdered to the spot where he was murdered, then I would welcome that case. The jury would see that the whole of the evidence was to the contrary in such a case. If you come to the conclusion that she conspired with Bywaters to murder her husband on that night, then you will convict her on that indictment if you come to the conclusion that she was urging on Bywaters. At this moment, however, she sits in the dock charged with being a murderess on the night of 3rd October, and it is for the prosecution to satisfy you that she is guilty. I suppose that the case for the prosecution is founded upon nothing but those letters written over a period of time, and founded outside that on nothing but guesswork, contradicted when you come to test it. I suppose the case is that there was an arrangement upon that night that Thompson should be murdered, that Mrs. Thompson was a party to it, and that Mrs. Thompson knew quite well as she was walking down the road near her home that at any moment her husband was going to be taken from her side and murdered in cold blood. I contend that every single action of Mrs. Thompson upon the night when the killing took place shows that she knew nothing of what was going to happen.

You have got to get into the atmosphere of this case. This is no ordinary case you are trying. These are not ordinary people that you are trying. This is not an ordinary charge of murder. This is not an ordinary charge against ordinary people. It is very difficult to get into the atmosphere of a play or opera, but you have to do it in this case. Am I right or wrong in saying that this woman is one of the most extraordinary personalities that you or I have ever met? Bywaters truly described her, did he not, as a woman who lived a sort of life I don't suppose any of you live in—an extraordinary life of make-believe, and in an atmosphere which was created by something which had left its impression on her brain. She reads a book and then imagines herself one of the characters of the book. She is always living an extraordinary life of novels. She reads a book, and although the man to whom she is writing is at the other end of the wide world—in Bombay, Australia, the Suez Canal—she wants his views regarding the characters in the books she has just read. You have read her letters. Have you ever read, mixed up with criticisms of books, mixed up with all sorts of references with which I shall have to deal, more beautiful language of love? Such things have been very seldom put by pen upon paper. This is the woman you have to deal with, not some ordinary woman. She is one of those striking personalities met with from time to time who stand out for some reason or another.

I desire to point out now that the only thing you are trying on this indictment—as to the actual alleged murder—is whether the prosecution have proved that Mrs. Thompson was in fact taking a real part in what happened on the night of 3rd October. As the

Closing Speech for Thompson.
Sir Henry Curtis Bennett

facts have come out in the case, as far as Mrs Thompson is concerned there are two verdicts on the indictment that you can find against her. She is either guilty of murder or she is not guilty. I ask you again to get into the atmosphere of the life of Mrs Thompson. I do not care whether it is described as an "amazing passion," to use the expression of the Solicitor-General, or as an adulterous intercourse. Thank God, this is not a Court of morals, because if everybody immoral was brought here I would never be out of it, nor would you. Whatever name is given to it, it was certainly a great love that existed between these two people. We read about love at first sight. But, after all, we are men and women of the world here. Don't you think it was a gradual process as regards these two people—friendship first of all, gradually leading into love? There has been much questioning by the prosecution as to the exact time of the two declaring each other's love, but that is beside the point. I suggest that the time was August Bank Holiday last year, on 1st August when an incident arose out of absolutely nothing—"sending for a pin"—and Mr Thompson lost his temper and threw his wife across the room. There was unhappiness, and the comforter was at hand. The man was ready to take her part, and he became from the friend the lover. You will remember the evidence as to the husband saying to the wife, "I am not going to give you up. You are my wife. You are mine. I am not going to let you go." Full of human nature, is it not? The two lovers agreed to wait for five years. Can you say that such a wait is the arrangement of murderers, or people who have made up their minds upon a certain date or dates to murder a man? The very last letter which was made so much of by the prosecution stated, "There are only three and three-quarters years left." Yet it is said that the person who was writing that letter on 1st or 2nd October was a murderess, by inference, not because she struck any blow as a murderess, but because she was planning murder the very next night.

Dealing with the letters, I ask you not to forget that although they have been combed and combed to find anything to suggest that Mrs Thompson is a murderess 33 out of 65 have not been put before you. In one of the letters there is this phrase—"All I could think about last night was that compact we made.... it seems so horrible to-day." Is it not palpable that the explanation they have given is the true one, that they had entered into some foolish compact to commit suicide, and not that they had contrived to murder the woman's husband? She talks there of death for herself and not for any other person. There is nothing in the letters to show anything but that Mrs Thompson was desirous of impressing on Bywaters that she was prepared to go any length to retain his affection. It is so easy to take bits out of letters in opening a case and to put them before the jury without their context and without the mentality

Bywaters and Thompson.

Sir Henry Curtis Bennett

of the prisoner being put before the jury, and say, ' What does that mean?" and to take the next reference and say again, " Oh! there is this, too." It is scarcely fair. If you take the letters and read them through, as I was so anxious you should do, what does it come to? At the most it might possibly make that woman guilty of one of the charges in the second indictment. They certainly do not make her a principal in the killing of Thompson on the night of 3rd October. In her letter of December, 1921 (exhibit 27), she says—" It is the man who has no right, who generally comforts the woman who has wrongs. . . . . . You will have the right soon, won't you? Say yes.' That is put before you, picked out as some evidence of murder in their minds. Is it not absolutely consistent with innocence? We all know if a thing is equally consistent with innocence then you will find it of an innocent description. What it means is this—" Thank goodness I shall be taken away and live with you either as your wife, if I am divorced, or as your mistress, if there is no divorce. You will then have the right." Referring to the porridge incident, I again quote the passage which has been read before—" I had the wrong porridge to-day, but I do not suppose it will matter, I do not seem to care much either way. You will probably say I am careless and I admit I am, but I do not care, do you?" You will remember that the evidence was that the porridge was prepared by Mrs Lester, and that Mrs Thompson occasionally had it, but her husband more often took it. One would have thought there was nothing in the reference to the wrong porridge, but in the witness-box yesterday when asked about it Mrs Thompson said, " I put that in with an object." Now this is the first time in this correspondence that you come to this extraordinary way of trying to keep the love of a man and trying to impress upon him that it is a love which will not die. It was an extraordinary way of showing, " I am prepared to go to any extreme to keep your love.'

The prosecution thought that the only way for them to prove whether those statements in the letters were true or untrue was to have the body of Thompson exhumed. What did they find? They found no possible trace of any sort or kind of poison. They found no trace of glass having been administered in that body. They found just what I hope they will find in my body and yours if ever we are exhumed. And having found that the result of the post-mortem examination was consistent with the suggestion I am now putting before you, that the statements were absolutely untrue that she had administered anything, I do complain that the prosecution are not generous enough to say, " We will let you have the whole benefit of that. It is true there is no sort of corroboration that you ever gave poison or glass to your husband." What would you think if you were sitting in the dock instead of in the jury box if nothing had been found that was not consistent with your innocence? When Dr Spilsbury was in the witness-box the prosecution got him to give

Closing Speech for Thompson.

Sir Henry Curtis Bennett

an answer to a question which was obvious to all before he said it "Oh, of course, it may be that poison was given and disappeared There are certain poisons that do not leave any trace." How is one going to deal with a case if it is going to be put in that sort of way?

The real truth about Mrs Thompson, as borne out by her letters, was that she was a woman who would go on telling any lies so long as she could keep her lover Bywaters You are men of the world and you must know that where there is a *liaison* which includes some one who is married, it will be part of the desire of that person to keep secret the relations from the other partner It is not the sort of thing that they would bring to the knowledge of their partner for life Happily, members of the jury, your body includes a member of the other sex, so that you will be able to discuss the matter from both points of view.

I come now to the "You must do something this time" letter The prosecution start with the idea that a man has been murdered, and then going back seven or eight months they find that written in a letter and they suggest that it refers to murdering a man But is not a passage like that exactly what you would expect to find written from one lover to another when it was a case of a woman going away and living with him? As to the sleeping draught illness, there is not the slightest suggestion that Mr Thompson was poisoned The woman who is supposed to be wishing for her husband's death searched amongst his belongings for the medicine and destroyed it As his lordship has said, it is a very long cry from wishing somebody is dead to becoming a murderess This woman was eight years older than the man and she realised that she might be losing the man Listen to the following sentence which she writes—"It was a lie—I would tell heaps and heaps to help you, but darling do you think I like telling them?" I ask you whether in that passage you do not get to the real heart of the woman Again I read another sentence—"This thing I am going to do for both of us will it make a difference?" Is not that exactly the sort of thing you read in a divorce court correspondence? Although through this woman's great love for the man she was prepared to leave her husband and risk everything, still at the same time, at the back of her mind and in her heart of hearts she felt—will the time ever come when he will bring it up against me and twit me with it, saying, "Well, you ran away to live with a man"? Is not that what the letter means! I submit that these things were not endeavouring to persuade to murder, but were a thousand miles from it

Dealing with the correspondence up to March, I ask, would you convict anybody of even some small offence on that evidence? Would you not say that the evidence was much more consistent up to then with innocence than with guilt? You would not send any one to prison for a month on that evidence With regard to the giving of quinine to Mrs Thompson it may be that Bywaters

Bywaters and Thompson.

Sir Henry Curtis Bennett

thought she was a woman to be pandered to. He knew the sort of woman she was, and he has described her to you as living in books and melodramatic. It is suggested that in the letters there are references to the death of Mr. Thompson. Unfortunately, there is a lot of loose talk amongst us all. We often hear the expression, "He should be shot," or "I would like to poison him," even in ordinary conversation. This was loose talk by Bywaters, and it was the sort of language a man who had an intrigue with a married woman might use. He may have said of the husband, "I wish he would die," but he did not mean it. Mrs. Thompson wishing to show him that she would back him up, because she loved him, so wrote the letters that she did write. If you get a woman like Mrs. Thompson, she may easily say, "I will back him up." You can test whether she was putting on paper facts or fiction by the evidence of Dr. Spilsbury and Mr. Webster, which was to the effect that she was not giving her husband poison or glass.

You will remember the references to "Bella Donna" in the letters. I hope that most of you gentlemen of the jury who have read the book have seen the play.

Mr. JUSTICE SHEARMAN—Are you going to put in the book? If you do, the jury will have to read the whole of it.

Sir H. CURTIS BENNETT—I do not wish to do that. I think your lordship gave a description of the book. I will if necessary put in the book.

Mr. JUSTICE SHEARMAN—Surely not. I don't think that is necessary. I hope not—I hope you will not put it in. You can deal with anything that has been given in evidence about it.

Sir H. CURTIS BENNETT—It has been suggested that the whole theme of the book is the slow poisoning of a husband in order that the wife may live with a wealthy man. Fortunately we have Mrs. Thompson's view of "Bella Donna." If it is to be suggested that the reference to digitalis means, "Is it any use for poisoning her husband" then you must look at her view of the woman in the book. She has described her as a monster. Is it suggested that Mrs. Thompson was slowly poisoning her husband? There is no evidence of it. Is it suggested that any one at her instigation was doing it, so that she might go off with Bywaters? There is no evidence of it. With regard to the phrase "You will never leave me behind again unless things are different." I submit that means that, unless the next time Bywaters comes home she has got a separation or divorce—unless she is his, and can be left behind as his wife or mistress—she will not be left at home at all; they will go away, they will take the risk and she will go anywhere. With regard to the passage, "I am not going to try it any more until you come back" and the reference to "the tea tasting bitter"—it is suggested that those statements mean "Murder him." Our answer is that it is "fiction," just as much fiction as "Bella

Closing Speech for Thompson.
Sir Henry Curtis Bennett

Donna." Turning to the subject of the aromatic tincture of opium found at Thompson's house, it is an amazing thing if this woman was desirous of her husband dying that when he was found in possession of something it was taken away from him and she refused to return it.

I again read the phrase, "The third time he found a piece," in reference to the alleged administration of glass, and I ask you to imagine what effect such a piece of glass would have in passing through the intestines. Did she ever use it three times? The evidence is that there is no trace of anybody ever having administered anything of the sort to Mr. Thompson.

Mr. JUSTICE SHEARMAN—Before the Court rises for the day I wish to offer you, members of the jury, this advice. Of course, you will not make up your minds until you have heard the whole case. The only other thing is, having regard to the surroundings for so many days, by all means look at the atmosphere and try to understand what the letters mean, but you should not forget that you are in a Court of justice trying a vulgar and common crime. You are not listening to a play from the stalls of a theatre. When you are thinking it over, you should think it over in that way.

The Court adjourned.

Fifth Day—Monday, 11th December, 1922.

Closing Speech for the Prisoner Thompson (continued).

Sir H Curtis Bennett—When we adjourned on Saturday I had almost finished dealing with the letters I wish to refer now to the letter of 28th August (exhibit 63), which contains this passage—

> Fourteen whole months have gone by now, darlint, it's so terribly long Neither you nor I thought we should have to wait all that long time did we? altho' I said I would wait 5 years—and I will darlint—it's only 3 years and ten months now

That letter, I submit, is a very important one indeed, because it shows what the mind of Mrs Thompson was upon that date, 28th August She was then saying to her lover, "We arranged five years, I am prepared to wait five years, and there are only three years and ten months to pass"
I next deal with the letter written on 12th September, in which Mrs Thompson refers to the fact that Bywaters is nearing England, and expresses the view that—

> This time everything seems different I don't hear from you much you don't talk to me by letter and help me and I don't even know if I am going to see you

Does that not show what I have been putting before you, that on 12th September Mrs Thompson had in her mind that Bywaters was not so fond of her as he had been and she was anxious to show him that she would go to any extreme to keep his love? Look now at the letter of 20th September (exhibit 28)—

> You say 'Can we be Pals only, Peidi, it will make it easier' Do you mean for always? because if you do, No, No a thousand times We can't be 'pals' *only* for always darlint—it's impossible physically and mentally
> If you still only mean for a certain time and you think it best, darlint it shall be so   We won't be our natural selves tho' I know—we'll be putting a curb on ourselves the whole time—like an iron band that won't expand

That is the woman writing on 20th September a letter which, of course, she had no idea would ever be used against her in this light writing what she is really feeling a fortnight before the tragedy It is suggested by the prosecution that there was not only a conspiracy but that she was a principal in the tragedy which took place on the night of 3rd October I submit that these last letters, one after another, show quite clearly that this charge which has been made

Closing Speech for Thompson.

Sir Henry Curtis Bennett

is ill-founded. Of course, the letters are prejudicial to the writer, all of them, but you have to be very careful that you do not allow prejudice to be turned into proof. These last letters do not prove at all what the prosecution seek to make them prove. In fact, they show that the submission I am making is the true one. In the same letter of 20th September there is this passage—

> You are jealous of *him*—but I want you to be—he has the right by law to all that you have the right to by nature and love—yes darlint be jealous, so much that you will do something desperate.

Start at the end of the story with the death and work back to that, and you can make what is an absolutely innocent expression in a letter appear to be a guilty one. Work back, as the prosecution have done, from the tragedy, and come to a letter written a fortnight before, and, because in that letter there is this phrase, "do something desperate," that means that the woman was trying to make the man return to England to murder her husband. Surely, if you look at the letters and all these references they are absolutely consistent with the story that both Mrs. Thompson and Bywaters have told. They are consistent with "Take me away, I care not where." Are you, because of the prejudice created by the reading of the extracts from these letters, going to say there is any evidence from them that this woman was a principal a fortnight afterwards in the murder of her husband? I come now to the letter (exhibit 60) which is said to have been written by Mrs. Thompson on 2nd October. That letter is one of the strongest documents that you could have against the suggestion that these two persons made a prior agreement before 3rd October that Thompson should be murdered. It is of the greatest importance to see what it was that was being written by Mrs. Thompson to Bywaters on the very day before the tragedy took place.

> Darlingest lover of mine, thank you thank you oh thank you a thousand times for Friday—it was lovely—it's always lovely to go out with you. And then Saturday—yes I did feel happy—I didn't think a teeny bit about anything in this world, except being with you—and all Saturday evening I was thinking about you. I tried so hard to find a way out of to-night darlingest but he was suspicious and still is—I suppose we must make a study of this deceit for some time longer. I hate it. I hate every lie I have to tell to see you—because lies seem such small mean things. There would be scenes and he would come to 168 and interfere and I couldn't bear that. Until we have funds we can do nothing.

Do the prosecution say that this letter, written on 2nd October, is evidence that these two people were intending murder next day, or the day after, or the week after? This woman is saying on 2nd October, "It is funds we want and until we have funds we can do nothing." They did not want funds for murder, but it was

Bywaters and Thompson.

Sir Henry Curtis Bennett

essential that they should have funds for the purpose of living together. Mrs. Thompson said that if she were to run away with Bywaters, as she wanted to do, she would have to leave her business. "Darlingest, find me a job abroad." "Murderess!" say the prosecution. "I will go to-morrow if you will find me a job, and shall not have one little regret. Help me to forget." And then the last letter written before the crime was committed—I should like to draw your attention to what was said by the Solicitor-General in cross-examining Mrs. Thompson on this letter on Saturday morning. I do not wish to make any remark which in any way can be considered to be improper about the cross-examination, because my learned friend was absolutely fair in dealing with both of the accused persons in the witness-box, but when the prosecution have to come down to a suggestion such as was made upon the last two paragraphs of that letter on Saturday morning, it is for you to say whether you think they have got a case which can be relied upon or not. The Solicitor-General put this passage to Mrs. Thompson, "He is still well, he is going to gaze all day long at you in your temporary home after Wednesday." The suggestion behind that, of course, was that Thompson was still well. Does that not show the danger of guesswork when people's letters are being looked at? When we come to see what the passage really meant, we find that it meant that the pathetic little bronze monkey was still sitting upon her desk and that opposite was the photograph of the ship that Bywaters had been on.

The next passage in the letter is, "Don't forget what we talked in the tearoom. I'll still risk and try if you will." The suggestion of the prosecution—and they have no evidence at all of it—is that in that tearoom in Aldersgate Street these two people were plotting murder. There is not one scrap of evidence. But having put all those letters before you and having created the prejudice those letters must create when first read without an explanation, the prosecution then say "The night of 3rd October Thompson dies and 'Don't forget what we talked about in the tearoom'"—and you members of the jury are urged to believe that they were talking about murder. Both the prisoners have been in the witness-box and have told you how the conversation was the same old story as to taking Mrs. Thompson away, as to her leaving her husband and risking all her future with Bywaters. Is it not shown that that is the way to look at the sentence when the last words of the letter read, "We only have three and three-quarter years left darlingest, try and help Peidi"? It is almost inconceivable that it can be suggested on that letter or to think that seriously the prosecution can say that it shows that these two people were plotting murder. The words show quite the contrary. Do you imagine that a woman who at that time, according to the prosecution, had got to the degree of having incited this man to the extent that the murder is imminent, would be writing "We have only three and

Closing Speech for Thompson.

Sir Henry Curtis Bennett

three-quarter years left"? If the story put before you by the prosecution be true, do you not think that you would find in these letters some references egging on, inciting, soliciting Bywaters to commit this murder? Yet you find, in my submission, exactly the opposite. There is not one reference in these letters which any one in this country dare say shows that the suggestion made by the prosecution is true.

I proceed now to deal with the night of the murder and I contend that everything points to the killing of Thompson being an unpremeditated act by Bywaters. It was an act by Bywaters, committed according to his own story because he was in fear of his own life—an act which he had not the slightest intention of committing one minute before it was committed. The letters provide the only evidence upon which the charge of murder is framed against Mrs Thompson. Everything that was done and said by her on that night shows as strongly as it can that not only did she not know the murder was going to be committed, but that she was horrified when she found her husband was killed. On 3rd October there was a family theatre party. The evidence is that Mr and Mrs Thompson were at the Criterion Theatre with Mr and Mrs Laxton, and, according to Mr Laxton, were happy and normal. Do you believe that that woman could have sat with her husband and the Laxtons the whole evening, happy and in normal condition, if there was to her knowledge going to happen the tragedy which did happen to her husband? I suppose the suggestion of the prosecution is that on the journey home Mrs Thompson knew that at some spot her husband was to be attacked and murdered. I must deal in the most serious way with such a suggestion. I venture to point out that there is not a bit of evidence to show that she knew anything of the sort. The evidence is that she had made an arrangement to go with her husband the next night to meet her maid at Paddington. Is that true or not true? Test it. The maid did arrive the next night, and did go to the house. Do you think this woman, if she was doing what the prosecution suggest would have made that arrangement? The prosecution declared that the tragedy took place at a dark spot, but as a matter of fact the spot was similarly lighted to the neighbourhood around. It was the proper and the best way home that the Thompsons took after coming from the theatre. She did not lure her husband into some dark by-way where a murder could be committed. I ask you to consider Bywaters' position. Was he going out to murder? He was at the Graydons for the purpose of getting his tobacco, and the last thing he did was to make an arrangement with Miss Graydon to take her to the pictures on the next night. Are you going to cast those facts aside and say that they are of no importance, and that there are those "awful letters"? Where is the evidence that this was the result of a conspiracy between the two, and that she was a party that night to what happened, or in leading her husband to the spot, knowing what was going to happen? I suggest that Bywaters made up his mind

Bywaters and Thompson.

Sir Henry Curtis Bennett

suddenly to see Thompson and settle the question of his leaving his wife. You all know how matters of that sort suddenly strike people, there is nothing extraordinary about it. Mrs Thompson's story that she was pushed aside and stunned is corroborated by her mother, who had felt the bruise.

Members of the jury, every step in this case, when you really come to look at it in the light of the evidence, is only consistent with the story of the defence being the true one. If Bywaters was acting in self-defence, then you need not consider the case against Mrs Thompson. If you even come to the conclusion that he is guilty of manslaughter, you need not consider the case against Mrs Thompson. It is only if you come to the conclusion, and are satisfied of it upon the evidence, that Bywaters is guilty of murder, that you have to consider whether Mrs Thompson was a party to that murder. The piteous plea of Mrs Thompson, "Don't, don't", her cry to the doctor, "Why did you not come sooner and save him?" and her statement to Mrs Lester, "If they allow him to come home I will make him better," are all consistent with the story of the defence. Every act of Mrs Thompson on that occasion was not only consistent with her story that she did not know that the murder was going to be committed, but that she was horrified when she found that her husband had been killed. Test the evidence, don't be satisfied with guesswork. It is quite clear that in her first statement to the police Mrs Thompson did conceal Bywaters' name, but I would remind you that you have to deal with human nature. One is apt to be high minded in a Court of justice, but we have after all, to deal with human nature. Mrs Thompson knew that her lover had attacked her husband. She did not know he had killed him, and in my submission, although it might be improper, any one of us would, if in the same position, do what has been done here. Of course, Bywaters protected Mrs Thompson, and, of course, Mrs Thompson protected Bywaters. Of course, one should always tell the truth, the whole truth, and nothing but the truth; but when in a murder case two people are sitting in the dock awaiting your verdict, is there anything in the fact that both keep from the police until a certain moment information about the other? Bywaters would not have been a man if he had not tried to shield the woman. Mrs Thompson would not have been a woman if she had not tried to shield her lover.

Mrs Thompson was taken to the police station and another statement was taken from her. A statement was taken from Bywaters, and next day, the 5th, a statement in writing. Still a denial by Bywaters of Mrs Thompson, and still a denial by Mrs Thompson that Bywaters was the man, and by an extraordinary chance, if the story of the prosecution is to be believed, when Mrs Thompson was being taken back to the C I D room she happened to pass the very room where Bywaters was standing, and she saw him. That is one story. The other story is that Mrs Thompson was actually taken into the room where Bywaters was, and they were confronted with one another

Closing Speech for Thompson.

Sir Henry Curtis Bennett

The woman said, "Oh God, oh God, what can I do? Why did you do it? I did not want him to do it. I must tell the truth." Is that the statement of a woman who was a party to the killing, or is it the statement of a woman who had protected her lover as far as she could from the police—the statement of an innocent person, who, having protected her lover, realised that the time for protection had passed and that she must tell the truth? The statement that Mrs Thompson then made to the police was exactly what she states to-day. A little later both these persons were charged. Bywaters, when charged, said, 'Why her? She was not aware of my movements." And where is the evidence in the case that she did know his movements on that night? It is all founded upon the suggestion that they had tea together, and that they may have there discussed the murder. All the evidence is to the contrary—that she did not know he was coming back that night. The statement of Bywaters himself was " I made up my mind at the last moment '

It will be for you to say whether the arguments I have put forward for your consideration are well founded or not. It will be for you to say, when you have heard the Solicitor-General address you again on behalf of the Crown, whether the prosecution have proved that either of these people is guilty of murder. I am only concerned with Mrs Thompson. It will be for you to say whether she is guilty of murder or whether all the prosecution have done is to show you a cloud of prejudice, and whether it may or may not be that upon some other indictment she may be found guilty. I have submitted as plainly as I can that upon this indictment, not only have the prosecution not proved she is guilty, but if you go through these letters and discuss them you will see they are quite consistent with the view I have put before you, and much more consistent, because there are many more references to running away and spending time together in the future, and waiting those three or five years that all these letters are consistent with the innocence of both the people in this trial. As far as Mrs Thompson is concerned, you do not have to consider the case against her until you are satisfied beyond all reasonable doubt that Bywaters is guilty of murder, a decision which, in my submission to you, you will never come to when you consider your verdict. I am loath to leave this discussion, because I am anxious to feel and know that I have dealt with the whole case as it is put against Mrs Thompson. I know I have risked your displeasure in taking up your time at such length, but you do not grudge a few hours one way or the other spent on something which means eternity. Of course, I cannot see what is in your minds, because I cannot tell whether the matters I have been discussing are matters that you don't want to discuss because you have made up your minds. But in asking this question I know one thing. I shall get your answer, and the answer to the question I have put is the answer that Mrs Thompson is not guilty.

Bywaters and Thompson.

Closing Speech for the Prosecution

The SOLICITOR-GENERAL—Members of the jury, you have listened to impressive and powerful appeals from my learned friends. Everything that devotion to the interests of their clients can suggest and every argument or plea that skilled advocacy can think of have been used, and I know that you will consider them with care and weigh every argument that has been put forward. I do not ask you to close your hearts to a single plea. But it is my duty to consider the case less passionately than the way my learned friends put it to you. It is no part of my duty to use a single word or to turn a single phrase that would divert your attention from the real facts of the case or to attempt to wrest your verdict by the interpretation or misinterpretation of a single letter or incident. But my learned friends have gone a little beyond an appeal to you which it is their duty to make. They have criticised and reproached me and my learned friends for our conduct or presentation of the case. They have suggested that counsel for the Crown, to use Mr. Whiteley's phrase, have laid before you a mass of irrelevant evidence, and presented it in an unprecedented and extraordinary way. Perhaps the first observation I should make is that, from some points of view, this is an unprecedented case, from others it is a very ordinary case. I think the real comment on their criticism is this—they have been good enough to say that we have laid the case before you fairly, and they have not taken a single objection either to the substance or the form of a single question we have asked. Their criticism is of the interpretation which we have thought it our duty to suggest is the right one of the letters. That is a matter so entirely for you that I shall say no more about it now. Mr. Whiteley also referred to my right of addressing you last. Was he afraid that his eloquence would be submerged by mine? If so, he may put his anxiety away for after everything I have to say there will be the cooling influence of my lord.

I ask you to treat the case as an ordinary one. It is indisputable that Mr. Thompson was killed that night by Bywaters, that Bywaters chose a spot a great distance from his own home, and went there deliberately. It was not an accidental meeting. He chose an hour after midnight which was about the most unsuitable hour anybody could have selected for a discussion, as he suggested it was his desire to have with Mr. Thompson. Bywaters chose a place which in itself was a suitable one for such a crime in the sense that there would not likely be many persons about. The whole of the circumstances in which he attacked Thompson suggest, at first sight, a case of deliberate murder. It will be for you to consider whether any of the arguments that have been put before you justify you in finding a less verdict than murder. It is said that Bywaters was

Closing Speech for Prosecution.

Solicitor-General

acting, not in pursuance of any intention to kill, that he had no motive which would move him to do that, and that, therefore, the verdict of the jury ought to be one of manslaughter. It is suggested to us still further that this is a case of justifiable homicide on the part of Bywaters, which means that he acted in self-defence. That suggestion was made by Bywaters in the witness-box, but it does not appear in either of his statements. It is a suggestion that requires for foundation the sort of evidence he gave in the witness box as to the apprehension he felt that Thompson was about to produce a revolver, and it must occur to you that if that was Bywaters' real defence then it would have appeared long before the hour at which he produced it or suggested it in the witness-box. I ask you, is there any evidence upon which you can reasonably or possibly come to the conclusion that he was acting in self-defence when he killed Thompson? In his own statement Bywaters does not even tell the truth. Referring to the actual struggle he says—

> The reason I fought that night was because he never acted like a man to his wife he always seemed several degrees lower than a snake. I loved her and I could not go on seeing her living that life. I did not intend to kill him, but only to injure him. I gave him an opportunity of standing up to me as a man but he would not.

I suggest to you that there can only be a verdict of murder in this case. At least four or five deep and probably fatal blows were inflicted. One of the blows was delivered 14 feet from the place where the attack began. Probably any one of them would have disabled Thompson. They were delivered with a weapon which could hardly be used by a violent man without running the grievous risk of immediate death on the part of the other man, and they were delivered with a force which was quite inconsistent with any other action than the intention to kill the man against whom they were delivered.

How does the case stand against Mrs. Thompson? I suggest that if she and Bywaters agreed to kill Mr. Thompson, and the husband was killed in pursuance of that agreement, then there must be a verdict of murder against Mrs. Thompson as well as against Bywaters. Again if Mrs. Thompson incited Bywaters to murder Thompson, and if, in consequence of that incitement, Bywaters did murder Thompson, similarly Mrs. Thompson is guilty of murder. I contend that if you find that in consequence of the instigation or even command of Mrs. Thompson the murder was committed, then she is guilty.

Mr. JUSTICE SHEARMAN—It is necessary, of course, to be careful of words, and I do not feel inclined to take the matter at large.

The SOLICITOR-GENERAL—I am not going to suggest to the jury that merely because some foolish or wild expressions were used in letters it is sufficient for you to say that in consequence of that the

Bywaters and Thompson.

Solicitor-General

murder was committed and Mrs. Thompson is guilty. I agree with my learned friends for the defence, that in order for you to arrive at a verdict of murder against Mrs. Thompson you must be satisfied that the persuasion lasted right up to—not the moment of the murder, but substantially right up to the murder, and was the continuing cause in consequence of which the murder was committed by Bywaters. If you think that the persuasion had no real connection with the murder, and that the expressions, however criminal and foolish, were not really the cause of the murder, then of course it is not a case of murder against Mrs. Thompson. What I ask you to consider is the progress of the idea found in the letters and to see how it was pressed by Mrs. Thompson on Bywaters, and how the idea continued right up to the very last moment. When you get to the time at which the two accused were in the tearoom together on 3rd October one would no longer expect to find correspondence passing between them, and if you find from the correspondence that the direction was continuing substantially up to the time of the murder, it is my duty to submit to you that that amounts to murder. It is suggested that the letters are consistent with something different from murder. Bywaters in the witness-box suggested over and over again that the statements in the letters all referred to a proposal to commit suicide. I do not suppose you will have much difficulty in dismissing that suggestion. My learned friend, Sir Henry Curtis Bennett, suggested over and over again that what was passing in the minds of those two persons was divorce or separation in order that she might go with Bywaters, and that all the other expressions were hysterical and extravagant utterances on the part of this woman. The view I suggest that you should consider is that there is no determination on the part of Mrs. Thompson to leave her husband or give him cause for divorce. For some reason or other they both seem to have put that out of the range of possibility. It may be that that was not a thing that Mrs. Thompson or Bywaters could contemplate, because if she left her husband she would not be able to continue in her employment, and neither she nor Bywaters had means. Mrs. Thompson seems from first to last to have done all she could to keep her connection with Bywaters from her husband. I do not find in the letters, when they are properly read, any real foundation for the suggestion that she was repeatedly trying to get her husband to divorce her, and did everything she could to convince him that it would be the best thing to get rid of her. That suggestion, like the suicide suggestion, does not seem to have been present in their minds. Right up to the very end the proposal in the letters is that her husband should be removed by poison. You will remember that in her examination-in-chief Mrs. Thompson did not disguise that a certain expression did refer to a proposal, either made in a moment of hysteria or perhaps almost as a joke, that her husband should be poisoned. At any rate the reference was to poison, however it began. In her letter she says, " I acquiesced in everything he said or did or

Closing Speech for Prosecution.

Solicitor General

wants to do. At least it will disarm any suspicion he might have if we have to take any drastic measures." It has been suggested that the drastic measures meant leaving her husband, but you, gentlemen, must be the judges of that.

It is important to remember the visits home of Bywaters, because you have only her letters; Bywaters letters have all been destroyed, and the correspondence was interrupted by his visits home, and what happened when he was at home you can only judge from the correspondence subsequently resumed. The first letter after he left home was that of 10th February, which you will remember begins ' You must do something this time." That letter was written to Aden, and Bywaters received it somewhere about March. If it is suggested that "You must do something this time" referred to the making of plans for running away with her, it is curious that the next paragraph refers to something not connected with divorce. It is the paragraph in which she relates her attempt to discover the prescription. "I told Avis about the incident only I told her as if it frightened and worried me. That can only mean that she wanted to create evidence at that time which might be useful in the case of something happening which might throw suspicion on somebody as having poisoned her husband. That part of the letter shows that Mrs. Thompson was interested in disarming suspicion, but if you have any doubt it will be dispelled after reading the last part— " It would be so easy darling—if I had things—I do hope I shall. How about cigarettes?' To suggest that all those passages are a question of hysteria or fun is a suggestion that you can exclude. If it is not all hysteria or fun, then you must come to the conclusion that she was proposing to him—arising, perhaps, out of a proposal from him—that poison should be administered. In a later letter there is a definite suggestion of some drug, medicine, or something " I suppose it is not possible for you to send it to me—not at all possible—I do so chafe at wasting time." That word " it " undoubtedly refers to something which was to injure her husband's health. On 14th March, as Bywaters was approaching this country, she wrote, ' I don't think I have shirked, have I? Except, darling, to ask you again to think out all the plans and methods for me." Shirked what, if not the enterprise they had entered into to poison her husband? Then she writes, " This will be the last time you will go away unless things are different. There will be no failure this time. If things are the same again I am going with you—if it is to sea I am coming too—and if it is to nowhere I am coming." You must consider whether that passage throws any light on whether there had been any discussion between Bywaters and Mrs. Thompson as to what was going to happen between herself and her husband, and if you think it does throw any light then you will give it its proper weight.

Then there is the letter containing the phrase, " Don't keep this piece." It is suggested that that was because it might come into her husband's possession. I am bound to say to you that this letter of 1st April is one that deals entirely with this idea now occupying so much of her attention, that her husband must be got rid of. The passage is full of crime. There is no other interpretation which can fairly be placed upon it. It is inconsistent with any other view than that she was proposing at this time an injury to her husband, not only to make him ill but eventually to make him so ill that, as she puts it herself, after he had a heart attack he would die under it. I suggest that these letters were being destroyed because his, like hers, referred to the subject of poisoning. In the next letter she has given up something "till you come home." I suggest that this was the idea of administering something to her husband. In her letter of 28th April she writes, "I used the light bulb three times." Sir Henry Curtis Bennett has poured ridicule on that and has said that it must be the imagination of a hysterical woman, because the use of glass would have left indications on the gullet or organs of the body. It was exactly with reference to that that Dr. Spilsbury was called. I called him as much to assist the defence as the Crown. It is complained that it was elicited that the administration of glass, even in large pieces, would not necessarily have left an indication in the organs of the body. I venture to say that that was a piece of evidence that the jury will think it desirable Dr. Spilsbury should have given. It may not carry the case any further, but it would have been wrong to have left you with the impression that an injury must necessarily have been found if glass was used.

Next comes the letter of 1st May (exhibit 19). It is quite plain that Bywaters had been writing, and, I submit, making observations to her about some drug which he had sent or suggested. Bywaters said it referred to quinine which he knew could not hurt, and which he had sent to pacify her in connection with the suicide proposal. There is a significant passage in the middle of the letter "I quite expected to be able to send that cable—but no—nothing has happened. I do feel so down and unhappy." Sir Henry Curtis Bennett said that this referred to a divorce or to adultery, but I submit that that letter is full of proposals as to the method in which her husband might be harmed.

The next letter, 18th May (exhibit 22), sets out an extract from 'Bella Donna' referring to the administration of cumulative poison and asks, "Is it any use?" That was a very important question for Bywaters to consider. Then she says, "Everything is destroyed—I don't even wait for the next arrival now." So dreadful were the suggestions contained in these letters, whatever they referred to, that she no longer thought it safe to keep any of them. They cannot have referred to their guilty relationship because it is their own case that they were repeatedly impressing on the husband that he should divorce her for adultery. I suggest that these letters

Closing Speech for Prosecution.

Solicitor General

were being destroyed because his, like hers, referred to the subject of poisoning. Then there is the letter in which Mrs. Thompson alludes to some weakness on her husband's part. Thompson fell ill on the ottoman at the foot of the bed and stated that he had another attack. Mrs. Thompson says, " I had to laugh at this, because I knew it could not be a heart attack.' How could she know that? On 23rd May Mrs. Thompson sends Bywaters a book, ' Bella Donna,' saying in her letter, " You may learn something from it to help us." She would not send the book to Plymouth merely to give him something to read.

Bywaters went to sea again on 6th June. It is at this time that she starts having her letters sent to the General Post Office in the name of Miss Fisher. On 4th July she writes to Bywaters—" Why are not you sending me something . . . if I don't mind the risk why should you?' Mrs. Thompson admitted to me in cross-examination that " something " was something to injure her husband—she was referring to something which Bywaters had suggested to her to which she first objected and in which she afterwards acquiesced. It is a serious piece of evidence against Bywaters if her statement is accepted, because she seems to have thought that the only way in which she could keep the love of Bywaters was by falling in with these suggestions that poison should be administered to her husband. Why did she think that this would keep Bywaters' love? Was it not because Bywaters was proposing this to her as the only way in which she could be his wife or live with him? From whatever point of view it is regarded this is a matter of the utmost importance. If the suggestion to give her husband something to make him ill came from Bywaters she not only responded to his suggestion and dotted the I's and crossed the T's of the idea he had mentioned but she concluded a letter which I must describe as being of the utmost importance with the startling postscript ' Have you studied bichloride of mercury?' Does a laundry steward in a ship even one interested in chemistry study bichloride of mercury? What did she mean? I suggest that that passage throws a little light upon the suggestion of Mrs. Thompson that all that she was doing was to humour the whims of her lover.

I would remind you that the letter of 20th September (exhibit 28) in which she says " Be jealous so much that you will do something desperate ' met Bywaters when he landed at Plymouth. As soon as he landed she telegraphed to him and got into touch with him on every occasion that she could right up to 3rd October. On 2nd October she writes to him and at the end of the letter there appears a sentence which repeated a phrase that had already appeared and which Mrs. Thompson admitted in the witness box meant what has been suggested it did—" Don't forget what we talked in the tearoom, I will still risk and try if you will—we have only three and three-quarter years left darlingest." When you review these

Bywaters and Thompson.

Solicitor-General

letters you are driven to the conclusion that right up to the end she was acquiescing in Bywaters' suggestions. She allowed him to think that she was prepared to co-operate with him in poisoning her husband right up to the end. She never undeceived him. In trying to reconstruct the conversation between Bywaters and Mrs Thompson, you can only draw inferences which can fairly be drawn by giving Mrs Thompson and Bywaters the benefit of any doubt there may be. Nothing I have said should give you reason to think that I wish to impress a single phrase, a single letter, beyond its proper importance. But when Mrs Thompson says she left Bywaters under the impression that she acquiesced in giving her husband something to make him ill, it is very significant. Is it possible that the anxiety Bywaters had evinced would evaporate when she came in fresh contact with her lover? Is it possible that the proposal to poison her husband was not discussed? I suggest that if the anxiety to injure her husband evaporated with the last letter Mrs Thompson wrote to Bywaters on his homeward journey, it will be your duty to say that Mrs Thompson is not guilty. These matters, however, are for the jury to decide. My duty is to suggest that on a fair reading of the letters and a fair construction of the meetings it is only possible to come to a conclusion that the same idea was present in their minds, that the same question was discussed then, and I am going to ask you to say that the discussions resulted in an agreement, the consequence of which was that Mr Thompson was killed.

Let us come to the day of the crime itself. I do not think it is relevant to consider what arrangements had been made by the Thompsons for 4th August. Of course, Mr Thompson would not know that he was going to be assaulted, and so would not break an engagement to meet the maid at Paddington. Nor does it throw much light on the matter that Bywaters made arrangements to take Mrs Thompson's sister to the pictures. He would not expose his guilt, he would be more likely to cover his guilt. It is rather inconsistent with his story that he had in his pocket that dreadful weapon with which the crime was committed. You have seen it, and you can say whether it was a handy or convenient thing to carry about. Not a single witness has been called to say that Bywaters was in the habit of carrying it. It is difficult to imagine that it would not have been the subject of jocular conversation if he had. I suggest that Bywaters' story about the knife has not been corroborated. Mrs Thompson has said in a statement that she knows nothing about the actual killing except that she was pushed aside. Her evidence now is not altogether inconsistent with the second statement she made to the police but certainly it is not consistent with her first statement. Nor is the evidence given by Bywaters consistent with any of his statements.

The case for the Crown is that there was an agreement between these two persons to get rid of Mr Thompson, or that, if there was

Frederick Bywaters

The Hon Justice Shearman
(*Photo Vandyk*)

Closing Speech for Prosecution.

Solicitor-General

not an actual agreement in terms, there was an instigation by Mrs Thompson to get rid of him on which Bywaters acted so as to kill him. Bywaters' case should be considered apart from the letters. Consider, first of all, whether he went there to kill Mr Thompson, in which case it is murder. Then you will consider Mrs Thompson's position. Take her admissions as to what she intended, what she proposed to Bywaters, her acquiescence in Bywaters' suggestion, and weighing everything carefully, as you will do on behalf of the prisoner, say whether she is not guilty of murder. You have an anxious task. The prosecution are under no duty to press anything beyond its fair value, but it is my duty to ask you not to shirk for one moment to give a reasonable construction of those letters and to every incident in the case, even though it results in your returning a verdict of guilty of wilful murder against the woman as well as the man.

Charge to the Jury.

Mr JUSTICE SHEARMAN—Members of the jury, there are several indictments in this case, only one of which has been presented, only one of which is before you, and that is the indictment of this man and this woman for wilful murder. The first case which you have to consider is as to the man, and I will come to that before I ask you to consider the case of the woman. The case presented is that these two by arrangement between each other agreed to murder this man, and the murder was effected by the man. Unless you are satisfied of that, namely, that they did it by arrangement in the way I shall explain to you, there would be no case against the woman. But with regard to the man, if you are satisfied that, without any arrangement with the woman, he intended to murder, then, of course, you can find him guilty of that, and that is why I am asking you to consider the case of the man first. But before I do that there are one or two observations I wish to make as to your duty. Of course, when a jury are summoned to try a case for murder, it is always an anxious time, it is as anxious for the judge as it is for the jury. But, whether it be a case of murder, or whether it be a case of petty theft, your duty is the same, and I want to explain to you what it is. In a phrase, you are there to convict the guilty and acquit the innocent. That means that you have two duties, you have got to look very carefully, patiently and sensibly, and acquit unless you are satisfied that the case is proved. On the other hand, if you are satisfied that the case is proved, it is just as much your duty, and an equally important duty, to convict, because if crime is not detected and conviction does not follow detection, crime flourishes. You have two duties: one is to protect the public by always convicting if you are satisfied that there is crime, and the other is to protect the accused by always acquitting if you think

Bywaters and Thompson.

Mr Justice Shearman

the evidence is unsatisfactory. I have only one word which I hope you will excuse me saying, it may be quite unnecessary—perhaps there are two things I should say to you. Of course we all of us in the last three or four days have been carrying on this work in a rather unnatural and unreal atmosphere. We are in a Court of justice, and Courts of justice in this country very properly are open to the public; it is the right of the public to come to a Court of justice and listen to the proceedings. Cases do arise where large numbers of the public want to come in, and they do come. It is inevitable that you should have been surrounded by a different atmosphere from that which prevails in the ordinary humdrum of the Courts, and you must throw that aside, try to escape from that, because this charge really is—I am not saying whether it is proved—a common or ordinary charge of a wife and an adulterer murdering the husband. That is the charge, I am not saying for a moment it is proved. We heard of flights of imagination in this case, and there was one that I cannot help alluding to. The whole of this case has very properly been conducted with studious moderation by the prosecution, which is quite usual and proper, and more fervently by the counsel for the defence, and that again, is quite usual and proper. When one heard the statement made that never before in the history of crime had anybody ever been charged with a murder when it was not suggested that that person had taken a hand in actually inflicting the blow, I sat amazed. These cases are not uncommon; I am not saying they are common cases. If the learned counsel who said so had been in this Court a few months ago he would have seen me sitting and trying one.

I do not say that cases like this are very usual, but there are cases of husbands who, in order to marry somebody else, want to get rid of a wife, and of wives who want to get rid of the husband. Let us say in the interest of the fair sex that they are more often on the other side, but such things are known and they are not unusual. Now, I have only one other observation about Sir Henry Curtis Bennett, he said, and indeed, I am afraid it has become now a precedent in these Courts, that he ' thanked God that you had to decide and he had not.' If that remark is intended to frighten you I hope it will not. We are dealing with law and justice here and I do not like invocations to the Deity. This case, we have no doubt, is as anxious a case as other murder cases. You will apply the ordinary principles of common sense and I will tell you exactly when there is any law. You may take it from me, that unless I mention there is any law, you will understand that I am talking merely about facts.

There is only one other observation I am going to make, and it has nothing whatever to do with counsel. You are told that this is a case of a " great love ", I am only using it as a phrase. Take one of the letters as a test. We have had for days an atmosphere, both in speeches and in questions, of this kind. Just at the

Charge to the Jury.

Mr Justice Shearman

end of a letter I shall have to allude to again comes this, " He has the right by law to all that you have the right to by nature and love " Gentlemen, if that nonsense means anything it means that the love of a husband for his wife is something improper because marriage is acknowledged by the law, and that the love of a woman for her lover, illicit and clandestine, is something great and noble. I am certain that you, like any other right-minded persons, will be filled with disgust at such a notion. Let us get rid of all that atmosphere, and try this case in an ordinary common sense way.

Now, what is murder? You will take the law from me. Murder is the intentional killing of a human being. You sometimes hear the words " malice aforethought." That does not mean it need be premeditated over a long time; all it means is that it is intentional. Did the person charged intentionally kill? In one of the statements made by the male prisoner he said, " I only intended to injure him and not to kill him." This much, however, is clear and this you may take from me, I do not think it will arise because the case made is that he went out to kill him, not to injure him. The law is clear that if a person goes out to injure anybody else with a deadly weapon (you have seen the knife) which any reasonable man would know might kill, then he is responsible for murder whether it was in his mind actually to kill or not because a person is taken to know the reasonable consequences of his own actions. That is all you have got to know about the law upon that. I shall say something more to you when I am dealing with the case of the woman, which you have got to take into consideration as a question of law but I will deal with that presently because I am asking you now to deal with the case of the man. I am not going to deal at length with the letters, and I have only one other point of law to put to you. Gentlemen, you know the facts of this case are extremely short and simple, the only length in the matter comes from the letters. As I told you, you will remember, in the case of statements made in the letters or the statements made by one not in the presence of the other which they had nothing to do with, they are not evidence at all against the other person, and the statements by the lady in her letters that she administered glass or something are not evidence against him. But when people go into the witness-box and admit that they received letters and answered them, anything said by the man is evidence against the woman, and anything said by the woman is evidence against the man, because they are represented by separate counsel who could have cross-examined them. You have noticed I daresay, in the course of the case that where the woman made statements they are mostly something excusing her and implicating the man, but in some of them, when the man is making statements they are always exculpating the woman. It is said that is chivalry and that is why he is doing it. What either of them says on oath is evidence against the other, but apart from that I am going to say very little about these matters, except that there are certain things that one has to

Bywaters and Thompson.

Mr Justice Shearman

take with regard to him (and you are now considering the case of the man alone) The man admits he gave her something, he says it was quinine, and the woman says in the witness-box—"He gave me something, and I do not know what it was" Certainly the woman says that the man wrote to her saying that it was "enough to give to an elephant," and the woman says yes, she did give something to the man If that meant to poison him or to make him die because he was unable to resist it in a heart attack it is common sense to say that would be murder just as much as the longest and strongest dose of poison It is useless to say that because he has got a weak heart I can give him a smaller dose and then it will be partly from his heart and partly from the dose A man with a weak heart is entitled to be protected from poison as well as anybody else She does say that he had given her something to give to the man and she admits, although I do not know that he does—I have not got it in my note—she admits that he did write to her saying, "Be careful not to leave any marks on the glass"

Now what were the relations between the parties at that time? Let us go back and think of it again with plain common sense The Thompsons had been married for some years and in June of 1921 this young lad went with them to the Isle of Wight I think it was attempted to be suggested to you that the man was merely friendly with the woman, that there was no love between them In one of the letters she sent to him (I think it is on 14th June, 1921) she says that she is writing this on this day because one year ago they had their first kiss when they were on a charabanc ride in the Isle of Wight, so it is pretty obvious that there were relations between them then There is another one in which she said she had had a quarrel with her husband over the old subject, "he was jealous of you" One thing, I think, is perfectly clear, at any rate, from the moment when he left the house as he says, by his own wish, as well as with the wish of the husband their relations were affectionate and they were clandestine from beginning to end, if one looks at the correspondence The first letter you have is exhibit 12 "Come and see me lunch time, please darling, he suspects" that is in August The next, the telegram, exhibit 10 "Wait till one, he's come," which is a note The husband is here so you must wait There is a letter the last letter of all, I think which is written one or two days before this man met his death, exhibit 60 "I tried so hard to find a way out to-night darlingest but he was suspicious and still is—I suppose we must make a study of this deceit for some time longer" Now, gentlemen the first thing you have got to make up your mind about—because this has a direct bearing upon the case put by him as well as by the woman—if it was clandestine how can you believe evidence that they were always talking to him and saying, "Give her up" and he said, "No, I will not give her up"? I think that being the relation between the parties you will have to ask yourselves what it means and why it

Charge to the Jury.

Mr Justice Shearman

was clandestine. It is said, you know, all they were writing about and a good many of the things they were saying were merely about going off together. Nothing prevents nowadays in this country a woman going away with another man except the divorce Court, and what else? The trouble, as is said in one of the letters, of ways and means. This man was in a respectable occupation, the woman was in a respectable occupation; if they were going off with one another even if they stayed in the same place, it might end in their losing their positions and having nothing to live upon. If it does not lead to that, it means it leads to scandal. It is part of the case that both said, 'We are going to keep this quiet because we cannot afford to risk our positions and our place in society, we must keep it dark," and the whole of the evidence is that from the moment he came back they saw each other every day except when the husband was at home, and it would have been suspicious if she had gone out. Those being the general circumstances of the case you will, of course, bear in mind whether you should believe the evidence, particularly the evidence this man has given, that she was always asking Thompson to grant a divorce and let them go off.

He comes home from his last voyage and, as I say, every day except when it is impossible without the husband knowing, they meet one another. Of course, as I have said before, these letters do show on the face of them—and you will hear more of that later—that whether he thought it melodrama or not, the lady was writing suggesting that she was poisoning her husband. On this particular day, by an arrangement made with her husband and other people, she goes to the theatre. She sees Bywaters. The two meet at 5.30. At six o'clock she tells us she had got to meet her husband and so goes off. At about seven o'clock he presents himself at Shakespeare Crescent, about two miles from the scene of where this unfortunate man met his death. He has a knife in his pocket; you must take the knife and see it. It would be in a leather sheath, which has disappeared. I do not know what has become of it, but, as you know, his evidence was that he always carried it about with him. It is a little difficult to put into any kind of pocket, except the side pocket. He said he always carried it in his overcoat pocket. It is pointed out that no other person had seen it. It is suggested by the prosecution that when he arrived, as he undoubtedly did—there is no dispute about that—at Shakespeare Crescent, two miles off the scene of the crime (if it was a crime)—the scene of this death—he had got this in his overcoat pocket. It is not suggested he showed it to anybody. There was possibly no reason he should if he had got it. It is suggested by the prosecution that the only reasonable inference is that he put it in his pocket for the purpose he had in view. He was there till eleven o'clock, or after eleven. I will read you presently his own statement; you know practically what it is, he was suddenly seized with an impulse to talk to this husband because he was so miserable about the wife, to talk to him about a separa-

Bywaters and Thompson.

Mr Justice Shearman

tion or a divorce—sudden impulse. It is said by the prosecution, nothing of the sort; he went out to lie in wait for the husband, and knew where he was coming. You have his own statement which I will read to you at length eventually. But what did happen, on evidence which is not contradicted, was this—It is a quiet road at half-past twelve at night, the husband and wife are coming down, she is next to the wall, her husband outside coming down on the pavement. In one of his statements Bywaters said he waited for them; in his sworn evidence he said he came up from behind. You will consider when coming up behind at that hour of night, if he were coming up—I am putting plain common sense considerations before you—do you think they would have heard him before he came up to them or do you think the blows were struck before they heard him? Whichever it was, the man is struck, as one sees from the bloodstains, and struck again probably in the front, because there is more blood there but he has gone a certain number of feet down the road; it is obvious he has got into the road then where there is a lot of blood which spurts out. he goes back and staggers and wobbles towards the wall and sinks down with his back against the wall. He went 46 or 47 feet in all, judging by the spots of blood; that is the way of it.

What is found on his body? There is found one blow, a wound which comes in behind the neck, administered it is suggested, by this weapon and is driven with such force into him that it comes out into his mouth. There is another one, driven with such force into the back that it reaches down to the spine. There is a third wound. It is suggested by counsel for the defence that it was inflicted from the front but there it is. it might be and very likely it was, inflicted from behind, and it cuts—not slashes, you recollect, but stabs—the gullet and cuts the carotid artery on the right side. From that blood gushes out with enormous force and renders death inevitable in a few minutes. I am putting aside the evidence of the man and the woman because you may think the whole of it is made up. I do not say you will think it is made up, but you might. All human evidence particularly of people who are defending themselves, is liable if they have an interest, to be uncertain so that the evidence of anybody who has an interest is to be scrutinised and the evidence of the bloodstains cannot be disputed.

Now, what happens afterwards? I am not going into the woman's case at all, except to the fact of her interest in the husband. I will deal with her evidence in detail later. The man goes away. The man who was killed sinks down, and even the doctor who comes up is under the impression—I will say something about it presently—that he has not been stabbed but it was a broken blood vessel or something of that sort, blood welling out from his mouth. it was an illness. Eventually the police come up and when the body is taken away the wounds are discovered. What does the man do? His evidence is that he ran away. A number of people come up

Charge to the Jury.

Mr Justice Shearman

and all their evidence deals entirely with the woman, so I am not saying a word about that with regard to the man because, again, statements made in evidence by other people with regard to the woman do not affect the man. So far the husband is killed, admittedly, and now the only two people present the wife and the lover, give evidence to show whether one or the other had inflicted the blow, or some third person or some entirely independent person had inflicted the blow. The police come upon the scene and these are his statements. The first one is admittedly now a tissue of lies. The police get the letters and have a suspicion of him and they get him to make a statement. " I have known Mr Percy Thompson for about four years," &c. (Reads statement, exhibit 5, page 37.) " After lunch she returned to business and I have not seen her since." That is to say, it was a concealment of facts. " Mr Thompson was not aware of all our meetings, but some of them he was." Do you think that is candid? " I have known for a very long time past that she had led a very unhappy life with him. This is also known to members of Mrs Thompson's family." That does not seem to be accurate. " I have written to her on two occasions. I signed the letters Freddie and I addressed her as ' Dear Edie ' " I think it is obvious, as was suggested by Sir Henry Curtis Bennett or Mr Whiteley, that that took the form of question and answer. Then he goes on, ' On the evening of Monday, 2nd October, I called on Mrs Graydon " (Continues reading.) " Before leaving I remember Mrs Graydon's daughter, Avis, saying that Percy (Mr Thompson) had 'phoned her up, and I gathered from the observations she made that he was taking his wife to a theatre that night and that there were other members of the family going." You notice that he had heard the same evening from Mrs Thompson—" When I left the house I went through Browning Road, into Sibley Grove, to East Ham Railway Station " (Continues reading.) " This statement has been read over to me, is voluntary and is true." It is not suggested that this was anything else but an intention to deceive the police. Later on he finds out she is there whether actually they are both together or he sees her there I do not know—there seems to be a conflict of evidence about that, it does not seem to me to make any difference. Then he says, " I wish to make a voluntary statement "—that is on the 5th October, the next day. (Reads statement, exhibit 6, page 39.) " I loved her and I couldn't go on seeing her leading that life. I did not intend to kill him. I only meant to injure him." I have already commented on that, if he stabbed him without any excuse or provocation then he is guilty. " I gave him an opportunity of standing up to me as a man but he wouldn't." In other words, he declined to fight. His statement was—it may not be true or parts of it—he would not fight. " I gave him an opportunity of standing up to me as a man but he wouldn't. I have had the knife some time, it was a sheath knife. I threw it down a drain when I was running through Endsleigh Gardens." Then I think there is only one other statement of any importance, to Detective Williams, on 6th October. He asked Williams "Have you a knife there? Have they found it? I told them I ran up Endsleigh Gardens, but coming to think of it, after I did it I ran forward towards the Wanstead Park along Belgrave Road, turned up a road to the right. I am not sure whether it was Kensington Gardens (where they lived) or the next road. I then crossed over to the left side of the road and just before I got to the top of the Cranbrook Road end I put the knife down a drain. It should easily be found." The importance of it is that he is admitting that his was the knife, and not the woman's, that did it. He again uses the expression, 'When I did it."

Now, let us come to his evidence in the witness-box. It is fair, I think, that I should read it to you. The part I am going to read to you there is no dispute about. There are several meetings I pass by altogether, but Mr Whiteley did read it to you quite properly, but as that was last week I had better read it to you again. He says he bought the knife in November 1921. As I say, gentlemen, all this as to the knife is entirely a question for you. It is pointed out that a sailor may have a knife of this sort; it is suggested that no reasonable man living in London carries a knife like that about in his pocket and it is suggested that the mere presence of the knife is very strong evidence of his intention—a knife of that description. I think you have seen it, but you may as well take it. He says, "I bought that in November, 1921; it had a leather sheath; I took it when I went abroad; I carried it in my inside right-hand overcoat pocket which I was wearing during October." She telephoned him on the morning of 3rd October; they went to Queen Anne's Restaurant to lunch and he met her at Fuller's shop at five o'clock. "I parted with her at Aldersgate Street Station at 5 30 I then went to Mrs Graydon's at Manor Park and I got there at half-past six to seven. I was in the same room all the time till I left about eleven o'clock. There were four members of the Graydon family there. I had a pouch with me which was a present from Mrs Thompson." Then there is a long discussion; I do not think I need read it to you. And then he goes on suggesting that Mrs Graydon knew the pouch had been given him by Mrs Thompson, and Mrs Graydon said, "We won't argue about it, she's one of the best," and he replied, "There is none better." That was introduced as showing that they were talking about Mrs Thompson. "After that I was naturally thinking of Mrs Thompson, I was thinking she was unhappy. I wished I could help her." (Continues reading evidence of Bywaters, page 54.)

Now, gentlemen, that is his case and that is the whole of the evidence with regard to it. Nobody questions that he inflicted those wounds, and now I think with regard to him you will have quite a

Charge to the Jury.

Mr Justice Shearman

simple task to arrive at your decision. First of all, it is the law that if you intentionally kill—intentionally—you are guilty of murder, but if you kill a person in legitimate self-defence, that is what is called " justifiable homicide." It is said by the prosecution that this story, that Thompson attempted to shoot Bywaters, is quite untrue. As a matter of fact, the policeman Geal said there was no weapon or pistol of any kind on the husband when his body was brought in. All of them say—all of the witnesses who were called—that, except for the stabs and the cuts there were no signs of a struggle on Mr Thompson's clothing. It is said on behalf of the prosecution, this story of the reason for their meeting and of the threat of the pistol is just a tale like other tales that are put up by prisoners in any crime. The prosecution say it is a story which no reasonable jury would think of believing, it is contradicted by the facts of the wounds themselves; it never appears at all till he is put in the witness-box, and it is such a story that you are entitled to reject entirely. If you think that is the truth you are entitled to acquit him altogether. He says that Thompson hit him and, if you believe that Thompson made an unprovoked attack upon him, and he only inflicted these stabs in self-defence, you will acquit him altogether. If you think it is a fabrication from beginning to end you will reject it. I will not say anything more about it.

There is something which requires a little consideration. I am telling you the law, you may take it from me. I am not speaking of facts, that is for you to decide and not for me. It is the law, that if a man, although intentionally, in the heat of blood kills somebody when he has had provocation, then the jury may, if they think that this provocation was the only thing that started the murderous impulse, reduce it to manslaughter. A man may flog you with a whip and, if you happen to have a pistol, and you take it out and shoot him, the jury may say the provocation was made; you never intended to shoot him. But that is a matter which you have to regard with great consideration. First of all, it is inconceivable that it would be any provocation for a man to say, " I will not allow you to run away with my wife." Provocation means blows or violence. But, then, in the middle of this story, he says, he hit me on the chest and then he put his hand behind he provoked me." I have dealt with the question of self-defence, but was there a blow at all? Is there any injury to this man or to his clothing? His own story is " I wanted to fight him, I waited for him "—he has got a knife, as we know, in his pocket—" I waited for him and he would not fight ", and then, in his second statement, where he says he looked upon him as a snake—" The reason why I fought with Thompson was because he never acted like a man to his wife. He always seemed several degrees lower than a snake. I loved her and I could not go on seeing her leading that life." Now, gentlemen, what is said by the prosecution is that there never was any provocation at all

Bywaters and Thompson.

Mr Justice Shearman

It is said that the true story is that he came at him from behind, whether he waited for him or whether he caught him up from behind. As regards Mrs Thompson's story, you are entitled to take that into consideration, it does not help him very much. And there is one other thing that I also wish to mention to you as regards him. Mrs Thompson says she was pushed aside and fainted and became senseless. I am going to deal with that when I deal with her, but she says when she did recover she saw a scuffle going on, which is equally consistent with a man who was defending himself—I mean if the story is true at all. She does not say in the least that there was any conversation. Here, again, in fact, her evidence that she was pushed violently aside does not look like what Bywaters said, that he went up there to have an amicable discussion with him about divorce. It is very odd, if they were to have an amicable discussion, that he pushed the lady so violently as to knock her head against the wall and render her, according to her view, senseless. There is, I think, only one other person who can throw any light on the matter and he is a man who was called, and he lived at a house somewhere opposite, and it was five minutes before he came out, and he heard Mrs Thompson in a piteous tone say, " Oh, don't, oh, don't " We will deal with that when we come to Mrs Thompson's case. It seems to me one cannot help saying rather to contradict the story. Mrs Thompson was rather contradicting the story that she did not see what was going on. But if you believe it and if Mrs Thompson was looking on it does not help the prisoner, and you may think it rather points to her seeing the murder. That is the story for the prosecution, but it is entirely for you and that is the whole of the evidence.

Now, may I just add this if you think that he really did this because he quite innocently had the knife and never thought of doing anything until he got there, or he did it because of this story which appears in the witness-box, he thought he was going to be shot and he did it in reasonable self-protection and he inflicted these stabs—if you think that then you will acquit him altogether. You will consider this matter very carefully if you think it was an intentional murder. If you think there is any foundation whatever for the story that there was an assault and provocation that is, a blow struck by the husband not in self defence of himself and that there was provocation in that way, you might find a verdict of manslaughter, but if you think that is a mere defence put up in order to escape retribution for what he had done and dismiss that story, then you will find him guilty of murder.

I have only one other matter to say to you with regard to this and, of course, it is my duty to say so at some time and I will say it now. Of course you know this is a man of good character. Sometimes evidence of this sort is put up—I am saying it quite

Charge to the Jury.

Mr Justice Shearman

frankly—because it is said "here is a young man, we are sorry for him, let us do something for him" Gentlemen, you know perfectly well, if you find him guilty of murder, what sentence I must pronounce, I never keep it back from the jury You know as well as I do that the prerogative of mercy, which is in other hands, does not rest with me nor with you, and even if you really think him a young and honest person and that he lost his head altogether, if you think that he was inflamed by sexual impulses and that the real truth of the matter is that he went out with the knife put it in his pocket in order to kill this man—went out and did kill this man and struck him from behind as said by the prosecution, without any provocation whatever—if you are satisfied of it, then, however unpleasant your duty is you must give effect to it That is the only way I can help you with regard to him, and, after the adjournment I will deal with the case of the female prisoner

Adjourned for a short time (Bailiffs being sworn)

Mr Justice Shearman—Gentlemen, I now turn to the case of Mrs Thompson a case which I have no doubt you will carefully and conscientiously consider being desirous of doing real justice Of course, if you should find that this was not a murder at all, there is an end of the matter It there never was any intention by the man to do it or if he never premeditated it, in the sense that he only did it because he was provoked by a blow—if you believe the story that he was struck by a blow and that so excited him that he did something that he had no thought of doing before and did not come there to do in fact it is a manslaughter, not murder, and there is an end of the matter, because the lady cannot be convicted of doing something which was done under provocation and never designed If you think it is a murder, then comes the question, is this lady a party to it?

Now, I am going to ask you to consider only one question in your deliberations and that is was it an arranged thing between the woman and the man? I quite accept the law of the learned Solicitor General that if you hire an assassin and say, "Here is money" and there is a bargain between them that the assassin shall go out and murder the man when he can the person who hires the assassin is guilty of the murder—it is plain common sense I also accept the proposition that if a woman says to a man 'I want this man murdered you promise me to do it' and he then promises her (she believing that he is going to keep his promise as soon as he gets an opportunity) and goes out and murders some one then she also is guilty of murder She is just as much guilty of murder if she sets loose an assassin as if she fires an arrow at a distance which pierces somebody's heart But I do not think that is quite the case you have got to consider here At half-past five she leaves him, telling

Bywaters and Thompson.

Mr Justice Shearman

him where she is going, and that she is coming back with her husband in the evening. If you think it was no surprise to her when she saw him that evening, and if you think that when she saw him there that evening he came there under her direction, under her information that she would be there about that time and that he was waiting there for their arrival under her direction and information that she had given him as to where she would be about that time—if you think she knew perfectly well as soon as she set eyes on him he was there to murder she is guilty of the murder too, because he was doing it under her direction with the hand that she was guiding. If you think he had that knife in his pocket intending to murder— of course, this question only arises if you think he had that knife in his pocket intending to murder that man that evening—and if you think she knew that he had it, I think it necessarily follows she would know that he was going to do it that evening. That is what I submit to you. Therefore, I think the only case I am going to ask you to consider is this, was she a party already to the murder in that sense that she was aiding and abetting it? The words are pretty plain. "Aiding and abetting" means giving a help to the murderer, if it actually took place.

And here it is that what I may call the necessary absence of evidence makes these letters of so much importance. Of course, you will understand that if two people agree to murder anybody, they do not make that agreement when anybody is listening. If they agree to murder, the crime will not take place if there is anybody looking on, and therefore it follows that when it is committed—if you think it has been committed—there should be no witnesses present. It necessarily further follows that in every case of such a description you have to infer from what is called circumstantial evidence, and you cannot have anything else. It rarely happens by accident—except by a fortunate accident in the course of justice—that a murder is committed when anybody is there to see it, and you have to gather from the evidence—and the short case for the prosecution is this—it really is a short case that for months these people had been corresponding, and for months this lady—we are only considering her case —had been writing to this man, inciting him to murder. I will deal with the letters, and deal with her explanation later on. It was suggested that she was always writing to him, and when he came back, the moment he came back, there were these frequent clandestine meetings—I am not going to remind you of what I said about these meetings being clandestine meetings, it is for you to judge, but I have given you a view which you may or may not accept, but I repeat, and must repeat in regard to her explanation, that she had been frequently talking to him about separation or divorce. If you think these letters are genuine, they mean that she is involved in a continual practice of deceit, concealing the fact of her connection with Bywaters, and not reiterating it with requests for her husband to

Charge to the Jury.

Mr Justice Shearman

let her go. That is for you, and not for me. I must also repeat what I say about the surrounding circumstances. Probably you will think that it is the fact that if she ran away with Bywaters she thought she might lose her position, and, having lost her position, there was nothing to live upon. The only question is was that what they were talking about in these letters? It is clear that if Providence should have removed the husband by a heart attack then they could have married and they could have kept their positions and the way was clear. The prosecution say that that was of enormous weight and one of the things that they were from time to time discussing, and it is said that they discussed it backwards and forwards in their letters. I am just going to refer you to some of those letters in which they discussed it. If you think that it is certain that they discussed it when he came back, and talked of what they would do in the future, it is said those letters not only throw a light upon the motive of the man and upon the motive of the woman, but they also throw a light upon the intention of their actions on the particular day and particularly the intention of her actions.

Now, let us turn to the letters. Again I am sure you will not think that I am taking any side in this matter; if you think I am taking any side in this matter, as I said you know as well as I do you can disagree with me without giving offence to me or anybody else, it is entirely a matter for you. I am anxious not to take a side, but if you think any of my opinions jump out in anything that I say, you will be perfectly at liberty to disregard them, because it is for you to decide it, because you are much better judges than I am. I do not want you to think, if I go into portions of the letters, that I am asking you to disregard the explanation of the letters. You will consider them very carefully. You will not consider that I am giving all the arguments on one side or the other.

I am going to read you certain extracts from the letters. All his letters—the letters from him—only breathe this insensate silly affection; they do not seem to help us very much that way. We are not now considering his case, but all these letters are written by her, and therefore they are evidence against her. It is said by the prosecution that from beginning to end of these letters she is seriously considering and inciting the man to assist her to poison her husband, and if she did that, and if you find that within a week or two after he came back the poisoning is considered no longer possible, he has no longer studied or has not studied bichloride of mercury, but has read "Bella Donna" without seeing how 'Bella Donna" can be of any use to him, they would naturally turn to some other means of effecting their object, and it is said to you they naturally would, when you find them meeting day after day, parting at half-past five, meeting the husband at six, and she telling him where they were going and he immediately, as soon as he gets ar

Bywaters and Thompson.

Mr Justice Shearman

opportunity, if you believe he waited for them coming back, and knew they were there—gentlemen, you may say here are circumstances following the long-studied incitement for him to help her to poison. He walks with her to the station and parts with her half an hour before she meets her husband and she then goes off with her husband. He clearly was waiting for the 11 30 train to Ilford—that is not disputed. He is there looking for them, knowing when they are coming. The evidence, so far as it goes, as to what was said at the house is that they were out at the theatre, and no more. He knew what train they were coming down by, although it is probably the natural train for anybody going to the theatre and returning to Ilford, and it is suggested when you find that is followed by a meeting within five or six hours of their parting, and the man, if you believe it, assassinated—then you are entitled to assume that she sped him on his errand, that when she saw him at any rate she knew he was coming and knew what he was after, that she, as soon as it was done—it is said by the prosecution—steadily told lies and concealed the whole of the facts. It is on that you are asked to draw the conclusion that she was a party to the act of Bywaters in killing her husband at that time and place. You will not draw it unless you are satisfied, and if you are satisfied you will draw it, and there is the whole matter.

Now, let us look at the letters. I am sure you know them and you recollect the whole of them. In exhibit 62 you find this "Yesterday I met a woman who had lost three husbands in eleven years, and not through the war two were drowned and one committed suicide and some people I know cannot lose one How unfair everything is" And then she breaks off. In exhibit 27— I am not going to comment. I am only going to call your attention to the facts "I had the wrong porridge to-day but I don't suppose it will matter, I don't seem to care much either way. You'll probably say I am careless and I admit I am, but I don't care, do you I gave way this week to him" Of course, you know these letters, as was quite properly pointed out, are full of the outpourings of a silly but at the same time wicked affection. There are all sorts of things in the letters other than alluding to poison and many other things which I am not going to refer to but mostly cases of affection and love—or other matters that I have already commented on which I believe to be matters of that description. In the same letter (exhibit 27) there is 'You know darlint I am beginning to think I have gone wrong in the way I manage this affair. I think perhaps it would have been better had I acquiesced in everything he said and did or wanted to do. At least it would have disarmed any suspicion he might have and that would have been better if we have to use drastic measures darlint—understand? Anyway so much for him I'll talk about some one else" Is that talking about divorce or is that talking about drastic measures —measures for removing him?

Charge to the Jury.

Mr Justice Shearman

Then in exhibit 15 there is this incident about his taking too much of some medicine "Some one he knows in town (not the man I previously told you about) had given him a prescription for a draught for insomnia and he'd had it made up and taken it and it made him ill He certainly looked ill and his eyes were glassy I've hunted for the said prescription everywhere and can't find it and asked him what he had done with it and he said the chemist kept it" Of course it is suggested she wanted to get hold of the prescription "I told Avis about the incident only I told her" (look at these words)—"as if it frightened and worried me"—not that it had frightened her, but she pretended it to convey that, and you will have to consider in a good many of these things whether she was genuine or acting "I told Avis about the incident, only I told her as if it frightened and worried me as I thought perhaps it might be useful at some future time that I had told somebody" It is said she is already preparing for witnesses in case there should be a murder case, that is what is said Then "It would be so easy darlint—if I had things—I do hope I shall How about cigarettes?" Then the next is an extract "Death from hyoscine poisoning, but how it was administered there is no sufficient evidence to show" Then there is another extract "Ground glass in box" —I only allude to it because somebody else alluded to it

Exhibit 16—"However for that glorious state of existence I suppose we must wait for another three or four months Darlint, I am glad you succeeded, oh so glad I can't explain, when your note came I didn't know how to work at all—all I kept thinking of was your success—and my ultimate success I hope I suppose it isn't possible for you to send it to me—not at all possible" Now, it is suggested he had written to her, you know—at any rate she understood he had written to her saying, "I have got something that would poison him or make him ill" "I suppose it is impossible for you to send it to me" She in her answer, you will recollect says 'He was to send something to make him ill, and I never intended to do it, although I said that to him" He said in his answer it meant "letters" Then she continues "Darlingest boy, this thing that I am going to do for both of us will it ever—at all make any difference between us darlint, do you understand what I mean Will you ever think any the less of me,—not now, I know darlint—but later on—perhaps some years hence—do you think you will feel any different—because of this thing that I shall do" The meaning of that is for you to judge, you will fully understand it is not for me to tell you what the letters mean, you are the judges of that, not I, there is no law about it whatever It is said the meaning of that is, "If I poison him is it going to make any difference to you afterwards", that is what is suggested is the plain meaning of the words

Exhibit 20—"Why do you say to me 'never run away, face

Bywaters and Thompson.

Mr Justice Shearman

things and argue and beat everybody' Do I ever run away? Have I ever run away? and do you think I should be likely to now? That's twice this trip, something you have said has hurt You will have to kiss all that hurt away—'cos it does really hurt—it's not sham darlint I'm not going to talk to you any more—I can't and I don't think I have shirked have I? except darlint to ask you again to think out all the plans and methods for me and wait and wait so anxiously now—for the time when we'll be with each other—even tho' it's only once—for 'one little hour,'—our kind of hour, not the song kind And just to tell you Peidi loves you always" Then she is referring to a lot of books you will see in the list "I think the 'red hair' one is true in parts—you tell me which parts darlint The Kempton cutting may be interesting if it is to be the same method" Then, "Will you be ready with every little detail when I see you—because you know more about this thing than I, and I am relying on you for all plans and instructions—only just the act I am not Why not go to 231 darlint, I think you ought to go as usual, it would be suspicious later if you stopped away without a reason known to them, and there is not a reason is there? You have not fallen out with Bill have you? What about Dr Wallis's case,—you said it was interesting but you did not discuss it with me Darlint about making money—yes we must somehow, and what does it matter how,—when we have accomplished that one thing—we are going to live entirely for ourselves and not study any one except ourselves"

Exhibit 50—"This time really will be the last you will go away—like things are won't it? We said it before darlint I know and we failed—but there will be no failure this next time darlint, there mustn't be—I'm telling you—wherever it is—if it's to sea—I'm coming too, and if it's to nowhere—I'm also coming darlint You'll never leave me behind again, never, unless things are different" Now, it is said that the meaning of that is, "If we get married you can go on your voyage and leave me behind, but if he is still alive I am coming away with you"

Exhibit 17—"Don't keep this piece"—that is at the top—"About the marconigram,—do you mean one saying Yes or No, because I shan't send it darlint *I'm not going to try any more until you come back*" What does that mean? "I made up my mind about this last Thursday He was telling his mother &c, the circumstances of my 'Sunday morning escapade' and he puts great stress on the fact of the tea tasting bitter, 'as if something had been put in it' he says Now I think whatever else I try it in again will still taste bitter—he will recognise it and be more suspicious still and if the quantity is still not successful it will injure any chance I may have of trying when you come home" The date of that letter, if you look at it again, is April Bywaters says "At some time in March I gave her" something which he says

Charge to the Jury.

Mr Justice Shearman

was quinine, and she says she does not know what it was. It is suggested the plain meaning of that is she tried that and failed. He says whatever it was it was only quinine but she does not know what it was.

Exhibit 18—"I used the light bulb three times, but the third time he found a piece—so I have given it up—until you come home." Of course, you know her explanation is that this was merely—I don't know what word to call it—swank—to show what a heroic person she was, that she was prepared to do all sorts of things which she was not in fact doing, and his explanation was always to exculpate her, and to say she was a melodramatic being. You will give what weight you think to it. Whether she gave all she said she did, or whether she only gave some of what she said she did or gave nothing at all—his explanation was to exculpate her. Her explanation as given by the Solicitor-General this morning is that, "He did send things which I was to give to my husband to make him ill, but I did not do it," in other words she said "He was expecting me to, I was not inciting him." Gentlemen, in this case we are only judging her, her case. I am saying you may disregard her or you may think it true, but, of course, you will bear in mind that if that she is exculpating herself and saying the man is the wicked person. "He sent me these things, and I did not pay any attention to him. When I wrote to him he thought I was trying to poison my husband, because to give him something when he has a bad heart is to poison him and she says, 'I kept it up and never undeceived him.'"

Exhibit 19—"I don't think we are failures in other things and we mustn't be in this. We mustn't give up as we said. No, we shall have to wait if we fail again. Darlint, Fate cannot always turn against us and if it is we must fight it—you and I are strong now we must be stronger. We must learn to be patient. We must have each other darlint. It's meant to be I know I feel it is because I love you such a lot—such a love was not meant to be in vain. It will come right I know one day if not by our efforts some other way. We'll wait eh darlint and you'll try and get some money and then we can go away and not worry about anybody or anything. You said it was enough for an elephant," and he admits you know he did say either in letters or by words that 30 grains of quinine were enough for an elephant—why an elephant should want 30 grains of quinine I do not know, or whether his explanation is true, or what she was writing that she had not succeeded—"perhaps it was but you don't allow for the taste making only a small quantity to be taken. It sounded like a reproach, was it meant to be." Then further on, "I was buoyed up with the hope of the 'light bulb' and I used a lot—big pieces too—not powdered—and it has no effect—I quite expected to be able to send that cable—but no—nothing has happened from it."

Bywaters and Thompson.

Mr Justice Shearman

Now, what is the cable? She says the cable was a cable stating she was going to get a divorce. It is not for me to say anything to you, but it is suggested that the cable was his death. "And now your letter tells me about the bitter taste again. Oh darlint, I do feel so down and unhappy." Then she says, "Wouldn't the stuff make small pills coated together with soap and dipped in liquorice powder—like Beecham's. Try while you're away." It is said that is asking him there to produce some poison with which they could poison this man without being discovered. 'Our boy had to have his thumb operated on because he had a piece of glass in it that's what made me try that method again—but I suppose as you say he is not normal. I know I feel I shall never get him to take a sufficient quantity of anything bitter." Then she says "No I haven't forgotten the key I told you before." Then further on—"You tell me not to leave finger marks on the box—do you know I did not think of the box but I did think of the glass or cup whatever was used." She says it is true he did write to her and ask her not to put finger marks on the box. Why finger marks? It is suggested by the prosecution that if this man is poisoned, and there is a trial, finger marks would display on the box who has handled the poison. 'Do experiment with the pills while you are away."

Exhibit 22—"It must be remembered that digitalin is a cumulative poison, and that the same dose harmless if taken once, yet frequently repeated, becomes deadly." I should not think you should bother much about what is in the book called 'Bella Donna.' The only point about it is, it is the case of a woman—nobody suggested she was like this woman, or the man was like this man. It is the case admitted on oath by herself that there is at the end of the book somebody poisoning her husband, or trying to poison her husband. "It must be remembered that digitalin is a cumulative poison and that the dose harmless if taken once, yet frequently repeated, becomes deadly." And there is this remarkable statement—"The above passage I have just come across in a book I am reading, 'Bella Donna,' by Robert Hichens. Is it any use? I'd like you to read 'Bella Donna' first, you will learn something from it to help us, then you can read the 'Fruitful Vine'." No doubt the letter about the "Fruitful Vine" was something similar, they write chiefly about so-called heroes and heroines, probably wicked people, which no doubt accounts for a great many of these tragedies.

Exhibit 26—"Why aren't you sending me something—I wanted you to—you never do what I ask you darlint—you still have your own way always—If I don't mind the risk why should you?" After the rest comes this—"Have you studied bichloride of mercury?" In answer to my question we were told it is what is called a corrosive sublimate, a poison with which those who unfortunately have to come to these Courts have to deal with.

Charge to the Jury.

Mr Justice Shearman

Then we come to this last letter at the end of September exhibit 60. It is quite obvious that that bit refers to a meeting, and, of course, quite properly, the Solicitor-General asked a question which was fully answered, and much point was made of it. It is no point in the case now—' Do not forget what we talked of in the Tea Room, I will still risk and try if you will,' and it is said it is poison or it is the dagger. ' We have got many things to consider shall we run away if we can get the money, or shall we try poison? We will talk it over.''

I think there is one other letter which I might refer you to exhibit 64, although the date we do not know. "I know what you say is really true, but darlint it does feel sometimes that we are drifting. Don't you ever feel like that—and it hurts so—ever so much. Yes, we are both going to fight until we win—darlint fight hard, in real earnest—you are going to help me first and then I am going to help you and when you have done your share and I have done mine we shall have given to each other what we both desire most in this world ' ourselves, isn't this right, but darlint don't fail in your share of the bargain because I am helpless without your help—you understand.'' That is certainly earlier in the year some time before this took place but there it is.

I should be wanting in my duty if I did not plainly explain to you that the meaning of these letters is entirely for you and you have to ask yourselves do they form a very strong case, and is she asking him clearly for his assistance to remove and murder her husband by the administration of poison? With regard to some of the statements, if they are accurate, they show that she administered it but the important part of it is that they were plotting and planning, and you have heard her explanation, that she did it because it was to please him to show how devoted she was to him. His story was "I thought she advised me to do it suggested I should do it, but I thought it was all vapour—melodrama." You bear in mind the force of those explanations but it is a strong case for your consideration that on each of those voyages while he was away they are discussing the removal of her husband by poison, and it is said again and I do not like to repeat myself, that that throws light, not only on the motive of what he did but it throws light on their intentions and their actions in what happened.

The rest is short. You will consider in saying whether you are satisfied what was done before, they met frequently. They met, as you know and only parted at about half-past five that afternoon, and at half-past twelve that night Thompson is lying dead and killed by the dagger of somebody. You have seen the weapon, I call it a dagger it is a weapon that has to be seized with the fist—it is a stabbing weapon—you have seen it, and you have

Bywaters and Thompson.

Mr Justice Shearman

got it Where is it done? Is it by accident that he comes up to her? All we know about that is that they were talking about a dance, and she was next to the wall I am not dealing with his case, I have done with it It certainly is in a lonely road which is obviously the direct way home, but it is in a road with no houses on one side except the house of one of the witnesses to whom I am going to call attention, and the back of other houses, and you have the circumstances of the killing which I mentioned to you when I was dealing with the other case That is all we know It is suggested by the prosecution that the moment she saw him there she expected him, and they ask you to be satisfied, they ask you to believe, that she saw it done What evidence is there of that? She denies it Of course, there is no other evidence

There is one other very curious piece of evidence to which I want to call your attention, and that is the evidence of Mr Webber He says he heard a noise, and these are his words he heard those words—" Oh don't, oh don't ' in piteous tones You know he is some way off, I am not saying it is true, it is for you to say whether it is accurate, or whether it is imaginary, or whether he has made a mistake but there is the evidence The voice was Mrs Thompson's " It was three or five minutes before I came out, and then I heard the doctor ask had he been ill ' Now, of course, again it is for you to say if you believe that, what the words mean, ' Oh, don't, oh don't,' in piteous tones, and it is made use of by her counsel as showing that she objected to the murder and was saying " Don't " Well, a remark of force, but it is a double-edged weapon, this evidence if you think it is accurate because if you think it means that when she saw him being stabbed or saw one of the stabs, she said " Don't, don't," it means that she was looking on, and she saw it all The evidence is incompatible with the story that she was senseless and only recovered—you know her story, I need not go into that matter again—if she was pushed aside and damaged by a fall (and there is independent evidence she had a bruise) That does not prove how the bruise was given, but her story is that she knew nothing of it She saw some scuffling a little way down, and she saw the back of the man running away, knowing who he was Of course, if that is so, it is impossible that she could be saying " Don't, don't," and she saw the blows struck I think it is entirely for you— I will not argue that Of course you will bear in mind that, if you think that is true the fact that she was saying " Don't, don't " at the end of it, would not protect her if she had summoned the man there and was only horrified when she saw the deed, and that he had compassed it These are things that will appeal to you or anybody else, you will weigh them But if you believe them you are in this difficulty, that it makes you disbelieve at once the whole of her evidence that she did not see it, and indeed, if you think, knowing what these wounds are like and what happened, it is almost

Charge to the Jury.

Mr Justice Shearman

incredible that she should not have seen what happened. It is a remarkable story for you to believe, that the sudden push against the wall rendered her senseless and stupefied. That is the story.

It is always relevant to see what is done before and after the deed. It is said by the prosecution that it was arranged he should run away, and she should go to the doctor. It is said that their letters are suggesting they were arranging how to avoid suspicion when it was done, and the letters bear that out. Now were they, do they bear that out?

I am going to read to you the evidence of the witnesses, which prove what Mrs Thompson said after the act was done. All the witnesses say she was very agitated, some of the witnesses say she did not know what she was saying. The witness Doris Pittard is called, and she says this—' I saw the woman running, and she met me and said, ' Oh, my God, will you help me, my husband is ill, he is bleeding.' I asked when it happened, and she said, ' I cannot tell you, when I turned to speak to him blood was pouring out of his mouth.' " That is the account of Doris Pittard. Not a word of anything more. " He is ill." You have got to consider whether this was genuine, or acting a part of the prearranged plan, whether it was out of control. All the witnesses agree that she was in a state of great agitation. Give what weight you think to that. Percy Clevely says she said her husband had fallen down. In cross-examination of Doris Pittard she said Mrs Thompson was running hard, she wanted help for her husband. Percy Clevely said she said her husband had fallen down and wanted help, he was ill, " I want to find a doctor." " I asked her how it had happened. She said some thing brushed past and he fell down ", not a word about another man. She asked for help, and she ran on in front, and she was agitated. John Webber says this, I have read part of it, and I will read it again, because I want you to have the whole of it ' I heard these words, ' Oh, don't, don't,' in piteous tones,' and then I asked the distance off—and it was the corner house, the next corner of the road. " The voice was Mrs Thompson's." Dr Maudsley says I asked the woman whether the man had been ill, and she said no. I said, ' He is dead.' She said, ' Why didn't you come sooner and save him.' I said ' Has he been under any medical man?' She said ' No, he often complained, but did not have one.' " He said he did not see the wounds—in other words, if you think that she had seen the stabbing, she is leaving the doctor in ignorance and under the impression that her husband was ill.

Those are the only four strangers who saw her. The rest are police officers. The first is Walter Mew. He said, " I went with her to her home. On the way she said ' Will he come back?' I said, ' Yes.' She said, ' They will blame me for this.' " There is no cross-examination about her statement. Then there is Police Constable Walter Grimes. He said, " I asked her, ' Are you in the

Bywaters and Thompson.

Mr Justice Shearman

habit of carrying a knife?' She said, 'No.' She said, 'I cannot explain what happened, I do not know, I only know he dropped down and said, 'Oh!'—I mean groaned or made an exclamation of pain.'" Then the next person that same night, you know, or soon afterwards, is his brother, Richard Halliday Thompson. He said, "She was very agitated. I knew he was dead. I said, 'What has happened?' She said, 'He was walking along and he suddenly became queer and said, "Oo-er"'"—that is how they wrote it down. "She said he complained of pains in his leg on the way to the station. She said she went for a doctor, and the doctor said he died from hæmorrhage." I think that is the last. These are all the statements I think until we come to the statements she makes to the police.

Now, gentlemen, you will doubtless bear in mind this, that all the witnesses say she is agitated; it is perfectly clear that she is concealing the truth on her own showing, if she knew that the man was there. Everybody, the strangers, thought that he was ill, and she keeps them in that opinion—everybody she meets from the time she starts to the doctor to the time she comes back. There is a series of deceptions as to the real facts of the case, if she knew them. It is said by the prosecution you cannot call witnesses to show what they did and what they were planning beforehand; but you can show from beginning to end that the woman is telling what is not true. It is said on the other side she said that because she was wanting to shield the man. You will give what weight you think to it; there it is. Was she really out of her mind or had she sufficient sense to know, whether agitated or not—I can well imagine that—she was carefully concealing what had happened? It is not decisive, but you are entitled to weigh that as a fact with all the other circumstances of the case.

Now we come to the statements. The important evidence is that of Inspector Sellars, and this is the gist of his evidence. At 11 a.m. the next morning he said he told her who he was, and he said, "I understand you were with your husband early this morning in Belgrave Road; I am satisfied that he was assaulted and stabbed several times. She said, 'We were coming,'" &c. (reading statement of Mrs Thompson p 35). That is her statement. That is at 11 a.m. on the next day, and she is obviously concealing a great deal of what she knew. She is taken through a room, and she sees that they have arrested Bywaters, or, at any rate, that Bywaters is in the police station. As soon as she sees him at the window she said, "Oh God! oh, God! what can I do? Why did he do it? I did not want him to do it." Now there, again, look at these statements. I do not want to, and you must not, use that against Bywaters, it has nothing to do with him. But again it is noticeable that she is throwing the blame on him, "Why did he do it?" and she is excusing herself. Then she makes certain statements. Now these statements are reduced into writing, there are two of

Charge to the Jury.

Mr Justice Shearman

them   Before I come to them there is one other witness, Mrs Lester   Mrs Lester says that that morning the prisoner said to her, "They have taken him away from me   If they would allow me to go to him I could make him better"—quite incomprehensible, you know, and carrying out the fact of the notion that she did not know he was dead   Do you think that she did not know he was dead or what had happened?   At any rate, you have that, that is the statement she made   Then the first statement, the first long statement they took from her runs as follows —(reads statement)   Then she is obviously questioned, you know by this time they had got some of these letters before them   Then she sees Bywaters there, and she says what I have read to you—"My God, my God, what can I do!   Why did he do it?   I did not want him to do it," and then she makes another statement   She says, "I will tell you the truth", it does not necessarily follow that she tells you the truth when she says she is going to tell you the truth, and then she makes a second statement—'When we got near to Endsleigh Gardens a man rushed out from the gardens and knocked me away from my husband   I was dazed for a moment   When I recovered I saw my husband scuffling with a man   The man I know as Freddie Bywaters was running away   He was wearing a blue overcoat and a grey hat   I knew it was him, although I did not see his face"   Now, when they are both charged Bywaters says he is not guilty, and she says nothing

Gentlemen, that is really the whole of the case   I ask your earnest consideration of it   I am not going to say another word to you about the case of the man   only to repeat that if you find the man guilty of murder, then you have got to consider   was this woman an active party to it   did she direct him to go   did she know he was coming, and are you satisfied that she was implicated directly in it?   Her story is that she knew nothing about it, it was a surprise, in fact, she was pushed aside, and she immediately fainted   She did not see what was going on, when a man pushed her against the wall she did not look up to see what happened, she swooned away, and then at the end she sees Bywaters going away   You know exactly what was done before the act, you know the fact of all the letters, and you know what she did after, and you know that her evidence is now that she knew nothing about it   In the letters she was merely saying she was poisoning her husband in order to make an appearance before Bywaters   Her whole case is, she says she is quite innocent of this matter, and that she is shocked at everything that has happened and had nothing to do with it   You will not convict her unless you are satisfied that she and he agreed that this man should be murdered when he could be, and she knew he was going to do it, and directed him to do it and by arrangement between them he was doing it   If you are not satisfied of that you will acquit her   if you are satisfied of that it will be your duty to convict her   Will you please retire and consider your verdict

Bywaters and Thompson.

Is there anything you want, gentlemen?

The FOREMAN OF THE JURY—I think there is, my lord, the prisoner's overcoat you wished us to have as well as the knife

Mr JUSTICE SHEARMAN—Yes, you have the knife In that bundle you will find copies of the signed statements which they made (Bundle handed to jury)

Verdict

[The jury retired at 3 32, bailiffs being sworn to take them in charge, and returned into Court at 5 43]

The CLERK OF THE COURT—Members of the jury, have you agreed upon your verdict?

The FOREMAN OF THE JURY—We have

The CLERK OF THE COURT—Do you find the prisoner, Frederick Edward Francis Bywaters, guilty or not guilty of the murder of Percy Thompson?

The FOREMAN—Guilty, sir

The CLERK OF THE COURT—Do you find the prisoner, Edith Jessie Thompson, guilty or not guilty of the murder of Percy Thompson?

The FOREMAN—Guilty

The CLERK OF THE COURT—You say they are severally guilty, and that is the verdict of you all Frederick Bywaters and Edith Thompson, you severally stand convicted of murder, have you, or either of you, anything to say why the Court should not give you judgment of death according to law?

Prisoner BYWATERS—I say the verdict of the jury is wrong Edith Thompson is not guilty I am no murderer, I am not an assassin

Mr JUSTICE SHEARMAN—Is there any question of law, Sir Henry, as to the sentence I have to pronounce?

Prisoner THOMPSON—I am not guilty

Sir H CURTIS BENNETT—No, my lord

Sentence.

Mr JUSTICE SHEARMAN—Frederick Edward Francis Bywaters, the sentence of the Court upon you is that you be taken from this place to a lawful prison, &c

Formal sentence of death was then passed on Frederick Bywaters

Sentence.

Mr. Justice Shearman—Edith Jessie Thompson, the sentence of the Court upon you is that you be taken from this place to a lawful prison, &c.

Formal sentence of death was then passed on Edith Thompson.

The Clerk of the Court—Edith Jessie Thompson, have you anything to say in stay of execution?

Prisoner Thompson—I am not guilty, oh, God, I am not guilty!

The prisoners were then removed.

Mr. Justice Shearman—Gentlemen, I thank you for your patient attention to a long and difficult case.

APPENDICES

Edith Thompson

APPENDIX I

Letters from Edith Thompson and Frederick Bywaters put in Evidence at the Trial.

INDEX TO EXHIBITS

Exhibit	Date	Page
9	30th September, 1922,	213
10	No date,	215
12	20th August, 1921,	162
13	3rd January 1922,	168
14	1st December 1921,	216
15	10th February, 1922,	170
15a	9th February 1922,	171
15b	8th February, 1922,	172
15c	5th February, 1922,	172
15d	6th February 1922,	172
16	22nd February, 1922,	172
17	1st April, 1922,	179
18	24th April 1922,	184
19	1st May, 1922	186
20	14th March 1922,	174
20a	10th March, 1922,	178
21	15th May, 1922,	189
21a	13th May 1922,	191
22	18th May, 1922,	191
22a	10th May 1922,	195
22b	6th May 1922	195
23	23rd May, 1922,	196
24	13th June 1922,	199
25	20th June, 1922,	202
26	4th July 1922,	205
27	No date,	166
28	19th September, 1922,	210
30	No date,	217
31	No date,	217
47 and 48	22nd September 1922,	213
49	11th August, 1922,	161
50	No date,	178
51	No date	195
52	14th July, 1922,	207
53	14th June 1922,	200
54	12th September, 1922,	209
55	No date,	212
55a	20th September, 1922,	213
58 and 59	25th September, 1922,	213
60	No date,	214
62	No date,	162
63	28th August 1922,	208
64	No date,	216
66	6th June, 1922,	198
67	7th June 1922,	198
68	9th June, 1922,	198
69	26th June, 1922,	205

Exhibit 49

August, 11th, 1921

Darlingest,—Will you please take these letters back now? I have nowhere to keep them, except a small cash box, I have just bought and I want that for *my own letters only* and I feel scared to death in case anybody else should read them   All the wishes I can possibly send for the very best of luck to day,

From PEIDI

Bywaters and Thompson.

Exhibit 12

Envelope—Mr F Bywaters, 11 Westow Street, Upper Norwood

[Postmark—Ilford 8 15, 20 Aug, 21]

Come and see me Monday lunch time please darlint He suspects
PEIDI

Exhibit 62

Envelope—Pour Vous

Darlint —Its Friday today—that loose end sort of day (without you) preceding the inevitable week end I dont know what to do—to just stop thinking, thinking very very sad thoughts darlint, they will come, I try to stifle them, but its no use

Last night I lay awake all night—thinking of you and of everything connected with you and me

Darlint I think you got into Marseilles last night did you? anyway I felt you did—perhaps you got my first letter, the other one you will get today

All I could think about last night was that compact we made Shall we have to carry it thro'? dont let us darlint Id like to live and be happy —not for a little while but for all the while you still love me Death seemed horrible last night -when you think about it darlint, it does seem a horrible thing to die, when you have never been happy really happy for one little minute

I'll be feeling awfully miserable tonight darlint I know you will be too, because you've only been gone one week out of 8 and even after 7 more have gone—I cant look forward can you? Will you ever be able to teach me to swim and play tennis and everything else we thought of, on the sands in Cornwall? you remember that wonderful holiday we were going to have in 22 and that little flat in Chelsea that you were coming home to every time and that 'Tumble down nook' you were going to buy for me, one day They all seem myths now

Last night I booked seats for the Hippodrome—the show was good—not a variety, but a sort of pierrot entertainment and 2 men opened the show with singing " Feather your nest " I wished we could just you and I—but we will yes, somehow we must I enjoyed the show immensely—you understand me don't you darlint I was dancing the hours, I was forgetting, but by myself in bed I was remembering

Altho its Friday Im not going anywhere I havn't been asked Darlint

Yesterday I met a woman who had lost 3 husbands in eleven years and not thro the war, 2 were drowned and one committed suicide and some people I know cant lose one How unfair everything is Bess and Reg are coming to dinner Sunday

Today is the Derby Cup and I have some money on 'Front Line' I dont suppose it will win, Im never lucky not in anything darlint, except in knowing you

I dont think Ill be able to buy that watch for you by Xmas, darlint, Id like to ever so much, but as things are, Im afraid I cant afford to,

Appendix I.

but the will and the wish to give is there and I know youll like that just as well

A man on the stage said this last night " Marriage is the inclination of a crazy man to board a lazy woman, for the rest of his natural life " Rather cutting I think, but there it came from a man

Au revoir darlint, until Monday, I'll write some more then and hope I'll be able to talk with you as well

---

Altho' I said Au revoir until Monday Darlint its only Saturday now We are opening Sats always now I don't like it a bit because Im thinking of that Sat about the 14th when you will be home but perhaps I'll manage to get that one off He s grumbling fearfully about it—' No home comfort whatever, you'll have to stop at home,' no other man's wife wants to gad the town every day ' They all find enough interest in their home ' Its his Saty off today

When I looked at you to say ' good morning " an irresistable feeling overcame me, to put my fingers thro your hair and I couldnt I love doing that darlint, it feels so lovely—you don t mind do you? most men dont like it, in fact they hate it, usually but I know youre different from most men When I got to 231 last night only Avis was in Mother and Dad had gone to Highbury to see Grandma, I believe she is sinking fast Avis said at the class Mel mentioned he had seen me " with a friend of yours " he said to Avis, but when Avis was telling me this she said " I asked him who it was and he wouldn't tell me " She didnt actually ask me to tell her, so of course I didnt mention you, but she knows I am sure

On the Friday you left, Mel rang me twice and both times I was out, he hasnt rung again

Yesterday I lunched opposite a Major and his typist Id love you to have been there The conversation consisted of " How extraordinary,' " really " and giggles She did manage to say—rather loudly too " I do wish I d come into my money soon, Im tired of being poor " I'm sure they would have amused you it reminded me of what you said Molly's stock of conversation consisted of

People tell me I have got fatter in the face this last fortnight, darlint do you put on flesh when your heart is aching I suppose you must if I am fatter because my heart aches such a lot When I lay awake at nights and think the small ray of hope seems so frail, so futile that I can hardly make myself keep it alive Its 12 noon now and I am going to get ready to go—no not home but to 41 to get dinner ready first and then do shopping and clean the bedroom and dust the other room and do God knows how many more jobs but I suppose they will all help to pass the time away If I could only go to sleep tonight and wake up tomorrow and find it was the 7 1 22 But I cant I know nothing ever comes right in this world, not right as we want it to be Its an awful sort of state to get into, this morbid feeling and I hope I shant give it to you darlint when youre reading this Perhaps I ought not to write at all when I feel like this, perhaps I'll feel better on Monday, anyway I'll put this away until then

---

I've had a funny sort of week end darlint I want to tell you all about it and I dont know how I am staying in this lunch time, especially

Bywaters and Thompson.

to write to you First of all on Sat at tea, we had words over getting a maid He wants one, but wont have Ethel 'because my people wont like it' he said I was fearfully strung up and feeling very morbid so you may guess this didnt improve things However at night in bed the subject—or the object the usual one came up and I resisted, because I didnt want him to touch me for a month from Nov 3rd do you understand me darlint? He asked me why I wasnt happy now—what caused the unhappiness and I said I didnt feel unhappy—just indifferent, and he said I used to feel happy once Well, I suppose I did, I suppose even I would have called it happiness, because I was content to let things just jog along, and not think, but that was before I knew what real happiness could be like, before I loved you darlint Of course I did not tell him that but I did tell him I didnt love him and he seemed astounded He wants me to forgive and forget anything he has said or done in the past and start fresh and try and be happy again and want just him He wants me to try as well and so that when another year has passed meaning the year that ends on January 15/1922, we shall be just as happy and contented as we were on that day 7 years ago These are his words I am quoting I told him I didnt love him but that I would do my share to try and make him happy and contented It was an easy way out of a lot of things to promise this darlint I hope you can understand I was feeling awful—I could have so easily died and I still feel awful today, how I wish you were here,—I think only you can make me hope on a little longer I got 2 letters in separate envelopes and 2 letters in 1 long envelope—today darlint, but I didnt like the L on the long envelope, even to curb other people's curiosity dont put that again darlint It was lovely to be able to talk to you I didnt feel any happier after doing so, but darlint you and I wont ever feel really happy until we have each other do you think?

The first page of your first letter amused me immensely I can imagine the bugler—also the condition of the other boys

I think I did tell you darlint I had 1 letter from Tilbury on Friday night and 1 long envelope from Tilbury Sat morning and 1 letter from Dover Monday morning

Darlint I dont like you to say and think those hard things about yourself and I certainly dont like that sentence of yours 'I've run away and left you' Dont please think them or about them Truly darlint, I dont, I know whatever you say—that its Fate—its no more your fault than it is mine that things are still as they are, in fact perhaps I really know, deep down in my heart, that it is more mine, but I try to stifle those thoughts, I only keep them locked up in my heart and I say to myself 'He wont even let it be my Fault this next time' Am I right darlint? its the only thought that makes me want to live on Darlint, you say do I remember? that Monday Oct 31 I'll never never forget it, I felt—oh I dont know how, just that I didnt really know what I was doing, it seemed so grand to see you again, so grand to just feel you hold my shoulders, while you kissed me so grand to hear you say just 3 ordinary commonplace words "How are you" Yes I did feel happy then

I am glad you liked "Maria" I thought it was lovely and yet I didnt expect you to agree with me about the ending I am glad you do darlint That's just what I thought it was a real live book, so sad tho'—I suppose thats what made it real—I'll never forget how I felt when reading it and I cried—oh such a lot Perhaps you do know how she felt darlint, I'm not sure, you know a man never feels like a woman about anything, but

Appendix I.

perhaps you know a little how she felt, because youre different yourself, anyway I know and I could feel for her

Darlint 3 years, 6½ years, no I m not going to imagine, Im just not going to,—3 months from now is absolutely the longest I am even going to try and imagine Im not going to look any farther forward and youre not either yet

I'm sorry you asked me about a photograph, really sorry, because I never make a good one, darlint, not even a natural one, when I pose, and I dont know that I will have one taken, even to please you—darlint you said " Yes," I didnt and why did you answer your own question for me— because you knew I would say ' No ' However I ll think about it You know Im really a coward Im afraid you wont like it—or perhaps see things in it you wont like You remember what you told me you thought of and felt about a photograph you had sent you on the ' Orvieto ' Thats why Im afraid

I will do as you say about when I want you, I ll even bruise myself, as you used and then take myself to Court for cruelty to myself, eh darlint?

I've thought about the hair torture and Im feeling quite prepared to undergo it now I dont vouch for how I shall feel when the time comes, so be prepared for a stand up fight—it'll be rather fun

I did laugh about the enclosed greeting card and Im sorry Im going to have another one of them even to show other people I dont think I like it connected with you but darlint I know its only the outside shell and its not the wish the real wish I shall get for myself—for only me to see

About books I have already sent out and obtained the ' Trail of 98 and am going to start it perhaps tonight no not tonight I think because Avis just phoned me and asked to go and see Grandma as Im the only one she has not seen and she keeps asking for me I suppose I shall have to go—altho I dont like it much, I'd far rather remember her as I saw her in the Summer They say she looks terrible now

I think the Guarded Flame is difficult to read and I dont know whether you will like it—W B Maxwell writes very strange books—some are very sensual—but in a learned kind of way I cant explain any better than that

Why dont you want your mother to ring me darlint? I should like to know about that seal on my letters darlint? break it if you want to, if you dont—well dont, but I am sorry you dont remember things I ask you about, things I want you to talk to me about Youll have to cultivate a better memory for some future date darlint, I shant be so lenient then I shant mind a bit darlint about the typed envelope as long as its not addressed as the one I received today was Yes, I think I do feel a bit no not cross—but what shall I call it—disappointed about the lady and the mail bag For a start I dont like the expression about the coffee and milk coming from you to me—from you to anyone else—perhaps yes and after all is she any worse for being a native—perhaps she is and perhaps she is not—anyway I dont know and I dont think you do and then you say ' If it had been one of the male sex ' Why ' it ' darlint, I thought you were beginning to think just a little more of us than you used

Thank you for giving me something at some future date, when both you and I are ready

I'm glad you told me you wouldn't worry about me darlint, Yes of course I will tell you everything, when the time comes but you wont worry about it, will you darlint, whatever it is, because I dont and wont

165

Bywaters and Thompson.

In that last note of yours you said 'you had been pushed to blazes for the last 3 hours' Do you know Darlint I can just hear you saying that, yes hear you really—its so like you

Yes, darlint, I shall say it and I mean it—you've not to feel like it, I wont have it, (I've stamped my foot here) so just forget and obey

PEIDI

Exhibit 27

[COPY]

Envelope—Unaddressed

Have told you before I put 10/- eh way on 'Welsh Woman' for the M'chester Cup, just because you liked it I expect you know the result The favourite won and it (the favourite) was the only horse I really fancied but as it was only 5 to 2 starting price, I didn't think it was worth the risk and then the dashed thing won

Darlint, its a good job you are winning some money at cards, for I can't win any at horses

I have won 14/9 on one race since you have been gone, I've forgotten which one it was

I've enclosed you several cuttings, please read them darlint, and tell me what you think of them The one I've marked with a cross I think very true indeed, but I'd like to know what you think about it

The part about 'a man to lean on' is especially true Darlint it was that about you that first made me think of you, in the way I do now I feel always that were I in any difficulty, I could rely and lean on you I like to feel that I have you to lean on, of course I dont want to really but its nice to know I can, if I want to Do you understand Note the part, 'always think of her first, always be patient and kind always help her in every way he can, he will have gone a long way to making her love him '

Such things as wiping up, getting pins for me etc all counted, darlint Do you remember the pin incident, on Aug 1, darlint and the subsequent remark from him ' You like to have someone always tacked on to you to run all your little errands and obey all your little requests ' That was it, darlint, that counted, obeying little requests—such as getting a pin, it was a novelty—he'd never done that

' It is the man who has no right who generally comforts the woman who has wrongs ' This is also right darlint isnt it? as things are, but darlint, its not always going to be is it? You will have the right soon wont you? Say Yes

The 'husband and dance partners' article also amused me, especially as things are I think I told you about him wanting to learn

Last Tuesday when Avis came across he asked her to teach him and she is coming across next Tuesday to give him his first lesson He wanted me to teach him, but I said I hadnt the patience, my days of dragging round beginners were over Of course this conversation led to us discussing dancing rather a lot and we talked about the nonstop We were talking of going as a set with our own partners and Avis detailed them all until she came to me and hesitated so I filled in the gap by saying ' Bill,' I felt

Appendix I.

like telling him who it really was and perhaps had Avis not been there I should have done but I didnt want to endure any more scenes especially in front of her You will find the photos with this letter, I havent looked at them and I hope they are so rotten you'll send them all back Is it horrid of me to feel like this? I suppose it is, but darlint I want bucking up today Ive made a bruise on each side of my left wrist, with my right thumb and finger but it doesnt do any good, it doesnt feel like you

We went to Stamford Hill to dinner on Sunday and had a very good time, and were given an invitation to dinner on *January 7th* to Highbury We accepted but all the time I was wishing and hoping (probably against hope) that circumstances would not allow me to go, do you understand? but I suppose I shall go

The last 2 Fridays I have been to the Waldorf and on the first occasion it was very foggy—all the trains were late, so had a taxi right to the avenue and got to Mother's at 10 20 He wasnt coming for me so I didnt matter much—but I expect they wonder what I do I have promised to go to the 'Cafe Marguerite' to dinner tonight Can you guess with whom? God knows why I said Id go I dont want to a bit especially with him, but it will help to pass some time away, it goes slowly enough in all conscience—I dont seem to care who spends the money, as long as it helps me to dance through the hours I had the wrong Porridge today but I dont suppose it will matter I dont seem to care much either way You ll probably say I'm careless and I admit I am, but I dont care—do you? I gave way this week (to him I mean) its the first time since you have been gone Why do I tell you this? I dont really know myself I didnt when you were away before, but it seems different this time, then I was looking forward—but now well I can only go from day to day and week to week until Jan 7th—then thoughts and all things stop How have you got on with 'The Guarded Flame' I expect by now you have it interesting—— I have persevered with 'Felix' and have nearly finished it Its weird—horrible and filthy—yet I am very interested You ll have to read it after I have finished I believe if I read this letter through before I sealed it you'd not receive it darlint I feel that Id tear it up it doesn't seem to me that Ive been talking to you at all—just writing to you but I feel like that today, and I know its rotten because you get this letter for Xmas and it wont be a very nice present will it darlint but its the best I can do Perhaps I'll leave this letter open and see how I feel by Wednesday the last day for posting it

———

Darlint, Monday—I recd greetings from you and a note 'I cant write to you' and Ive been expecting to talk to you for a long time I wanted to I wanted you to cheer me up—I feel awful—but I know darlint if you cant well you cant—that's all to be said about it, but I always feel I cant talk to you when I start but I just say to myself he s here with me, looking at me and listening to what I am saying and it seems to help darlint, couldnt you try and do this, I feel awfully sad and lonely and think how much you would be cheering me up but perhaps you'll think I'm selfish about it all and I suppose I am, but remember when you are thinking badly or hardly of me your letters are the only thing I have in the world and darlint, I havnt even all those

We had—was it a row—anyway a very heated argument again last night (Sunday) It started through the usual source, I resisted—and he

Bywaters and Thompson.

wanted to know why since you went in August I was different—'had I transferred my affections from him to you' Darlint its a great temptation to say 'Yes' but I did not He said we were cunning, the pair of us and lots of other things that I forget, also that I told lies about not knowing you were coming on that Sat He said Has he written to you since he has been away,' and when I said 'No' he said 'That's another lie' Of course he cant know for certain, but he surmises you do and Im afraid he'll ring up and ask them to stop anything that comes for me so I must get Jim on my side You know darlint I am beginning to think I have gone wrong in the way I manage this affair I think perhaps it would have been better had I acquiesced in everything he said and did or wanted to do At least it would have disarmed any suspicion he might have and that would have been better if we have to use drastic measures darlint—understand? Anyway so much for him Ill talk about someone else Have you guessed with whom I went to the Cafe Marguerite? If not you will by the following 'Isnt your sister jealous of you'

Me—My sister—why should she be?

He—It seems to me you see more of her fiance than she does herself

Me—Hows that and what do you know about it anyway

He—Well I saw you going down Ilford Hill the other evening and he was holding your arm—did you go to a dance together

Me—Oh shut up and talk about something else

But darlint he wouldn't he kept on coming back to you and I'd gone there to forget and instead of forgetting I was remembering all the time

I went to lunch with Mr Birnage today At the next table 2 girls were discussing *Flemings* Oh a jolly fine place I think Good food, a nice band, and plenty to drink The *other one*——Yes I like the place very much but my boy wouldnt be seen inside it It reminded me of you with a glass of bass was it? and Avis with a glass of water

Goodbye for now darlint, I'll try and be more cheerful when I write to Marseilles You say 'Dont worry'—just dance—If I only could

PEIDI

Exhibit 13

Envelope—Mr F Bywaters, P O R M S "Morea," Plymouth

[Postmark—London, 3 Jan 22]

Darlint, I've felt the beastliest most selfish little wretch that is alive Here have I been slating you all this trip for not talking to me and I get all those letters from Marseilles darlint, I love them and don't take any notice of me, I know I am selfish—and you ought to know by now, I told you haven't I? heaps of times Now what have I got to talk to you about, heaps of things I believe—but the most important thing is, that I love you and am feeling so happy that you are coming back to England, even tho perhaps I am not going to see you—you know best about that darlint, and I am going to leave everything to you—only I would like to help you, can't I Of course he knows you are due in on the 7th and will be very suspicious of me from then, so I suppose I won't be able to see you—will I? You know darlint, don't have the slightest worrying thoughts about letters as " to be careful I've been cruel " to myself I mean

Appendix I.

Immediately I have received a second letter, I have destroyed the first and when I got the third I destroyed the second and so on, now the only one I have is the " Dear Edie " one written to 41, which I am going to keep It may be useful, who knows? By the way I had a New Year's card, addressed to me only from " Osborne House, Shanklin "

About the 15th darlint, which will be the 14th as that is the Sat I am going—*as far as I know*, I have to book the seats this week

Darlint, I've surrendered to him unconditionally now—do you understand me? I think it the best way to disarm any suspicion, in fact he has several times asked me if I am happy now and I've said " Yes quite " but you know that's not the truth, dont you

About the photos darlint, I have not seen them, so I don't understand about " waiting for you " please destroy all you don't want and when you come to England, show me what I look like, will you yes, I was glad you promised for me, darlint, as I most certainly should have refused myself and I should have hated myself for refusing all the time Darlint, I never want to refuse you anything, its lovely for me to feel like that about you, I think by this you can understand how much I love you

The French phrase darlint if I can remember rightly was " I cant wait so long, I want time to go faster "

You used iron and I used my heel and its such a long time ago, or seems so since I asked a question to which your " I did that " is the answer, that, I have forgotten what my question was * Yes, darlint I did wonder about you and the " Cale " and was nursing all to myself quite an aggrieved feeling against you for not telling me, but your letter explained I feel glad you didn't transfer, darlint Ive got no special reason for feeling glad—but I am About the fortune teller—you have never mentioned " March " before darlint, you've said " Early in the New Year," are you gradually sliding up the year to keep my spirits up? darlint, I hope not I'd sooner be sad for ever and know the truth than have that expectant feeling of buoyancy for a myth

Darlint Ill do and say *all* and everything you tell me to, about friend, only remember not to do anything that will leave me behind by myself

About the Stewardess, Im glad you went to the cabin with her what is it I feel and think about you? I have *someone* to lean on—if I need anyone and she had too darlint, had'nt she? someone to lean on and help her, even against her own inclinations

I know I am right? Darlint, I didnt think it fair about the fight altho most people are disgusted with boxing (women I mean) I always tried to look upon it as something strong and big and when you told me about that I thought If amateurs even do that sort of thing, then professionals must and I felt disappointed

Thanking you for those greetings darlint, but you wont always be " The man with no right " will you—tell me you wont—shout at me—make me hear and believe darlint about that " Do you " I believe I felt about the worst I have ever felt when that happened I think when I noticed what I had done I had a conscience prick and felt " I dont care what happens and I dont suppose he does really " but you would care wouldnt you darlint? tell me yes, if I really thought you wouldnt darlint I shouldnt want to die, I just want to go mad

---

* I have no explanation to offer of this sentence —Fd

Bywaters and Thompson.

Why have you never told me what you thought of your own photos darlint, you are a bad bad correspondent really darlint I absolutely refuse to talk to you at all next trip if you dont mend your ways Darlint, are you frightened at this—just laugh at me

I think you misunderstand me when you think I thought you were cross with me for going out No, darlint, I didnt think you were cross for that, but cross because something happened or might have happened to me, that would happen to any girl who took the risks I take sometimes

Yes, I enjoyed John Chilcote ever so much, I admire the force in the man that made him tackle such a position against such odds

The man Lacosta in the "Trail of 98" I didnt give a thought to, he was so vile I didnt think of him at all, and Id rather not now darlint

I am reading a book that I think you will like darlint 'The Common Law" by R W Chambers We were at 231 for the coming of the New Year darlint—I wondered if you were wondering the same as I What will the New Year give to two halves—to you and I Last night 231 all came over to me and did not go until gone 1 and then I had the clearing up to do and consequently am feeling a bit tired today

If I only had you here to put my head on your shoulder and just sleep and dream and forget Darlint come to me soon, I want you so badly— more and more

Your cable has just come in, thank you darlint and I think you might get to Plymouth earlier than expected, so am wishing this off

Goodbye and good luck darlint from

PEIDI

I feel quite big, being a member of the Morea darlint

Exhibit 15

Envelope—Mr F Bywaters, P & O R M S ' Morea," Aden

[Postmark—London, 10th Feb 22, 2 30 p m]

Darlint——You must do something this time——I'm not really impatient——but opportunities come and go by——they have to——because I'm helpless and I think and think and think——perhaps——it will never come again

I want to tell you about this On Wednesday we had words——in bed ——Oh you know darlint——over that same old subject and he said——it was all through you I'd altered

I told him if he ever again blamed you to me for any difference there might be in me, I'd leave the house that minute and this is not an idle threat

He said lots of other things and I bit my lip——so that I shouldn't answer——eventually went to sleep About 2 a m he woke me up and asked for water as he felt ill I got it for him and asked him what the matter was and this is what he told me——whether its the truth I dont know or whether he did it to frighten me, anyway it didnt He said—— someone he knows in town (not the man I previously told you about) had given him a prescription for a draught for insomnia and he'd had it made up and taken it and it made him ill He certainly looked ill and his eyes

Appendix I.

were glassy I've hunted for the said prescription everywhere and cant find it and asked him what he had done with it and he said the chemist kept it

I told Avis about the incident only I told her as if it frightened and worried me as I thought perhaps it might be useful at some future time that I had told somebody

What do you think, darlint His sister Maggie came in last night and *he told her*, so now there are two witnesses, altho' I wish *he* hadn t told her——but left me to do it

It would be so easy darlint——if I had things——I do hope I shall

How about cigarettes?

Have enclosed cuttings of Dr Wallis s case It might prove interesting darlint, I want to have you only I love you so much try and help me PEIDI

Exhibit 15a

Extract from *Daily Sketch*, 9th February, 1922, page 2, column 1

With headnote —

"Curate's Household of Three
"Mystery of his Death still unsolved
"Wife and Doctor
"Woman asked to leave the Court during man's evidence"

"Death from hyoscine poisoning, but how it was administered there is not sufficient evidence to show"

This was the verdict last night at an inquest at Lingfield after remarkable evidence and searching cross examination

The three principal figures in the case are—

The Rev Horace George Bolding (39), curate of Lingfield (Surrey) Parish Church, found dead on his bed in his dressing gown on January 4 Described by parishioners as "Happy, jovial, one of the best of good fellows, and a regular sport"

Mrs Bolding, about 35, the widow, who was in London with the only child, a boy, at the time of her husband's death

Dr Preston Wallis, a ship's surgeon, who, separated from his wife, had stayed some time with the Boldings, and who was called to the bedroom and found the curate dead

On page 15, column 3, the report is concluded with the following headnote —

"Helping the Doctor
"Why Curate's wife often went about in his Chair
"Practice that dwindled"

Bywaters and Thompson.

Exhibit 15b

Extract from *Daily Sketch*, 8th February, 1922, page 2, column 1

With headnote—

"Poisoned Curate
"Resumed Inquest to day following Analyst's Investigation"

Then follows a short paragraph referring to the inquest on Mr Bolding to be held on the 8th February, and referred to in Exhibit 15a

---

Exhibit 15c

Extract from *Sunday Pictorial*, 5th February, 1922, page 2, column 1

With headnote—

"Poison Chocolates for University Chief
"Deadly Powder posted to Oxford Chancellor
"Ground Glass in Box
"Scotland Yard called in to probe 'Serious Outrage'"

Then follows a paragraph dealing with chocolates sent anonymously to Dr Farnell, the Vice Chancellor of Oxford University, which were examined by an analyst resulting in the discovery that some of the sweets had been bored underneath and filled with ground glass and what is believed to be an insidious form of Indian poison

---

Exhibit 15d

Extract from *The Daily Mirror*, 6th February, 1922, page 3, column 4

With headnote—

"University Mystery of Poisoned Sweets
"Oxford Vice Chancellor on Deadly Gift
"Postmark Clue
"Powder containing Indian Drug in Police hands"

Here follow some details which refer to the same matter as is reported on Exhibit 15c

---

Exhibit 16

Envelope—Mr F Bywaters, P & O R M S "Morea," Port Said

[Postmark—London, February 22, 1922, 5 p m]

Darlint, I've been beastly ill again this week—only with a cold tho, but it was a pretty rotten one, pains all over me I caught it from him, I asked

Appendix I.

him when he had his if he would sleep in the little room and he said " No, you never catch my colds, I always catch yours " so we remained is we were and I caught it badly

Darlint in a hundred years you'd never guess what happened on Sunday —I'll tell you, but you mustn't laugh I was given my breakfast in bed, I think he was feeling sorry about not sleeping alone when I asked him, so did that

Darlingest boy, it is four whole weeks today since you went and there is still another four more to go—I wish I could go to sleep for all that time and wake up just in time to dress and sit by the fire —waiting for you to come in on March 18, I dont think Id come to meet you darlint it always seems so ordinary and casual for me to see you after such a long time—in the street, I shall always want you to come straight to our home and take me in both your arms and hold me for hours—and you can't do that in the street or a station can you darlint I think Bill is leaving Bombay today I wonder if you have played any matches and I wonder and want to know so much who has won

Darlint, did anything happen in Bombay—or did any kind of conversation happen whatever referring to me at all I felt terribly lonely all this week, darlint—a kind of " dont care, cant bother to fight " sort of a feeling

Im just waiting for a gorgeous long letter from you when will it come, I suppose not for a long time yet, I do so want you to talk to me today, I keep on looking at you to make you talk, but no words & not even thoughts will come

I am looking now darlint, hard at you and I can hear you say " dont worry Chere " to Peidi

Darlint, pleased, happy, hopeful and yet sorry—thats how I feel, can you understand? Sorry that Ive got to remain inactive for more than another whole month, and I had thought by that time I should be seeing you for just as long and every time you wanted me However, for that glorious state of existence I suppose we must wait for another three or four months Darlint, I am glad you succeeded Oh so glad I cant explain, when your note came I didn't know how to work at all—all I kept thinking of was your success—and my ultimate success I hope

I suppose it isnt possible for you to send it to me—not at all possible, I do so chafe at wasting time darlint He had a cold last week and didnt go in, but came up to meet me about 5 Of course I didnt know he was coming and it was funny—our Monkey was on my desk—which must have been and Im confident was noticed

Miss Prior told him we had not worked after 5 since last year and he mentioned this to me—as much as to say " How do you account for saying you worked late some weeks ago " I didnt offer any explanations

On the evening that I told you we had words—about you—he asked me for your address which I gave him and which he wrote in his note book, he also asked me what had happened to the Xmas greeting letter you sent and when I said I kept it he said " Why, you never do keep letters from people " so I answered " I kept it for bravado, I knew youd miss it and know I had kept it and one of these days ask me for it "

He also said " Have you anything whatever belonging to him—anything mind you " (I knew he meant our monkey) " I have nothing whatever belonging to him " I said—darlint it wasn't a lie was it, because the

Bywaters and Thompson.

monkey belongs to *us* doesn't it and not to you or to me, and if it was a lie I dont care, I'd tell heaps and heaps and heaps to help you even tho I know you don't like them

Darlint that reminds me you said in one of your letters "It was a lie and Peidi I hate them," about something I had or had not told you and I forget which, but I am sure I told it to help us both

That hurt ever such a lot when I read it darlint, it hurts so much that I couldn't talk to you about it at the time

Darlint, do you think I like telling them, do you think I don't hate it, darlint I do hate this life I lead—hate the lies hate everything and I tell so many thats what hurts—it hits home so hard—if only I could make an absolutely clean—fresh start—it would all be so different—Id be so different too darlint and we're going to start a new fresh clean life together soon darlint arent we tell me we are tell me you are confident—positive we are, I want telling all the time—to make me hope on

Darlingest boy this thing that I am going to do for both of us will it ever—at all, make any difference between us, darlint do you understand what I mean Will you ever think any the less of me—not now, I know darlint—but later on—perhaps some years hence—do you think you will feel any different—because of this thing that I shall do

Darlint—if I thought you would Id not do it, no not even so that we could be happy for one day even one hour, Im not hesitating darlint—through fear of any consequences of the action dont think that but I'd sooner go on in the old way for years and years and years and retain your love and respect I would like you to write to me darlint and talk to me about this

---

Exhibit 20

Envelope—Mr F Bywaters P & O R M S "Morea," Plymouth

[Postmark—London, E C , 14 Mar 1922]

Don't you think this is funny darlint? Mr Lester the old man, is failing fast and hardly knows anyone now

He doesn't know me Avis was over to tea the other day, and was toasting some Sally Luns in front of their fire, and he said to her—"I don't know who the lady of this house is but she is a beautiful woman, and such a good woman to her husband' I don't know whether I feel honoured or otherwise

He is moving to new offices in Eastcheap next week, and henceforward will use Fenchurch Street Station More bad luck darlint we never seem to have any good, do we? I've got 10/ each way on a horse to day, it's supposed to be a cert but I don't expect it will win because I've backed it Before I forget—can you let me know about what time you will arrive in London on 18th We are going to a party at Mrs Birnages on that day, and if you were in early I might squeeze an hour to be with you

On Sunday the 19th we and Avis are going to Stamford Hill to dinner —we shall arrive at L'pool St at 12 22 and catch the 10 37 or 11 7 p m back from Liverpool St at night Darlingest boy, when you do get to London—if I don't see you until you want to see me—you won't do as you did before, will you? please, pour moi We'll want all the spare money you

Appendix I.

have to "celebrate" at least I'm hoping we will You're not going to do anything this time, without me are you? You can't imagine how I'm looking forward to the first time we—not, quarrel, but are cross with one another—then 'the making up'

You are going to love me always aren't you—even when you're cross with me and when you are I'll ruffle all your hair lots of times until you have to melt—and smile at me—then you'll take me in both your arms and hold me so tight I can't breathe, and kiss me all over until I have to say "Stop, stop at once'

Why do you say to me ' Never run away, face things and argue and beat everybody" Do I ever run away? Have I ever run away? and do you think I should be likely to now? That's twice this trip something you have said has hurt You will have to kiss all that hurt away—'cos it does really hurt—it's not sham darlint

I'm not going to talk to you any more—I can't and I don't think I've shirked have I? except darlint to ask you again to think out all the plans and methods for me and wait and wait so anxiously now—for the time when we'll be with each other—even tho' it's only once—for " one little hour "— our kind of hour, not the song kind

and Just to tell you

(PEIDI) Loves you always

Since finishing my letter to you I have a confession to make—

To day I've been into the Holborn Restaurant—no don't be cross darlint, not to lunch—

I got off the 'Bus at Southampton Row to go and pay the piano account and ran into Mr Derry outside the Holborn Rest Do you know whom I mean? The " White Horse " man

He wanted me very much to have lunch with him there and I only got out of doing so by saying I had mine However I consented to go into the buffet with him and had a guinness with a port in it and two ports afterwards—so with nothing to eat since 9 p m last night you may guess how I felt when I got back here, oh I forgot to say I had 1 lb of French almonds as well—he knows from previous experience that I don't like chocolates You're not cross are you darlint? No, you musn't be, not with Peidi

A note from you this morning darlint it bucked me up ever so I can't say for certain that I shall be at 168 any time after 5 30 It depends on how busy we are If you wire me " Yes " I will go to Fenchurch Street and wait until you come If you wire ' No " I'll wait until I hear further from you—perhaps you could 'phone me—Bill got home at 3 p m —perhaps you will too—I'm impatient now—if only I could shut my eyes and then open them, and find it was Friday night

I have sent off to you to day two parcels—one small and one large per pels post Let me know if you receive them, I wasn't expecting you to get in early—or I could have posted them a day before

Oh darlint even the looking forward hurts—does it you? every time I think of *Friday* and onwards my inside keeps turning over and over— all my nerves seems like wires continually quivering

Bywaters and Thompson.

The "non stop" for Thursday is off Thank God or anybody Reg has gone to Derbyshire and Avis's partner is down with the 'flu, I am glad—even so—at any rate I shan't be tired to death when I see you—all Wednesday—all Thursday and all Friday and then—The Fates—our luck will decide
PEIDI

Remember how I've been looking forward and when you remember—you'll be able to wait just a little longer, eh darlint?
This is Friday and on Monday I'm expecting a huge mail from you—you'll have had all my letters—and if you are not able to talk to me darlint at least you'll be able to answer all my questions—now just keep up to scratch or I'll be cross, no I won't, I don't think I could be somehow—"cross" wouldn't be the right word—it would more often be hurt"
When we were at Mrs Manning's her sister asked him to go over there the following Sat and when she asked me I hesitated, so she said I've already asked Percy and he said Yes," so of course I did I've mentioned this to him in front of all at 231, and he didn't question it, but a few days later said " he wasn't going "—he wouldn't have me making arrangements to go anywhere without first consulting him, and obtaining his consent The next morning I sent Beatty a card saying it was impossible to keep our promise to see her on Sat In the afternoon I went home and had a general clean up everywhere The sun was shining in the windows beautifully—it was a typically English spring day and I did so want to be in the park with you darlint He didn't come home till 5 30 p m darlint I do hope you don't mind me relating to you all these trivial little incidents that happen I always feel I wanted to talk to you about them
Gordon was staying in Ilford last week end, and was on my train on Monday morning His greeting was " I never got that cigarette case you promised me at Xmas " and my reply was ' I did not have a new one then, and haven't still—but when I do you shall have the blue one " I have heard darlint that the Stoll film Syndicate have secured the rights to show " Way down East " in Suburbia—so we may be able to see it together after all We're going to Bessie's to dinner this Sunday and then follows Monday, when I shall hear from you, such a big budget I hope I'll write again after the week end darlint
Au Revoir
PEIDI

I saw Bill on Friday darlint He looks very thin I think—in the face Bombay and you were not mentioned at all—that horse I backed lost of course Will you tell me how many letters you have got at Marseilles Wed the last day for posting was fearful here—gales and snow storms, and I believe the next day no Channel boats ran at all I hope nothing went astray I wrote three letters and one greeting, posted separately Enclosed are some cuttings that may be interesting I think the " red hair " one is true in parts—you tell me which parts darlint The Kempton cutting may be interesting if it's to be the same method Altho' it's Monday darlint the mail from Marseilles is not yet in, I'm expecting it every moment, I wish it would hurry up and come I will put this away now until you have talked to me, and then I will be able to talk to you for another long time

Appendix I.

The mail came in 12 noon, and I thought I would be able to talk to you after then—but I don't think I can. Will you do all the thinking and planning for me darlint—for this thing—be ready with every little detail when I see you—because you know more about this thing than I, and I am relying on you for all plans and instructions—only just the act I'm not. I'm wanting that man to lean on now darlint and I shall lean hard—so be prepared.

In this case I shan't be able to rely wholly on myself and I know you won't fail me. I can't remember if I only sent one letter to Port Said, if it was a very long one perhaps there only was one, but even if there wasn t—it doesn't matter much, does it? There would be no identification marks in it either for you or me, and the loss of one letter seems such a small thing when you and I are looking forward to such big things darlint, this time? Yes! About "The Slave" I didn't know what to make of that girl—yes I think she is possible—perhaps and apart from being happy with her body—he was quite happy seeing her with those jewels. They were 2 similar natures—what pleased him—pleased her—not English at all, either of them. She stooped low—to get back that Emerald—but darlint wouldn't all of us stoop low to regain something we have loved and lost. I know hers was without life, but that was because she had never lived herself and she didn't live did she? not in the world as we know living—she just existed in her casket of "live things," as she knew them. I don't know if you will understand this, it seems a bit of a rigmarole even to me. I asked you in one of my letters it seems ages ago, whether I should send you a book to Norwood, or keep it for you—you never told me. When you read my letters do you make a mental note of all the questions I ask you. I don't think you do, because I seem to have asked you heaps and heaps of things that you never mention. Darlingest boy, when you get my letters and have read them are you satisfied? Do you feel that I come up to all your expectations? Do I write enough? *Just don't forget to answer this and also don't forget I won't, I won't I won't let you bully me*

Why not go to 231 darlint, I think you ought to go as usual, it would be suspicious later if you stopped away without a reason known to them and there is not a reason is there? You haven't fallen out with Bill have you? What about Dr Walis's case you said it was interesting but you didn't discuss it with me. Darlint, about making money—yes we must somehow, and what does it matter how—when we have accomplished that one thing—we are going to live entirely for ourselves and not study any one except ourselves? Of course I'd not like to sacrifice any one that has been or ever still is dear to me—but I've no other scruples darlint—except actually robbing my own flesh and blood and perhaps one or two persons that are even dearer to me than my own flesh and blood. Yes It must be done—we must get up high darlint not sink lower or even stop where we are—I'd like to see you at the top—feel that I'd helped you there—perhaps darlint in my heart right deep down I don't want to stop in a hat shop always—if things are different. If they were to remain as they are now—yes I should—it takes me out of myself but when we are together—I'll never want to be taken out of myself because myself will be you as well and we can't ever be parted can we? If we have to be in person we shan't be in mind and thought. About that flat—I'm afraid its going to be difficult to get one unfurnished—they all seem to be furnished—I've been looking for a long time now. Darlint could I get a furnished one at first

Bywaters and Thompson.

until you come home next time and look for an unfurnished one in the meantime   I don't want to furnish it all by myself I want you to be with me, everything we do must be together in future and you see darlint it would have in it everything I like and perhaps lots of things you don't like   That musn't be—If I want something I like and you don't then for that one thing   you must have something that you like and I don't   This is right, isn't it?   It must always be " give and take " between us, no misunderstandings about trivial things—darlint plain words perhaps hard ones but nevertheless plain ones they're always the easiest to fight and then we're pals again——

[Part of letter apparently missing here—continues]—not over the object 'jewels" but over other things   take for instance Ambition—social and otherwise   Yes, I can imagine her real—but Aubrey—I could shake him—no go—no initiative of his own—just standing and looking on at other people calmly taking what could have been his, away in front of his eyes —oh an ass—nothing more   I agree with you over Ameau he could have had her—with jewels—but he didn't read her quick enough when he did, it was too late   I think Sir Reuben—you seem hard on him for his spite on Caryll—over his first wife—but I suppose its natural darlint—I suppose all of us right down deep would like to hurt someone when we have been hurt

---

Exhibit 20a

Extract from *The Daily Mail*, 10th March, 1922, page 7, column 7

With headnote—
 " Girl's Death Riddle
 ' Tales of London Night Life
 " Beautiful Dancer Drugged
 ' Visit to a Chinese Restaurant "

Then follows a report of the inquest held on the 9th of March in the course of which Mr Oswald, the West London Coroner, addressing the jury on the opening of the inquest said, that it was suspected Miss Kempton died from cocaine poisoning, and he had been also told there was a suspicion of cyanide of potassium

The inquiry was adjourned till 17th April for an examination of the contents of the stomach to be made by Dr Spilsbury

---

Exhibit 50

Darlingest Boy, This will be the last letter to England—I do wish it wasn't, I wish you were never going away any more, never going to leave me—I want you always to be with me

Darlint, about the doubt—no I've never really doubted—but I do like to hear you reassure me   I like you to write it   so that I can see it in black and white and I always want you to say, " Please do believe darlint that I don't really doubt   its just a vain feeling I have to hear you say things to me   nice things—things that you mean

Appendix I.

which most people don't   I wonder if you understand the feeling
—perhaps you don't—but I always say and think and believe nobody on this
earth is sincere   except *the* one man—*the* one who is mine

Pride of possession is a nice feeling don't you think darlint—when it exists between you and me

I sent you the books darlint, all I felt were worth reading   I hope you'll think of me when you're reading them and I hope you'll talk to me about them

After tonight I am going to die   not really   but put on the mask again darlint until the 26th May—doesn't it seem years and years away?   It does to me and I'll hope and hope all the time that I'll never have to wear the mask any more after this time   Will you hope and wish and wish too darlint   pour moi

This time really will be the last you will go away   like things are, won't it?   We said it before darlint I know and we failed   but there will be no failure this next time darlint, there mustn't be   I'm telling you   if things are the same again then I'm going with you wherever it is   if its to sea   I'm coming too and if its to nowhere—I'm also coming darlint   You'll never leave me behind again, never, unless things are different

I've sealed up your envelopes and put them away   I did not look at them—except at a small slip of paper I found in one of the small pockets   I did read that—and then put it with the others—did you know it was there darlint—it was about a chase—a paperchase I think and a request not to be wakened early

I'm beginning to think I'm rather silly to have asked you for them—because you do love me—I know that—Do you think I am silly?

I slept on your letter last night darlint unopened I had no chance to read it but got up at quarter to six this morning to do so   Darlint you can't imagine what a pleasure it is for me to read something that you have written   I can't describe it   Last night darlint—I didn't think of you (Because you once told me not to) but I hope you were thinking of me   Its much harder to bear when you're in England than when you're away   This must be au revoir now darlint in the flesh at all events—not in the spirit Eh!   We are never apart in that

Here's luck to you in everything especially in the thing concerning two halves—one of whom is

PEIDI

I always do and always will love you whatever happens

Exhibit 17

Envelope—Mr F Bywaters, P & O R M S 'Morea' Bombay

[Postmark—London EC, 1 Apl 22, 2 30 p m]

I believe I insufficiently stamped the first Marseille letter I sent   If I did darlint I ever so sorry   I hate doing anything like that   You know dont you

I think Thursday was the worst day and night I ever remember   All day long I was thinking of the previous Thursday, and contrasting my feelings, one day with the other—the feelings of intense excitement and those of deep depression, and then when night came it was worse—it was awful I was fighting all night long to keep your thoughts with me darlint I felt all the time that you were not with me—didnt want to be Just had withdrawn yourself, and try as I would I couldn't bring you back Darlint, tell me what was happening on Thursday I cried and cried and cried, until I eventually went to sleep but I had heard the clock strike five before I did so, and then Friday morning I saw your sister and she just gave me one of those looks that are supposed to wither some people and then I felt that the whole world was up against me and it wasn't really much good living Still, that fit of depression is on me and I cant shake it off Perhaps on Monday when the mail is in I shall feel bucked up a bit, also I got your complaint badly since Thursday—all my teeth ache and my head and neck Is yours better now darlint? I hope it is Lily had a dream the other day that the Birnages came to 168 to warn me that he was going to murder me—as he had found out I had been away from home for a night with a fair man (her expression)

She didnt know any more than this as she woke up On Wednesday I met Harry Renton and he told me he was giving up his flat and going to live at Woodford—did I know any one that wanted it—

Darlint it is just the thing we wanted I do wish I had been able to take it just three rooms unfurnished 35s per week including electric light, in Moscow Court, Kensington Its a very nice one I practically chose it for him myself two years ago That boy's fearfully ill really The Doctor has ordered him to live in the country else consumption through his shoulder wound, will take hold of him We went to lunch at "Manchester," but I only had one hour darlint and a wretched man sat near me who absolutely reeked of scent It was overpowering I can understand a woman using such a lot, but a man—oh! its beastly To day I'm going home to entertain Dad He is coming to dinner and to help him with a job after and Mother and Avis are coming up to tea Darlint, this writing is awful I know I hope you will understand it I know you'll understand me, and how I'm feeling Ive got to get thro that weekend again

Au revoir until Monday darlint I wish you could say "I love you cherie"

Thank you 20 times darlint—the mail is in and I've got such a budget I wish we weren't quite so busy—Its Easter week—and usually the busiest week in all the year and it seems as if its going to live past its reputation this year

---

Before I talk to you about your letters darlint, I want to say one or two things that I forgot last week, When Avis came over on Wed although it was 11 30 before she went *he* insisted on seeing her to the tram and when I offered to come with him he was most emphatic in his "No" I expect he wanted to ask her about you—had she seen you? Did she know if I had etc? I didnt ask her anything about it and she volunteered no information Also, you remember her telling me you had a diamond ring on—she added "on his engagement finger" I said, Why, is he engaged? and she said "Probably He was always knocking about with some girl or other before he knew me, and now he doesn't see me and he probably does the same"

I do laugh at some of the things that are said A thought has just struck me—may I ask you? Yes, of course I may Darlint, has your

Appendix I.

head "turned again to its proper place"? I thought of the expression "she has absolutely turned your head," and really darlint I can't possibly imagine *anyone* "turning your head" if you didn't want it to be turned—let alone me—therefore the only conclusion I have come to is that if it is turned, you wanted me to turn it and only I can turn it back again Do you want it turned back again?

I saw Molly this morning—darlint if you saw her you say at once—the same as you did about the girl in the "Strand" Do you remember? What is she doing to herself? She looked awfull—her face and lips are rouged terribly and thick black lines pencilled under her eyes—and her face is fearfully thin fallen in under the cheek bones Perhaps its working in the West end She certainly looks years older than her years and I shouldn't say she was pretty now—Oh darlint I do think it is a shame don't you?

Darlingest boy, I'm so sorry you thought I was silly—about those things from Australia—darlint—although I know—I feel I am—I didn't want you to think so—but you do and I feel worse I feel small and petty and truly darlint I did not want them from any feelings of jealousy that I might entertain

I'm not jealous—certainly not of her—darlint—I thought perhaps you wouldn't give them to me—I thought you might say No I won't give them to you—but I will destroy them" and when you did give them to me I loved you such a lot—more and more and more every time I thought about it

---

About that Thursday—had there been anywhere to stop in Ilford—I should have said, "Take me there, *I won't* go home" and you would have said, "Yes I will" but darlint before we had arrived at the Hotel, I should have thought about things and so would you and I can hear you say just when we reach the door ' Peidi, you're going home ' pour moi—just this once darlint and I should have gone

Darlint you're not and never will be satisfied with half and I don't ever want to give half—all every ounce of me that lives to you

You say you're sorry for some things that happened Yes! I suppose I am in a way but darlint, I feel I don't do enough I want to show you how large my love is and when it is something you want and you do want it just at that moment don't you—I want to give it you—I want to stifle all my own feelings for you

Darlingest boy you said to me " Say no Peidi, say No ' on Thursday didn't you—but *at that very moment* you didn't wish me to say " No " did you? You felt you wanted all me in exchange for all you I knew this—felt this—and wouldn't say " No " for that very reason

Half an hour afterwards or perhaps even ten minutes afterwards you'd really have wanted me to say " No " but not at that especiall moment

Darlint I feel that I never want to withhold anything from you—if you really want it and one of these days youre going to teach me to give all and everything quite voluntarily—arent you? Please darlint

Darlint I do know how much you do love me—how much I love you and I'm pleased too because its a lot for me and a lot for you Its such a lot it hurts—terribly hard sometimes—just when I think and think and hope without much thought of that hope ever being realised

Bywaters and Thompson.

About the watch I'm so so glad it keeps good time and that you always wear it—I always want you to—go to sleep on it darlint, please pour moi—I always wear something you gave me now—both by day and at night What is it? do you know I suppose in a way the barber was right darlint—he does know you better than I do—that part of you that lives on ships but I know you—the inside part that nobody else sees—or knows and I dont want them to yet awhile at any rate

I do hope you're feeling better now darlint, in one of your letters you say you have had a tough fever—oh darlint—dont go and get ill—it will worry me such a lot because I cant be with you Do try and not get ill pour moi darlingest bo

When I marked the paragraph about photos in Felix, I certainly was thinking of my photo—dont be cross—altho you say you like them darlint I dont really—especially that one that I look so fat in Tear it up please To please me and then tell me you have done so You can keep one I dont mind that one so much but I dont really like it and I hate the other one Of course by now you will have finished Felix You wont like Mrs Ismay although you said previously that you thought you would You also say she wants to tell Felix she takes drugs but hasn't the courage to You will also have found out by now that this is wrong That is the last thing on earth she wants to tell anyone

---

Darlingest boy never mind about the news being ordinary It is you talking to me and that is all I want and if it is ordinary it is interspersed with little bits that are'nt ordinary that are for me only—such bits—as " I love you "—always Chere " and " I'm always with you in thought Chere "—that shows darlint that even though you write about ordinary things you are thinking of extraordinary things My letters must always appear ordinary to you in most parts if you think like that, but I have to tell you everything that happens I feel I must I always want to and those things are always ordinary to me Things are always the same—the same old round—unless you are in England and then its a different world—a joyous world that hurts at the same time

---

You say you thought you were going to hear nothing from me except that first letter and you felt that is all you deserved Darlint, to me such a thing is never a thought really Whatever I feel about not hearing from you at any time, I think would never influence me to not write you All I think and feel—if I want to—and darlint I always want to I know I said once that " I'd never talk to you again "—but darlint you really dont think I mean it do you because I dont If I didnt hear from you for a whole trip—unless you told me not to—I should still talk to you and try to do my share if I felt I wanted to

Darlint if you *dont deserve* a thing (and I dont think that will really ever be) you will always know that because you dont deserve it—you will always get it Does this sound contrary? Mother wasnt cross a bit about the Cigarettes in fact she laughed it off as a huge joke and said I had three yesterday and they didnt hurt me Yes darlint about the writer and K 5, I did laugh to myself—thats why I told you but I dont like laughing by myself I want you to be there to laugh with me

Just those little jokes all to ourselves

Appendix I.

Yes, you are a bully—but sometimes—only sometimes I like it   I like being told to do this by you   I didnt like you to bully me about a wet fur collar tho', darlint

---

I read the copy to your Mother and thought when I was reading it " what a pedestal he is on when he is writing this and I am the only one that can fetch him down but when I came to the last two paragraphs I thought " this is more like the boy I know—not like the shell "   I'm glad you softened a bit

I have returned copy—thank you darlint   The part that hurt most was " that *woman* "

I could hear the tone in which it was said and it hurts such a lot—I had to cry altho I tried not to   Why didn't you tell me that on Thursday? there would have been time then for you to kiss all that hurt away and now I shall retain it until you come back again

You didn't mention anything about what I wrote regarding your Sister   Why not?

Darlingest boy—is she your Mother any judge of whether " I'm no good," and if she is has she any right to judge me   Whether she or any-one I knew were good or bad I shouldn't judge them

Darlint I love you such lots and lots and the mail to-day made it more—by that mail I knew you loved me more—yes more than you did

It must be au revoir until Aden now—Je suis fache you have to wait such a long time to talk with me but darlint I am always with you wondering what you are doing and feeling and loving you every minute of always

PEIDI

Dont keep this piece

About the Marco ngram—do you mean one saying Yes or No, because I shant send it darlint I'm not going to try any more until you come back

I made up my mind about this last Thursday

He was telling his Mother etc the circumstances of my " Sunday morning escapade " and he puts great stress on the fact of the tea tasting bitter " as if something had been put in it ' he says   Now I think whatever else I try it in again will still taste bitter—he will recognise it and be more suspicious still and if the quantity is still not successful—it will injure any chance I may have of trying when you come home

Do you understand?

I thought a lot about what you said of Dan

Darlint, don't trust him—I don't mean don't *tell* him anything because I know you never would—What I mean is don t let him be suspicious of you regarding that—because if we were successful in the action—darlint circumstances may afterwards make us want many friends—or helpers and we must have no enemies—or even people that know a little too much Remember the saying, " A little knowledge is a dangerous thing "

Darlint we'll have no one to help us in the world *now* and we musnt make enemies unnecessarily

He says—to his people—he fought and fought with himself to keep conscious— ' I'll never die, except naturally—I'm like a cat with nine lives " he said and detailed to them an occasion when he was young and nearly suffocated by gas fumes

I wish we had not got electric light—it would be easy

I'm going to try the glass again occasionally—when it is safe Ive got an electric light globe this time

Bywaters and Thompson.

Exhibit 18

Envelope—Mr F Bywaters, P & O R M S "Morea," Aden

[Postmarks—London, E C , Apr 24, 1922, 5 30 p m , Aden, 7 May, 1922]

I think I'll tell you about the holidays darlint—just what I did—do you want to know? or will you say its all ordinary common place talk—I suppose it is—but after I have discussed the ordinary things, I may be able to really talk to you On Thursday we left at 1 and I went to the Waldorf to lunch and stayed on until the dance tea—I only danced once—a fox trot—I don't feel a bit like dancing darlint—I think I must be waiting for you We left the Waldorf at 6 20 and met Avis at 6 30 and went with her to buy a costume—getting home about 9

On Friday I worked hard all day starting that ' Good Old fashioned English housewife's occupation of spring cleaning," not because I liked doing it—or believe in it, but because I had nothing else to do and it helped to pass the time away I started about 9 30 and went to wash and dress about 20 to 6—

Dad took us to the E H Palace to the Sunday League Concert in the evening and we stopped the night at 231

In return for this I booked for us all at Ilford Hippodrome on Saturday The show was good and a girl—in nurses uniform appearing with Tom Edwards sang " He makes me all fussed up "

Of course Avis remarked about you and the song also Molly was sitting behind us with another girl and a boy—is she affected in her conversation? She was very much on Saturday and I wondered if it was put on for my special benefit

Avis came back to stay the rest of the holiday with us Bye the way, we, (she and I) had a cup of tea in bed on Sunday—we always do when she is stopping with us

Mother and Dad came over to me to dinner—I had plenty to do On Monday Mr and Mrs Birnage came to tea and we all went to the Hippodrome in the evening Bye the way—what is " Aromatic Tincture of Opium '—Avis drew my attention to a bottle of this sealed in the medicine chest in your room *

I took possession of it and when he missed it and asked me for it—I refused to give it him—he refuses to tell me where he got it and for what reason he wants it—so I shall keep it till I hear from you

I used the " light bulb " three times but the third time—he found a piece—so I've given it up—until you come home

Do you remember asking me to get a duplicate of something— I have done so now

On Sunday we were arguing about the price of " Cuticura " Avis is quite certain when she bought it, not for herself, (her own words) it was 10½ Mother said when she bought it for you it was 1/- and I said the same

The remark was passed—" you all in turn seemed to have bought it for him "

I had another mysterious parcel this Easter—a large gold foil egg filled with chocolate about 2 lbs by the weight—still with no word or

---

* The room Bywaters had occupied when he lodged with the Thompsons —Ed

Appendix I.

even a name attached, posted in the City E C 2 to 168   I suppose it's from the same source as the Xmas parcel—but I haven't and shan't acknowledge it   What did you think of " Edwina's Shoes " ?

Darlint, do you like this term of endearment   I shan't tell you why I ask, but you'll probably notice it one of these days, ' Carissima "

Thank you for sending back the time table, darlint, but why do you think I might want it—when you are away—you know very well I shant —why did you say that ?   I understand the wire now—but I certainly didn't read it like that at the time   won't the Post Office put in a full stop mark then ?

I had a funny dream the other night darlint—you had taken me out somewhere and saw me home and persisted in coming in

Eventually you and I slept in your little bed—in the morning I woke early and went into the big room and found Harold was sleeping with him —you were unbolting the front door in your pyjamas to get out quickly when he came down the stairs, so you went into Mrs Lester's room   She didn't like it a bit and you thought you had better make a clean breast of it and came up to him and told him what had happened—there was a fight—I don't remember how it went—in Dad and Mother were there with him and they had been discussing things and wouldn't let me stop there   I don't know what became of me or of you

---

I've been reading a very very interesting book, darlint, I want you to read it after me and give me your opinion—not just a few lines and then " Dismissed "—but your real opinion of every one of note in the book   Read and remember it carefully will you ?   pour moi

It's called ' The Fruitful Vine " by Robert Hitchens, and it's very very nice and the subject is interesting—not lovely—like the ' Common Law " or " The Business of Life "—it's too sensual for that but " the one act " in the book would lead to hours and hours of discussion—even now I have finished it—I am not sure whether she did right or wrong and I am not sure which man I really liked—one man was calm strong and clean—not sensual at all but selfish, very, and the other was absolutely different,— sensual, a lover in every sense of the word and yet I liked him at least I liked heaps of things about him and connected with him—lots of his little speeches—actions

You must tell me everything you think about it, it's rather long 500 pages and there are several passages that I have marked—some I have queried for you to answer others I have just marked—because they have struck me as being interesting to us or to me, I'm very anxious to know what you think of it   what shall I do with the book ?—send it to you ?

I think I have never found it so difficult to talk to you before   all the times you have been away—I am just dried up waiting to see you and feel you holding me

It is Friday now and altho I had a mail in from you——about 11 30— I still don't feel like talking darlint, I'm not disappointed—not a little bit— in fact I'm pleased—ever so pleased—at the difference when I read all you say to me I feel you are with me—just looking at me and telling me all those things about yourself and it feels lovely darlint—so different from before and I wonder if its going to last—or shall I have a letter from

Bywaters and Thompson.

Plymouth saying "I'm not going to answer your questions Peidi and I don't mind if you are cross about it" Youre not going to say that any more are you?—darlint *please don't*, I said I wouldn't ask again didn't I, but I'm doing so—you see, I don't mind what you think—all I know and feel is that I love you so much——I must go on asking and asking not minding whether my pride is hurt—always asking until you consent

Darlint do you remember being very proud once? I remember and I gave way first—write and tell me if you remember the incident and what it was

Its not going to happen again tho' is it? Mr Carlton said to me at 11 30 to day—"I have news from your brother for you"—I wasn't thinking of the mail being in and said "How have you got news?" and he just gave me your envelope. I thought the remark rather strange and can't quite make out if he really thought it was from my brother—or was being sarcastic You get into Bombay to day—just 5 more weeks—I wish they'd fly

I had a doctor s bill in yesterday—I took it in myself as it happened so of course I kept and shall pay it myself—without saying it is even in and then there can be no question of who's to pay it can there

You want me to pay it, don't you darlint—I shall do so

Why that passage in your last letter The last time we met, we were *pals*, weren t we Chere? why the question darlint if you had wanted to write it you should have *stat d* it as a fact

Of course we were pals, we always are and always will be while this life lasts—whatever else happens and alters our lives—for better or for worse —for either or for both of us we shall always remain that darlint—don t ask me the question again—it hurts

On Saturday we went to the dinner party at the Birnage's—it was a very posh affair for a private house—full course dinner and she cooked everything herself—I think she is awfully clever

Yesterday I thought I should have gone mad with faceache—I took 24 Asparins—in 6 lots of 4 during the day and made a pillow of thermogene at night—I didn t get a scrap of sleep tho'

Has your pain gone darlint? I think you must have left it with me, I thought I might get a letter from Suez to day otherwise I wouldn't have come up to town to day

I think I want you here to take care of me—it seems more than ever before—shall be so glad when we get nearer the 26th May just that darlint nothing more

PEIDI

Exhibit 19

Envelope—Mr F Bywaters P & O R M S Morea, Port Said

[Postmark—London, E C May 1, 1922, 6 15 p m]

Darlingest Boy I know

If you were to hear me talk now you would laugh, I'm quite positive and I should be angry—I've got practically no voice at all—just a little very high up, squeak

It started with a very sore throat and then my voice went—it doesn't hurt now—the throat is better but it sounds so funny I feel like laughing

Appendix I.

myself but altho you'd laugh darlint you'd be very kind wouldn't you? and just take care of me I know you would without asking or you answering—but you can answer because I like to hear you say it

About those fainting fits darlint, I don't really know what to say to you

I'm beginning to think its the same as before—they always happen 1st thing in the morning—when I'm getting up and I wasn't ill as I should have been last time, altho' I was a little—but not as usual

What shall I do about it darlint, if it is the same this month—please write and tell me I want to do just what you would like

I still have the herbs

" I like her she doesn't swear "

This is what you write—do you like her because she doesn't swear or was that bit an afterthought I'm wondering what you really think of a girl—any girl—even me who says—damn and a few stronger words sometimes—or don't these words constitute swearing as you hear it

Of course I was glad you did as you did with her I should never be glad at any other way darlint, whatever the object or the end in view

Talking about " Felix " darlint can't say I was disappointed in the end because I didn't expect very much of him You say you expected him to do a lot for Valevia—I didn't—he was too ordinary—too prosaic to do anything sensational—he'd do anything in the world for her if it hadn't caused comment but when it did—he finished Do you remember the railway station scene when her husband appeared, and took command of the proceedings Felix was nowhere and he allowed himself not only to go home, but to be ordered to go home by Mr Ismay What were your feelings for Mr Ismay—did you like him? About the word you starred—I can't say I actually know the meaning of the word only of course I guess but you can tell me darlint I certainly shan't ask anyone else

Darlint isn't this a mistake Je suis gâche ma pauvre petite amie This is how you wrote it

I was glad you think and feel the same way as I do about the " New Forest " I don't think we're failures in other things and we musn't be in this We musn't give up as we said No we shall have to wait if we fail again Darlint, Fate can't always turn against us and if it is we must fight it—You and I are strong now We must be stronger We must learn to be patient We must have each other darlint Its meant to be I know I feel it is because I love you such a lot—such a love was not meant to be in vain It will come right I know one day, if not by our efforts some other way We'll wait eh darlint, and you'll try and get some money and then we can go away and not worry about anybody or anything You said it was enough for an elephant Perhaps it was But you don't allow for the taste making only a small quantity to be taken It sounded like a reproach was it meant to be?

Darlint I tried hard—you won't know how hard—because you weren't there to see and I can't tell you all—but I did—I do want you to believe I did for both of us

You will see by my last letter to you I havn't forgotten the key and I didn't want reminding—I didn't forget that—altho' I did forget something last time didn't I altho it was only small

We have changed our plans about Llandudno—it is too expensive we are going to Bournemouth July 8th, and while Avis was over last night he asked her to come with us The suggestion was nothing to do with me—

Bywaters and Thompson.

it was his entirely and altho' I wouldn't have suggested such a thing for the world—I'm glad—because if things are still the same and we do go—a third party helps to make you forget that you always lead the existence we do

Au revoir for the week end darlint

The mail was in this morning and I read your letter darlint, I cried—I couldn't help it—such a lot it sounded so sad I cried for you I could exactly feel how you were feeling—I've felt like that so often and I know

I was buoyed up with the hope of the "light bulb" and I used a lot—big pieces too—not powdered—and it has no effect—I quite expected to be able to send that cable—but no—nothing has happened from it and now your letter tells me about the bitter taste again Oh darlint, I do feel so down and unhappy

Wouldn't the stuff make small pills coated together with soap and dipped in liquorice powder—like Beechams—try while you're away Our Boy had to have his thumb operated on because he had a piece of glass in it that's what made me try that method again—but I suppose as you say he is not normal, I know I feel I shall never get him to take a sufficient quantity of anything bitter No I haven't forgotten the key I told you before

Darlint two heads are better than one is such a true saying You tell me not to leave finger marks on the box—do you know I did not think of the box but I did think of the glass or cup whatever was used I wish I wish oh I wish I could do something

Darlint, think for me, *do* I do want to help If you only knew how helpless and selfish I feel letting you do such a lot for me and I doing nothing for you If ever we are lucky enough to be happy darling I'll love you such a lot I always show you how much I love you for all you do for me Its a terrible feeling darlint to want—really want to give all and everything, and not be able to give a tiny little thing—just thro' circumstances

You asked me if Deborah described her feelings rightly when she was talking about Kullett making love to her

Darlingest, boy, I don't think all the feelings can be put on paper because there are not words to describe them The feeling is one of repugnance, loathing not only of the person but of yourself—and darlint when you think of a man and a woman jointly wrote that book it's not feasible that the words used would be bad enough to express the feelings The man Author wouldn't allow the woman Author to talk too badly of Kullett—do you think? I still think that nobody can express the feelings—I'm sure I couldn't—but they are there, deeply rooted and can never be plucked out as circumstances now are unless they (the circumstances) change Did you notice any similarity in 2 girls names in two books that you recently read and the utter dissimilarity in their natures (I don't think I spelt that word rightly) I didn't know that you would be in London a month this time—altho I had a little idea

That month—I can't bear to think of it a whole four weeks and things the same as they are now All those days to live thro for just one hour in each

All that lying and scheming and subterfuge to obtain one little hour in each day—when by right of nature and our love we should be together for all the 24 in every day

Appendix I.

Darlint don't let it be—I can't bear it all this time—the pain gets too heavy to bear—heavier each day—but if things were different what a grand life we should start together Perhaps we could have that one week I could be ill from shock—More lies—but the last Eh darlint

Do experiment with the pills while you are away—please darlint

No we two—two halves—have not yet come to the end of our tether" Don't let us

I'm sorry I've had to use this piece of paper but the pad was empty—I sent the boy for a fresh one and they will have none in until tomorrow

We have started on the 5th week of your absence now—each week seems longer than the last and each day the length of two

Do you know darlint that the Saturday I usually have off when you are home is Whit Saturday and I shan't be able to see you nor on the Monday following

Three whole days—and you so near and yet so far—it musn't be darlint—we musn't let it somehow

Good bye now darlint I can't write any more You said you have a lump—so have I in fact its more than a lump now

Good bye until Marseilles next week I do always love you and think of you
PEIDI

Exhibit 21

Envelope—Mr F Bywaters, P & O R M S Morea, Marseilles, France

[Postmark—London E C 15 May, '22, 5 30 p m]

My very own darlingest boy

I received the mail this morning—but am not going to answer it yet—I've got several other things I want to tell you, and talk to you as well I had no time to read your letter alone, so what do you think I did darlint I got on the top of a bus—back seat by myself and went to Hyde Park Corner in my lunch hour and read it I couldn't stop in—in the lunch hour—it was such a glorious day in fact it has been a beautiful week end—warm and sunny—quite warm enough to wear very thin clothes and not feel cold I do love this weather—it's not too hot yet—but even when it is I'm not going to grumble—this winter has been terribly long and cold, *and lonely* Do you know darlint I won 30/- on Paragon in the City and Sub and lost 20/- in each of the 2000 gns 1000 gns and the Jubilee Money was never made to stop with me

When you've been in England have you ever seen "Les Rouges et Noirs" They are all ex soldiers—running a concert party—like the Co-optimists and impersonating girls as well as men

Men usually dressed as women—especially in evening dress—look ridiculous—but these were splendid—very clever and very funny—I did laugh such a lot—it was really dancing through the hours We went with Mr and Mrs Birnage He has made *him* an agent for the Sun Life privately and now draws commission on any policies he gets—it has been about £750 premiums up to now and he draws 1% on some and ½% on others Miss Prior's sister lost her husband quite suddenly and as I happen to be her stamp—Miss Prior asked me to go up west and buy some mourning for her—a costume—a silk frock and a cloth frock—jumper—shoes stockings and gloves It was a nice job and when I got back—there were some

Bywaters and Thompson.

widows hats with veils at the back and nobody including Miss Prior had the pluck to try them on—they all say it is unlucky—so because of it being unlucky to them I thought it might be lucky to me and tried them all on

I think they all think terrible things are going to happen to me now—but darlint I am laughing I wonder who will be right, they or I? Talking about bad luck—Mother came over to hang some clean curtains for me and in moving the dressing table—the cheval glass came off the pivot and smashed the glass in a thousand pieces—This is supposed to mean bad luck for 7 years—I am wondering if its for us (you and I) or her What do you think about it? Darlint I've bought a skirt—cream gabardine—pleated to wear with a sports coat—It looks lovely—are you pleased?

Do you know the skirts are going to be worn longer?

I shall have to wear mine a wee bit longer—if I don't want to be hopelessly old fashioned—but it won't be very much, will you mind? On Friday Mr Birnage came up and took me out to lunch again I left him at 2—and was astonished when at 4 p m they said a gentleman wanted to see me upstairs—and on going up found it was him waiting to take me out to tea I went—but I didn't really want to—I shan't go too often darlint You said you were home for a month this time—does that mean that you are going to sail on the 23rd June

Darlint I hope not—I do so want to be with you—even if its only for a little while on June 27th 1922 Our first real birthday Are you getting in on the Friday again this time?

You mentioned about a boy and a girl and a chocolate incident in one of your letters—you said " I smiled and thought a lot " what did you think—you didn't tell me and I want to know

Darlingest boy—I like Montelmont as well as Turkish Delight " Cupboard Love " did you say? I am glad you didn't like Waring—I thought perhaps you might—just a little—I didn't a bit I was cross with Deborah—several times darlint—especially for sending him away that first time but I admired so much the will power she had to do so—didn't you? You say " Deborah " was more natural than " Maria " No I don't think so—they were two very different types—but both were absolutely natural according to their mode of living Deborah was primitive—Maria civilised more—but both natural—darlint don't give " Maria's " place in you to anyone else Admire others *as much but not more* pour moi—I loved Maria and I admired Deborah

---

I don't know whether Avis liked the books or not—but if you asked her why she did or did not she couldn't say could she do you think—she couldn't discuss each character as we do—she wouldn't remember enough about them—she would only remember the general theme of the book—so why ask? Yes I like Desboro (in the Business of Life) mostly—why should we not agree about him darlint—I should like to argue with you over him—shall we? Yes and when?

In a book I have just read which I am going to lend you there are two characters—whom you and I must copy—only if things are never got to be right darlint if they are always as they are now—I want you to remember what I have written I shall be like and do what Dolores does and you must do what Cesare does—Of course what I do will be from a different motive from Dolores and you must fight like Cesare—but darlint

Appendix I.

don't ever let go—keep tight hold—bring up and take care of pour moi and then it won't matter much what happens   I shall have given you something for you only—my all

You will probably wonder what I am rambling about—I shan't tell you   I shall wait until you read the book and then you will find out for yourself   To day its 3 weeks before you're in England—I'm trying to get thro the time—without letting it feel too hard—only I hope you will hurry to England
and PEIDI

Exhibit 21a

Extract from *Daily Sketch* 13th May, 1922 columns 1 and 2

With headnote:—

  'Holiday—Then Death Pact
  "Passionate Farewell Letters in Seaside Drama
  'Women's Sacrifice'

The newspaper reports proceedings at an inquest held on George William Hibbert who was found dead in a gas-filled room at Brighton—and by his side lay Maud Hibbert, wife of his youngest brother, unconscious

---

Exhibit 22

Envelope—Mr F Bywaters, P & O R M S "Morea" Marseilles, France

[Postmark—London E C, 18 May, 22, 2 30 p m]

'It must be remembered that digitalin is a cumulative poison, and that the same dose harmless if taken once, yet frequently repeated, becomes deadly'

Darlingest Boy,
   The above passage I've just come across in a book I am reading "Bella Donna" by Robert Hichens   Is it any use   In your letter from Bombay you say you asked a lot of questions from Marseilles   I hope I answered them all satisfactory Darlint   I want to   I want to do always what will please you   I can't remember all you asked   I have nothing to refer to everything is destroyed   I don't even wait for the next arrival now About the Co Optimists, I remember the song quite well and darlint if you can only be practically true to me—I'd rather not have you at all and I won't have you   Whats more now I'm the bully aren't I? but it's only fun darlint—laugh   Yes a lot pour moi   I've heard nothing at all from your Mother   I've seen your sister several times   Darlingest boy you must never question me being still here   However hard (even the hardest you can possibly imagine) things are, while you still say "B B Peidi" I shall hang on—just, because you want me to and tell me to   Don't ever question me again   You have often said a thing as a question when you have known it is a fact   Why is that Darlint?   *Don't ever doubt*   I'll always love you—too much perhaps but always, and while you say stay I shall

Bywaters and Thompson.

I shall ask you about the laugh in the Buffet but when shall I? I'm not clear about what you write. Do you mean me to ask you when I see you this time or to wait until things are perhaps different. You say "I'm not bullying I'm deciding for you Chere". Darlint, that's what I like. Not that hard tone "You must, you shall" But the softer tone I know you can use especially to me. Yes, I like you deciding things for me. I've done it so long for myself. Its lovely to be able to leave it all to someone I know will not go wrong—will do the right thing pour moi always. You will wont you darlint. I lean on you not on myself when you are here. Now I'll talk a bit about the book "Beyond the Shadow". I did like very much, only it was hardly a possible story do you think Marian was an ideal woman and under her circumstances too ideal too unnatural too careful of other peoples' opinions. It reminded me of the book you lent me "The Way of these Women". Do you remember the man and the woman who didn't take their fate into their own hands although they could have done so easily. Too careful of the opinions of their so called friends and the world. When Geoffrey remembered he should have taken her away mastered all her protests and carried her off They were made for each other he was married to another *through no fault of his own*. He had plenty of the most necessary thing money and he just drifted. Darlingest Betty wasn't a little fool she loved as much as her nature allowed and it wasnt her fault but fate, that Geoffrey didn't love her and because he didn't (and he knew himself he didn't) why did he marry her. For sensual reasons thats all—to gratify himself. He knew she worshipped him and he was flattered. I didn't like him very much Marian was lovely. The few moments of joy she had with him before she died could never compensate her for her life utterly spoiled, but darlint "It is better to have loved and lost than never to have loved at all". Marian would not have liked any to have told Geoffrey of the incident before the accident. He would have asked her to marry him again, and she would have felt he was only doing it from duty and thats not a nice feeling to have darlint—for life, is it? I agree with you about Chambers endings darlint but the endings are not the story. The end is written to please nine out of ten people who read his books. You and I are the tenth and he doesn't cater for us darlint, we are so few. Do as I do. Forget the ends lose yourself in the characters and the story and, in your own mind make your own end. Its lovely to do that darlint—try it, and you must not be scathing about a particular author that I like. I wont have it you hear me—I'm bullying you now. I'll ruffle all your hair darlint until you're really cross. Will you be with me about anything ever?

Yes! we will be cross with each other and then make it up—it will be lovely. I shall have to stop for a little while now darlint. I have a ton of work to do. I do hope we are not quite so busy when you are home. Au revoir for now darlint.

One more day has gone by.—I'm counting the days now darlint. What are you doing now I wonder its Thursday about 12 noon and I've squeezed 10 minutes to talk to you. Today is fearfully cold again and very windy—I hate wind. For the last 4 days it has been 82 shade and 112 sun and today shade temp is down to 52—what a country to live in—hurry up and take me away—to Egypt if you like—but anywhere where its warm.

The book I'm reading "Bella Donna" is about Egypt—I'd think

Appendix I.

you'd be interested in it—although I don't think you would like the book—at least I hope you wouldn't—I don't

Do you remember telling me to do the "Scamp" for the Derby? Well I was rather hard up that week—so only put on 5/- each way I got 20 to 1 price

Yesterday was the first time the 'Scamp' came out and it failed miserably at a mile—the papers say it is a non stayer and made a very poor show and the price to-day is 33 to 1 What luck

I dont think I previously told you that old Mr Lester——fell in the fire and gashed his head

He was taken to Hospital and is still there—that is 10 days ago Reports at first said he wouldn't live through each night—but he has recovered after all Dont some people exaggerate?

Darlint I do feel so miserable to day I think its the weather—it has been so bright and sunny and makes you feel quite cheerful and today is cold and dull and I feel cold too—not in the flesh—in the body inside I mean— that sort of feeling that only one person in the world can alter for me—why aren't you here to do it? I want you so badly to lean on and to take care of me to be kind and gentle and love me as only you can

Goodbye darlingest boy—I'll write again before the mail closes for Marseilles

PEIDI

Supposing I were to meet your mother in the street darlint, what should I do? What would you want me to do?

Answer this please, particularly

PEIDI

———

When I asked you that question darlint I had already seen your Mother—but I really wanted to know what you would like me to have done

As it was—I hardly knew what to do—I couldnt pass her unrecognised without being absolutely rude so I just said "Let me smell, how are you?" and passed on I didn't stop to shake hands She had a large bunch of red roses in her arms and she had that tall man with her—I forget his name

Seeing her with red roses reminded me of you darlint, you like red ones dont you?—you told me so once—so do I, but not as much as one flower theyre all finished now isnt it a shame Ive taken the tussore to be made up darlint and was told that it was the best quality they have ever handled Ive also had a new navy costume made I dont think you will like it because its a long coat—but I bought a cream gabardine skirt (not serge) to please you darling so I thought I could please myself this time Am I right? I wonder if I shall wear the tussore costume with you darlint I dont mean once or twice but always I dont know I dont feel even optimistic about things I cant darling—not like I did before That hand of fate is always held up at me blocking out the future If I could only be certain? Darlingest boy pour moi be very very careful coming in this time Things and people have become much more vigilant Understand? I dont want to lose any tiny minute of you, they will probably be so few, but even a few is so much better than none at all remember that darlint Im very very anxious to know if you are getting in on the Friday I cant possibly wait over the week end—do let me know as soon as you can find out yourself Bill got in on Friday darlint about 3 p m home and came up to tea yesterday We had it out in the garden He started the

Bywaters and Thompson.

conversation about—— and said if he knew where to plant it he would get some and we talked a lot about it   I wanted to change the conversation quickly but *he* would continue   On Saturday darlint I did something which you would have said made me look old—gardening all day   It passes the time away   Old Mr Lester died last night   All their side of the house the blinds are drawn   I havnt drawn mine and Im not going to   I think they think Im a heathen   'Will it be under the year' you say   I wish I could be certain—feel certain—but I cant darlint   I keep on saying to myself 'Yes! Yes! It must, it shall be 'Yes,' and I have that feeling deep down all the time that it will be 'No'   Your letter today made me feel miserable darlint, I felt how much I wanted to be with you, so that I could love you that 'Mothering feeling' came over me   You dont know what its like   I do love you so much—more than anyone can know   Is that how you feel?   By now darlint you will have heard from me several times   Yesterday you passed Suez and got my Port Said letters   Im so sorry its a long time from Marseilles to Bombay, when you hear from me, but I cant do anything to help it can I darlint?   You'll be able to talk to me a long time this week to post at Marseilles because youll have all my letters to answer   Yes darlint, I want you and love you such a lot just as much as you do   I want you to hold me and kiss me   Yes always   When you do see me darlint you will, you must, darlint   It doesnt matter where we meet, perhaps a Buffet but it musn't matter, we musn't think of other people being there we must just live for each other in that first minute   Dont forget darlint   Dont just say how are you " Chere "   It so prosaic and were not are we?

I dont know whether Im sorry or pleased about you sailing on the 9th   Its so hard to say now   If things are the same as now perhaps I shall be pleased   If we are successful I shall probably be sorry   I shall want you so much through that time I think   It will be awful to think of you miles away   Darlingest boy, get that ankle well quickly I do want to play tennis with you some time this year—dont bother about the blessed old football—it always makes it give out and isnt ankle spelt with a 'K' it looks so funny with a 'c'

All June—all July—all August—you'll be home again Sept 9   I wonder if we shall have that week together darlint, by the sea—Sept isnt too late is it?

Ive got a real longing for you to take me to Tunbridge Wells   Ive only been there once and I did like it so much

Could you take me darlint for a week-end—or even for a day?

In one of your letters you say 'and you are mine Peidi, arent you?   I shall always try to keep you,' darlingest boy what do you mean by that? especially the last part, I dont understand it, will you tell me?

Of course Im yours—you know that, without the ? mark and why will you say these things in the form of a question when you know they are a fact—it hurts darlint

Dont forget to tell me what you mean by the last part   I really want to know

Goodbye darlingest boy—for now and Marseilles—the next letter to England—Hoorah! I do love you so much and miss you more than you can ever know—its the whole of me—all my life—just all I live for now

PEIDI

Appendix I.

Exhibit 22a

Extract from *Daily Sketch*, 10th May, 1922, page 3, column 3

With headnote—
 "Girl's Drug Injections
 "Mysterious Death after Doses of Cocaine and Morphia"

Then follows a report of an inquest on Lilian May Davis, when evidence was given that she took injections of cocaine in the daytime and morphia at night for sleeplessness. Dr. Spilsbury gave evidence that he made a post-mortem examination and could not assign the cause of death.

Exhibit 22b

Extract from *Daily Sketch*, 6th May, 1922 page 15, column 3

With headnote—
 "Patient Killed by an Overdose
 "Woman Dispenser's Error of Calculation.
 "Ten Times too Strong, Multiplied by a Hundred instead of by Ten"

The report refers to an inquest on Arthur Kemp, who died from an overdose of sodium antimony tartarate, prepared by a woman dispenser.

Exhibit 51

Envelope—Mr F Bywaters, P & O R M S "Morea"

[Postmark—London, 1922 (remainder undecipherable)]

The mail is in darlint, but I havent had an opportunity to read it yet Im fearfully busy Miss Prior is in Paris and I've tons to do, but, darlint when Ive read it I will answer it, even if I have to give it to you by hand Im sure I shant have time to do it to day and I do want you to get something from me at Plymouth—even if its only a few lines Friday, Ill see you shall I? Today to Friday four more days to live—no not live—exist thro You are getting in Friday arent you darlint? do say 'Yes' Are you going to answer my letters to you at Marseilles please do darlint I dont want you to say what you did last trip *You wont* darlint because Ive asked you not to On Saturday Mr Carlton took me home by road It wasnt his car but a friend of his A real posh car youd have liked it Im afraid if Miss Prior knew she might want to give me the sack However I shant tell her and Im sure he won't Also Bess and Reg came down quite unexpectedly on Sunday and we went for a ride from about 3 till 9-30 Bess asked after you Darlint I had a terrible shock when the Egypt went down Nobody said the name of the boat they just said a big P and O liner Imagine what I felt can you? I have sent you a parcel to Plymouth containing 2 books 'The Fruitful Vine' and 'Bella Donna' Read 'Bella Donna' first will you please whilst you are in England if

Bywaters and Thompson.

possible and keep 'The Fruitful Vine' until we are parted again. Also in the parcel is something I forgot last time. I dont suppose you really want it but because I promised and forgot I got it this time. Forgive me for forgetting. You have, havnt you darlint? And there is a pocket of Toblerone. I bought two. Sent you one and kept the other myself. Will you eat it Thursday and I will mine. Darlingest boy will you send the enclosed P C as instructions attached in your name. I hav sent one in mine or rather in my 'used to name' that sounds funny doesnt it. After all whats in a name. Nothing at all except 'Peidi.' I saw your Mother again last Wednesday. I was with Harry Penton and behind her and purposely kept so.

It has been frightfully hot this weekend. The sun has been fierce and I dont want a neck like I had at Shanklin. I shall have to get a sunshade. What about Whit Saturday? We shan't be able to be together. He doesnt go in. I thought of asking for a day off, say Wed the 31st, what do you think? Bill brought Miss Ashley home. Did you know? He says she is very mean. I saw Carpentier on the afternoon of his fight he was over the road at Pagets. The Police had to guard his car. He looks very lined and old for his age. Young Mr Paget (you remember me telling you about him) says the fight was a frost and very unfair. Carpentier took an unfair advantage while the Referees were intervening. You wouldnt like me a bit today darlint. 'Why' did you say? Because Ive got my foulard frock on. Its so hot, and that reminds me the black frock with the white beads that I always wear when you take me out I thought I would wear it out for every day this Summer. Its too conspicuous to keep for next winter and when I've got some spare cash Ill buy another frock for you to take me to dinner in, but I wont wear the blk and white until you say I may so write and tell me what you think also darlint, let me know about Wed 31st because I must give them a little notice as we are so busy. On Sunday I cooked a chicken my very first attempt at poultry. It was all very nice—I think—stuffing and bread sauce etc and then a gooseberry pie. I thought about you the whole time and wished I had cooked it for you. Dont be too disappointed with this letter darlint, I havnt time to really talk to you, but I will and give it you when I see you. Its been a fearful rush to get even this in, and I do hate to rush when I'm talking to you. Au revoir darling for 4 more days. I love you such a lot—just as much—no more than you love   PEIDI

Written on back of envelope—

Did you receive a pencil slip in letter to Marseilles

Exhibit 23

Envelope—Mr F Bywaters, P O. R M S 'Morea,' Plymouth

[Postmark—London, E C, May 23, 1922, 3 p m]

So it wasnt G M M.C* it was G A M C this time darlint, I was sur

---

* "Good morning, ma Chere," &c

Appendix I.

prised I got it at 4 20 p m , Monday   Also I managed to read your letters
   I dont know how tho'   you are wrong about the scent quite
try and guess again   I dont use scent at home   other people smell it
   Darlint, one day last week I went to Frascati to lunch and took one hour and 10 minutes   it was a fearful rush—it was a man that I have known for years by sight but never better until a few weeks ago
the usual type of man darlint   that expects some return for a lunch However, that doesnt matter, this is what I wanted to tell you   he wanted to buy a box of chocolates and I said   I'd rather you didnt thank you '
   He—' Now what earthly difference is there in you accepting from me a box of chocolates to a lunch
   I— Oh its not that—its just that I dont like chocolates '
   He—' Good God, you're the first girl I've ever heard refuse chocolates that she didnt have to pay for   Are you sure you dont like them or is a pose? '
   Darlingest boy what do you think of that?   Can you imagine me posing especially over chocolates   However he ended up in buying me a pound of ' Marrons Glace '   Have you ever had them, they are chestnuts in syrup, I really did enjoy them
   Now about your letters   I cant say if you are right or wrong about Molly   I dont know her sufficiently to say and I do hate to judge other people by appearances   I'd much rather dismiss them from my thoughts altogether   I had already sent you 2 books to Plymouth darlint, the only two I have read since you've been away   I'd like you to read ' Bella Donna ' first you may learn something from it to help us, then you can read ' The fruitful Vine "—when you are away   You say you think, I think, you dont talk enough about books and things to me Darlingest boy I'm not going to say anything at all about anything—I'm just going to be thankful for what I do receive   think to myself
   " I must not be impatient perhaps they wont always be crumbs "
You havnt read a book with the term " Carissima ' in   at least not the book I have read it in   I do so much wonder if you will like " The Fruitful Vine," and who you will like in it—its quite different from anything I have ever read before —Darlingest, you really must tell me all and everything you think about the book and the characters and especially the motive   I do want to know so much   Your news about—from Bombay —and waiting till next trip made me feel very sad and downhearted—it will be awful waiting all that time, 3 months will it be—I cant wait   Yes, I can   I will, I must   I'll make myself somehow   I'll try to be patient darling   You talk about that cage you are in   that's how I feel   only worse if it can be so   because mine is a real live cage with a keeper as well   to whom I have to account every day, every hour, every minute nearly
   " The fate of every man have we bound about his neck " (I dont know if I've got it quite right—you can tell me later on   but the meaning is right)
   Have we darlint? have we the fate of one—or we two halves I dont know—I darent think   its like making sand pies at the sea-side they always topple over   We havnt fixed up anything about Bournemouth yet   they are too expensive for Avis and him   I dont care per-

sonally   . I'd sooner not have a holiday   I really looking forward with dread, not pleasure   I'll always be thinking first of Shanklin and then of our tumble down nook

I'm going to post this now and risk whether it gets to you in time, wire me how many letters you receive—there should be two—then I should have answered all yours darlint and shant have to give you anything by hand   I didnt like the idea   but thought that it would be force of circumstances I've got a feeling inside me   of sinking   do you know what its like   its a feeling of great excitement   probable excitement but not positive Au revoir for such a short time that will seem so long till Friday

PEIDI

Exhibit 66

[COPY TELEGRAM]

Office of Origin—Barbican, London City   Office Stamp—Tilbury, 6 June, 1922, Essex
Handed in at 10 36   Received here at 10 52

To—Bywaters, Steamer Morea, Tilbury Dock

Failed again perhaps 5 o'clock to night

Exhibit 67

[COPY TELEGRAM]

Office of Origin—London C T O   Office Stamp—Tilbury, 7 June, 1922, Essex
Handed in at 12 34   Received here at 12 46

To—Bywaters, Steamer Morea Tilbury Docks

Have already said not going 231 see you and talk six

Exhibit 68

[COPY TELEGRAM]

Office of Origin—London Cit S   Office Stamp—Tilbury, 9 June, 1922, Essex
Boatage assured
Handed in at 9 35 p m   Received here at 10 a m

To—Bywaters, Steamer Morea, Tilbury Docks

Send everything Fisher care G P O call Monday

Appendix I.

Exhibit 24

Envelope—Mr F Bywaters, P & O R M S ' Morea," Marseilles, France

[Postmark—London, E C, 13th June, '22, 4 30 p m]

Darlingest Boy,
    I'm trying very hard—very very hard to B B   I know my pal wants me to
    On Thursday—he was on the ottoman at the foot of the bed and said he was dying and wanted to—he had another heart attack—thro me
    Darlint I had to laugh at this because *I knew* it couldn't be a heart attack
    When he saw this had no effect on me—he got up and stormed—I said exactly what you told me to and he replied that he knew thats what I wanted and he wasnt going to give it to me—it would make things far too easy for both of you (meaning you and me) especially for you he said
    He said hed been to 231 and been told you had said you were taking a pal out and it was all a planned affair so was the last Thursday you were home and also Tuesday of last week at Fenchurch Street—he told them at 231 a pal of his saw us and by the description he gave of the man I was with it was you
    Thats an awful lie darlint because I told him I went to F St for Mr Carlton and saw Booth and spoke to him and I asked him the next day if Booth mentioned me and he said no—nothing at all
    We're both liars he says and you are making me worse and he's going to put a stop to all or any correspondence coming for me at 168   He said " Its useless for you to deny he writes to you—because I know he does "—hence my wire to you regarding G P O
    He also says I told him I wrote to you asking you not to see me this time—he knows very well I said last time—but I think he has really persuaded himself I said this time
    I rang Avis yesterday and she said he came down there in a rage and told Dad everything—about all the rows we have had over you—but she d d not mention he said anything about the first real one on August 1st—so I suppose he kept that back to suit his own ends   Dad said it was a disgraceful thing that you should come between husband and wife and I ought to be ashamed   Darlint I told you this is how they would look at it—they dont understand and they never will any of them
    Dad was going to talk to me Avis said—but I went down and nothing whatever was said by any of them   I told Avis I shd tell them off if they said anything to me   I didnt go whining to my people when he did things I didnt approve of and I didnt expect him to—but however nothing was said at all
    Dad said to them " What a scandal if it should get in the papers " so evidently *he* suggested drastic measures to them
    On Friday night I said I was going to sleep in the little room—we had a scuffle—he succeeded in getting into the little room and on to the bed - so I went into the bathroom and stopped there for ½ an hr—he went down stairs then and I went into the little room quickly—locked the door and stopped there all night—I shd have continued to do so—but even a little thing like that Fate was against us—because Dad was over on Sat and

asked me if he could stay the night—suggested he should sleep with *him* in the big bed—but Dad would not hear of it—so sooner than make another fuss—I gave in

On Saturday he told me he was going to break me in somehow—I have always had too much of my own way and he was a model husband—and in future on *Thursdays* the bedroom was to be cleaned out

He also told me he was going to be master and I was to be his mistress and not half a dozen mrs (his words) I dont exactly know how to take this—Darlint, do you know Avis said to me—Miss M'Donald saw you with Freddy last week—of course I denied it—but she described my frock—anyhow it turned out to be on Wed—so of course it was all right—but you see we are seen and by people who know us and cant hold their tongues Avis said she was upset because you had gone for good—she said she could hardly realise it She also said that *he* said at 231 'I thought he was keen on you (Avis)—but now I can see it was a blind to cover his infatuation for Edie"

Darlint its not an infatuation is it? Tell me it isnt

I dont think theres anything else heaps of little things were said that I cant remember but you can judge what they were—because you know me and *him*

Im writing a letter to Marseilles darlint—this is only a summary of events

---

Exhibit 53

Envelope—Mr F Bywaters P & O R M S 'Morea,' Marseilles, France

[Postmark—London, E C 14 June, 1922]

Darlint Pal,

Ive come to the conclusion that you and I do absolutely mad things especially I

I never have a thought about having those letters sent to G P O I called there on Monday and was told that unless I could prove I was Miss P Fisher I couldnt have them

I thought, this is a devil of a mess and wondered what to do

Eventually I decided to have some cards printed (this cost me 6/6) dont laugh, darlint and I also got Rosie to address an envelope to me at 168 in the name of Fisher

The card and envelope I showed to the man at the G P O today—fortunately it was a different man from yesterday Darlint I think it would be best to address all letters there until I tell you otherwise, dont you? The watch I received quite safely darlint—you say in your letter it goes 10 minutes a day *fast* this isnt right is it? It should be slow

However yesterday I took it back and they promised to put it in order for me I shall probably send it to Sydney—is this what you wish Also the cheque I received but not until today of course—I will try and cash it tomorrow and let you know the result In any case I will put the money on the Hunt Cup for you and for me The Oaks money has not been paid out—I dont think we shall get it—at all—Jim tells me the man got 7 days for obstructing the Police and he (Jim) cant get hold of him now Have also sent what you asked me for—hope you get it safely

Appendix I.

Darlingest boy, dont forget to answer the note I gave you on your last night in England Ill feel much happier if I know Im so glad youre not sorry this time, no Im not a bit I really begin to feel that I am doing something just a little for you—not exactly doing something for you but giving you something—a part of me, for you and no one else—write and tell me that not only are you not sorry this time but youre glad really glad—*because I am*

———

Mr Carlton likes my hair cut—he noticed it and told me so immediately he saw me, I told you nobody but Lily did didnt I—do you? you never said

———

I wonder how my own pal is feeling—I m feeling very blue myself—an inactive sort of drifting feeling, that cant be described—I suppose its really reaction—I longing to hear from you next Monday—I hope its a lot

On our birthday you will be left Aden on your way to Bombay—you'll be thinking of a girl whose best pal you are in England wont you—Ill think of you—all day every little minute—and keep on wishing you success as I cant be—Perhaps you can and as you say you are still hoping darlint—so shall I Time hangs so dreadfully and just because I want to work it away we are not busy this week and are leaving at five I suppose we shall thro the Summer now Darlint, how can you get ptomaine poisoning from a tin of salmon? One of our boys Mother has died with it after being ill only three days

One year ago today we went for that memorable ride round the island in the char-a-banc do you remember? Last night when I went to bed I kissed you goodnight in my mind because that was the first time you kissed me

Darlint this month and next are full of remembrances—arnt they?

I went to 49 last night and sat and listened to ailments for about 2 hours—its awfully exhilerating especially when you feel blue I also had a small row with them He asked why Graham never came to see us and I said "Why do you ask for him to come round when you know he's not allowed to"

This led to words of course and I was told that neither his mother nor his Father would tell him not to speak to me—my retort was that I knew his Father would not but It would take more than any of them to convince me his mother would not, and I wish to God I didnt have to go there—I feel really bad tempered when I come away

I was taken faint in the train this morning—I didnt quite go off though—On Saturday I'm going to see a Doctor, I think it is best that I should—I dont like doing these silly things in public places—I've got my costume home—it looks very nice—Im ever so pleased with it—but I dont want to wear it—I wish you could see me in it—what would you like me to do? Next week I'll be writing to the other end of the world to you darlint—I wish you didnt ever have to leave England, even if I didnt see you I should feel happier and safe because you would be near—but the sea and Australia sounds years and years apart. I do so much want my pal to talk to and confide in and my own man to lean upon some times

———

Have just come from the Bank They cashed the cheque for me after a difficulty—asked me if I was F Bywaters—I thought it best to tell the

Bywaters and Thompson.

truth—as they might ask me to write signature, so I said, "No" "Did you endorse the back?" "No"—"Just write your name on this paper please" I did so, and they then asked me what authority I had from F Bywaters to cash the cheque I had your letter with me—showed it them—and they paid out So much for that incident—What a mess we do get into!

I shall have to close now darlint, goodbye until Sydney—I always loved my only Pal and I do love so much my own boy—think of this all the time you are in Australia—I shall be thinking of you and wishing you were with

PEIDI

Written in pencil on plain envelope

Varzy 1st
Stafford 2d
Crubenmore 3rd

Darlint,
 We must give up horse racing
 We have lost between us

30/ each way Stamp
20 , , Montserrat
10/ ,, Pondoland
(£6)

and won about 10/ on Crubenmore on which I had 2/6 each way for luck

I used £3 10 0 from cheque, 30/- from my own money and 20/- from Derby winnings for the £6, so I have the £5 untouched

Don't send me any more money please darlint

Goodbye and good luck

always,

PEIDI

Exhibit 25

Envelope—Mr F Bywaters P & O R M S "Morea Sydney Australia

[Postmark—London E C June 20, 1922, 1 30 p m]

Darlingest Boy I know

This time last year I had won the sweep stake for the Gold Cup, this year I have lost £1 10/ eh way Kings Idler and the result is Golden Myth at 7 to 1, Flamboyant 20 to 1, and Ballyheron 8 to 1 I'm not going to bet any more—even in horse racing the fates are against me

You get into Marseilles tonight I wonder how you're feeling darlint, very blue—or not feeling anything at all—just drifting—its hard either way isn't it?

I wish you had taken me with you darlint—I don't think I will be able to stay on here all alone—there seems so much to contend with—so long to "dance" when you'd rather die and all for no definite purpose Oh I'll pack up now, I can't talk cheerfully—so I shan't talk at all goodnight darlint

Appendix I.

It's Friday now, darlint nearly time to go, I am wondering if you remember what your answer was to me in reply to my "What's the matter" tonight of last year

I remember quite well—"You know what's the matter, I love you" but you didn't then darlint because you do now and its different now, isn't it? From then onwards everything has gone wrong with our lives—I don't mean to say it was right before—at least mine wasn't right—but I was quite indifferent to it being either right or wrong and you darlint—you hadn't any of the troubles—or the worries you have now—you were quite free in mind and body—and now through me you are not—darlint I am sorry I shouldn't mind if I could feel that some day I should be able to make up to you for all the unhappiness I have caused in your life—but I can't feel that darlint—I keep on saying to myself that ' it will—it shall come right "—but there is no conviction behind it—why can't we see into the future?

When you are not near darlint I wish we had taken the easiest way—I suppose it is because I can't see you—can't have you to hold me and talk to me—because when you are in England I always want to go on trying and trying and not to give up—to see and feel you holding me—is to hope on, and when I can't have that I feel a coward   The days pass—no they don't pass they just drag on and on and the end of all this misery and unhappiness is no nearer in sight—is anything worth living for?

There are 2 halves in this world who want nothing on earth but to be joined together and circumstances persistently keep them apart—nothing is fair—nothing is just—we can't even live for ourselves—can we?

I suppose the week end will pass somehow—the only thought that helps is that you will talk to me on Monday

Goodbye darlingest boy—I do wish you were here

Its Monday now darlint, that day you came up and took me to lunch at the Kings Hall do you remember?

Things are very quiet here and Mr Carlton has taken 2 or 3 days off this week.   He told me he would come up about Thursday—to fix up the outing on Saturday—that was the day last year that you and Avis came to an understanding—I wonder if that's the right way to put it

Nothing happened over the week end darlint except that Dad came up on Saturday and did not go home in the evening   It's becoming a regular thing now—I wonder why?

When you are in Australia—darlint you will tell me all you do and where you go—everything—I want to know

I shall be in Bournemouth when you're in Australia think about me darlingest boy—it won't be the holiday I anticipated will it? I certainly shant learn to swim neither shall I be playing tennis it won't be nice at all—because I shan't even be able to escape things and beings by going up to town each day—but it's one of those things that have to be gone thro in this life I lead and all the railings against it won't alter a tiny bit of it—so I must dance thro somehow   Are you going to see Harold? if you do try and knock a bit of sense into him please darlint pour moi and write and tell me what he is doing,—how is he getting on—everything—he writes such nonsense that you can't tell from a letter what he really is doing   He's written to Doris Grafton and tells her, he is sending over her passage money and she is to come out and marry him—and a lot more of rot like that—darlint I'm sure he's not normal sometimes

Bywaters and Thompson.

See what my pal can do for me, please

Won't you have a long time to wait for a letter from me this time, Darlint? I have been looking at the mail card and see you do not arrive in Australia until July 22nd—I'm so sorry—I wish I could afford to cable you a long long letter to somewhere before Sydney, or better still, to be able to phone to you and hear you say "Is that Peidi?"

I went to see a doctor on Saturday he asked me lots of questions—could he examine me etc—I said no—then he said are you enciente? to which I replied "No, I think not," but explained to him how I felt. Eventually he came to the conclusion that I have "chronic anæmia"—which will probably turn to pernicious anæmia if I am not careful

I asked him exactly what this was and he said, "all your blood every drop turns to water"

I also asked him if it was a usual thing for any one to have and he said "No" only much older people suffer with it, as a rule—only younger people, when they have had an accident and lost a lot of blood, have you had one? he said

I said 'No'—because it wasn't really an accident and I didn't want to tell him everything—he might have wanted to see my husband

But I expect thats what has really caused this anæmia—because I lost an awful lot of blood

The doctor says I must drink Burgundy with every meal—4 glasses a day—I don't know how I am going to do that—I hate the stuff

He has given me some medicine as well and a box of pills to be taken until I am ill

Darlint are you disappointed it is only that? tell me please

I've just come back from getting the Marseilles Mail at the G P O

What an utterly absurd thing to say to me 'Don't be too disappointed"

You can't possibly know what it feels like to want and wait each day—every little hour—for something—something that means "life" to you and then not to get it

You told me from Dover that you were going to talk to me for a long time at Marseilles and now you put it off to Port Said

You force me to conclude that the life you lead away from England—is all absorbing that you havn't time nor inclination to remember England or anything England holds

There were at least 5 days you could have talked to me about—if you only spared me 5 minutes out of each day. But what is the use of me saying all this—it's the same always—I'm never meant to have anything I expect or want. If I am unjust—I am sorry—but I can't feel anything at present—only just as if I have had a blow on the head and I am stunned—the disappointment—no, more than that—the utter despair is too much to bear—I would sooner go under today than anything

All I can hope is, that you will never never feel like I do today—*it's so easy to write* "try to be brave" its so much harder to be so, nobody knows—but those who try to be—against such heavy odds

It's more to me than anything on this earth—to read what you say to me—you know this darlint, why do you fail me? What encouragement is it to go on living and waiting and waiting

Appendix I.

Perhaps I ought not to have written this—perhaps I ought to have ignored having a scrap only, altogether—but how I feel and what I think I must tell you always

Darlint I hope you will never never never feel as miserable as

PEIDI

Exhibit 69

[COPY MARCONIGRAM]

Deld Date 26 June, 1922

No 2   MOREA   26 Jun 1922
 P   7
Handed in at   LONDON   13 35
                                    V W B   10/2   A G S
Via Eastern Radio—26th

To—BYWATERS Steamer Morea Bombay radio

M H R   27621   PEIDI

Exhibit 26

Envelope—Mr F Bywaters P & O R M S 'Morea,' Freemantle, Australia

[Postmark—London, E C   4 July, 1922]

Darlingest Boy,

First of all last Sunday week a lady I dont know her name—we all call her '2 jam pots high' asked after—"that nice curly headed boy" We met her in Ilford in the evening—I said when I last saw you—you were quite well   I wasnt by myself Darlint—*he* was with me

I felt quite jealous that she should remember you all this time   Then last Wednesday I met your mother and she cut me   I wasn't prepared for it either—I saw her coming towards me and thought ' as she spoke to me last time we met that there is no reason why she shouldn't this time " And as she came up I just smiled bowed said ' How do you do "—she just took no notice whatever and walked on   I can't explain how I felt—I think I wanted to hit her more than anything—things get worse and worse —instead of just a tiny bit better each day

On Thursday afternoon I went to the G P O for the Port Said Mail and encountered the first man that I saw before—he handed me a registered envelope from you (which contained the gaiters—thank you very much darlint) and told me if I had an address in London I couldn't have letters addressed to the G P O —I told him I hadn't—but I dont think he believed me anyway he didnt give me your Port Said letter and I hadnt the patience to overcome (or try to) his bad temper

I went again on Monday and got it a different man was on duty—when I read it—I didnt feel very satisfied darlint it didn't seem worth waiting all that time for—24 days—however I wont talk about it—you ought to know by now how I feel about those things

Bywaters and Thompson.

In one part of it you say you are going to still write to me because it will help, in another part you say—"Perhaps I shant write to you from some ports—because I want to help you" I dont understand—I try to—but I cant—really I cant darlint—my head aches—aches with thinking sometimes

Last Friday last year—we went to see "Romance"—*then* we were pals and this year we seem no further advanced

Why arnt you sending me something—I wanted you to—you never do what I ask you darlint—you still have your own way always—If I dont mind the risk why should you? whatever happens cant be any more than this existence—looking forward to nothing and gaining only ashes and dust and bitterness

I'm not going to ask dad about you at all—I not going to say anything to anybody—they can all think the worst of me that is possible—I am quite indifferent

Miss Prior is on holiday and the only person in this world that is nice to me is Mr Carlton—I have had 2 half days off and am having another to-morrow afternoon—all this time off makes me think of last year—when you were with me—rushing home to see you

I've had a brandy and soda some mornings—about 11 30 and a half bottle of champagne between us—other mornings and I learn such a lot of things that are interesting too

This morning on the station I saw Molly—talking and laughing with Mr Derry—in case you dont remember the name—it's the little man in the "White Horse"

I've never seen her talk to him before altho she has passed me on the platform talking to him several times (me talking to him I mean) I bowed —said good morning to him as I passed and have since been wondering if they have told each other what they know about me

Never mind, a little more bad feeling cant hurt—there is such a lot of it to contend with will you tell me if youd rather I didnt write?

                            PEIDI

Have you studied "Bichloride of Mercury"?

                  231 Shakespeare Crescent,
                    Manor Park, E 12
                      June 13th 1922

Dr Fred,

I have just received a letter from my sister in Melbourne she encloses a letter received from Harold in which he says he has got a job in the "Ehto Cafe" 85 *Ackland Str* St Kilda, Melbourne, he has just been working there for a week at the *time of writing* and has got £2 a week with board and lodging so he ought not to want for much, he works from 9 a m to 1 p m then he is off duty till 6 p m he then goes on again from 6 till 10 p m according to this he has plenty of time to come down to your ship and get hold of the bag so might I suggest you write him from Freemantle and tell him to come along and see you and get the bag, this would avoid having to send it to Box Hill but I'll leave it to you to make the best arrangement you can, and I've no doubt you will Well now what of the voyage so far, are you comfortable and a full ship, and does there seem a prospect of making say half a fortune this trip I hope you will be successful and do yourself a real bit of good this trip as it is a long one and that next time we meet you will be able to report progress

Appendix I.

Well, I dont think I've much more news to tell you
So will conclude with best wishes from us all for your health and prosperity, and again thanking you

I am,

Yours etc

W E GRAYDON

Exhibit 52

Envelope—Mr F Bywaters, P & O R M S "Morea," Colombo

[Postmark—London W 1 July 14, 1922 7 15 p m]

Darlingest boy—you worry me so much—what do you mean you say " I want to be in England to look after you " I can understand that and I want you to be here also—but you then say ' I want you to look after me too " Whats the matter darlint, are you ill? is any thing the matter that I could help you in at all I do believe youve been ill——oh darlint why are you such miles away—why arent we together—so that I could help you Would you like a pillow? the pillow that only Peidie can give you—Id love to have you here now so that I could give it you Do tell me whats the matter darlingest boy—I shall worry and worry all the time until you write and tell me Its Thursday and Ive just come from the G P O with the Aden mail Isnt it late this time darlint it's usually in on a Monday or at latest Tuesday However Ive got it and thats all that really matters Darlingest boy didnt I say a long time ago " Dont trust Dan " Of course I didnt mean that in the sense you have told me he couldnt be trusted in but my instinct was right wasnt it? You will be careful wont you darlint pour moi? I dont want to ever know or think that my own boy is in any predicament of that sort——because Ill be too far away to help wont I? The thought of anything like that makes my blood cold—Ill be always worrying Im writing this letter rather early to Colombo—because Im going away tomorrow and I shant have an opportunity of writing to you again for a fortnight Perhaps I could manage a letter card tho anyway you'll understand wont you darlint pal? I dont mind a bit pencil as long as its words on paper——it doesn't matter——because they're what you say and think and do——a letter darlint is like food only you have food everyday to keep you alive and I have a letter every how many days? 14 sometimes and I have to keep alive on that all that time About Bella Donna——no I dont agree with you about her darlint—I hate her——hate to think of her——I dont think other people made her what she was—that sensual pleasure loving greedy Bella Donna was always there If she had originally been different—a good man like Nigel would have altered her darlint—she never knew what it was to be denied anything—she never knew " goodness " as you and I know it—she was never interested in a good man—or any man unless he could appease her sensual nature I don't think she could have been happy with nothing —except Baroudi on a desert island she liked—no loved and lived for his money or what it could give her—the luxury of his yacht the secrecy with which he acted all bought with his money—that's what she liked

Yes she was clever—I admire the cleverness—but she was cunning there is a difference darlint I don t admire that—I certainly don t think she would ever have killed Nigel with her hands—she would have been found out—she didn't like that did she? being found out—it was that secret cunning in Baroudi that she admired so much—the cunning that matched her own

If she had loved Baroudi enough she could have gone to him—but she liked the security of being Nigel's wife—for the monetary assets it held

She doesn't seem a woman to me—she seems abnormal—a monster utterly selfish and self living

Darlint this is where we differ about women

I usually stand up for them *against* you and in this case its the reverse but honestly darlint I dont call her a woman—she is absolutely unnatural in every sense

---

You do say silly things to me—' try a little bit every day not to think about me '—doesn't that ' trying ' ever make it worse—it does for me always

About the age passages in ' The Fruitful Vine '—I marked them because as I read they struck me as concerning you and I

Darlint I didn't do it with malice every passage in any book I read that strikes me as concerning 2 pals I mark—it doesn't matter what they are about

I hadn't mentioned the subject any more had I?

My veriest own lover I always think about the ' difference ' when I'm with you and when I'm away sometimes when I m happy for a little while I forget—but I always remember very soon—perhaps some little thing that you might say or do when we're together reminds me   Sometimes I think and think until my brain goes round and round   ' Shall I always be able to keep you   8 years is such a long time—it's not now—it's later —when I'm ' Joan ' and you're not grown old enough to be ' Darby ' When you've got something that you've never had before and something that you're so happy to have found—you're always afraid of it flying away—that's how I feel about your love

Don't ever take your love away from me darlint—I never want to lose it and live

If it gets less and gradually fades away—don't let me live to feel without it   It feels a bigger fuller greater love that I have for my own and only lover now

PEIDI

Exhibit 63

Envelope—Mr F Bywaters, P O , R M S " Morea," Port Said

[1½d stamp—London, E C , Aug 28, 6 15 p m , 1922]

Darlingest boy, today is the 27th and its on a Sunday, so I am writing this in the bathroom, I always like to send you greetings on the day—not the day before or the day after

Fourteen whole months have gone by now, darlint, its so terribly long   Neither you nor I thought we should have to wait all that long time did we? although I said I would wait 5 years—and I will darlint— its only 3 years and ten months now

Appendix I.

Many happy returns and good luck darlingest boy—I cant wish you any more can I? every day I say 'Good luck to my Pal' to myself

PEIDI

Exhibit 54

Envelope—Mr F Bywaters, P & O R M S "Morea,' Marseilles, France

[Postmark—London, E C , Sept 12, 1922, 5 30 p m]

Darlint Pal,

I've got nothing to talk to you about—I cant think about anything at all—I can't even look forward to seeing you Now you are nearing England—I keep contrasting this home coming with the previous ones I have been buoyed up with hope, bubbling with excitement Just existing with an intense strung up feeling of seeing you and feeling you holding me in your two arms so tightly that it hurts but this time everything seems different I don't hear from you much you don't talk to me by letter and help me and I don't even know if I am going to see you

Darlint, I'm an awful little beast I know—I don't want to be either—but I feel so hopeless—just drifting—but it you say No I won't see you ' then it shall be so, I'm quite reconciled to whatever verdict you send forth and shall say to myself ' It is for the best it must be so '

Darlint you do love me still tho' don't you? and you will go on loving me even if we don't meet Things here are going smoothly with me—I am giving all—and accepting everything and I think am looked upon as ' The Dutiful Wife ' whose spirit is at last bent to the will of her husband '

This isn't sarcasm or cynicism its exactly how I feel I had a little letter from you—by what you said it was written on the 28th of July Ive had nothing—further there are heaps and heaps of questions in my letters to you

I wonder if you will answer them or are they already *dismissed?* On Saturday I was so ill I had to stop away—its not very often I give in so much as stopping away from business but on Saturday I really had to I m quite alright now tho' darlint

I don't think I told you I bought a fur coat—at least part of it It was 27 gns and I had £13 saved up—so I borrowed £15 from the account and am paying it back at £1 per week—the debt is only £10 now

Also I've had to fall back on wearing lace shoes—no don't make a race darlint, they are rather nice ones—I wanted grey and could get nothing at all in my usual style—only with one or two straps across—and I don't like these—even if they hid my foot I shouldn't—they look loud, so I bought lace ones only to wear with cloth clothes tho' darlint—not with silk

Yesterday you were at Suez—I suppose you got my Port Said letters there and on Friday or Saturday, you will get these—I think the mail facilities favour you more than me darlint

Darlingest pal—do let me hear an awful lot from you next week—I'm just existing now—I shall live then

Darlingest, only lover of mine—try to cheer me up

PEIDI

Bywaters and Thompson.

Exhibit 28

Envelope—unaddressed

(After 19th Sept 1922)

I think I'm fearfully disappointed about you not getting in on Friday darlint I'd been planning to get off early—rush to Ilford and do the shopping and rush up to meet you—having had my hair washed in the luncheon hour instead of at night—as I should have said and now all that is no use—so I shant have my hair washed—it must wait until the next Friday—that will mean an extra hour with you—do you mind me having a dirty head for a week darlint—its very very dirty I've been hanging it out especially for now

Why are you so late this time—oh I hate this journey, I hate Australia and everything connected with it—it will be 109 days since Ive seen you—and you didnt answer my question about China and Japan next time I suppose it is right—or you would have told me—it will be worse then

I was surprised about you going home this time darlint—so surprised I couldnt believe I had read rightly at first

You ask me if Im glad or sorry—darlint I dont know how I feel about it—Im glad for you darlint—because you know I always felt responsible for the break, I dont think Im glad for myself tho', I think I'm harbouring just a small petty feeling of resentment against them—I've tried so hard not to—and I think I didnt at first, and its only just this last time

You say you have reasons darlint I dont know them and you dont tell me them—so I cant be influenced by them one way or the other Tell me them—it'll help darlingest You say you suppose you deserve the Sydney letter—didnt you get 2 darlint—I was sorry as soon as I had posted the first I do hope you got the 2nd

Darlingest boy—pal—you're horrid to be cross about the Turkish Delight —you are really—I'm sorry I wrote that—but just think darlint—you know that is what everyone else would have said or thought and I'm mixed up with all the "everyones" so much that I forgot at the moment, that I was talking to someone different If you are still cross—soften a wee teeny bit and forgive Peidi and try and accept her excuse for erring Darlint —you know "to err is human to forgive divine," and Im certainly not going to even hazard a guess why you are not bringing any delight or cigarettes this time, in case I err again or am misunderstood Please tell me I think I must have been reading 'The Firing Line' at the same time as you—I finished it last Sunday Why didn't you like it as well as the others darlint?

I liked it—but I liked the villain as they call him, too, Louis Malcourt

I've read it before—ages and ages ago only I was stuck for something decent to read and asked Avis to bring along something belonging to me that they had at 231—she brought that

I've read "Monte Christo" darlint—but neither of the others you mention

You're going to get me some books this time arent you? please darlint

---

Darlingest boy—I don't quite understand you about 'Pals' You say 'Can we be Pals only, Peidi, it will make it easier'

Appendix I.

Do you mean for always? because if you do, No, no, a thousand times We can't be 'pals' *only* for always darlint—its impossible physically and mentally

Last time we had a long talk—I said, "Go away this time and forget all about me, forget you ever know me, it will be easier—and better for you"

Do you remember—and you refused, so now I'm refusing darlint—it must be still 'the hope of all' or 'the finish of all'

If you still only mean for a certain time and you think it best, darlint it shall be so—I don't see how it will be easier myself—but it shall be as you say and wish, we won't be our natural selves tho' I know—we'll be putting a kerb on ourselves the whole time—like an iron band that won't expand Please don't let what I have written deter you from any decision darlint—I don't want to do that—truly I'd like to do what you think best

---

I don't sleep much better now—the nights seem so long—I sleep for an hour and lie awake for 2 and go to sleep again for another hour—right thro' the night

A doctor cant do me any good darlint—no good at all—even the most clever in the land—unless that doctor is you and it cant be, so Im not going to waste any more money on them I want you for my doctor—my pal—my lover—my everything—just all and the whole world would be changed Im very anxious to know about missing the ship at Sydney I heard about it from Avis last night—she said 'Oh I suppose he was drunk' Darlint, thats a lie isn't it—you promised me once that it would never be 'too much' Im worrying about it—231 have made me worry—by putting things into my head

Send my letters to 168 as before darlint—I'll risk it and I have a difficulty in getting them at the G P O The Marseilles letter was marked all over "Not known" and initialed about 5 times, I think, and they always question me closely as to not having a permanent address I'll expect a letter on Monday morning at 168

Im not very keen on the sound of "I went home to my cousin's every night—quite domesticated" It sounds like a sneer—I wonder if you did sneer when you wrote it

---

Now about that Wednesday I mentioned—Im disappointed I thought you told me you'd never forget "Dont spoil it" and yet you can remember a trivial incident like that Monday when I was with Harry Penton Do you remember now? taking me to a quick lunch at Evans and coming into 168 and then meeting your Mother up West and then ringing me and asking me what I was doing that evening—and I was going to tea at The Waldorf You went and slept at Norwood that night and didn't come back to me until the Friday You sound very despondent when you say about "Time passes and with it some of the pain—Fate ordained our lot to be hard" Does some of the pain *you* feel pass with time? Perhaps it does—things seem so much easier to forget with a man—his environment is always different—but with a woman its always the same

Darlint my pain gets less and less bearable—it hurts more and more every day, every hour really

"Other ways only involve the parting of you and I, Peidi, nobody deserves anything more than I do"

Bywaters and Thompson.

I don't understand this part—try and explain to me please—have you lost heart and given up hope? tell me if you have darlint—don't bear it all alone

Darlingest, about you being unnatural—I don't know—I don't think its unnatural to give something without wanting to receive in return—I never did—but I think at one time—you would have thought so

From the way your acquaintances argue—they are judging you from how they know you I think, but I know quite a different boy from them— he's a pal—not an ordinary sensual sort of creature made in the usual mould of men

Let them know you as they like darlint—Im selfish enough to want to be the only one who really knows her pal

---

I think I must be fearfully dense—also my memory has left me in the lurch—because I dont understand what you mean by your question " Peidi do you think you could live with a replica—you once said No "

When did I say it and what do you mean—what does the question refer to? Its a puzzle to me darlint, but I accept the rebuff my memory has given me and hope you will overlook this omission

Darlint that's the worst of saying something " is always good "—it invariably lets you down after this statement

Please explain

Now I'm going to be cross—*Dont bully me*—I never said or even suggested that I should cultivate the Regent Palace Hotel and there was no need whatever for you to have hurled forth that edict and then underlined it Ask to be forgiven—you bully! (darlint pal)

No, I dont think the man who mistook me for " Romance " was decent darlint, but I do think he was quite genuine in mistaking me, I dont think it was a ruse on his part

Yes, darlint you are jealous of *him*—but I want you to be—he has the right by law to all that you have the right to by nature and love—yes darlint be jealous so much that you will do something desperate

Ive not sent a wire to Plymouth to you—Ive changed my mind—I see you left Gibraltar on the 19th and perhaps you will get in Saturday morning —then I shall send you a wire to Tilbury to meet me in the afternoon—if its at all possible for you

Before I finish up this letter Ive got a confession to make Darlingest about the watch—I didnt send it to Plymouth—purposely

I felt that you were not going to come and see me this time and the feeling was awful—horrid and I felt that if you refused I couldnt make you

And then I was tempted—I thought, " Yes I can make him—I wont send his watch—I'll tell him if he wants it—he's to come to 168 and fetch it

Darlint, was it small? if it was, real big love must make people think of small things because real, big love made   PEIDI

Exhibit 55

Darlint Pal, please try and use—pour moi, and dont buy a pouch, je vais, pour vous—one of these days

(ad)   PEIDI—

Appendix I.

Exhibit 55a

Extract from *Daily Sketch*, 20th September, 1922, page 2, column 4

With headnote—
' Chicken Broth Death
" Rat Poison Consumed by Fowl Kills Woman "

The report states—
" That death was due to consuming broth made from a chicken which had eaten poison, containing a rat virus, was the medical explanation at the resumed inquest at Shoreditch yesterday on Mrs Sarah Feldman (34) of Reliance Square, Horton "

Exhibits 47 and 48

[TELEGRAM]

Office of Origin—London City, S   Office Stamp—Tilbury Essex, 22 Sep 22
Handed in at 9 28   Received here at 9 48

To—Reply Paid Bywaters Steamer Morea, Tilbury Dock

Can you meet Peidi Broadway 4 p m

Envelope addressed—Bywaters, s s " Morea "   Reply Pd

Exhibits 58 and 59

[TELEGRAM]

Office of Origin—London City, S   Office Stamp—Tilbury, Essex, 25 Sep 22
Handed in at 10 3 a m   Received here at 10 16 a m

To—Bywaters Steamer Morea, Tilbury Docks

Must catch 5 49 Fenchurch Reply if can manage

Exhibit 9

[ORDER]

From Carlton and Prior,
    168 Aldersgate Street,
        London, E C 1

September 30, 1922

Come *in* for me in ½ an hour

PEIDI.

Bywaters and Thompson.

Exhibit 60

Plain envelope

Darlingest lover of mine, thank you, thank you, oh thank you a thousand times for Friday—it was lovely—its always lovely to go out with you

And then Saturday—yes I did feel happy—I didn't think a teeny bit about anything in this world, except being with you—and all Saturday evening I was thinking about you—I was just with you in a big arm chair in front of a great big fire feeling all the time how much I had won—cos I have darlint, won such a lot—it feels such a great big thing to me sometimes—that I can't breathe

When you are away and I see girls with men walking along together —perhaps they are acknowledged sweethearts—they look so ordinary then I feel proud—so proud to think and feel that you are my lover and even tho' not acknowledged I can still hold you—just with a tiny ' hope '

Darlint, we've said we'll always be Pals haven't we, shall we say we'll always be lovers—even tho' secret ones, or is it (this great big love) a thing we can't control—dare we say that—I think I will dare Yes I will ' I'll always love you '—if you are dead—if you have left me even if you don't still love me, I always shall you

Your love to me is new, it is something different it is my life and if things should go badly with us, I shall always have this past year to look back upon and feel that ' Then I lived ' I never did before and I never shall again

Darlingest lover, what happened last night? I don't know myself I only know how I felt—no not really how I felt but how I could feel—if time and circumstances were different.

It seems like a great welling up of love—of feeling—of inertia, just as if I am wax in your hands—to do with as you will and I feel that if you do as you wish I shall be happy, its physical purely and I can't really describe it—but you will understand darlint wont you? You said you knew it would be like this one day—if it hadn't would you have been disappointed Darlingest when you are rough, I go dead—try not to be please

---

The book is lovely—it's going to be sad darlint tho, why can't life go on happy always?

I like Clarie—she is so natural so unworldly

Why ar'nt you an artist and I as she is—I feel when I am reading frightfully jealous of her—its a picture darlint, just how I did once picture that little flat in Chelsea—why can t he go on loving her always—why are men different—I am right when I say that love to a man is a thing apart from his life—but to a woman it is her whole existence

---

I tried so hard to find a way out of tonight darlingest but he was suspicious and still is—I suppose we must make a study of this deceit for some time longer I hate it I hate every lie I have to tell to see you— because lies seem such small mean things to attain such an object as ours We ought to be able to use great big things for great big love like ours I'd love to be able to say ' I'm going to see my lover tonight ' If I did he would prevent me—there would be scenes and he would come to 168 and

Appendix I.

interfere and I couldn't bear that—I could be beaten all over at home and still be defiant—but at 168 it's different It's my living—you wouldn't let me live on him would you and I shouldn't want to—darlint its funds that are our stumbling block—until we have those we can do nothing Darlingest find me a job abroad I'll go tomorrow and not say I was going to a soul and not have one little regret I said I wouldn't think—that I'd try to forget—circumstances—Pal, help me to forget again—I have succeeded up to now—but its thinking of tonight and tomorrow when I can't see you and feel you holding me

Darlint—do something tomorrow night will you? something to make you forget I'll be hurt I know, but I want you to hurt me—I do really—the bargain now, seems so one sided—so unfair—but how can I alter it?

———

About the watch—I didn't think you thought more of that—how can I explain what I did feel? I felt that we had parted—you weren't going to see me—I had given you something to remind you of me and I had purposely retained it If I said 'come for it' you would—but only the once and it would be as a pal because you would want me so badly at times—that the watch would help you not to feel so badly and if you hadn't got it—the feeling would be so great—it would conquer you against your will

Darlint do I flatter myself when I think you think more of the watch than of anything else That wasn't a present—that was something you asked me to give you—when we decided to be *pals* a sort of sealing of the compact I couldn't afford it then but immediately I could I did Do you remember when and where we were when you asked me for it? If you do tell me, if you don't, forget I asked

How I thought you would feel about the watch, I would feel about something I have

It isn't mine, but it belongs to us and unless we were differently situated than we are now, I would follow you everywhere—until you gave it to me back

He's still well—he's going to gaze all day long at you in your temporary home—after Wednesday

———

Don't forget what we talked in the Tea Room I'll still risk and try if you will—we only have 3¾ years left darlingest

Try & help

PEIDI

———

Exhibit 10

[ORDER]

From Carlton and Prior
168 Aldersgate Street
London E C 1

————19

Wait till one he's come

PEIDI

Bywaters and Thompson.

Exhibit 64

Plain envelope

Darlingest boy, thank you—

I know what you say is really true, but darlint it does feel sometimes that we are drifting Don't you ever feel like that—and it hurts so—of ever so much

Yes, we are both going to fight until we win—darlint, fight hard, in real earnest—you are going to help me first and then I am going to help you and when you have done your share and I have done mine we shall have given to each other what we both " desire most in this world " ourselves, isn't this right, but darlint don't fail in your share of the bargain, because I am helpless without your help—you understand

Darlint, this is the one instance in which I cannot stand alone I cannot help myself (at first)—the one instance when I want a man to lean on and that one man is and can only—always—be you

Please, please darlint take me seriously—I want you to—I wanted you to before and you didn't Tell me when you see me next time that you will darlint, *for certain*, remember Peidi is relying on *you* and *you* understand me and know I mean what I say and tell me you know I *wont fail* or *shirk* when the time or opportunity comes

---

Darlint you say you are looking forward to Thursday night, is this really true? somehow I feel it isnt, I have done ever since the 9th and when I think about it I feel more so about it You have not asked me all the time you've been home to go with you—except to a dance—which I refused—because I want to wait for that time—that *first dance* until it will be a real pleasure, *without* any pain and it can't be just now darlint can it? and when you said you'd take me to lunch and then didn't come and I'm wondering—I can't help it darlint if I've done right in asking you to take me out And apart from this feeling that I have, there is that ever present question of money—darlint you've never told me this time once about money—what you had and what you spent and I felt hurt—horribly darlint, especially about the suit—last time you told me about the coat—but not this time—why the difference darlint?

And as I haven't any money to give you, at least not much and perhaps you havn't any I wish you weren't going to take me out darlint and even now its not too late—if you'd only tell me, be quite frank about it darlint, I'll understand—surely you know I will I didn't intend to mention this darlint, but neither you nor I must harbour thoughts that each other doesn't know, must we, we must be one in thoughts and wishes and actions always darlint, so I have   Please understand how I feel and know I love you
                                Peidi

Exhibit 14

Peninsular & Orient Steam Navigation Company
S S Morea

Bombay,
1st December, 1921

Dear Edie,

Do you remember last Xmas you wrote to me wishing me all the best

Appendix I.

I never wrote you so this year I'm going to make sure of it, I want to wish you all that you can wish yourself I know all those wishes of yours will run into a deuce of a lot of money Such items as fur coats, cars and champagne, will be very prominent on the list—anyhow, good health and I hope you get it Have a very real good time, the best that is possible I shall be about 2 days this side of Suez Never mind I will have a drink with you Once more the very very best at Xmas and always

Yours very Sincerely,
FREDDY

Exhibit 30

Gomme

Darling Peidi Mia,

Tonight was impulse—natural—I couldnt resist—I had to hold you darling little sweetheart of mine—darlint I was afraid—I thought you were going to refuse to kiss me—darlint little girl—I love you so much and the only way I can control myself is by not seeing you and I'm not going to do that Darlint Peidi Mia—I must have you—I love you darlint—logic and what others call reason do not enter into our lives, and where two halves are concerned I had no intention darlint of doing that—it just happened thats all—I'm glad now chere—darlint when you suggested the occupied carriage, I didn't want to go in it—did you think that perhaps I did—so that there would have been no opportunity for me to break the conditions that I had stipulated—darlint I felt quite confident that I would be able to keep my feelings down—I was wrong Peidi I was reckoning on will power over ordinary forces—but I was fighting what? not ordinary forces—nothing was fighting the whole of me Peidi you are my magnet—I cannot resist darlint—you draw me to you now and always, I shall never be able to see you and remain impassive Darlint Peidi Mia Idol mine—I love you—always—always Ma Chere Last night when I read your questions I didn t know how to answer them—I have now Peidi?

Darlint I dont think I can talk about other things tonight—I want to hold you so tightly I'm going to tonight in my sleep Bon Nuit Ma Petite, cherchez bien pour votre   FREDDY

Exhibit 31

Peidi Darlint

Sunday evening, Everybody is out and now I can talk to you I wonder what you are doing now my own little girl I hope that Bill has not been the cause of any further unpleasantness darlint Darlint little girl do you remember saying " the hope for all " " Or the finish of all " Peidi the finish of all seems terrible even to contemplate What darlint would it be in practice? Peidi Mia I love you more and more every day—it grows darlint and will keep on growing Darlint in the park—our Park on Saturday, you were my " little devil "—I was happy then Peidi—were you? I wasn't thinking of other things—only you darlint—you was my entire world—I love you so much my Peidi—I mustnt ever think of losing you, darlint if I was a poet I could write volumes—but I not—I suppose at the most Ive only spoken about 2 dozen words today I dont try not to speak—but I have no wish to—Im not spoken to much so have no replies to make

Darlint about the watch—I never really answered your question—I only said I wasnt cross I cant understand you thinking that the watch would draw me to you—where you yourself wouldnt—is that what you meant darlint or have I misunderstood you The way you have written looks to me as though you think that I think more of the watch than I do of you darlint—Tell me Peidi Mia that I misunderstood your meaning

Darlint Peidi Mia—I do remember you coming to me in the little room and I think I understand what it cost you—a lot more then darlint than It could ever now When I think about that I think how nearly we came to be parted for ever,—if you had not forfeited your pride darlint I dont think there would ever have been yesterday or tomorrow

My darlint darlint little girl I love you more than I will ever be able to show you Darlint you are the centre—the world goes on round you, but you ever remain my world—the other part some things are essential—others are on the outskirts and sometimes so far removed from my mind that they seem non existent Darling Peidi Mia—I answered the question about the word " Idle " on Saturday—I never mentioned it

Yes darlint—I remember you being asked if you had found " The great lover " It was when you sang " A Tumble Down Nook "

What have I found darlint? The darlingest little sweetheart girl in the whole world and " The Only Pal " Now darlint pal—Im anxious about Avis—I hope you have found out all there is to know of the other night—I want you to tell me Supposing she did stay with some fellow and she tells you and asks you not to tell anybody—are you going to tell me Peidi?

Darlint I'm enclosing a slip for you for the books in case I am unable to get them myself—also will you get the " Tempting of Paul Chester " Alice and Claude Askew There is 13/- to pay on the others—but darlint I hope to be able to get them myself, also and principally I want to drink Beaune with you

Good night now darlingest—dearest little sweetheart and big pal
FREDDY

APPENDIX II.

Letters from Edith Thompson not put in Evidence at the Trial.

Envelope—Mr F Bywaters, P & O R M S "Morea," Aden

[Postmark—London, E C , Dec 6, 1921 , 2 30 p m]

Darlingest boy I know,

I saw in the paper yesterday you touched Aden on the 28th, I suppose tomorrow or Sunday you will arrive in Bombay & I believe Bill left today, perhaps you will just manage to see him tho

I am feeling very blue today darlint, you havn't talked to me for a fortnight, and I am feeling worried, oh I don't know how I'm feeling really, it seems like a very large pain that comes from that ceaseless longing for you, words are expressionless—darlint, the greatness, the bigness of the love I have makes me fear that it is too good to last, it will never die, darlint don't think, but I fear—how can I explain—that it will never mature, that we, you & I will never reap our reward in fact, I just feel today darlint, that our love will all be in vain

He talked to me again last night a lot, darlint I don t remember much about it, except that he asked me if I was any happier I just said I suppose as happy as I shall ever be, & then he frightened me by saying—oh I don t think I'll tell you

---

I left off there darlint—thought—thought for ½ an hour & I will tell you now He said he began to think that both of us would be happier if we had a baby, I said No, a thousand times No " & he began to question me, and talk to me & plead with me, oh darlint, its all so hard to bear, come home to me—come home quickly & help me, its so much worse this time He hasn't worried me any more, except that once I told you about, darlint do you understand what I mean? but things seem worse for all that You know I always sleep to the wall, darlint, well I still do but he puts his arm round me & oh its horrid I suppose I'm silly to take any notice, I never used to—before I knew you—I just used to accept the inevitable, but you know darlint, I either feel things very intensely or I am quite indifferent just cold—frozen

But to write all this is very selfish of me, it will make you feel very miserable—you can't do anything to help me—at least not yet, so I'll stop

What else can I talk about? only ordinary things darlint, but to talk about even those perhaps will help to deaden the pain We went to the theatre in the week to see " Woman to Woman " at the Globe I had the tickets given me Darlint, it was a lovely play, I think I liked it as much as " Romance " altho the plot is not the same I have written you a description of it—I should like you to discuss it with me, but better still I should like to see it again with you, but I cant, so I have talked to you about it, that's the next best thing, isn't it darlint?

Bywaters and Thompson.

Also I finished the book "The Trail of 98" & liked it ever so much, I have also written to you, about it Darlint you have quite a lot of mail from me at Aden, I think, I do hope you will feel pleased—not too miserable, I don't want you to, darlint, just forget all the miserable things I've said to you

Its been terribly cold here, & foggy—thick real old fashioned fogs for 4 days I've had & still got such a bad chilblain on the back of my heel —its been there a fortnight now & I cant get rid of it I think I've tried 5 different things The worst of it is any shoes I have—the tops of them cut it—the chilblain, right in half

Darlint, have you written to the 'B I Co' yet, please do—I want you to, you know—if we are going to win, we must look forward understand darlint?

Yesterday I was taking a country buyer to Cooks, St Pauls, & passing the "Chapter House" he said to me "Would you care for a glass of wine here, its quite a nice place" Imagine darlint, me being told its quite a nice place I said "No thanks," really I'd rather not" & yet if it had been anywhere else I should have said "Yes" Do you know, darlint, when you were home last time we didnt go there once, I feel sorry when I think about it I should like to have gone, but we will next time, say "Yes" darlint I do so hope you'll be home longer than a fortnight this next time Isn't it funny the feelings we have about going into the places with strangers that we have been in together I feel very strongly about it, I *couldn't* no I simply couldn't go & sit in either of those corner seats at the Strand without you nor at the Holborn, nor "Chapter House," nor the "Coronetion" nor anywhere else, where you & I have been & *talked*, really talked Do you remember us talking together in the "Chapter House" one Friday night, about my life being happy, living with only 2 people besides myself I don't remember what I answered then—Yes, I believe I do, but the answer would not be the same today, it would be with only 2 people, 2 halves, one whole, darlint, just you & me, say "Yes, it's right, & it will be so," I want telling so many times darlint

What do you think he is going to learn dancing—to take me out to some nice ones, wont it be fun—as the sing says "Aint we got fun," while you are away About myself darlint, its still the same & I've not done anything yet—I don't think I shall until next month, unless you tell me otherwise, after you get this letter, or the one I wrote previously

---

Darlint I got a letter, or rather 2 in 1 envelope on Saturday morning You say that you can't write but you will try from Port Said Is this correct? The envelope of these is stamped Port Said No, you're quite right darlint, when you say you cant talk to me, you can't, these letters are only writing, they are not talking, not the real talking I was looking forward to

Why is it? darlint, what is the matter? you do still feel the same, don't you? Oh say Yes, I feel so sad & miserable about it I seem to be able to talk to you always & for ever, but you, I don't know, you don't seem the same as when you were away before, you did talk to me a lot that trip, but this time you don't seem to at all Why is it darlint? You do still feel the same don't you? Am I horrid to expect so much, tell me if I am but darlint I feel that I could give all, everything & I can't read

Appendix II.

between the lines of your letters this time that you even want to accept that all

One part that did amuse me was over the argument That expression "I do love 'em, etc" made me think of old times, you remember the Shanklin times, when neither of us had any cares, or worries, personal ones I mean, altho' we hadn't learned to know ourselves or each other, which were the best times darlint? now or then, just tell me, I shant mind That was a funny dream you had, wasn't it? I wonder what it means or if it means anything Why do you tell me not to get excited darlint, do you think I would I don't think I should darlint, over that, you & I have too much at stake, to take too many risks But I don't think there is any risk, darlint, it doesn't *seem* so at any rate, but I feel that I could dare anything, and bear everything for you, darlint

That's all now, darlint, I've got such a great lump come in my throat & I'll have to swallow it somehow Peidi does want you now

---

Envelope—Mr F Bywaters, P & O R M S "Morea," Marseilles

[Postmark—London, E C , Jan 24 1922, 1 30 p m]

Darlingest boy I know,

I got your note and enclosure from Tilbury and a letter—a real nice one from Dover this morning

Yes, darlint, it was real lovely on Thursday—just to be with you for longer than that one hour just to let time slide for a little longer than usual I'm ever so glad I had you on Thursday—it would have been so hard —yes, much harder than it is now for you to go away without being with you for just that short time

Darlint don't we set store by just those few hours—can you imagine what a whole long day will be like? Hours seem like Paradise days will be like well I don't know, because I've never had days before

This is a vile nib, but I haven't another

That feeling I had & still have about you going darlint I can't explain—not even to myself—first of all I feel that I shall want you & shall need you to lean on & you wont be there & then darlint—the " drifting feeling " that I told you about before—I think is mainly responsible I think —if next time—(I mean in March)—things are just the same—we'll feel further apart still, because darlint, I did feel apart this time—its no use making myself say I didn't But darlint that was your fault—yes, it was & you're going to say " It was " & take all the blame—because I said so— but its not going to happen again—you're not going to let it are you darlint, you're going to tell me every tiny little thing both when you're away & when you come home—even if some things are silly & you're cross about & you're still going to tell me Yes, I've said " Yes " for you, so you must darlint Darlingest boy, I didn't go to 231 on Friday—I did want you so much—just to take care of me & help me to get thro , I'll tell you about it

About 10 30 or 11 a m I felt awfully ill—I had terrible pains come all over me—the sort of pains that I usually have—but have not had just lately—do you understand

Bywaters and Thompson.

These continued for about an hour & I stuck it somehow—feeling very sorry for myself—until about 12 o'c I went off then into a faint They managed to get me to with brandy—then I went off again, & again, making 3 times in all Everybody here was fearfully frightened & eventually sent for the doctor He told them to partially undress me & give me a hot water bottle—refilling it every half an hour

At 3 30 p m he came in again and as I was no better Jim took me home in the motor Darlint I was lying flat on the floor inside with the water bottle

When I got home I went straight to bed & about 7 something awful happened, darlint I don't know for certain what it was, but I can guess, can you, write & tell me

On Saturday, I felt a bit better, but not much I didn't know what to do or take to get better & I looked awful In the evening I dressed & went out & really enjoyed myself, meeting heaps of people I knew & hadn't seen—some for 2 years It was a very cosmopolitan crowd darlint & I do wish I had been with you there I'm so certain sure you would have enjoyed it I've enclosed you a menu & programme, *not ours*, but an extra one I got Uncle to give me On the back you will see names of artistes " Evelyn Clifford & John Humphries " They are husband & wife & friends of Mr Carlton & they sang a song the following of which I remember

    He   One little word
    She   Cheri
    He   heads to two little words
    She   Ma chere
    He   Two little words lead to 3 little words
    Both   I love you

It was nice, darlint, you would have liked it

Yesterday darlint was an opportunity lost, it was a thick, a very thick fog—the worst London has known for years He went to bed about 8 30 with a headache—I stayed up in front of the fire until 10 30 with you darlint—thinking of you & thinking of us & thinking of that " Glorious Adventure " that you are helping me with You are aren't you?

Everything was alright on Thursday night I had an escort from the station I didn't go to sleep at all that night, no not once, not even when it was time to get up

Darlingest boy, I'll talk to you again by Wednesday Don't worry about me now, I'm feeling much better, but a teeny bit disappointed

                                                                             PEIDI

Envelope—Mr F Bywaters, P & O R M S "Morea," Marseilles

[Postmark—London, E C , Jan 28, 1922, 2 30 p m]

Darlingest boy, its Wednesday now, the last for posting to Marseilles

I'll be thinking & thinking, wishing such a lots of things tomorrow—late —when I shall know you have arrived You will help me darlint you won't fail me this time I'm feeling very very hopeful to-day—that " bucked " feeling darlint, you know it, I know, but I also feel how much I miss you—miss so much even that one little hour

Do you remember the songs darlint " One little Hour," did you like it —well if you did when you first heard it, you dont now, because **darlint**

Appendix II.

you've changed, you're different—not a bit like the boy I remember at Shanklin on the last Friday, do you remember darling "I love you," I do & then it was that "One little Hour" kind of love, oh yes it was, but those kind of things that were pleasures to you then are, just sordid incidents now aren't they—I mean with everybody—but ourselves

Darlint, about the other song you never mentioned if you liked the words I didn't buy it to send to you especially, it belonged to me—no to both of us, & it still does Not since you've been gone darlint have you had a nice tidy head, I've done it purposely not once a day but 2 or 3 times, it's nice I like doing it So you'll have to, darlint Just say I'm not to, & I will Do you remember our Sat morning the snowballs & the sweets & the drinks in that 'low common place" for a woman to go

Darlint you know you called me " fast " & the man in the confectioners thought I was terrible spending all your money & darlint I will be terrible, when you have a lot of money for me to spend All those motor cars & fur coats & champagne you wished me at Xmas I'm going to have one of these days, eh darlint—because you're the only one that I'll let buy them

I went to E H S on Monday night for the parcel & as I had time to spare (I didn't want to get home before 7) I walked back along the High St to the Broadway—very narrowly missing Mrs Bristow & bumping into Cossy I dare say everyone at 231 knows I was in the High St now

On Monday night we went into the Birnages for a hand of cards They were very nice, but the strain of keeping out family matters (owing to the rift with Lily) was rather trying

Darlint, I got your cable this morning, thank you so much the clock indicates handed in at ¼ past 7 p m on Tuesday Is this right? It's later than it always has been

The weather here is frightfully cold again, the wind blows so hard, & I miss you to hold me in the train

Will you do something for me darlint, yes, I know you will if its possible I want a slide for the back of my hair to match the comb, do you think its possible to match

I can't possibly wear my usual one & the comb together Try for me please darlint

Have you finished " The Common Law " yet, I expect you have & don't forget to write me a long discussion on it, I want to hear exactly what you think of her ideas & what you think about her giving in

The giving in part was rather significant to me darlint, because as you remember saying to me " But you would if I asked & wanted you to "

Darlingest boy, please excuse me now—I've just had a ring from Avis & Mother was taken ill last night with " flu " & temperature 105—the doctor is afraid of pneumonia—so I'm just going down to Manor Park It's 12 30 now I love you darlint & am living for Monday when you will be talking to me I hope it will be a long long time   PEIDI

Envelope—Mr F Bywaters, P & O R M S "Morea," Aden

[Postmark—London, E C , Jan 31, 6 15 p m , 1922 Stamps—2d]

27th January, 1922

My very best wishes darlint and hopes for many real happy ones later
PEIDI

Bywaters and Thompson.

Envelope—Mr F Bywaters, P & O R M S "Morea," Aden

[Postmark—London, E C , Feb 15, 5 30 p m , 1922 Stamp—2d]

I was so pleased to get your letter, darlint, it came on Friday mid day Miss Prior took it in & examined the seal—all the time she was bringing it down the stairs I was looking at her Darlint, you say I cant know how you feel, when you failed cant I darlint? dont I know didn't I fail once? I do know darlint its heartbreaking to think all the schemeing —all the efforts are in vain But we'll be patient darlint the time will come we're going to make it just you & I our united efforts darlint, I shall be very very interested in all you will have to tell me I can understand darlint how difficult it must be—all that underwork I wonder if I could do any more I believe I could somehow women usually can in these things but I'm counting on you putting all my faith in those persuasive powers that I know you possess, because you've used them on me Darlingest Boy you say " Am I right " I dont know it's what I think happened—darlint— but I dont know, I've never had any experience in such matters and I never discuss them with members of my sex as so many girls do therefore I suppose I m rather ignorant, on such subjects but I'll tell you everything about it when I can look at you & you mustnt be cross with me darlint about getting up I can say I did know it was dangerous or whether I didn't I just didn't think about it at all, I fought and fought with myself to make myself keep up & I think I succeeded, darlint Put yourself in my place darlint & see how you would feel if you thought by stopping in bed and not making an effort a doctor would have been called in would have said well what have you & I think he would someone else not you would have taken both the blame & the pride for the thing they did not do

I imagine how I would feel about it, I'm afraid darlint I would not have been able to keep silent Please dont worry, darlint I'm alright really now—only a bit shaky—& I dont like the way you say " It was ridiculous for you to get up " etc because I'm not going to let you bully me so please take note monsieur & dont transgress again

Darlint that Friday night you wouldn't have " gone under to anything " would you and left me by myself I understand how you felt, but cheer up darlint it wont always be like that & all we get in future darlint, we shall appreciate the more because we have had to climb so many stiles in ' Our glorious adventure " & have fallen the other side so many times, that when we dont stumble when we land on our feet oh wont it be gorgeous darlint the thought of it is the only thing that keeps us up sometimes eh, I understand darlint the one pal you've got understands everything

It is as if our thoughts & minds & actions were just one even tho' we are miles apart Do you feel like that darlint I do when I'm doing anything by myself I always think & say to myself that you are doing it & thinking it with me

Darlint when you are home next time you must ask your sister to play that song for you because it wont matter that she does know who gave it you then will it & I shall never be able to play it so darlint please do

Fancy darlint you doing such a dreadful thing as to discuss those truly awful matters with me I am ashamed of you Am I? you know & darlint

Appendix II.

I am glad you altered (in your own mind) that word *good* to fortunate because you also have to utter the word " Bad " to unfortunate

I've been reading a perfectly glorious book darlint ' The Business of Life " by R W Chambers It is very like in detail " The Common Law " but in the *one* question it is exactly opposite

I did enjoy it so much I believe I liked it better than " The Common Law " no I'm not quite certain Anyhow I want you to read it & tell me what you think of it if you liked it better etc it seemed to me more human in many ways, than the other one

Shall I send it to your home for you to read over weekend March 18th or shall I keep it & give it you I'd like to send it to you now, I'm so anxious for you to read it

Darlint is my letter to Bombay awaiting you on your arrival, or do you have to wait a week for it, I believe you do This morning I think you arrive and you'll see Bill & I ll be thinking of & about you all this coming week, darlint such a lot I know you'll be careful you said you would

I want to tell you about a dream I had last week I received a letter by hand by Avis & the envelope was addressed in Harry Renton's writing only inside was a letter from you

It wasn't your writing darlint it was a large round hand just like a schoolboy's I read & read for a long time not recognising from whom it came until I came to the word Peidi & then I called out " Why its from my own boy " I dont know if I did really, but I did in the dream

Even now I cant determine in my own mind whether you sent the letter to him to send on to me or whether he got hold of it somehow

Tell me what you think girlint There's nothing but ordinary every day things to tell you darlint oh except one thing just that I love you so much but you know that dont you darlint I wish you were here that I could tell you but you will be one day each day is gradually dragging on

PEIDI

Envelope—Mr F Bywaters, P & O R M S ' Morea," Marseilles, France

[Postmark—London E C , Mar 6, 6 15 p m 1922 Stamps—1½d , 1½d , 1d]

My Darlingest boy

I was so pleased to get letters from you last Monday I hadn't expected any—as I got that note—after the Port Said letter & thought it must have been posted at Aden Darlint if you were 1½ hours out from Port Said how did you post it?

In your letter you say you felt I had been ill, darlint I told you not to worry & you mustn t when will you do what I ask you?

I suppose I have been ill probably more so than I thought but I wouldnt give way because I wanted to keep that illness all to ourselves thinking that helped to keep me up

I certainly did receive your cable in time to get you an answer, but darlint, it never entered my head that you would expect one I am so sorry if I disappointed you it was not intentional

You see darlint, I had told you in my Marseilles letter about it I thought I could write in full in my Bombay letter & what could I put in a cable darlint only " Dont worry better " & you would still have worried I hope you are not now anyway there is no need

Bywaters and Thompson.

On Sunday I was ill—as usual—& I did feel really ill darlint, I think it was worse than before what happened The only effects I feel of anything is a languid lazy sort of feeling—no energy—just pale & limp but all that will be altered when you are in England I didnt stop away from 168 because I thought of your letters and I knew they would forward them to 41 if I was not there so I managed to get in every morning & went early & then Mater got ill & I had no time to think of myself

Darlingest boy dont talk or think about losing me that will never happen will it? if I go you will too wont you? You say ' I must let you know of all those things that you ask me & I have forgotten "

Darlint, do I forget to answer anything I dont remember forgetting anything & I try not to forget anything that we ever say to each other or do with each other or ask each other

Tell me what I have forgotten & I'll answer everything Darlint you say you realise what it was for me after Aug 5th I am glad you do, in a measure, it was & still is too awful, I darent think too much I should always be weeping & that wouldn't do, would it? because you told me to dance only sometimes to dance is much harder than to sit & think

Do you remember the cutting I once showed you—where tell me? " Eyes that tell of agony untold Lips that quiver with unuttered pain A heart that burns with misery " & grief etc

Darlint do you remember anything happening to me on Nov 7th I do & I think you will We have just got the Doctor's bill in for it here & he has charged 10/6d so Heaven knows what he will charge for Friday Jany 20th I dont know whether to offer to pay or let 168 pay, what would you do?

I have bought " the Red Planet " by W J Locke & am reading it but am disappointed in it & I think it is the one that you have read & which you thought was " The Rough Road " anyway it is a war story and I'm not very keen

Do you remember I told you I had been ill with a bad cold well I managed to shake it off a bit—but last Sunday brought it back again—so I slept in the little room of my own accord, last Saturday I went to see " The Co optimists " at the Palace Theatre W & was awfully disappointed in them I had heard them raved about & suppose I expected too much

Darlint I'm beginning to think that I expect too much always of people & things in fact too much of life altogether do you think I do? darlint if you do think so do you think I always will? I have enclosed you a sheet of sketched Millinery that we had done I had to write 100 of these how would you like the job?

Twelve of us, mostly Stamford Hill people & Reg & Bess went to a private dance at Shoreditch Town Hall last week, he came too Darlint I enjoyed it—do you know it hardly seems possibly that I could to me & I'm sure it does not to you I enjoyed it dancing with Reg & Mr Philpot —they are both good dancers & now he wants us to make arrangements for 8 of us to go to the Nonstop March 16, 22 I suppose I shall go I shall have to, but I wouldn't if you were in England would I? I am living for you to come home this time darlint, (sorry) every time you go away the two months seem to grow longer and longer

I suppose you left Bombay on Saturday for England only 3 more weeks By the way I heard that a boy from the " Malwa " knocked Mr Moore right down a ship's gangway & rather hurt him I didn't hear what he did it for

Appendix II.

To-day I finished the "Turkish Delight" its all gone now & I'm sorry I was so greedy but I know I'll get some more soon   Enclosed is a cutting that reads as if it might be you?   What do you think?

Last Saturday we went over to Tulse Hill—to Mr Manning's—I went to his office and helped him with his books until 5 p m & then met *Mater & Dad*   Avis & we all went together   None of us this time managed to carry away a prize (it was whist) it is unusual as one of us usually manage to take one   There was no mail in on Monday this week—perhaps there will be later in the week—I do hope there will be I'm longing to hear you talk to me, but darlint longing much more for you to be here to see you, for you to hold me tight so tight I cant breathe   Au revoir darlint

PEIDI

Envelope—Mr F Bywaters, P & O R M S "Morea," Marseilles, France

[Postmark—London, E C , Mar 7, 12 30 p m , 1922   Stamps—2d , 1d]

27th

You know all & everything I wish you darlingest & myself

I was very very sorely tempted to buy myself a birthday present from you today   They looked so lovely everywhere you go you see them now, but then I thought next birthday you will be in England to buy them for me so I refrained, altho' it was hard

Good bye darlint—you have all my love

PEIDI

Envelope—Mr F Bywaters P & O R M S "Morea" Plymouth

[Postmark—London, Mar 14, 5 p m , 1922   Stamp—2d]

Je suis Goche darlint & disappointed   I said in my previous letter I was sending 1 large & 1 small parcel

I have only sent 1, the large one

Lunch time I went to Queen Vic St to get some "Toblezone" to send with the tissue paper (a small pcl) but finding "Toblezone" is out of stock for a few days therefore I've not sent the tissue, but I'll give it you when we meet

Au revoir darlint, I'm consumed with impatience

PEIDI

Envelope—Mr F Bywaters, P & O R M S "Morea," Marseilles, France

[Postmark—London, Apr 4, 6 15 p m , 1922   Stamps—2d , 1d]

First of all darlingest about Thursday   He knows or guesses something—how much or how little I cant find out   When I got home & went upstairs I found him not there

As I was getting into bed a car drew up outside & he came in looking, well you know how with that *injured air of mystery on his face* attempted to kiss me and then moved away with the expression "Phew—drink" He had been to a Theatre—he had a programme—what I imagine is—waited for me on the 11 30 found I wasn't on it & caught the next—of course was surprised to find me home If he has any sense he could easily put 2 & 2 together Your last night last time & your last night this time—I went to a theatre on both occasions

He says he caught the 11 55 but there is no such train in my time table—there used to be Tell me what you think about this please darlint

I must tell you this talking about rates at 231 last night Avis said 'if you dont pay they'll take you to prison" He said 'No they wont I'll see to that Avis "Well they'll take your wife He (under his breath altho I heard it) ' A good thing too" He's never even said " What did you see or how did you enjoy yourself" Oh its a rotten spirit Avis came over to tea on Sat & said " The last time I came Bess & Reg were here" *He* Bess is supposed to be here to-day—but she doesn't know she hasn't been asked (1 note—asked Bess to come down for the week end as Reg would be away—but she replied by Thursday to 168 that she couldn't come as he was coming home at noon Sat) He didn't ask me if we enjoyed ourselves or if Bess was coming so I didnt mention it

After Avis had gone I said A remark you passed at tea time about Bess what do you mean by it I want to know" *He* "You want to know do you—well you shant you can just imagine how much I know & how much I dont & I hope you'll feel uncomfortable about it "

I'm afraid I let go then & said several things in haste perhaps it would have been better had I held my tongue & finished up with " Go to Hell "— you can only keep good tempered when you—getting what you want a case of sugar for the bird & he sings I was told I was the vilest tempered girl living & ' you used not to be, but you're under a very good tutor" now it seems That was Saturday I went to bed early & how I got through Sunday I dont know living with banging doors & sour silent faces will turn me grey

---

It was funny at 231 on Friday I didn't go down till 8 15 just had some tea in Lpool St Buffet & read the paper Mother asked me to have a cigarette almost immediately I got in & I said, 'Where did you get these they look posh" *She* 'Never mind I had them given me

Me Well I dont suppose you bought them—where did you get them

She Fred Bywaters gave them to me

Me Has he been down here?

Dad Yes he's been 3 or 4 times

Me Oh I sorry I missed him next time he comes remember me to him & say if he lets me know when he's coming to 231 I'll come too

Dad He's sailed now, went out today By the way " Have you had a row with him?

Me Have I no, the last time we met we were pals (this is right isnt it darlint)

Dad Has Percy had a row with him then

Me Yes—he did

Dad & is it over yet I thought it was when Percy came back to say good bye just before Xmas

Me No, its not over & not likely to be—but still I'm sorry I didn't see Freddy I should like to have done very much

Dad Yes, I sure you would & I'm sure he would like to see you

Mother What do you think of the fags

Me Not much they are scented & I dont care for such posh ones

Appendix II.

Mother was quite indignant with me darlint & said " If they'd been given to you you'd like them, so I said " Would I " & smiled Darlingest boy, you know why I smiled

He came in then & mother offered him one—he looked & said " Amlve " Oh they're doped cigarettes

Mother What do you mean by doped

He The tobacco is grown on opium fields

Can you imagine me seeing the joke—inside me—all by myself when are we going to see the joke together darlint Oh mother said something about " By the way he spoke "—I said to Avis, he must not have seen Edie (meaning you)

Avis came to tea Sat as I've already told you & went again at 7 30 to keep an appointment she said

In the afternoon we went shopping together & she spoke about you a lot She seemed to be quite friendly with you

She mentioned she saw you on the station every morning & what a lot it must cost you for fares & it would be cheaper she thought if you lodged in East Ham & then they would be able to see more of you

Also you had on a diamond ring & seemed to have plenty of money altho ' I know writers dont make more than £5 per trip she said " she also told me you asked after Peggy & that she told you all about it & that she went round & had a drink with you she didn't see why she shouldn't as you could be pals (her interpretation) if nothing else

She said lots of small things connected with you—which aren't important & I didn't remember

---

Darlint what a poor quality Mail card this time—not a bit like the usual

Are you Oxford or Cambridge the former I expect—men nearly always are Well they didn't win & I m glad because I'm Cambridge & I won 5/- on Sat over it

By the way I had 5/ eh way on Leighton on Saturday for the Newbury Cup & the meeting was abandoned owing to the course being covered with 6 inches of snow

Au revoir darlingest boy

Envelope—Mr F Bywaters, P & O R M S " Morea," Marseilles France

[Postmark—London, E C Apl 5 2 30 p m 1922 Stamps 2d , 2d , 1d]

I didn't get your letter first thing in the morning darlint I felt a wee bit disappointed but supposed you'd been too busy with work that must be done & I was prepared to wait till next Monday to hear from my own man, but at 12 15 just as I was going to leave your letter came It bucked me up such a lot I thought to myself well it will help me to get thro the ' inevitable weekend " & it did help me darlint All the time I felt miserable & downhearted I was thinking to myself ' when you go to 168 on Monday you ll have a real letter to read again I shall read it every morning until I get another one from you just as I say " good morning " to you No not to you but to your picture & ruffle your hair & make you cross first thing in the morning (Is this right) Darlint that ache which you and I share & you speak about—yes its awful—not a sharp stabbing pain that lets you know it is there & then goes—but just a numb feeling a feeling of inactivity like a blind that is never more than half raised just enough to torment you with the sight of a tiny bit of light & sunshine

About what you told me—No I dont think it will worry me—but I cant help thinking about it can I? after all darlint—but for me it never would have happened I'm always the cause of pain to you & perhaps to myself as well but always to you ever since you just knew me you've never been really happy & perhaps had you known me less you might have been

Darlint I dont think you told me everything that you & others said on that Thursday—you didn't because you thought it would hurt, but if I promise it wont hurt, will you write & tell me please I want to know everything I do tell you everything that is said about you dont I?

Why didn't you recognise your sister on Thursday you must darlint pour moi—you know what you promised to do for me & she's my sex—forget she's your sister think she's me when you meet her & be courteous I'm ever so sorry you didn't recognise her whatever is ever said or ever happens connected with them & me dont forget this Does this sound like a lecture? I dont what it to be I just want you to remain as I know you now, not to revert to you I knew last year

Of course darlint I love all you've said about me, about giving up what people cherish most for me about those horrid thoughts that people have that you will stamp out I love all that darlint I feel proud when I read it that you say it about me—proud that I have someone that thinks so much of me—its so nice darlint I've never had anyone quite like you (like you were once yes, but not as you are now) When & if you do write to your Mother I want a copy of the letter please, yes I do & you must send me one you've not to ignore this subject or dismiss it in the usual manner Remember I sent you a copy once about the hat for Mavie you're not going to charge her for it are you? if you were then you're not to give it her please from you & me I'd like you to

Darlingest boy I received a telegram from you on Friday G M M C always stop—dont worry Now am I very dense or are you a little too vague, because I dont know what "Always stop" means Please tell me darlint I can only think you mean we will always stay together is this it?

I'd like you tell me darlint just how you feel when you move out of dock—what are your thoughts when you begin to move when you must realise that you'll not on England or anybody connected with you & England for 2 whole months

You told me you were sailing about 2 & about that time I began thinking how you were feeling if you were hopeful and not too down-hearted & I thought about everything connected with the last fortnight, some things I was sorry about & some things pleased How did you feel? This you went was'nt like the last time darlint I had a pain but it was a different one—not a physical one at all—just a pain that you & I were parted again, even tho it was only for 2 months I dont want ever to be parted from you not even for one day, not one minute really I always want to be where I can see you feel you holding me

Darlint couldnt Marie help us at all if I have to leave here, perhaps she would if you asked—you know I could do practically anything to earn just enough to keep myself for a little while

Appendix II.

I don't want to give in darlint oh I do want to have you so much & if we give in people will only laugh & think us failures & we're not are we—tell me we're not going to be—we're going to succeed you & I together even tho' we fail in " Our Glorious Adventure "

We'll fight to the last while there's an ounce of strength & will power left—fight to live our life, the life you & I will choose together—we're not cowards to shirk & hide behind a cloak of previous misfortunes—we'll take the bull by the horns & shape something good & clean out of something bad

---

I cant help this paper being another colour—its the only pad the stationer had in stock

A lady has just come in whom I have not seen for 5 years nearly, she has since been married & had 2 children one of which & her husband has died She says I dont look any older—but I'm sure by the way she said it, she doesn't think it I wonder why people will pay doubtful compliments they dont mean

Today is April 4th & the snow is falling in thick lumps & laying in some places—the weather has stopped trade & made everybody miserable What poet was it who wrote Oh to be in England now Spring is here " I wish he were alive & feeling miserable as I on this nice English Spring Day

Dont forget darlint when you are reading the books that the Shulamite comes first The ' Woman Deborah " after

I wonder if you will notice anything in " The Woman Deborah " I await your remarks

Jim fetched my case from Barking & left it at 41 for me, he was going down to Ilford

Darlint the Turkish Delight is lovely this time much better than the last lot

Enclosed is one that you sent me it is a fortnight today hasn't it kept well I have tended this one especially to send you—cut its stalk and given it fresh water with salt in every morning

Darlint tell me you love me & how much—keep on telling me make me feel all the time you do, its a long time 2 months darlint & I want telling heaps & heaps of times, no not because I doubt but because I like to feel that you're always thinking it

Darlingest boy I do love you—yes always while this life lasts so much —oh so much I cant tell you—but you must know you do know darlint, that there never has been anyone I love at all only just you, there is such a difference—Good bye until Bombay

(Good luck)

PEIDI

Darlingest boy,

11 45 a m 5/4/22—I've just read your cable—it came first thing this morning I believe—but I didn't feel up to the mark—so I didn't go up until 11, & then I was beseiged by people wanting this done & that done

It was nothing much darlint just a few fainting fits one after the other nothing whatever to worry about so please dont

I notice it says " Good afternoon so you quite expected me to get it on the 4th but it wasn't recd in London until 7 48 p m

Anyway—whatever time it came I was pleased to get it Pleased to know that when you sent it you were thinking about me

Bywaters and Thompson.

I've got to post this to day darlint, I dont suppose you'll get this one till Friday but I hope when you do you'll feel its all you want

I'd love to look at you now—*you* I mean—no, no substitute they (substitutes dont satisfy) but I'll wait I'll not say with patience, because darlint I'm not patient am I—but I know you understand

PEIDI

Envelope—Mr F Bywaters, P & O R M S 'Morea," Bombay, India

[Postmark—London E C   Apr 12 1 30 p m , 1922 F]

I just wanted to write a few lines to you darlint before we close here for the holidays—from Thursday 1 oc till Tuesday 10 oc

Friday—Saturday—Sunday—Monday—4 whole days darlint with nothing whatever to do but think, & only you can know what those thoughts will be

If I only had all that time to spend with you darlint can you imagine what it would be like—I cant & can't possibly imagine such a long time—I suppose it would only seem like 4 hours—instead of which it will now seem like 4 years—but perhaps it wont always be like it eh—I'm going on hoping so—hoping hard—are you too? You havent given up yet have you? please dont darlint?

We're fearfully busy here—I was here till 7 the last 2 nights & still we have such a lot to do before the holidays—

Darlingest boy—I love you such a lot & want you such a lot oh so badly—why arent you here to hold me tightly & make me feel how much you love me—its such a starving sort of feeling darlint—just living on a picture

I do want you so much—I want comforting darlint & only you can do that for

PEIDI

Envelope—T E F Bywaters Esq Writer P & O S S ' Morea," Marseilles

[Postmark—London, E C   10 My   22   Stamps—2d 30 centimes, 30 centimes]

11 Western Street,
Upper Norwood
S E 19
May 9th 1922

Dear Mick,

Just a few lines in the hope that you wont have gone yet   I really haven't had any time for writing or anything else   Mum has been very ill for about three weeks Doctor coming every day, so you can guess I have been pretty well occupied   But Im glad to be able to tell you she is alright now   The tables have turned & now the doctor is visiting me I am a walking Chemists shop with all the muck he is dosing me with

Just one thing I want to tell you Mick   The night before you left well of course I couldnt help hearing it said   But leaving out what you said to Mum even but I happened to hear a little remark which I think concerned me   It was this " My sister ' '   They only want me for what they get out of me "   Well you know best yourself whether this is true or not

Appendix II.

But all I can say is that if it were true I have been very patient in waiting for what I get from you Its true last time home you bought me some jewellery but if you are regretting that well, it can easily be remedied

About your laundry the whole lot including collars comes to 3/6d

Mum wants me to tell you she had your letter but it came at a rather bad time she being that day at her very worst and of course the contents & tone of letter did not tend to improve matters as she was suffering from a nervous breakdown together with blood poisoning

I hope you have had a good trip & that you are keeping quite well

Love from all

Your affectionate sister,

FLOPRIE

Envelope—Mr F Bywaters P & O R M S Morea," Sydney, Australia

[Postmark—London, E C, Jun 2 1922, 3 30 p m Stamp—1½d]

Since I have posted the first letter to Sydney darlint a whole night & a whole day has gone by & Ive been thinking & thinking such a lot & feeling so awful about it—I couldnt sleep for one little minute—thinking about you & what you would think of me & how you would feel when you received it

I am sorry darlint—but I wrote how I felt it was awful—& sometimes when you feel so terrible you write & think very unjust and bitter things your feelings at the time carry you away they did me please please, darlingest boy forgive me

Pals should never feel hard & cross with one another—should they? & we are still pals in spite of that letter, aren't we? do write and tell me it makes no difference—I shant feel "right" with myself until you tell me it has made no difference, I feel an awful beast about it I wish I had not posted it at once but kept it for a day then I should have torn it up Please forgive me & try to excuse your pal She did feel so awfully down in the world when she found that or felt that the best pal a girl ever had had forgotten or neglected her

She'll try hard not to transgress again

PEIDI

Envelope—Mr F Bywaters, P & O R M S "Morea,' Melbourne, Australia

[Postmark—London, Jun 23, 1922 2 30 p m Stamps—1½d , 1½d]

Today is Friday darlint by the *day* not the date the day you took me to lunch at the Holborn—first time when I let you see and told you some things that no one else knew I wanted to ask you if you remembered anything about last Wednesday—I'm not going to tell you—just tell me if you do remember & what it is

Nothing else of any importance has happened darlint since I talked to you last—we still argue about you & I suppose we always shall Tonight we are going to a Garden Party & Fete in aid of the Seamens Orphanage at Wanstead

Mrs Birnage & her people are on the Committee & she is partaking in the some of the amusements I believe & tomorrow is the outing—so perhaps

Bywaters and Thompson.

this week end will pass a little more quickly I shall still have to wait 5 days after Sunday—to hear from you Darlint I havent sent your watch on to you, because you have not told me what to do about it & I especially asked you so I shall keep it until I do hear

It was rather funny on Tuesday Mr Dunsford offered to take me up in the Car and let me stand on the roof of it to see the Prince on the next day—of course I was rather bucked about it and told *him* on the Tuesday evening He did make a fuss—said he objected & a lot more nonsense & asked how I was going to get on to the roof—I darent tell him Mr Dunsford was going to hoist me up—he would have been " terribly shocked " so I said I could climb up by a rope ladder at the side of the motor

However I went in spite of all objections & saw everything beautifully it was rather fun

Last week on one evening I went up West to buy a frock for the outing —I did so—I think you would like it—it is pale mauve voile embroidered in grey on the bodice & on the skirt & a sash of darker mauve ribbon It was from the shop I saw the White & jade frock I told you about & I asked them if they had still got it—they had & showed it to me—it was lovely & so was the price—12 guineas—so it had to stay in the shop

I was looking into a shop window up there & went to move away & found your sister & her fiance standing beside me, also looking in the window

I suppose she was trousseau hunting of course she's not coming to town after she is married is she?

Darlint, your own pal is getting quite a sport

On Saturday I was first in the Egg & Spoon race & first in the 100 yards Flat race & 3rd in the 50 yards Flat race

Everybody tells me Im like a racehorse—can get up speed only on a long distance & my reply was ' that if a thoroughbred did those things then I felt flattered "

The I was M C for the Lancers we stood up 10 Sets had some boys in from an adjoining cricket field I sat on the top of the piano & made a megaphone of my hands & just yelled—nothing else—Mr Carlton said all that shouting was worth 2 long drinks afterwards so I had 2 double brandies & Sodas with him

We had a very good day indeed In fact I think I enjoyed the actual outing better than last year—until we got to Lpool St coming home & then *he* started to make a fuss—says I take too much notice of Dunsford & he does of me & created quite a scene I am really sick of this sort of thing— he gets jealous & sulks if I speak to any man now

Darlint, if were ever together for always & you get jealous I'll hate you—I shant be your pal

Im so stiff & sore today I can hardly move I left the house 10 mins earlier than usual this morning—to make certain of catching my train I was so stiff

This time last year you were able to rub me & gradually take that stiffness away do you remember?

It was rather fun on Thursday at the Garden Party—They had swings & roundabouts & Flip Flaps cocoa nut shies Aunt Sallies—Hoopla & all that sort of things I went in for them all & on them all & shocked a lot of people I think I didnt care tho' & going home Mr Birnage said he'd

Appendix II.

like some fried Fish and potatoes—I'd got rather a posh frock on—wht georgette & trd with rows & rows of jade ribbon velvet & my white fur & a large wht hat, but all that didnt deter me from going into a fried fish shop in Snaresbrook & buying the fish & chips

Getting it home was the worst part—it absolutely smelt the bus out I didnt mind—it was rather fun only I wished you had been with me I think 2 halves together would have enjoyed themselves—better than 1 half by herself

---

Today is your birthday & our birthday—Darlint I wonder if you are thinking about it at all, I am

I sent you greetings by cable this time it was the only way I could celebrate darlint I wanted you to receive it on the exact day but Im afraid you wont its not my fault darlint its the fault of that ship of yours not being within radio range of either Aden or Bombay on the 27th

---

Darlingest own Pal, I love you heaps & heaps more than yesterday and such a lot less than I shall tomorrow

---

Miss Prior is going away tomorrow I expect I shall have plenty to do then until I go away

Only 2 more days before I hear you talk to me I hope its a lot—I do so want it to be

Goodbye for now darlingest pal to

PEIDI

Envelope—Mr F Bywaters P & O R M S " Morea " Melbourne, Australia

[Postmark—London 27 Jun, 1922 Stamp—1½d]

June 27/1922

The birthday of the Palship of 2 halves

This is the real birthday darlint just the same as I always wish I wish today & hope everything will not always be in vain

The birthday of the best pal a girl ever had

Many happy returns darlint may everything you undertake in your life be successful

PEIDI

Envelope—Mr F Bywaters P & O R M S " Morea," Fremantle Australia Macdonald Hamilton & Co 10 Aug 1922 Fremantle W A

[Postmark—London, Jul 12, 1922, 3 30 p m Stamps—1½d , 1½d]

Darlint Pal,

I dont think Ive got anything to tell you just the ordinary things happen every day & I somehow dont think you want me to talk to you about those I went to Henley last Thursday—with the Woldorf man—I previously had the invitation but refused on the plea of business but on the Tuesday night

Bywaters and Thompson.

Mr Carlton asked me if Id like Thursday off so I rang up & made arrangements to go We got there about 12 30 and had lunch at Phyllis Court at the invitation of an M P Mr Stanley Baldwin—it poured with rain all the afternoon & was altogether miserable—I got home by 6 45 p m

I've had a lot of time off this fortnight 2 Sats 3 half days & last Thursday & go about 4 every day—I dont know what to do with myself—why are you not in England when Miss Prior is away—look what a lot of time we could have together Last Saturday I was ill—the first time since I told you about it last trip—in the evening I went to the Doctor & told him he seemed pleased—I suppose because his pills had done their work I felt terribly bad & could not have gone to business had I had to do so—fortunately I had the morning off

It wasnt the same sort of ill feeling that it was that time before tho

On Saturday we go for our holiday Shall I call it? It wont be what I anticipated will it no swimming lessons or tennis or anything that Id really enjoy However I must make the best of it & dance—Im so tired of it all tho—this dancing and pretending

I've not packed my peach sports coat I dont want to wear it this time—so Ive left it behind

This is the last day for posting mail to Fremantle & Ive not had your *promised* letter from Aden

If it is at the G P O lunch time—perhaps I ll have some more to talk to you about before I post this

I'll leave it for a little while anyway

Avis has just been round here & I was in the office having a brandy & soda with Mr Carlton, he asked her to have one too—I think she feels very flattered am I horrid I really believe I am—tell me—but everything in this world seems so topsy turvy—Id give anything to be her—free I mean & I think she'd change places with me this minute if we could—but we cant—so I mustnt moan it'll become a habit

By the way I told you about Molly & Mr Derry

I think it was Tuesday he said to me " So you know that young lady I was talking to the other morning?

Me No I dont know her

He But she knows you & all about you

Me Oh, probably lots of people know me & about me that I'd rather not know

He I believe you're jealous

Darlint, just try & imagine me being jealous of her talking to him of all people I have to laugh right out loud when I think about it Some men have such a high opinion of themselves & their charms that I'm afraid I cant climb up to them

I wonder what " my only pal " is doing now & how he is feeling—when I try & contrast my feelings of going away this year to those of going away last year—I really wonder if Im living in the same world—I suppose I am—but its not the same world to me darlint—that world last year didnt contain a pal—just one only, to whom I need not wear a mask—but this year does—altho he is still so very far away that I go on wearing that mask to everyone I meet—every day—I wonder if there ever will be a time when I shall appear as I really am—only you see me as I really am—the " pretence me " is my ordinary every day wearing apparel the " real " me is only visible for such a very short time when you're in London Darlingest

Appendix II.

Boy—I cant bear to think of you being in England and not seeing me—must we be so very strict & stern—cant you imagine what your only pal—(no, not pal—Im talking to you darlint as the girl that loves you, Im talking to my veriest own lover not as & to a pal) will feel like knowing youre in London, & expecting to see you at every turn & really knowing deep down in her heart that she wont. Must you be so cruel darlint? See me once—for one whole day together for all that time & I wont mind if I dont see you any more the whole time you are in London I cant bear it if you go away without seeing me again—nearly 4 more months after September—that makes it January 1923 its too long to wait Darlint—too much to ask of any human being—especially is it too much to ask of you and I—we're not ordinary human beings—we're apart—different—we've never known pleasure —real pleasure I mean in anothers company—until we knew each other— weve had so few pleasures—& so many rebuffs—every one that is added now makes it harder

Am I selfish? No I dont think its a selfish feeling cos its for both of us—Im fighting for our rights to break down that reserve that youre going to build up against yourself & between

PEIDI

Letter Card (Bournemouth)—To Mr F Bywaters, P & O R M S 'Morea," Colombo

[Postmarks—Bournemouth 8 p m, 27 Jul London, 29th Jul 22
Stamps—½d ½d ½d

Mackinnon & Mackenzie, Colombo 25 Aug 1922, 9 15 a m

27/6/21

Today is 27th M H R
Chorley today last year

PEIDI

Darlingest Pal,

I'm on the Boat that has been all round the I of W landed at Ventnor —Id rather go there than Cornwall I think please take me—He says were coming next year—are we?

Envelope—Mr F Bywaters P & O R M S Morea' Colombo

[Postmark—London E C, Jul 31, 1922 6 15 p m]

Postcard (unaddressed)

29th

I am leaving for London today
This day last year I was at Kew with my pal
I shan't post this in B'mouth, probably shan't get an opportunity I love you so much darlint, I always shall

PEIDI

Envelope—Mr F Bywaters, P & O R M S "Morea," Bombay

[Postmark—London, E C, Aug 4, 1922, 4 30 p m Stamps—1d, 1d, 1d]

The bestest pal a girl ever had

Bywaters and Thompson.

I wonder if you remember what today *by the day* is I keep on thinking about it & of you & wondering if youre thinking as well about leaving me all by myself at 41 for good, when Morris Avenue corner became one of the treasured spots in our memory   Last Tuesday was the memorable 1st such a lot seems to have happened in that little time—& yet such a little—everything that we wanted to happen hasnt & everything that we didnt want to happen has

However perhaps this coming year will bring us the happiness we both desire more than anything in this world—& if it doesnt? we'll leave this world that we love so much—cling to so desperately

We are finishing at 168 at 1 p m today   I dont know what the dickens I shall do with myself   everyone I know is away—I cant even get a lunch or a tea out of anyone—or even a few hours amusement

Last holiday breaking up I had a Pal waiting for me—a Pal that really wanted to see me for myself alone & who really wanted to take me to lunch —for nothing

On Tuesday you're starting for home—how I shall count the days now & look forward so much—I dont know to what because you say you wont see me—but I shall hope & hope & hope that before Sept 23rd you'll melt just a teeny weeny bit towards your pal   I wonder if youve got anything to tell me   or do you still feel very reticent about all your doings while you're away

On Sept 24th I wonder if you would like to remember to her that it is Avis's birthday—I know shed like to remember

Dont say I didnt tell you in time this year

I am enclosing a piece of the evidence of the " Russell " Case

Have you read it all?   I have found it very interesting & a portion of the evidence on enclosed slip struck me as being very similar to evidence I could give—does it you?

I've wished & wished all the time it has been on that she could be proved innocent but the jury have found her innocent in the case of the 2 co respondents mentioned—but she will come up for trial again regarding the " man unknown "   Write & tell me what you think about it please darlint

Darlingest Boy, have you destroyed that photo that I asked you to last trip—you've never mentioned it—neither have you acknowledged my request—is it one of those things that you have—dismissed? "   I had an absolutely rotten holiday—the Boarding house was terrible—" Ladies are requested not to smoke in the house "—no drink allowed indoors and not too much grub—even for ladies—I was sorry for the men

However we made the best of a bad job—there were 27 in the house & not a very sociable crowd either or rather they were too quiet   I think Avis & I managed to liven them up a bit   We did some mad things—climbed a tree in front of a row of Boarding Houses & had our photos taken up it (Avis & I I mean) everyone in the Bdg Hses were watching us from the windows & had donkey rides up & down the front   the people stopping in our Boarding Hse could hardly believe (they said) I'd been married as long as I had & I was the age I am   they said I only seemed a child   I felt glad they thought this pour vous—altho I really felt very old & miserable & lonely all the time I was away

Bournemouth is a very stiff starchy place—not a bit like the Island—Im very glad we didnt go there last year—that is one holiday I can look

Appendix II.

backward on & think I thoroughly enjoyed the holiday & myself in an impersonal way You'd like Ventnor Darlint when we complained to the people there about B'mth being stiff—no smoking no drinking—(by the way there is only 7 licenses granted to the whole of B'mth & Boscombe & its a very big town 90,000 inhabitants) they said " There's nothing like that about Ventnor—you can walk about naked if you like " Thats the place for us we said & this man recommended us to a very nice Boarding Hse right on the front with 2 front lawns very like Osborne Hse last year

We said to the Pier Master at Ventnor " I suppose youre going to dust us for 2d going off & 2d going on (they do in B mth) as well " & he said " Oh, no, we want your Company here & not your money " & shook hands with us

Darlint I do so want a holiday *with you* next year please—I must do the wages now—last holiday you came with me to draw them didn't you?

Do you still love me as much? I do you—no more

PEIDI

Envelope—Mr F Bywaters, P & O R M S "Morea, Aden

[Postmark—London, E C, Aug 15, 2 30 p m , 1922 Stamps—1½d , 1½d]

Do you know darlint, I dont think I can talk to you very much—I dont feel like it a bit—I want to see you & feel you—not to imagine you & then talk, its so awfully hard

When I came back to 168 I went to G P O & got a letter & the discussion on the book from Bombay & a note from Colombo—I havent heard any more—I wonder if you have written to me since & when I shall get it if you have—it seems such a long time since you went, three or four times longer than when you go to Bombay, and now you have already started home & I am writing to Aden—a month is 12 when you're not in England & it will always be the same darlint—that will never alter, whatever else does

I meant to have mentioned before that the Turkish Delight last time was stale—not a bit nice Darlint, I'm not ungrateful and I'm not looking a gift horse in the mouth—as you might think I'm just telling you this so that if you liked you could tell the old chap from whom you bought it, what you thought of him I should want to I know & I think you will too Dont be cross anyway will you?

I've read one or two books while you've been away—& Ive not marked them—Ive wanted you to find the small things that interest us, out for yourself Ive got the " House of Baltazar " now & have just started it The two you ordered for me, never came in—the girl still says they werent ordered there—so I didnt bother—I didn't want to do it for myself—I wanted you to do it for me—so Ill wait until youre in England again

On Tuesday we went at 2 & I went to the " Waldorf " to tea—& while waiting in the vestibule by myself a gentleman came up to me—raised his hat & said " Good afternoon, are you Romance? " I thought he was mad & turned away & sat on a couch—he followed & continuing the conversation said " Im sorry if youre not, but I have an appointment here with a lady with whom Ive corresponded thro a " Personal Column," she calls herself " Romance " & she was to wear a black frock & a black lace hat " I was wearing the blk frock with the roses on it & the lace hat you like) Then he moved away & later I saw him at a table with a girl in a blk frock with steel beads & a black lace hat, so I supposed he was speaking the truth, altho at the time I doubted it

I think it was rather funny dont you? Darlingest boy, Ive shown my beads & said that Miss Prior gave them to me, do you mind? I did it because I can wear them more often now—they are very much admired

I think this is rather funny dont you? While I was away I wrote to 168 for Rosie's & the Dunsford's private addresses & *he* made ever such a fuss about it—said I was too familiar & deceitful—because I couldnt say what I wanted to on a post card to him (Mr D.) at 168. We had a right royal battle about it & I was told I was impudent & all sorts of things bad & that I must have a very good tutor—that is quite a favourite phrase and is often used

Anyhow he sulked for 2 days and on the Sat. Avis came down and during the course of conversation she said to him, "My friend Bessie Hughes saw you in Lyons in Bishopsgate the other Friday evening" *He* 'Oh did she, its quite possible' *It is* Yes & you were with a short fat girl in a brown costume with a white stripe (This is Miss Tucknott) *He* Oh yes, I took her in to have something to eat as it was late after working at the office & it was my last night in town for a fortnight I told him afterwards that I was not the only one who was deceitful, but he wont have it. We've been chipping him about Miss Tucknott ever since & I believe he thinks Im quite jealous

Ever since Ive been back in Ilford Ive had most awful nights rest I havent been able to sleep for more than an hour together & even when I do that I dream—sometimes theyre not very nice dreams. They are nearly always about you. One night I dreamed that you had married Avis— because she found out how much was between us (you & I) & threatened to tell everybody unless you married her—another night I dreamed I had been to a theatre with a man I knew—I had told you about him & you came home from sea unexpectedly & when you found me you just threw me over a very deep precipice & I was killed,—sometimes Ive dreamed worse things than these & waked up in a fearful fright

It reminds me of this time last year do you remember I didnt sleep hardly at all for 3 weeks then

I think I read your letter from Bombay thro again—destroy it & then talk to you about it for next week's mail & Ill also talk to you about Dolores then

I dont think I can now, I feel too sad—no not really sad—but Im in a deep depression that only one person in this world can light

Do you know who that is darlint? Just the best Pal of

PEIDI.

Envelope—Mr F. Bywaters, P.O. R.M.S. "Morea," Aden

[Postmark—London, E.C., Aug. 18, 5 30 p m, 1922. Stamps—1d., ½d.]

I was reading the book & I could understand her so well—I should do the same—exactly for the man I love—but you must love him darlint—real & deep & true—because your honour is such a sacred thing—your only covering, that you would only lose it to an "anybody" for a man you really loved

Appendix II.

You ask if it is sufficient reason that a good woman knows she is wanted, that she sins Yes I think this right in a measure A good woman who had no husband or lover—either had never had one or one that had died—would sin with a man whom she knew wanted her & she would willingly give herself—because she felt that she was wanted *so much wanted enough* darlint, but a good woman who had a husband or a lover who really loved him & whom she really loved—would never sin with another man—because she felt that other man wanted her Have I explained the difference, darlingest boy, Ive tried to

I didnt like Theo myself—but I think he was a good man & would have been a fine man if he had had a child He was terribly selfish darlint I know, but then every man is selfish in life as well as in fiction, to be selfish is part of their nature Cesare I loved, I think he was fine —he certainly loved Dolores very very much—but it still didnt make her love him You say you dont understand Dolores because she wrote when she came back " All that she told you is true, I sent her to tell you " (Nurse Jennings)

What about Lady Sarah Ides didnt you like her?

About Dolores darlint—I dont agree with you at all about her not loving her husband You think she loved Cesare—because she gave all—darlingest boy she didnt give herself in the true sense of the word She loved her husband so much that she would do anything in the wide world —anything in her power—to give him pleasure She felt for him—as well as for herself—she knew what his pleasure would be if she gave him a child—she also knew more than he did—she knew it was not thro her she didnt have a child—it was thro him—he was the Fruitless Vine & she the Fruitful & because of this she degraded herself in every way for him

Darlint, if she hadnt loved him, it would have been the easiest thing in the world for her to have said " It is your fault Theo (that is what she called him isnt it), not mine & he would have probably loved her so much more & she would have been so much happier—instead of which she makes the supreme sacrifice—(darlint it is the supreme sacrifice to give yourself to someone you dont love) for her husband's sake, to make him happy—as well as herself—it was a *big* thing to do darlint, tremendous & it is always the same darlint & will always be the same—*nothing* is too much to do for the man you love—nothing is too much to give—no not even yourself

I can feel with her & live with her darlint & I did—all the time I certainly think she wronged Cesare more than she did her husband & I think she realised she had & that is why she wrote that

She wanted Cesare to see how much she had wronged him—how bad she really felt she had been towards him

Had she have loved him—she would never have said or written that— she would have gone anywhere with him—to the ends of the world—she wasnt a woman who was ruled by convention He, Cesare was just a man who could help her to give her husband what he (& she) wanted most in this world & because Cesare loved her enough to want her & take her as she was—she used him—thats all there is about it darlint

About the Marcelli darlint, you say you like her in one breath & in another you say you quite understand Cesare wanting to break away from her These two sentences are absolutely opposite

I think you said you liked the Marcelli—to please me—I think you thought " If I say I *dont* like her & could understand Cesare's feelings in

Bywaters and Thompson.

trying to get away from her " Peidi will be hurt—she will think of her position & mine in relation to the Marcellis & Cesare s with regard to age so I will say I like her   Oh I hated her—she was a beast a vampire—Oh I cannot bear her—darlint I should have been much more pleased if you had said you hated her

I like " Carissima " better than yours darlint—it sounds so like the " Great Lover," so much like Cesare as I imagine him

---

Envelope—Mr F Bywaters, P & O , R M S " Morea ' Aden

[Postmark—London, E C , Aug 23, 1 30 p m , 1922   Stamp—1½d]

Thank you for your wishes on the 27/6/22 darlingest boy

It seemed such a strange day to me, I did want to wish you ' Many Happy Returns " for yourself first—then for we two darlint—in person that day—but I couldnt—so I sent the ' Radio "

Darlint, tell me what you thought when you were first told there was a message for you—before you knew what the message was   I thought about you such a lot that day & wondered if I did right in sending it   I thought perhaps it would give you a shock—that perhaps you would think it was something to do with " Health " either mine or his

---

About Dolores darlint—you say " Forget her romance in connection with you "

I said it would be as her case with me darlint, because I felt it would be so good to do something for you—to give you something to live for & cherish all your life—you could be happy then darlint—I know youll say you couldnt—but think a little—Im sure you could—you could live in a memory and with a replica

However, while you still tell me to hope—I shall forget about Dolores

---

Talking about " Scamp " darlint, Im a bit fed up with him   While I was away he ran in the Steward's Cup at Goodwood & I made sure he would win it especially as I was away & couldnt back him—so I thought about it & sent a wire to Rosie to do £1 each way for me & then the wretched thing didnt win

---

Darlint remember when the ' Morea " is due in England, both 231 & 41 will sure to try & find out if you are still on her or if you have stayed in India as you said

I went to the Regent Palace to tea the other day darlint with Lily Im trying to overcome that horror of the place & she asked me to go & I didnt want to say No, I felt very uncomfortable all the time I was there tho', & I did try hard not to think of previous experiences there

---

Its rather funny sometimes at 41   The attacks continue so I am told of course I know differently—but I say nothing & laugh all to myself right deep down inside   They always happen after " words " or " unpleasantness "

A Phrenologist at Boscome told him he would live to be quite an old man

Appendix II.

Darlint, I've used all my perfume shall I buy some myself, or shall I wait for you to do it for me

I'd really like you to do it best but I'll do just whichever you tell me to do

Goodbye for another week darlint Pal I do hope I shall hear from you soon—I've had nothing since Colombo—& Im starving now You havent forgotten your Pal in England have you? her name is

PEIDI

— —

Envelope—Mr F Bywaters, P O R M S "Morea" Port Said

[Postmark—London E C Aug 29, 3 30 p m, 1922 Stamps—1d, ½d]

Darlingest, I got a letter from you last Thursday, from Fremantle I think, I dont think there was anything in it that I can talk to you about —you say you are longing for that letter from me that you will get in Sydney—well darlint, Im longing to get a letter from you—a real letter, one in which you're going to tell me such lots and lots of things perhaps you will when you have heard from me I always feel that you write better to me when you have heard from me And then another thing that strikes me is this—in most of your letters you say "We are getting into so & so tonight" That makes me think that a few hours before you get into a Port, you sit down & write to me as a duty Don't you ever feel that you'd like to write a few lines to me & then leave it & write again when you feel like it Thats how I do darlint, & then when it comes to the last day for posting, I havnt got to sit down & write as a duty

About books—I havnt read Mrs Marden "—I should like to, but I have read " Martin Conisby's Revenge " quite lately & I wasnt very keen on it—it didnt seem up to Jeffrey Farnol's standard I dont think I have read

The Chronicles of an Imp " & yet the title is familiar However I dont think the book would appeal to me very much from the title Why did you leave out " The Common Law " when you were naming the list of books that you have read & liked Didnt you like it sufficiently to let it remain in your memory? For want of a nice book to read I got hold of ' Septimus " & read it again

It is very amusing—have you read it? if not I ll send it to you

Im now reading Eden Philpotts " Secret Woman " darlint Im not very keen—it takes a lot of reading—its very dry & you know the " Secret Woman " practically at the commencement—if you've got any sense

Darlint, a little news that you wont like

Blouses are fashionable again, no more jumpers—I've saved the " little green one " for you, do you want it? Im longing for Sept 23rd to come, although you say I shant see you, just to know you are in London will be good

I wonder what you're going to say to my first letter to you at Colombo

I'll be awfully anxious to get your answer—be kind to me darlint— our pleasures together are so few—no, I'm going to stop now—because I shall start railing against Life & Fate & everything—& I do want to try not to— I want to B B only for you darlint—cos I know you will be pleased with

PEIDI

Bywaters and Thompson.

Envelope—Mr F Bywaters P O R M S "Morea" Marseilles France

(Seal on back " P ")

[Postmark—London, E C , Sep 11, 2 30 p m , 1922 P   Stamps—Three 1½d]

Today is Sept 7th darlint, do you remember it last year—I think it was the day the "Morea" left England—am I right? I had rather a shock this morning—I am enclosing you the cause of it—just as I received it   Do you know anything about it? I dont suppose you do darlint, but Im just asking   Im sure if you had reasons for not wanting to see me—you'd tell me and tell me the reasons—you couldnt resort to letters of this description   I dont think it can be from anyone I know—or from any relation of mine, because I am addressed as " P " you will notice—& no one knows you call me anything but "Edie"   Also darlint I cant help noticing that it is posted in the *West End on a Wednesday*   Write and tell me what you think about it & if you have no use for the letter—destroy it—because I dont want it   I cant talk to you very much darlint—it seems such a long time since you really talked to me and nothing can break down this barrier but a real long talk with you—I am so looking forward to it   Avis was over last night and told me you had seen Harold   She also said that they (231) were looking forward to the "Morea" coming in—to hear all about Harold from you & when I said "But I understood he was not coming to England"—she said "Oh that was a lot of rot he was talking I expect he has thought better of it since we all think we'd like to die at certain times but we all get over it and I suppose he has done the same by now"   She also told me that the "Morea" is due for China & Japan next trip—is this so? darlint—its even longer than Australia isnt it?—Oh I cant wait all that time its awful here in England without you

There has been some unpleasantness with Mrs Lesher—she is not attempting to get out and its nearly 2½ years now—so *he* told her if she wasnt out by *Dec* (she promised to get out for certain by this September) he would take the matter to Court   We have had our solicitors advice on this matter & he says—she wouldnt have a leg to stand on—2½ years is tons of time for anybody to find something else   But I suppose she is waiting for something at the same figure (30/- a month) & of course she will never get it   However she's horrid to me—of course she cant do anything to irritate him, as he hardly comes into contact with her—but I do—& she's so nasty—she refuses to take anything in at all—not even bread or milk & has told the window cleaner only to do her side of the house

Its awfully awkward—I have to rush home on Friday nights & do all my own shopping, carry potatoes etc—because if I only ordered them & had them sent she wouldnt open the door when they came   She wouldnt open the door to Bill the other day when he brought a parcel up for me & she wont open it to the Laundry—so I have to take it & fetch it   She's done some very petty things this last fortnight—I didn't believe she would—especially after what Ive done for her & Norah   I am trying to get Ethel to come up from Cornwall now—I dont know if I shall be successful—I do hope so—I shant be able to stand this state of things much longer Darlint   I hope I havent bored you with all this—I have just thought perhaps I have —after I had written it all   Forgive me if I have, I didnt intend to—I just

Appendix II.

tried to make you live in my life   Will you write & tell me if I am to send your watch to you at Plymouth & the books   I have had it put right and often wear it myself at 168—the strap is so big it comes nearly up to my elbow—also I have had a gold buckle put on it—did you notice it was only R G   I didn't when I bought it—or I should have had it altered at the time —however it is done now

Dont forget to write from *Marseilles* & tell me what to do   Darlingest pal I love you more & more—I always shall Ill never alter

PEIDI

Envelope—Miss P Graydon   C/o Messrs Carlton & Prior, 168 Aldersgate Street, E C 1

[Postmark—London, W 1, Sep 6, 3 15 p m, 1922 A]

September 6th

If you wish to remain the friend of F Bywaters, be careful   Do not attempt to see him or communicate with him, when he is in England

Believe this to be a genuine warning from

A WELLWISHER

Envelope—Mr F Bywaters, P O R M S ' Morea ' Plymouth

(Seal on back ' P ')

[Postmark—London, 5 p m, 20 Sep 1922   Stamps—½d and 1d]

Do you know Darlint Im getting fearfully disappointed today   I had hopes of hearing from you—but there is nothing yet   I went to G P O yesterday and they told me there was nothing for me—that was quite disappointing enough, but I thought perhaps you were late at Marseilles & it would be in to-day (Tuesday)   When I asked for the letters for me to day & was told there was none, I asked if the mail by the " Morea " was in & was told it was—but was not yet sorted—so now Ill have to wait until tomorrow—as its no use me getting letters after business hours—I have nowhere to keep them for safety   However I hope time will fly till tomorrow

This afternoon I sent you a parcel of books to Plymouth—I thought perhaps it would be too late to catch you—if I waited to hear from you   And darlint something was in the parcel for you—I couldnt remember if you told me your hair brushes were worn out—or if it was some one else— was it you? & do you like the " Mason Pearson " brush like wire on a rubber cushion   On Saturday I had very solemn warning that you were expected home this week end & you were sure to visit 231 (This Gran Mother) & when I said I understood you were not coming to England any more—I was told " Oh that was all bluff—just an excuse to make it easier to take you out that night "

I have been amusing myself making jam—chutney & mincemeat with the apples from the garden   Most people who have tasted it think I have been very successful & Norman wants to borrow me as his cook   Im getting rather proud of myself darlint—but I wish I was doing it to

Bywaters and Thompson.

share with you—it would be worth more to me than the whole world's praise This morning I had a letter from Ethel and she says she will come up to me at the end of the month—thats something anyway—Im beginning to hate this drudgery—it doesnt even help to stifle thoughts now

I think Ill send you a wire to Plymouth to ask you to send Plymouth letter (if I am to have one) to 168 One letter cant matter can it darlint anyhow I'll risk it But Ill wire you because perhaps you wont open this before you leave

Its 5 now darlingest—Ill put this away till tomorrow Im thinking about such a lot

PEIDI

Darlint darlint pal—Im so happy Ive heard from you—such a lot it seems like the very first time I have really heard since you have been gone I dont know what to say to you—I really dont—but you know how I feel dont you? Today is the 20th and Ive got tons of work to do—it is statement day and its also nearly H—so I must post this now I will talk to you properly and answer your letter—& keep it until you tell me where to send it—you will wont you? One thing I must say—darlingest pal—Im a thought reader—I must be—you'll think so too when you get your parcel at Plymouth Must it be pals only darlint? if you say "Yes" it shall be

PEIDI
(still loves you)

Plain Envelope

Darlingest boy I know can I wish you all & everything you wish me
Here's luck to us both in " The Glorious Adventure " may our next meeting be real, darlint real & true & happy Ill let you have your own way about writing darlint if you think it really best & I'll quite understand

Goodbye & good luck darlint, the very very best luck that could happen to you darlint and

PEIDI

Plain Envelope

Darlingest Boy

Thank you—ever, ever so much for all those things I received—are they all for me tho? there seems such a lot & what am I to do about them? Wear them now? or wait, I know when you sent them you wanted me & expected that I would wear them, but now—well I suppose its not to be

Ive nothing to talk about darlint, not a tiny little thing—Life—the Life I & we lead is gradually drying me up—soon I'll be like the " Sahara "—just a desert, like the ' Shulamite " you must read that book, its interesting—absorbing, arent books a consolation and a solace? We ourselves die & live in the books we read while we are reading them & then when we have finished, the books die and we live—or exist—just drag on thro years & years, until when? who knows—Im beginning to think no one does—no not even you & I, we are not the shapers of our destinies

I'll always love you darlint,

PEIDI

Appendix II.

Plain Envelope

Darlint, I did have a doubt about Australia—doesnt doubt show great love sometimes? I think it does, its that sort of doubt I had—perhaps "doubt" is the wrong word—its fear more—fear of losing you—a woman is different for a man—a man says "I want it—I'll take it—a woman wants to say that—but an inborn feeling of modesty is it? makes her withhold her action perhaps you'll not understand this Men are carried away on the moment by lots of different actions, love, hate, passion, & they always stand by what they have done

Darlint, Australia frightens me, memories with faces, return & humans cannot control their own Fate

Supposing Fate has it written down that you & I are never to be happy, you'll fight against it but you'll have to give in & perhaps you'll come back perhaps you wont Darlint I'm going to forget there is such a place from the day you sail this time, till the day you return

On the evening you said to me ' Au revoir" in January—you told me you still had something—something in connection with Australia All the time you were away I wondered why you mentioned it what made you remind me about it

Darlint before you go this time send me everything connected with Australia & when you *come back to me from Australia* I'll give them all back to you, to do with what you like

Whatever you think about this will you talk to me about it please darlint

Nothing nothing on this earth ever will make a teeny scrap of difference to our love

Darlint, it is real & for all time too large—too great—too grand for anything to destroy it

I'll keep those things, at least for you to see the first time, but darlint if its possible for us to go out this Thursday, I'm going to wear one set, & on the day you come home I'm going to wear the other set Yes, you want me to? or not?

Why and how was I a ' little girl '—darlint I always feel that I want you to take care of me to be nice to me, to fuss hold me always in your 2 arms tight, ever so tight, & kiss me, keep on doing it darlint

An organ outside now, playing "Margie"

Darlint I'll try not to be cynical hard I'll try always to be just a " little girl " a tiny little girl that you call

PEIDI

Plain Envelope

Oh darlint I do want to thank you so much, heaps & heaps, heaps for everything—you're much too good to me darlint in that way really you are

At any rate Ill be able to think of you every morning & every evening because I'll be able always to wear silk now, & the beads no darlingest boy I cant say ' thank you " enough everybody wants me to leave them to them in my Will—I feel proud ever so proud when anybody admires anything you have given me

Bywaters and Thompson.

The lilac set I like best of all, I told you this before, but I must tell you again, they are for Thursday first & then only for the first & last times I am with you I dont think you can possibly know how much I thank you, but I dont mind if you dont know, because *I* know how much.

Darlingest boy, I got your note this morning, if you felt it was awful on Saturday & you wanted to die, how do you think I felt? its indescribable, all the pain that this deceit and pettiness causes

Yesterday I thought was too awful to beat, I dont know how I got thro the day, my mind and thoughts I had to make frozen, I darent think, not about anything, I should have run away, I know I should I felt quite sure

Saturday at 5 30 it was terrible, every time I see you, the parting is worse, on Saturday it was awful, so bad I couldnt B B any longer, I had to cry all the way to 41

I keep on asking myself " Will it ever be any different " things seem so hopeless, do they to you?

You said in your note " What am I saying dont let this make you too miserable Chere "

Darlingest nothing that you say like that can ever make me feel more miserable than I do, just try & think darlint that Peidi always feels as badly about things as you do perhaps worse, circumstances always have to be considered & remembered

Will you think this always darlint perhaps it will help I am going to see you tonight arent I, just for that " very little while," its the only few minutes of the day that is worth living

---

When you shook hands on Saturday I felt sick with pain, that that was all you & I could do, just imagine shaking hands, when we are all and everything & each other, to each other, two halves not yet united

---

Have you thought any more about that ' leave it at night " for

PEIDI

Plain Envelope

Darlingest boy I know always and ever, after all I shant be with you on our birthday—darlint I shall think of you such a lot & you will too eh?

I want to leave every little thing to you darlingest boy, I know you will decide and do what is best for two halves, only I should like to know all your thoughts & plans darlint, just to help me beat up & live, no exist thro this life, until it is time for us to be joined together Could you write to me from Marseilles & tell me everything Am I selfish? I believe I am because I am always thinking of myself & yet right deep down in my heart I want to do what is best for you

Its fearfully hard to decide, thats why I want you to pour moi & whatever you say or do I shall accept without fear or doubt or question, & think all the time, even if it seems wrong to me that you know it will, at some indefinite period be, best for us This is right isnt it?

It gets harder and harder every time doesnt it I seem to have lived years & years in that little one from 27 6 21 to now

Goodbye darlingest—I want you to have every success in everything

Appendix II.

darlint, you know that dont you? if only I could help you in that success, but I cant, so you must go on by yourself and know always that you are loved and trusted by

PEIDI

Plain Envelope

Darlint, it doesnt seem possible you are home again I cant realise it, I tried all last night I did not close my eyes once—just thinking & feeling all over again how I felt when I saw you By the time you read this I shall have asked you to do something for me I didnt like doing it myself, darlint, in fact I cried all the time, but after it was done I felt easier, & after you have finished it for me I shall feel easier still Darlint, dont be cross about it, its better I am sure & I was thinking all the time to myself "the next real one I have perhaps Ill be able to keep for always I wasnt very nice last night when you were leaving me darlint, I know, but Ill try and be patient, 2 hours after 7 weeks seems so short I put the violets in my hand bag last night until I went to bed at 9 p m & then put them in water They are quite fresh this morning, I wore them & they are now beside our monkey on my desk I dont think I thanked you properly for the sweets darlint but I was so pleased to see you, everything flew, you understand, I know

I have not put *his* ribbon on again yet—it will cause comment if I do so am leaving it for a little while

Thank you for G M M C wire this morning Dont forget *I want you always* so be careful, & good luck darlint

PEIDI

Envelope—Mr F Bywaters P O R M S 'Morea" Marseilles France

(On back)—I burnt this sealing it —PEIDI

[Stamps—Three 1½d]

---

well let us accept it then—and bear the hard part as willingly as we enjoy the natural part Darlint, I didnt think you wanted to go into the other carriage—but I suggested it because I felt there would be less temptation there—not only for you but for me too—do you think it is less pleasure to me, for you to kiss me & hold me, than it is for you to do so? I think its more pleasure to me than it can possibly be to you—at least it always feels so & darlingest, if you had refrained from doing these things (not perhaps last night—but at some time before you went) I am not above compelling you to—darlint I could, couldn't I, just the same as if the position was reversed—you could compel me to—because we have no will power I felt thats how it would be darlingest lover of mine—I was strong enough in spirit, until I was tempted in the flesh & the result—a mutual tumble from the pedestal of "Pals only" that we had erected as penance for ourselves No darlint, it could never be now—I am sure that you see that now dont you? intentions—such as we had—were forced—unnatural—& darlingest we are essentially natural with each other—we always have been, since our first understanding Why should we choose to be as every other person—when we're not—is every other person such a

Bywaters and Thompson.

model that you & I should copy them? Lets be ourselves—always darlingest there can never be any misunderstandings then—it doesnt matter if its harder—you said it was our Fate against each other—we only have will power when we are in accord, not when we are in conflict—tell me if this is how you feel As I said last night, with you darlint there can never be any pride to stand in the way—it melts in the flame of a great love—I finished with pride Oh a long time ago—do you remember? when I had to come to you in your little room—after washing up I wonder if you understand now I feel about these things—I do try to explain but some words seem so useless Please please lover of mine, dont use that word I dont like it—I feel that Im on a pedestal & that I shall always have to strive to remain there & I dont ever want to strive to do anything anything with or for you—thats not being natural & when you use that word—thats just how I feel—not natural—not myself Would you have me feel like this just so that you could use a term that pleases you & you only? Tell me

Do you remember me being asked if I had found " The Great Lover "? Darlingest lover of mine—I had & I d found ' The Great Pal " too *the best pal a girl ever had* One is as much to me as the other, there is no first and second they are equal

I am glad you held me tightly when you went to sleep darlint I wanted comforting badly—I cried such a lot—no I wasnt unhappy—I look a sight today

Darlingest—what would have happened had I refused—when you asked me to kiss you? I want to know

M H R   27621   from
PEIDI

Plain Envelope

Order from Carlton & Prior

168 Aldersgate Street,
London, E C 1   19

(Written in pencil)—

Mr Carlton has gone out to lunch now & I must wait until he comes back—Miss P is not back yet—do you mind waiting there—Im sorry to ask you to wait such a lot but its awkward today—I had a terrible half hour

PEIDI

Order from Carlton & Prior

168 Aldersgate Street,
London, E C 1   19

(The following written in pencil)—

I rang you to-day—but you were out

It was only to say goodbye—I am going away again in the morning—I didn't ask you to drink my health this time home somehow I thought you would refuse Perhaps I shall get my appointment in Bombay this time—I hope so I failed before

APPENDIX III

Royal Courts of Justice, Thursday 21st December, 1922

COURT OF CRIMINAL APPEAL

REX
v.
FREDERICK EDWARD FRANCIS BYWATERS

Before—The LORD CHIEF JUSTICE OF ENGLAND,
Mr JUSTICE DARLING, and
Mr JUSTICE SALTER

JUDGMENT

The LORD CHIEF JUSTICE—This appellant, Frederick Edward Francis Bywaters, was convicted at the Central Criminal Court, together with a woman named Edith Jessie Thompson, of the wilful murder of Percy Thompson, and he was sentenced to death. He now appeals against conviction, and in accordance with the practice of this Court it is right that this appeal should be dealt with at once, and it will not then be necessary that this appellant should have the ordeal of listening to the appeal in the other case.

Now the learned judge, in his summing up to the jury, spoke of the charge as a common or ordinary charge of a wife and an adulterer murdering the husband. That was a true and appropriate description. The case is a squalid and rather indecent case of lust and adultery, in which the husband was murdered in a cowardly fashion partly because he was in the way and partly, it would seem, because such money as he possessed was desired by the others. There is no need to recapitulate the facts of the case. The woman, Mrs Thompson—to whom I refer for the present purpose only in describing so far as it is necessary to describe the events which preceded the commission of the crime, prejudging nothing as to what may be said on her behalf in that appeal—was the daughter of a Mr Graydon, and is twenty nine years of age. In 1915 she married Percy Thompson, who, at the time of his death, was thirty-two years of age. There were no children of the marriage. They occupied part of a house at 41 Kensington Gardens, Ilford, and there was evidence, upon which it is not necessary to dwell, that there came a time, at any rate, when she and her husband ceased to be upon good terms. The appellant Bywaters was twenty years of age last June. He was employed as a ship's writer, and apparently he had known the Graydons for two or three years, and in the year 1921 he stayed with Mr and Mrs Thompson at the Isle of Wight, and then after

Bywaters and Thompson.

wards in their house at Ilford. In August of last year Bywaters told his mother that Mrs Thompson led a very unhappy life with her husband, and asked his mother how Mrs Thompson could get a separation, and there is evidence that he met Mrs Thompson twice at the warehouse where she was employed—once eighteen months ago and once on Friday, the 29th September of this year. That was the day upon which Bywaters' new period of leave started. There was further evidence that he and Mrs Thompson were seen together at a neighbouring teashop on the 29th September and on the 3rd October, and that letters had been taken for Mrs Thompson from the warehouse to Bywaters. On Tuesday, the 3rd October, Mr and Mrs Thompson went to a theatre with Mr Thompson's uncle. This appellant, Bywaters, was at Mr Graydon's house in Manor Park that night, and in the course of the evening it was mentioned that the Thompsons had gone to the theatre. Bywaters left about ten o'clock or a little later, and the place where Mr Thompson was afterwards killed was some 2 miles and 370 yards from the house of the Graydons, and was not at all on the appellant's way home. Mr Laxton left the Thompsons at the Piccadilly Tube station at about a quarter to eleven that night, and they made their way to Ilford, and as they were going in the direction of their home Mrs Thompson went running to a passer by in a state of great agitation and made a statement. I do not at present enter into that statement, because it is not necessary. Mr Thompson had been killed, and when the police came and took his body to the mortuary he was found to be wounded in many places: on the left side below the ribs there were four slight cuts on the skin which had gone through his clothing, there were two slight cuts on the front of the chin, two slight cuts on the right side of the lower jaw, and a slight cut on the right arm. There was a stab in the back of the neck 2 inches deep and $1\frac{1}{4}$ inches wide, a stab at the back of the neck $2\frac{1}{2}$ inches deep and $1\frac{1}{2}$ inches wide, a stab in the centre of the neck 1 inch wide and $2\frac{1}{2}$ inches deep, which penetrated down and opened the gullet. The doctor was of opinion that the fatal wound in the neck was received from behind, but he was doubtful about it.

Now to pass over further evidence, no small part of the evidence in the case undoubtedly consisted of a remarkable correspondence between the appellant and Mrs Thompson. Few of his letters had been preserved, I think only three. Many of her letters had been preserved, and those letters were undoubtedly used as some material helping the jury to arrive at a true conclusion with regard to this appellant. It is not necessary for me in dealing with his case to enter further into the nature of the contents of those letters, but it is said by Mr Whiteley, who has argued this appeal on behalf of the appellant, that it was wrong in this case that the appellant and Mrs Thompson should be tried together. That is the first ground of his appeal. Now, it has been held again and again by this Court—the cases are so numerous that it is not necessary to refer to them—that it is a matter of judicial discretion whether two persons shall or shall not be tried separately. In this case the learned judge, exercising his discretion, decided that the present appellant and Mrs Thompson should be tried together. In the opinion of this Court, there was no ground at all for unfavourable criticism of that decision. On the contrary, this was clearly a case in which, in the interests of justice, it was desirable that the two prisoners should be tried together. It is said that the effect of trying the two prisoners together was that many of the letters

Appendix III.

written by Mrs Thompson to the appellant were used as material from which the jury might draw a conclusion unfavourable to Bywaters. But exactly the same thing would have happened if the prisoners had been tried separately. It is not to be supposed that if the learned judge had come to the conclusion that Bywaters should be tried separately the prosecution would not have made use of those letters. It was further said that the result of trying the two prisoners together was that Mrs Thompson became, as otherwise she might not have been, a witness in the case in which Bywaters was being dealt with. No doubt, if the result of trying two persons together who might have been tried separately is what has been called in the cases referred to by Mr Whiteley a miscarriage of justice, this Court will interfere. But what is meant by a miscarriage of justice? That means that a person has been improperly found guilty. It is idle to suggest that a miscarriage of justice has taken place if the prisoner, against whom there is ample evidence, and, indeed, overwhelming evidence, suffers, in the opinion of the defence, some incidental disadvantage because a fellow prisoner, who would not otherwise have been a witness, does go into the witness box. No doubt, in cases where the defence of one accused person is to incriminate another accused person, that is a good reason for not trying the two persons together, but that was not this case, and, in the opinion of this Court, it was helpful in the administration of justice, which knows no other object except to arrive at a true conclusion, that Mrs Thompson's evidence should have been given as assisting the members of the jury to come to a right conclusion in the case, not only of herself, but also of Bywaters. Now, in the course of the complaint under this head, Mr Whiteley said that there was no evidence at all that Mrs Thompson did anything to aid and abet the actual commission of this crime on the night of the 3rd October. That is a matter which may have to be considered in the next appeal, but, so far as that argument is employed on behalf of Bywaters, speaking for myself, I am not prepared for a moment to admit that there was no evidence that Mrs Thompson aided and abetted the actual commission of this crime. Upon the whole, so far as this first ground of appeal is concerned, the learned judge, as we think, exercised his discretion and exercised it wisely and well in holding that these two prisoners should stand their trial together.

The second ground of appeal was that as the learned Solicitor General appeared as leading counsel for the prosecution, he had, and exercised, the right of reply, and it was contended that at any rate, since the passing of Lord Denman's Act, the Criminal Procedure Act of 1865, the law officer of the Crown has not a right of reply. Support for that proposition was sought to be derived from cases in which the prerogative of the Crown in relation to the provisions of statutes dealing with similar matter has been considered. The argument fails, for this quite simple reason: the Act of 1865 is not dealing with this matter at all, and it was long after 1865 that the resolution of the judges referred to by Mr Whiteley was come to, namely, in the year 1884. That was not an enabling resolution; it was a resolution which had a limited effect, and it was this: that in those Crown cases in which the Attorney or Solicitor-General is personally engaged, a reply where no witnesses are called for the defence is to be allowed as of right to the counsel for the Crown and in no others. That is the existing state of the law. If the law is to be altered, it must be altered elsewhere, but at present, when the law officer of the Crown,

Bywaters and Thompson.

whether he be the Attorney-General or the Solicitor-General, appears in a Crown case—which is no mere accident—what it means is that those who have had to deliberate upon the matter have come to the conclusion that it is a case in which, in the interests of justice, it is right that a law officer of the Crown should appear—when a law officer of the Crown does appear, then, according to the exercise of his discretion, he may exercise the right which at present he lawfully has; and again, applying that matter to the facts of this particular case one cannot see any ground for the suggestion that the defence was prejudiced by what the learned Solicitor-General, in a speech of studious moderation, did

Finally, it is suggested that there was misdirection. The summing up in the case of Bywaters fills, in the transcript of the shorthand note, an enormous number of pages. It is not denied by Mr Whiteley that the questions relating to Bywaters were fully and clearly put again and again, and, in the opinion of this Court, in the particular and minor matters to which Mr Whiteley has taken exception, there is no ground whatever for the complaint of misdirection.

As to the complaint that evidence was wrongly admitted, I have already dealt with that in dealing with the letters. The complaint there is with regard to the letters and I make this further observation about them only; it matters not for this purpose whether Mrs Thompson had really done or attempted the various acts which in those letters she said or suggested that she had done or attempted. It matters not whether those letters show, or, at any rate, go to show, that there was between this appellant and Mrs Thompson any agreement tending to the same end. Those letters were material as throwing light, not only upon the question by whom was this deed done, but what was the intent, what was the purpose with which it was done. Therefore not to mention other grounds, those letters were most material upon the allegation of the appellant, by way of afterthought, that what he did was done in self defence. I say "by way of afterthought," because when one looks at the statement which he made at an early stage, after his arrest upon the 5th day of October (exhibit No 6)—and Mr Whiteley has already read the passage this morning—what he said was this—" The reason I fought with Thompson was because he never acted like a man to his wife. He always seemed several degrees lower than a snake " That is not merely not the same thing as saying—" The reason I fought with Thompson was in self defence, because he appeared to me that he was going to shoot me ", it contradicts that reason It is something which excludes that defence

In all these circumstances not to dwell further upon the evidence in a very ordinary though a very painful case, in the opinion of this Court this appeal fails upon every ground and must be dismissed

Appendix III.

Royal Courts of Justice, Thursday, 21st December, 1922

COURT OF CRIMINAL APPEAL

REX

v

EDITH JESSIE THOMPSON

Before—The LORD CHIEF JUSTICE OF ENGLAND
Mr JUSTICE DARLING, and
Mr JUSTICE SALTER

JUDGMENT

The LORD CHIEF JUSTICE—This appellant, Edith Jessie Thompson, was convicted at the Central Criminal Court, together with the last appellant, Frederick Edward Francis Bywaters, of the wilful murder of Percy Thompson, and she was sentenced to death. She now appeals against conviction. The charge against her was in point of law that she was what is called a principal in the second degree, that is to say that she was a person present at the commission of the offence who aided and abetted the commission of the offence, and, to put it in a slightly different way, the point of the charge against this woman was that she incited and aided and abetted the commission of this crime upon the night of the 3rd day of October. Now, before I come to deal with the argument that has been presented on behalf of the appellant by Sir Henry Curtis Bennett, it is necessary, as shortly as possible to review some of the facts of this essentially commonplace and unedifying case. The appellant, Edith Jessie Thompson, is twenty-nine years of age. She is the daughter of a Mr Graydon, and seven years ago she married Mr Percy Thompson, the man now dead, the only person who in this case excites any sympathy.

At the time of his death he was thirty two years of age. They lived in a part of a house at Ilford, called No 41 Kensington Gardens, and the evidence was that the appellant and her husband were not on good terms with each other. She was employed as manageress to a firm of milliners in Aldersgate Street, where she received a salary of £6 a week in addition to a bonus. Some time ago, a considerable time ago, the appellant made the acquaintance of Bywaters, a young steward on a liner, whose case was dealt with this morning. He had stayed with them elsewhere and in their own house, and it is quite obvious from many portions of the evidence that the terms upon which she and Bywaters had come to be, long before the 3rd October of this year, were terms of the most culpable intimacy. Bywaters was from time to time absent on his ship. It is not necessary even for the sake of clearness to examine closely the chronology in the case, but

Bywaters and Thompson.

there were periods when he was at home and there were periods when he was away, and the periods when he was away are to a great extent covered by a remarkable and deplorable correspondence, full of the most mischievous and perilous stuff. In August of last year Bywaters, according to the evidence, made a statement to his mother about the unhappy life of Mrs Thompson, and the evidence showed, if the jury accepted it, as they apparently did, that on more than one occasion Bywaters had called at the warehouse where Mrs Thompson was employed, that he had kept up this protracted correspondence with her. The letters which are actually made exhibits began with the 11th of August, 1921, and they continue right down to the 2nd October, 1922—that is to say, the day before the commission of the crime—and the evidence further was that after an absence of some weeks, Bywaters began a new period of leave on the 29th September last. There was evidence that he was with the appellant at a neighbouring teashop upon that day, and again upon Tuesday, the 3rd day of October. That was the day upon which the crime was committed. On that Tuesday, the 3rd October, the appellant and her husband went to a theatre with the husband's uncle, Mr Laxton. Upon that same evening Bywaters went to the house of the appellant's father, and it appears to have been mentioned at that house that the Thompsons had gone to the theatre. Bywaters left about ten o'clock or a little after ten. Somewhat later the appellant and her husband with Mr Laxton, went to the Piccadilly Tube station, about a quarter to eleven. There, it was said, they were apparently on good terms, and it is clear from what followed that they made their way home by train to Ilford. Shortly before midnight a Miss Pittard was walking with Mr and Mrs Clevely from Ilford station, and their way took them through a road called Belgrave Road, and when they were between De Vere Gardens and Endsleigh Gardens, both places not far from Kensington Gardens, where the Thompsons own house was, Mrs Thompson came running to him. She was agitated and incoherent. She said—"Oh, my God, will you help me, my husband is ill, he is bleeding." And she said he was on the pavement, and asked those persons to go or take her and get a doctor. They took her to the house of a doctor, Dr Maudsley, and then Mrs Thompson ran back. A witness was called named Webber, who lived about 30 or 40 yards away from that place, and he said that as he was going to bed he heard a woman's voice, a voice which he now recognised as Mrs Thompson's voice, calling in piteous tones, "Oh, don't, don't." He went outside, and three or four minutes later he saw three persons coming from Dr Maudsley's house. Mrs Thompson was in front running and sobbing. He followed, and found Mrs Thompson and Mr Thompson. He asked her if he could help, and she said, "Don't touch him, don't touch him, a lady and a gentleman have gone off for a doctor." Miss Pittard and Mr Clevely then came up, and they found the appellant kneeling down by Mr Thompson, who was lying upon the footpath in Belgrave Road with his back propped against the wall. The place was dark. Mr Clevely struck a match, and Miss Pittard asked Mrs Thompson what had happened, and the appellant answered, "Oh, do not ask me, I do not know. Somebody flew past, and when I turned to speak to him blood was pouring out of his mouth." A few minutes later Dr Maudsley arrived, and he found that Mr Thompson was dead. He thought he had been dead then about ten minutes. Mrs Thompson was standing by his side, and he described her as being confused,

Appendix III.

hysterical, and agitated. He asked her if Mr Thompson had been ill coming home, and she said "No." He told her that Mr Thompson was dead, and she said "Why did not you come sooner and save him?" The doctor made no examination then. He saw the blood. He did not see any wound, but he sent for the police. A police sergeant took the appellant to her house, and on the way she said, "Will he come back? They will blame me for this." Now, the place where the body was found was about 50 yards from the Thompsons' house and 1250 yards from Ilford station. It was an indirect way from the station to the house. The police came, took the body to the mortuary and undressed it, and it was examined, and a great number of wounds were found upon it. The most serious wounds were three stabs apparently inflicted from behind, one of which penetrated down to and opened the gullet. Mr Thompson's brother was sent for, and shortly before two o'clock in the morning he arrived at Mrs Thompson's house. She told her brother in law that Mr Thompson was walking along and suddenly came over queer and said "Oh!" and that on the way from the station he had complained of pains in his legs, and that she had met a lady and gentleman and had gone for a doctor, and when they got back he was dead.

At three o'clock in the morning two police sergeants went to Mrs Thompson's house and saw her. She was asked if she could explain what had happened on the road, and she said, "I do not know, I cannot say, I only know that my husband suddenly dropped down and screamed out 'Oh!' I then rushed across the road and saw a lady and gentleman, and asked them if they would help me, and they went with me for the doctor." She was asked whether she could account for the cuts on her husband's neck, and she said, "No. We were walking along, and my husband said 'Oh,' and I said 'Bear up,' thinking he had one of his attacks." He then fell on her, and walked a little further. He then fell up against the wall and then on the ground. She was asked if her husband carried a knife, and she said "No." She was asked if she was carrying a knife in her handbag, and she said "No." She was also asked if she or her husband saw or spoke to any person in Belgrave Road, and she said, "No, I did not notice any one." About eleven o'clock in the morning of the 4th October Inspector Hall saw Mrs Thompson at her house, and she told him "We were coming along Belgrave Road and just passed the corner of Endsleigh Gardens when I heard him call out, 'Oh er,' and he fell up against me. I put out my arms to save him, and found blood which I thought was coming from his mouth. I tried to hold him up. He staggered for several yards towards Kensington Gardens and then fell against the wall and slid down. He did not speak to me, I cannot say if I spoke to him. I felt him, and found his clothing wet with blood. He never moved after he fell. We had no quarrel on the way, we were quite happy together. Immediately I saw blood I ran across the road to a doctor's. I appealed to a lady and gentleman who were passing, and the gentleman also went to the doctor's. The doctor came and told me my husband was dead. Just before he fell down I was walking on his right hand side on the inside of the pavement nearest the wall. We were side by side. I did not see anybody about at the time. My husband and I were talking about going to a dance." That evening Mrs Thompson was taken to the police station, and on the 5th October she made a statement which became

Bywaters and Thompson.

exhibit No 3 at the trial. I shall not read it all, but it is to be observed that in that statement made when she went to the police station she says this "I have always been on affectionate terms with my husband. I remember Tuesday, the 3rd October, we both went to our respective businesses that day; I met my husband by appointment at a quarter to six in Aldersgate Street." She then describes how they went to the theatre and how they came home, and then she describes or purports to describe what took place, and she says, amongst other things, this—"I cannot remember whether I saw any one else there or not. I know there was no one there when he staggered up against me." She went on to speak of Bywaters and her knowledge of Bywaters. She said, "I am not in possession of any letters he wrote to me. I have destroyed them all, as is customary with me with all my correspondence. When he was at home in England we were in the habit of going out occasionally together without my husband's knowledge." According to that statement she had not seen Bywaters that night; she did not associate Bywaters with what had taken place, and she was on good terms with Mr Thompson, her husband. Now it happened that at the police station she saw Bywaters, who had been taken to the police station, and was in the library as she passed, and she then said, "Oh God, oh God, what can I do? Why did he do it? I did not want him to do it. I must tell the truth." And then she made a further statement, which is exhibit No 4. In that short statement she said this—"When we got near Endsleigh Gardens a man rushed out from the Gardens and knocked me and pushed me away from my husband. I was dazed for a moment. When I recovered I saw my husband scuffling with a man. The man who I know as Freddie Bywaters was running away. He was wearing a blue overcoat and a grey hat. I knew it was him although I did not see his face." The two were afterwards charged together. The knife with which these wounds had been inflicted was found in a neighbouring drain, and I do not think I need dwell upon the rest of the evidence. Dr Spilsbury said that all the wounds except the one on the arm of Mr Thompson were stabs.

The appellant Bywaters gave evidence first and Mrs Thompson gave evidence, and I shall have to refer in a moment to the denials she made. She said, among other things, that she first fell in love with Bywaters in September, 1921, and that she had told her husband that she had given him cause for divorce. The jury, having heard the whole of the evidence, both that which I have summarised and much else, came to the conclusion that the appellant was guilty of wilful murder.

Now, what are the pleas that are put forward on behalf of the appellant in this appeal? Sir Henry Curtis Bennett at the outset stated, and very frankly stated, that before he came into Court this morning he had decided to abandon that ground of appeal which rested upon the allegation that this appellant and Bywaters ought to have been tried separately, but were in fact tried together. That ground of appeal is not persisted in. But Sir Henry says—he puts it in more than one way, but it is really the same contention illustrated and sought to be enforced from different points of view—that in order that this appellant might properly be convicted of this crime there ought to be evidence showing not merely that as between her and Bywaters there was a community of purpose in this matter, but that that community of purpose continued right up to the

Appendix III.

crucial moment when the crime was committed, and in regard to that complaint Sir Henry relies especially upon two matters. He relies first upon the letters and the use to which they were put or not put, and secondly, he relies upon certain portions in the summing up, where he says the learned judge not only misdirected the jury in the sense of inviting them to find what they could not find, but also omitted to direct the jury in the sense that he did not adequately put before the jury what the defence of the appellant was. With regard to the letters in the opinion of this Court there was more than one ground upon which the use of these letters could be justified. It is enough for the present purpose to say that they could be justified upon this ground—that by means of them the prosecution were seeking to show that continuously over a long period, beginning before and culminating in the time immediately antecedent to the commission of the crime, Mrs Thompson was, with every sort of ingenuity by precept and by example, actual or simulated, endeavouring to incite Bywaters to the commission of this crime. I am not going to read those letters. There is a great mass of them. Many of them were read at the trial. They begin in the summer of 1921, and they continue until the 2nd October, 1922, that is to say, they continue until the day before the day upon which this crime was committed. Now, what is it that those letters may reasonably be regarded as showing? First of all, they show a passionate and, in the circumstances, a wicked affection between Mrs Thompson and Bywaters. Secondly, they contain what purport to be accounts of efforts which have been made, sometimes without the assistance of Bywaters, sometimes with the assistance of Bywaters, to get Mr Thompson out of the way. Thirdly—and this is a thread that runs through the whole skein of these letters—there is the continual entreaty and hope that that which they both desire will somehow be accomplished. Now in the opinion of the Court, the theory that these letters so far as they purport to describe attempts made upon the life of Mr Thompson, are mere nonsense—" Vapour," as Bywaters calls them—" Melodramatic nonsense," as learned counsel has thought fit to call them—is a theory which cannot be accepted. But however that may be, if the question is, as I think it was, whether these letters were evidence of a protracted, continuous incitement to Bywaters to commit the crime which he did in the end commit, it really is of comparatively little importance whether the appellant was truly reporting something which she had done, or falsely reporting something which she merely pretended to do. I am not going to read them, it is not necessary, but reference may, perhaps, be made to one of them, which is the last. By this time Bywaters was back in this country. The appellant and Bywaters were meeting. They had ample opportunity of conversation and arrangement of any plan in which they might be interested, and upon the 2nd of October the appellant wrote to him—" I tried so hard to find a way out of to-night, darlingest, but he was suspicious and still is. We ought to be able to use great big things for great big love like ours." And again—" Darlint, it is funds that are our stumbling block—until we have those, we can do nothing." That is not the only passage in the later correspondence in which the appellant refers to the importance of money. Then she goes on—" Darlint do something to-morrow night will you? something to make you forget. I'll be hurt I know, but I want you to hurt me—I do really—the bargain now seems so one-sided—so unfair—but how can

Bywaters and Thompson.

I alter it" And finally, the last passage—"Don't forget what we talked in the tearoom I'll still risk and try if you will—we only have 3¾ years left darlingest" Now, it cannot be said that those letters were not evidence against the appellant in support of the charge which the prosecution were making up against her

I pass to the summing up The complaint against the summing up, which is a very long summing up, is that it did what it ought not to have done, and it omitted to do what it should have done Is there any ground for that criticism? Let me refer to one or two, and only to one or two passages The case for the prosecution was that the appellant and Bywaters were acting together The case for this appellant was that the letters she had written were nonsense, and that what took place on the night of Tuesday, 3rd October, was to her a great surprise At the very outset of the summing up the learned judge put the question for the jury in this clear and simple form—"The case presented is that these two, by arrangement between each other, agreed to murder this man, and the murder was effected by the man Unless you are satisfied of that, namely that they did it did it by arrangement in the way I shall explain to you there would be no case against the woman" Then the learned judge deals with the case against the man, and, to come to a later page, he says this—"Now I am going to ask you to consider only one question in your deliberations, and that is, was it an arranged thing between the woman and the man," &c (reading to the words) "if you are satisfied" I pause there to say that one of the incidental criticisms offered upon the summing up is that it does not expressly say in so many words the burden of proof is upon the prosecution, but again and again and again the learned judge says that everything depends upon the jury's being satisfied of something, which apart from technicality is the same thing as saying that the prosecution have to prove their case "If you are satisfied that there was,' &c (reading to the words) "that is what I submit to you" Now, the criticism which is offered upon that passage is that there was no direct evidence that she had informed Bywaters that she would be there with her husband at that time There was no direct evidence that he was there at her invitation, or upon information given by her That is quite true But in view of all the rest of the evidence, both as to what happened before the commission of those acts, and as to what happened immediately after the commission of those acts, it was obviously open to the jury to infer that that which was done was done as the result of preconceived arrangement, and that is what the learned judge is putting here, making it plain again and again and again that they are to be satisfied before they draw that inference And he pursues the same matter He says on the next page—"The short case for the prosecution is this, that for months these people had been corresponding," &c (reading to the words), "inciting him to murder" In the next sentence the learned judge goes on to say—"I will deal with the letters and deal with her explanation later on", and it is complained that in that part of his summing up he says, "I know when you have letters the jury want to hear what the judge says about the letters' I cannot help thinking that far too much stress has been laid upon that particular phrase It seems no more than this—"I have not forgotten the letters, I know you will expect me to deal with them" And when the learned judge comes to deal with the letters, what is it that he

Appendix III.

says? Let me refer to two other passages. He says this, having referred to a letter—"The meaning of that is for you to judge. You will fully understand it is not for me to tell you what the letters mean. You are the judges of that, not I. There is no law about it whatever." And yet again he says—"I should be wanting in my duty if I did not plainly explain to you that the meaning of these letters is entirely for you." In view of those warnings, it seems to me to be impossible that the learned judge could be understood to have meant by his former phrase, "You will take your view of these letters from me." Again to pass to another passage, the learned judge says this—'It is said by the prosecution that from the beginning to the end of these letters she is seriously considering and inciting the man to assist her to poison her husband, and if she did that, and if you find that within a week or two after he came back the poisoning is considered no longer possible, he has no longer studied or has not studied bichloride of mercury, but has read 'Bella Donna' to see if 'Bella Donna' can be of any use to him"—I pause to say there that a remark was made as to the view which she expressed upon a leading character in that story, and it is also to be observed that she recommended that book to be read by him as a book which might prove useful to him hereafter—"they would naturally turn to some other means of effecting their object," &c (reading to the words) "a meeting which only finished when there was a discussion in the tearoom"—that is the discussion referred to in the last paragraph of the last letter. And again—"You are entitled to assume—it is entirely for you to say whether you are satisfied—you are entitled to assume that she sped him on his errand," &c (reading to the words) "you will not draw it unless you are satisfied.' And finally, at the close of the summing up the learned judge once more repeats the warning. It is on the last page of the summing up—"You will not convict her unless you are satisfied that she and he agreed that this man should be murdered," &c (reading to the words) "he was doing it.' The matter could not be put more strongly than that—"If you are not satisfied of that you will acquit her. If you are satisfied of that it will be your duty to convict her."

Taking that long summing up as a whole and reading one part with the rest of what the learned judge says, in the opinion of this Court it is not possible to found upon it any unfavourable criticism. The case was clearly put before the jury. There was simple evidence, partly direct evidence, partly evidence from which inference might properly be drawn, and upon that evidence, in a case which exhibits from beginning to end no redeeming feature, the members of the jury have convicted the appellant. In the opinion of this Court there is no reason to interfere with that conviction, and this appeal must be dismissed.

CPSIA information can be obtained at www.ICGtesting.com
Printed in the USA
LVOW060412060313

322907LV00003B/70/P

9 781275 103849